Anti-Inflammatory Diet for Beginners: 1000+ Easy, Tasty & Low-Budget Recipes to Beat Chronic Inflammation, Detox Your Body & Feel Better Than Ever /21-Day Meal Plan Included/

By
Lester C. Collings

Contents

Introduction

When your body recognizes anything alien, such as an invading bacterium, pollen from plants, or a chemical, your immune system is triggered. The result is an increase in inflammation. Your health is protected by occasional inflammatory episodes that target genuine intruders. You may have inflammation even if you don't have a foreign invader in your body. Inflammation might then work against you. Many disorders, including cancer, heart disease, diabetes, arthritis, depression, and Alzheimer's disease, have chronic inflammation. Food, not medicine, is the most effective anti-inflammatory tool.

Chemicals included in some foodstuffs have the potential to initiate or exacerbate inflammation. Fresh, healthy meals are less likely than processed or sugary foods to contribute to this. Fresh fruits and vegetables are an important part of an anti-inflammatory diet. Antioxidants abound in many plant-based diets. However, certain meals may generate free radicals. One example is food that is routinely fried in hot frying oil.

An anti-oxidant is a compound found in food that aids the body in destroying free radicals. Free radicals are generated naturally by human activities, such as metabolism. Free radicals in the body may be exacerbated by stress and smoking, among other things. Free radicals may damage cells. Inflammation that results from this damage is more likely, and it may lead to a wide range of illnesses. However, ingesting antioxidants may also be advantageous since they are produced by the body and aid in eliminating hazardous contaminants. Anti-inflammatory foods are prioritized above pro-free radical foods in a diet designed to reduce inflammation. Omega-3 fatty acids, which are found in oily fish, lower the amounts of inflammatory proteins in the body.

Recommendations for easing the transition to a new diet may be found here. Go shopping for various fruits, veggies, and healthy snacks each week. Eventually, you'll be able to give up fast food for wholesome, home-cooked lunches. Mineral water may be utilized instead of sugary sodas and other sugary drinks. Before using them, supplements like cod liver oil or a multivitamin should be discussed with your doctor. The daily routine should include 30 minutes of moderate exercise. Lack of sleep may exacerbate inflammation. Therefore good sleep hygiene is critical. Many ailments are made worse by chronic inflammation and may benefit from an anti-inflammatory diet as a complementary therapy, as detailed in this book's recipes.

Chapter 1: Anti- Inflammatory Diet

These days, the anti-inflammatory diet is all the rage, but it's not a fad. First, following an anti-inflammatory diet entails consuming genuine, complete, and unprocessed foods to support a healthy inflammatory response in your body. Reduce your chances of chronic bodily pains, persistent indigestion, and illnesses like fibromyalgia, heart disease, and cancer by lowering inflammation in your body.

So, what is inflammation precisely, and why are you trying to prevent it?

You've probably encountered inflammation if you've ever had a cold, injured your ankle, or skinned your knee. Your body's normal and essential reaction to external stresses such as damage or illness. The reaction normally switches off after your body gets the stressor under control. When the inflammatory response does not cease functioning and continues to operate long after the initial need has passed, it may result in harmful chronic inflammation.

You'll be well on your way to encouraging a healthy inflammatory response if you regularly eat foods like vividly colored fruits and vegetables, herbs and spices, and healthy fats.

It would help if you avoided or restricted meals that might create a detrimental inflammatory response and consume anti-inflammatory nutrients.

Refined carbs, such as crackers, cakes, and bagels; foods containing gluten meals with added sugars; and foods containing Tran's fats, such as fried foods, are all known to induce inflammation.

1.1 What is the definition of inflammation?

The inflammatory reaction is perfectly natural and essential to the body's healing process. It's simply how the body provides nutrients and increases immune activity in places that have been injured or infected.

Your immune system develops an inflammatory response if you are exposed to an infectious pathogen or suffer tissue injury or damage. Inflammation, for example, kicks in when you cut your finger, and it turns red and swollen, and it's a lifesaver. Blood flow to areas in need of healing rises. Pain becomes more intense as a warning that something is amiss with the body. Eicosanoids (also known as prostaglandins, prostacyclins, thromboxanes, and leukotrienes) are secreted to battle unwanted external invaders like germs while simultaneously repairing damaged tissue. Anti-inflammatory chemicals are generated to switch the immune response after being eliminated under normal conditions.

Chronic inflammation causes a variety of signs and symptoms, including:

- Aches and pains throughout the body

- Stiffness that persists
- Joint function loss
- Consistent swelling
- Continual indigestion
- diarrhea regularly
- Continual skin breakouts

Chronic inflammation behaves like a slow but lethal poison over time, causing overactive inflammatory chemicals to harm your body while you go about your regular activities.

Other chronic inflammation-related illnesses and ailments include, but are not limited to:

- Allergies
- Asthma \Cancer
- Crohn's disease is a chronic inflammatory bowel illness.
- Fibromyalgia
- Irritable bowel syndrome (IBD)
- Heart problems
- Kidney disease
- Psoriasis
- Arthritis rheumatoid (RA)
- Stroke
- Inflammation-Producing Foods

According to research, one of the biggest contributors to chronic inflammation is your food. Certain foods may promote inflammation in the body, and eating them regularly can lead to chronic inflammation. Avoiding inflammatory meals is equally as essential as including anti-inflammatory items in your diet.

End Products of Advanced Glycation (AGEs)

Researchers have discovered chemical interactions in the body that result in pro-inflammatory compounds known as advanced glycation end products (AGEs). AGEs are created through food preparation and do not occur in nature. All AGEs have been found to promote inflammation, regardless of their source.

Highly processed, refined foods like Frankfurters, bacon, and powdered egg whites are rich in AGEs.

- Prepackaged foods that have been preserved, and pasteurized, such as white flour, cake mixes, processed cereals, dry milk, dried eggs, pasteurized milk, and canned or frozen pre-cooked meals that have been conserved, pasteurized

- Mayonnaise, cream cheese, butter, margarine, and dried fruits

Tran's fatty acids

- Tran's fats are the most inflammatory of all fats.

- Pro-inflammatory prostaglandins are produced as a result of these lipids.

- Fried and deep-fried dishes (typically cooked in hydrogenated shortening) are Tran's fats. Margarine and shortening are also high in Tran's fats.

- Dairy-free creamers

- Biscuits

- Baked products including cakes, pie crusts, and cookies (particularly those with icing)

- Baked goods

- Crackers, chips, and other snack items identify hydrogenated as an ingredient.

1.2 Foods that cause inflammation

Saturated fatty acids Saturated fats are unhealthy fats found in meat, high-fat dairy products, and eggs. Although saturated fats provide vital vitamins and minerals, they may cause inflammation, as shown by their capacity to raise fibrinogen and CRP inflammatory indicators in the blood.

Fatty acids with omega-6. Excessive consumption of omega-6 fatty acids causes inflammation, induces blood clotting, and may cause cells to multiply uncontrollably, even though they are unsaturated and considered necessary in tiny amounts. Omega-6 fatty acids are prevalent in the current diet due to excessive intake of meats and vegetable oils such as maize, safflower, soybean, and cottonseed, widely found in processed meals and fast foods.

Lampshades Although fruits and vegetables are highly healthy, some nightshade foods, such as potatoes, tomatoes, eggplants, ground cherries, and tomatillos, may increase inflammation in certain individuals.

1.3 Inflammation-Reducing Foods

Fortunately, several nutrients may assist your body in fighting inflammation. The most effective anti-inflammatories may be bought in the supermarket, not the drugstore! Your best chance is to stick to the supermarket's perimeter to discover fresh, unadulterated items. Look for brilliantly colored fruits and vegetables, herbs and spices, and meals high in healthy fats. Let's look at all the anti-inflammatory foods you should stock your pantry with.

Vegetables and fruits

Phytochemicals and antioxidants, both of which have anti-inflammatory properties, are abundant in fruits and vegetables.

Although not needed for life, phytochemicals are plant-derived substances with several health advantages, including lowering the risk of cancer, heart disease, and diabetes. Phytochemicals are essential for plant defense and survival. These powerful compounds aid plants in their resistance to bacterial and fungal infections, free radical damage, and continual exposure to UV radiation from the sun. Fortunately, the compounds found in plants permeate your body's tissues, protecting against sickness.

Fatty Acids Omega-3

In the body, omega-3 fatty acids have an anti-inflammatory action.

These fatty acids are transformed into eicosanoids, which are hormone-like compounds. Eicosapentaenoic acid (EPA) and docosahexaenoic acid (DHA) are the two most powerful omega-3 eicosanoids (DHA). Dilating blood arteries, preventing blood clotting, and lowering inflammation benefit EPA and DHA. Fatty fish such as albacore tuna, anchovies, Atlantic herring, halibut, lake trout, mackerel, sardines, striped sea bass, and wild salmon are rich in omega-3s.

Probiotics are found in flaxseeds and flaxseed oils, walnuts, soybeans, and tofu.

There are millions upon millions of naturally occurring bacteria in the human body. Bacteria have a terrible reputation, yet the correct bacteria, such as lactobacilli and Bifidobacterium, may help you stay healthy and prevent illness. These bacteria help maintain the immune system's strength and ability to fight disease and sickness. They also contain anti-inflammatory properties in the intestine, which may aid with constipation, diarrhea, inflammatory bowel disease, and irritable bowel syndrome.

Consuming foods like Lactobacillus acidophilus, which contains high quantities of beneficial probiotics (the name probiotics means "for life"), may help good bacteria thrive. Probiotic bacteria in your body are increased by fermented milk products like yogurt, kefir, and other soy-based drinks. To ensure you're getting enough probiotics, look for "live and active cultures" on the label.

Protein (Light)

Clean protein comes from lean meats, white flesh poultry, and eggs, which are low in pro-inflammatory lipids. Coldwater fish provide a good source of protein and anti-inflammatory omega-3 fatty acids.

Soy meals, beans, lentils, whole grains, seeds, and nuts are examples of vegetable proteins that minimize the presence of pro-inflammatory agents in the body while also providing phytochemicals and antioxidants.

Garlic

Garlic is a very effective anti-inflammatory food. It includes compounds that crush the body's inflammation-causing molecules. Consequently, frequent garlic intake may help lessen the pain and inflammation associated with osteoarthritis and rheumatoid arthritis and asthma symptoms.

Curcumin

Curcumin is a compound present in turmeric, a

yellow curry spice.

Curcumin has been suggested to have antioxidant,

anti-inflammatory, and perhaps anticancer properties. Curcumin may have anti-inflammatory and anticancer characteristics, according to preliminary data from animal studies. However, there is presently very little study evaluating the impact of curcumin intake on disease risk in people.

Ginger

Turmeric's cousin, ginger, is a tropical plant. Gingerols, one of the plant's ingredients, is thought to block a variety of biochemicals that cause inflammation, particularly in osteoarthritis and rheumatoid arthritis. Fresh ginger gives meals a subtle spiciness and mellow sweetness, and it's a great spice to use in stir-fries and dipping sauces.

1.4 Anti-Inflammatory Diet's Main Advantages

According to research, eating an anti-inflammatory diet may help relieve the symptoms of various diseases.

The formation of plaque in the arteries is known as atherosclerosis, and it is quite prevalent among the elderly. The researchers discovered a correlation between subclinical atherosclerosis and heart disease-related mortality; following an anti-inflammatory diet may assist people with type 2 diabetes decrease certain inflammatory markers. Individuals with type 2 diabetes who follow the Mediterranean diet solely report fewer inflammation symptoms than those who do not follow an anti-inflammatory diet.

The Mediterranean diet and the anti-inflammatory diet have a lot in common. The Mediterranean diet emphasizes low-fat dairy products and the selection and preparation of protein-rich meals. Mediterranean diet followers favor plant-based proteins such as beans, nuts, and seeds, which may also offer enough dietary fiber. As previously stated, antioxidants are necessary for our diets to help prevent or postpone cell damage. You should choose vegetables and fruits of various colors to help manage inflammation and deliver consistent energy. Minerals and vitamins, vital fatty acids, dietary fiber, and beneficial phytonutrients should all be included in an anti-inflammatory diet.

Furthermore, following an anti-inflammatory diet might assist you in preventing becoming obese. An anti-inflammatory diet warns against eating too many calories, leading to fat tissue buildup and obesity.

Obesity and an inflammatory diet may be linked in numerous ways. One inflammatory diet consumes more refined carbs, processed meats, and junk food. Because of the low-calorie content and lack of fiber in these meals, a person will have to compensate for the calorie deficit and lack of satiety by eating more. Two, someone who eats an inflammatory diet may spend more time sitting inside, encouraging them to consume more calories and move less.

An anti-inflammatory diet, in particular, may aid people who are already suffering from inflammatory

disorders. Anti-inflammatory diets that exclude refined sugars and carbohydrates, for example, may lead to type 2 diabetes, metabolic syndrome, and obesity. Instead, an anti-inflammatory diet recommends eating whole grains like brown rice, which is high in fiber and low glycemic index.

In this way, following an anti-inflammatory diet improves one's long-term health. In an anti-inflammatory diet, saturated and trans-fatty acids are avoided in omega-3 fatty acids. Unhealthy fat consumption has been linked to an increased risk of cardiovascular disease. One of the negative consequences of bad fats is that they deposit on the inside walls of blood vessels, narrowing them and raising blood pressure. Increased blood pressure may harm blood vessels and other organs that respond to a higher than normal blood flow rate. The anti-inflammatory diet encourages heart-healthy oils like olive oil and flaxseed.

With this in mind, an anti-inflammatory diet is essential for long-term blood pressure management.

An anti-inflammatory diet may also help with weariness. The inflammation indicates that the immune system is working. Histamine levels rise when the immune system gets completely dedicated, making a person feel sleepy, tired, and cranky. The immune system's operations are supposed to cause weariness, which allows your body to slow down and preserve energy. Fatigue is also thought to aid rest and healing rather than limiting the body. An anti-inflammatory diet helps to reduce or eliminate inflammation, which reduces or eliminates the immune system's fatigue-causing effects.

An anti-inflammatory diet, which has nothing to do with obesity, may help you lose weight. You might be overweight or on the verge of being obese even if you are not obese. Unintentional weight gain and other non-dietary reasons, such as sedentary lifestyles, blame on the high consumption of refined carbs and sugars. Refined carbohydrate foods are deficient in nutrients, meaning that one must eat more calories than required to meet calorie requirements. Furthermore, refined carbohydrate foods lack fiber, causing people to overeat about their physical size since they don't feel full. Fortunately, an anti-inflammatory diet excludes refined carbs and promotes other nutrient-dense foods, meaning that harmful sugars and carbohydrates are avoided. Following an anti-inflammatory diet also has indirect advantages.

One of these advantages is that a person will feel more settled due to dietary choices that reduce inflammation. Pain, weariness, swelling, and immobility are some of the symptoms of inflammation.

Inflammation, in this context, may lead to absence from work or school. Inflammation may cause pain at work or school, making it difficult to concentrate. An individual's chances of achieving desired attention at work or school will improve if dietary sources of inflammation are addressed.

An anti-inflammatory diet may help you sleep better. Diet may contribute to poor sleep quality or an inconsistent sleep pattern in various ways. When you eat a diet that raises inflammation, you'll have trouble sleeping regularly, and when you do, it'll be of poor quality. An inflammatory diet may lead to eating problems, such as getting up in the middle of the night to eat, disrupting the quality and length of sleep. You may need frequent episodes of brief sleeping due to weariness, which will disrupt your night's sleep. Fortunately, an anti-inflammatory diet may help you sleep better by reducing inflammation and ensuring that your meals are balanced in terms of calories and minerals.

Finally, an anti-inflammatory diet encourages diversity and choice, enabling other dietary regimens to draw inspiration. An anti-inflammatory diet reduces or eliminates inflammation while still providing the nutrients and calories required for daily consumption. Several diets, such as vegan and Mediterranean, match the anti-inflammatory diet. An anti-inflammatory diet enables people to make their own choices, which is a key aspect of the success of any dietary strategy. Because of availability, cost, cultural relevance, and seasonality, openness in a dietary plan are required.

1.5 Shopping List for an Anti-Inflammatory Diet

On the first day of an anti-inflammatory diet, you don't have to clean out your refrigerator. The first step is to take stock of what you already have. You should also make a list of everything in the kitchen and pantry.

Some of the foods you already have on hand may have anti-inflammatory properties. During this inventory, you must identify any food that does not meet the criteria and either donate it or throw it away. Below is a complete list of anti-inflammatory foods that may be beneficial.

- Eggs With Animal Protein
- Sardines
- Bison And Grass-Fed Beef
- Breasts And Thighs Of Chicken
- Herring
- Salmon (Wild)
- Mackerel
- Lamb
- Veggies
- Asparagus
- Arugula
- Avocados
- Artichokes
- Beets
- Peppers (Bell) (Any Color Or Variant)
- Green Beets
- Bok Choy, Broccoli, And Other Asian Greens

- Sprouts From Brussels
- Rabe Broccoli (Rapine)
- Cabbage (Green And Red Variants)
- Cauliflower
- Carrots
- Chicory
- Celery
- Chard (All Variants)
- Chives
- Cabbage From China
- Cucumbers
- Greens From Collards
- Green Dandelion
- Radishes Daikon
- Escarole \Endive
- Garlic
- Fennel
- Jicama
- Leeks
- Kale (All Types)
- Mushrooms
- Lettuce (All Varieties Except Iceberg, Which I Dislike)
- Mustard Leaves
- Olives (Fresh, Not Canned)
- Okra
- Radicchio
- Onions
- Pumpkin
- Parsnips
- Radishes
- Leaves Of Radish
- Romaine
- Scallions
- Rhubarb \Rutabagas
- Sea Vegetables (Nori, Dulse, Kombu, Wakame, Kelp)
- Shallots
- Sprouts

- Spinach
- Potatoes Dulces
- Squash (All Variants Like Winter And Summer Varieties)
- Tomatillos \Tomatoes
- Turnips
- Greens From Turnips
- Watercress
- Zucchini
- Yams
- Fruits
- Apples
- Bananas
- Apricots
- Oranges With Blood
- Blackberries
- Cantaloupes
- Blueberries
- Coconut
- Cherries
- Currants
- Cranberries
- Dried Fruit (No Sugar, Sulfur, Or Other Additions)
- Grapefruit
- Dates
- Berries Of Goji
- Figs (Fresh) (Fresh)
- Guava
- Grapes
- Kiwi
- Melon With Honeydew
- Limes
- Lemons
- Muskmelon
- Mangoes
- Oranges
- Nectarines
- Peaches
- Papayas
- Persimmons
- Pears
- Pineapples
- Watermelon
- Pomegranates
- Plums
- Raisins
- Prunes
- Raspberries
- Tangerines
- Strawberries
- Seeds And Nuts
- Almonds
- Seeds Of Chia
- Nuts From Brazil
- Ground Flaxseed
- Cashews
- Seeds Of Hemp
- Hazelnuts
- Nut Macadamia
- Brazil, Almond, Cashew, Pumpkin, Pecan, Walnut, And Sunflower Butter
- Nuts Of Pine
- Pecans
- Seeds Of Sesame
- Seeds From Pumpkins
- Paste Of Tahini
- Seeds From Sunflowers
- Walnuts
- Spices And Herbs
- Pepper Ancho
- Leaves Of Bay
- Basil
- Cardamom
- Freshly Ground Black Pepper

- Seeds From Celery
- Pepper Cayenne
- Powdered Chili
- Chervil
- Powdered Chipotle
- Red Chilies
- Cinnamon, Ground Or Sticks
- Coriander Cilantro (Ground)
- Cumin
- Cloves
- Curry Powder With Dill
- Powdered Five-Spice
- Seeds Of Fennel
- Fresh Garlic
- Masala Garam
- Gomasio
- Fresh And Ground Ginger
- Marjoram
- Lemongrass
- Powdered Mustard
- Mint
- Seeds Of Mustard
- Oregano
- Nutmeg
- Parsley
- Paprika
- Flakes Of Red Pepper (Crushed)
- Turmeric
- Rosemary
- Black Peppercorns
- Saffron
- Sage
- Anise Star
- Sea Salt
- Thyme
- Tarragon
- Legumes And Beans

- Garbanzo Beans/Chickpeas
- Green And Brown Lentils
- Peas (Snow, Green, And Sugar Snap)
- Condiments
- Vinegar Balsamic
- Oil From Avocado
- Miso Made With Chickpeas
- Aminos De Coco (Soy Sauce Alternative, Gluten-Free)
- Unsweetened Cocoa Powder
- Coconut Flesh (Fresh)
- Shredded Coconut, Unsweetened Flakes
- Coconut Oil Is A Kind Of Vegetable Oil.
- Olive Oil (Extra Virgin)
- Yogurt With Coconut
- Oil From Flaxseed
- Raw Honey
- Hemp Oil
- Kimchi
- Medjool Dates With Horseradish
- Vegetable Broth With Low Sodium (Organic)
- Pickles
- Mustard, Dijon Mustard, Or Whole Grain Mustard
- Almond Extract (Pure)
- Vanilla Extract (Pure)
- Authentic Maple Syrup
- Vinegar Of Red Wine
- Apple Cider Vinegar, Unfiltered
- Sauerkraut
- Tomatillos (In A Glass Jar Or Sundried)
- Salsa
- Hot Sauce Or Sriracha Sauce
- Vinegar Of White Wine
- Grains (Gluten-Free)
- Amaranth
- Pasta With Chickpeas
- Pasta With Brown Rice
- Buckwheat

- Teff

- Spaghetti With Chickpeas

- Millet

- Quinoa (White, Red)

- Rolled And Steel-Cut Gluten-Free Oats

- Rice From Sorghum (Black, Wild, Brown)

- Milk Without Dairy

- Hemp-Based Milk

- Milk From Almonds

- Coconut Milk For Cooking (In BPA-Free Cans)

- Cashew Cream

- Oat Milk (Only From Gluten-Free Oats)

- Coconut Cream

- Beverages

- Purified/Filtered Water

- Teas With Herbs (Any Tea That Is Good For Detoxification)

- Tea (Green)

- Green Juices That Have Been Freshly Squeezed And Pressed

- Baking Flours Without Gluten

- Almond Meal

- Almond Meal With Coconut Flour

- Oat Flour Without Gluten

- Flour From Chickpeas (Garbanzo Bean)

- Snacks

- Chocolate (Dark)

- Cocoa

- Cocoa

- Lipoic Acid (ALA)

- Extract Of Curcumin

- Extract Fish Oil

- Extract Of Ginger

- Resveratrol

- Spirulina

1.6 Meal Plan

Week 1

MONDAY
Breakfast: Tropical Green Smoothie
Lunch: Slow-Cooker Vegan Split Pea Soup
Dinner: Brown Rice Pasta with Creamy Carrot "Marinara"

TUESDAY
Breakfast: Avocado Toast with Greens
Lunch: Brown Rice Pasta with Creamy Carrot "Marinara" **(leftovers)**
Dinner: Whitefish Chowder

WEDNESDAY
Breakfast: "Choose Your Adventure" Chia Breakfast Pudding
Lunch: Slow-Cooker Vegan Split Pea Soup **(leftovers)**
Dinner: Quinoa Flatbread Pizza

THURSDAY
Breakfast: Strawberry Sunshine Smoothie
Lunch: Whitefish Chowder **(leftovers)**
Dinner: Baby Bok Choy Stir-Fry

FRIDAY
Breakfast: "Choose Your Adventure" Chia Breakfast Pudding **(leftovers)**
Lunch: Baby Bok Choy Stir-Fry **(leftovers)**
Dinner: Buckwheat-Vegetable Polenta

SATURDAY
Breakfast: Blueberry-Millet Breakfast Bake
Lunch: Buckwheat-Vegetable Polenta **(leftovers)**
Dinner: Tasty Fish Tacos with Pineapple Salsa

SUNDAY
Breakfast: Blueberry-Millet Breakfast Bake **(leftovers)**
Lunch: Poached Chicken Wraps
Dinner: Classic Butternut Squash Soup

SNACKS
Pick one to two snacks per day. If you aren't hungry between meals, don't feel obligated to snack.

- Piece of fruit
- Handful of nuts or seeds
- Mug of herbal tea or bone broth (Basic Chicken Broth)
- Baked Zucchini Chips
- No-Bake Chocolate Chip Granola Bars
- Crudités with Roasted Fennel and Sunflower Seed Pesto*

Week 2

MONDAY

Breakfast: Tropical Green Smoothie

Lunch: Classic Butternut Squash Soup (leftover from Week One)

Dinner: Coconut Chicken Curry

TUESDAY

Breakfast: Maple-Tahini Oatmeal

Lunch: Coconut Chicken Curry (leftovers)

Dinner: Home-Style Red Lentil Stew

WEDNESDAY

Breakfast: "Quick Greens and Cauliflower Bowl

Lunch: Gluten-Free Ramen "To Go"

Dinner: Sesame-Tuna with Asparagus

THURSDAY

Breakfast: Butternut Squash Smoothie

Lunch: Home-Style Red Lentil Stew (leftovers)

Dinner: Slow-Cooker Chicken Alfredo (here)

FRIDAY

Breakfast: Tropical Green Smoothie

Lunch: Slow-Cooker Chicken Alfredo (leftovers)

Dinner: Homemade Avocado Sushi

SATURDAY

Breakfast: Maple-Cinnamon Granola

Lunch: Cream of Broccoli Soup

Dinner: Root Vegetable Loaf with Cumin-Roasted Cauliflower

SUNDAY

Breakfast: Maple-Cinnamon Granola (leftovers)

Lunch: Cream of Broccoli Soup (leftovers)

Dinner: Vegetable Spring Roll Wraps

SNACKS

Pick one to two snacks per day. If you aren't hungry between meals, don't feel obligated to snack.
- Crispy Roasted Chickpeas*
- Carrot and Raisin Salad*
- Half an avocado (sprinkled with sea salt)
- 1 or 2 Medjool dates, sliced open and spread with nut or seed butter
- Apple topped with nut or seed butter
- Crudités with Creamy Lentil Dip*, or purchased hummus or guacamole

Week 3

MONDAY

Breakfast: Strawberry Sunshine Smoothie

Lunch: Herbed Tuna Cakes

Dinner: Quinoa-Lentil Salad

TUESDAY

Breakfast: Quick Greens and Cauliflower Bowl

Lunch: Brown Rice Congee

Dinner: Almond-Crusted Honey-Dijon Salmon with Greens

WEDNESDAY

Breakfast: "Choose Your Adventure" Chia Breakfast Pudding

Lunch: Brown Rice Congee (leftovers)

Dinner: Carrot-Ginger Soup

THURSDAY

Breakfast: "Choose Your Adventure" Chia Breakfast Pudding

Lunch: Quinoa-Lentil Salad (leftovers)

Dinner: Yam-Bean Burgers

FRIDAY

Breakfast: Avocado Toast with Greens

Lunch: Carrot-Ginger Soup (leftovers)

Dinner: Sardine Donburi

SATURDAY

Breakfast: Gluten-Free Toast with Toasted Coconut Sunbutter

Lunch: Glorious Creamed Greens Soup

Dinner: Yam-Bean Burgers (leftovers)

SUNDAY

Breakfast: Tropical Green Smoothie

Lunch: Glorious Creamed Greens Soup (leftovers)

Dinner: Apple-Turkey Burgers with Garlicky Sautéed Greens

SNACKS

Pick one to two snacks per day. If you aren't hungry between meals, don't feel obligated to snack.

- 1 cup of any soup leftovers
- 1 or 2 pieces of Quinoa Flatbread spread with nut butter, or purchased hummus or guacamole
- Half a steamed sweet potato mashed with coconut oil, hemp seeds, and sea salt
- Crudités with Veggie Pâté*
- Chocolate-Avocado Pudding*

Chapter 2: Breakfast

1. Egg Kale with Caressole

Preparation time: 10 minutes

Cooking Time: 17 minutes

Servings: 6

Ingredients

- 1 tablespoon of avocado oil
- 1 onion
- 5 kale leaves
- 1 clove of garlic
- 2 tablespoons of lemon juice
- ½ teaspoon of salt
- 9 eggs
- 2 tablespoons of water
- 1½ teaspoons of rosemary
- 1 teaspoon of oregano
- ¼ teaspoon of black pepper
- ½ cup yeast

Instructions

Add the oil to the saucepan and sauté for 1 minute. Sauté onion for 2 minutes until tender. 14 teaspoon salt, greens, garlic, lemon juice agitate.2 minutes more cook time. Click Cancel.

Meanwhile, combine the eggs, water, 14 teaspoons of salt, pepper, and nutritional yeast. Stir in the onion and kale combination. Rinse the inner pot and add 2 cups of water inside. Cooking sprays a spring from a pan. Move the egg to a spring form pan. Set the pan on the steam rack and cover. Manual or Force Cook button, 12-minute timer. Quickly release pressure until the timer beeps, then open the lid. Remove the pan from the pot and cool for 5 minutes. Chopping, serving.

Nutritional facts

Calories 45| Carbohydrates 7 g| Proteins 1 g| Fats

g| Sodium 21 mg |

2. Raspberry Steel Cut Oatmeal Bars

Preparation time: 5 minutes

Cooking Time: 15 minutes

Servings: 6

Ingredients

- 3 cups of steel-cut oats
- 3 eggs
- 2 cups vanilla almond milk
- ⅓ cup of erythritol
- 1 teaspoon of vanilla extract
- ¼ teaspoon of salt
- 1 cup of raspberries frozen

Instructions

Mix all ingredients except raspberries in a medium bowl. Combine all ingredients and fold in raspberries. Cooking oil in a cake pan. Cover the oat mixture with aluminum foil. Place the steam rack into the Instant Pot with 1 cup of water. Place the oat pan on the rack. Fix the lid. Set the timer to 15 minutes. Quickly remove pressure until the float valve drops, then unlock the lid. Remove the pan and foil from the inner pot. Let cool fully before cutting into bars.

Nutritional facts

Calories 48| Carbohydrates 5 g| Proteins 4 g| Fats 1 g| Sodium 23 mg |

3. Blueberry Vanilla Quinoa Porridge

Preparation time: 2 minutes

Cooking Time: 1 minute

Servings: 6

Ingredients

- 1½ cups of dry quinoa
- 3 cups of water
- 1 cup of frozen blueberries
- ½ teaspoon stevia powder
- 1 teaspoon pure vanilla extract

Instructions

Rinse the quinoa carefully in a fine-mesh strainer until the water flows clear. Inner pot: quinoa, water, blueberries, stevia, vanilla Mix well. Fix the lid. Set the timer to 1 minute on the Manual or Pressure Cook button. Quickly remove pressure until the float valve drops, then unlock the lid. Allow quinoa to cool slightly before serving.

Nutritional facts

Calories 45| Carbohydrates 7 g| Proteins 1 g| Fats 1.2 g| Sodium 21 mg |

4. Buckwheat Ginger Granola

Preparation time: 10 minutes

Cooking Time: 10 minute

Servings: 8

Ingredients

- 1½ cups of groats
- 1½ cups of rolled oats
- ⅓ cup of walnuts
- ⅓ cup of coconut
- ¼ cup of coconut oil
- 1" piece of ginger
- 3 tablespoons of date syrup
- 1 teaspoon of cinnamon
- ¼ teaspoon of salt

Instructions

There should be plenty of a medium-sized mixing basin with all the ingredients (save the coconut). Stir in coconut oil, ginger, date syrup, cinnamon, and salt. Pour into the cake pan. In the inner pot, put 1 cup of water and a steam rack. Place pan on rack. Fix the lid. Set the timer to 10 minutes in Manual or Pressure Cook mode. Quickly remove pressure until the float valve drops, then unlock the lid. Spread the granola on a large sheet pan and chill for 1 hour. It will crisp up.

Nutritional facts

Calories 44| Carbohydrates 4 g| Proteins 4 g| Fats 2 g| Sodium 27 mg |

5. Orange Cinnamon Oatmeal Muffins

Preparation time: 7 minutes

Cooking Time: 15 minute

Servings: 6

Ingredients

- 3 cups oats
- 1 teaspoon baking powder
- ¼ teaspoon salt
- 1 teaspoon cinnamon
- ¼ cup vanilla almond milk

- ¼ cup orange juice
- 3 cups mashed bananas
- 1 egg
- ¼ cup erythritol

Instructions

Add all ingredients and toss thoroughly.6 silicone muffin cups in a cake pan. Fill the muffin tins with the oat mixture Cover with foil. Place the steam rack into the inner pot with 1 cup of water. Place the muffin pan on the rack. Fix the lid. Set the timer to 15 minutes. Quickly remove pressure until the float valve drops, then unlock the lid. Remove the pan from the inner pot and the foil on top. Let the muffins cool for 15 minutes. They'll stiffen up as they cool.

Nutritional facts

Calories: 212| Carbohydrates: 24 g| Protein: 3 g| Fat: 4 g| Sodium 196 mg |

6. Coconut Chocolate Oatmeal

Preparation time: 5 minutes

Cooking Time: 6 minute

Servings: 4

Ingredients

- 1 cup of oats
- 1 can of coconut milk
- 2 cups of water
- ½ cup of cacao powder
- ½ cup of erythritol
- ⅛ teaspoon of sea salt

Instructions

Add the oats, coconut milk, water, cacao powder, erythritol, and salt to the inner pot. Fix the lid. Set the timer to 6 minutes on the Manual or Pressure Cook button. Quickly remove pressure until the float valve drops, then unlock the lid. Allow the oatmeal to cool slightly before serving.

Nutritional facts

Calories: 202| Carbohydrates: 14 g| Protein: 5 g| Fat: 6 g| Sodium 186 mg |

7. Banana Date Porridge

Preparation time: 5 minutes

Cooking Time: 4 minute

Servings: 4

Ingredients

- 1 cup groats

- 1½ cups vanilla almond milk
- 1 cup water
- 1 large banana
- 5 pitted dates
- ¾ teaspoon cinnamon
- ¾ teaspoon vanilla extract

Instructions

A banana, dates, cinnamon, and vanilla are in the inner saucepan. Fix the lid. Set the timer to 4 minutes on the Manual or Pressure Cook button. Quickly remove pressure until the float valve drops, then unlock the lid. Let the porridge cool slightly before serving it in bowls.

Nutritional facts

Calories: 112| Carbohydrates: 26 g| Protein: 2 g| Fat: 5 g| Sodium 106 mg |

8. Blueberry Banana Baked Oatmeal

Preparation time: 5 minutes

Cooking Time: 7 minute

Servings: 6

Ingredients

- 3 cups of oats
- ¼ teaspoon of salt
- 2 bananas
- 2 eggs
- ⅓ cup of xylitol

Instructions

Mix the oats, salt, bananas, eggs, and xylitol in a medium bowl. Lightly spray a cake pan. Add oat mixture to pan. 11 cups of water into the inner pot. Put a steam rack in the inner pot and the pan on it. Fix the lid. Set the timer to 7 minutes on the Manual or Pressure Cook button. Quickly remove pressure until the float valve drops, then unlock the lid. Wait 5 minutes before serving the porridge.

Nutritional facts

Calories: 172| Carbohydrates: 26 g| Protein: 5 g| Fat: 5 g| Sodium 186 mg |

9. Banana Steel Cut Walnut Oats

Preparation time: 2 minutes

Cooking Time: 4 minute

Servings: 4

Ingredients

- 2 cups of oats

- 2½ cups of water
- 2½ cups of vanilla almond milk
- 3 bananas
- 1½ teaspoons of cinnamon
- 1 teaspoon of vanilla extract
- ¼ teaspoon of salt
- 4 tablespoons of walnut pieces

Instructions

Stir in the steel-cut oats, other ingredients and salt. Fix the lid. Set the Instant Pot to Pressure Cook for 4 minutes. After 15 minutes, quick-release any leftover pressure until the float valve lowers, then open the lid. Each plate of oats is topped with 1 tablespoon of chopped walnuts.

Nutritional facts

Calories: 182| Carbohydrates: 44 g| Protein: 4 g| Fat: 8 g| Sodium 156 mg |

10. Spinach and Artichoke Egg Casserole

Preparation time: 10 minutes

Cooking Time: 18 minute

Servings: 8

Ingredients

- 12 eggs
- ¼ cup of water
- 4 cups spinach
- 1 can of baby artichoke
- 1 tablespoon of chives
- 1 tablespoon of lemon juice
- ¾ teaspoon of salt
- ½ teaspoon of black pepper
- ¼ teaspoon of garlic salt

Instructions

Cooking spray in a round glass bowl. Whisk the eggs and water in a medium bowl, then add the spinach, artichokes, chives, and lemon juice. Pour the mixture into the pan. In the inner pot, add 2 cups of water and the steam rack. Set the pan on the steam rack. Fix the lid. Set the timer to 18 minutes. Quickly remove pressure until the float valve drops, then unlock the lid. Allow it cool for 5 minutes before slicing and serving.

Nutritional facts

Calories: 202| Carbohydrates: 20 g| Protein: 5 g| Fat: 8 g| Sodium 176 mg |

11. Coconut Almond Granola

Preparation time: 5 minutes

Cooking Time: 7 minute

Servings: 8

Ingredients

- 1½ cups of rolled oats
- ½ cup of unsweetened shredded coconut
- ¼ cup of monk fruit sweetener
- ⅛ teaspoon of salt
- ¾ cup of almond butter
- ¼ cup of coconut oil

Instructions

Mix oats, coconut, sweetener, and salt in a medium bowl. Mix in the almond butter and oil. Prep cake pan with nonstick spray. Add the oat mixture to the pan and 1 cup of water to the Instant Pot inner pot. Place the steam rack inside and the pan on top. Fix the lid. Set the timer to 7 minutes on the Manual or Pressure Cook button. Quickly remove pressure until the float valve drops, then unlock the lid. Remove the pan from the inner pot and cool thoroughly before serving.

Nutritional facts

Calories: 155| Carbohydrates: 25 g| Protein: 4 g| Fat: 8 g| Sodium 126 mg |

12. Pumpkin Quinoa Porridge

Preparation time: 2 minutes

Cooking Time: 1 minute

Servings: 4

Ingredients

- ¾ cup dry quinoa
- 2 cups water
- ¾ cup pumpkin purée
- ¼ cup monk fruit sweetener
- 1½ teaspoons pumpkin pie spice
- 1 teaspoon pure vanilla extract
- ¼ teaspoon salt

Instructions

Rinse the quinoa in a fine-mesh sieve until the water flows clear. Quinoa, water, pumpkin purée, and salt to the inner saucepan. Mix well. Fix the lid. Set the timer to 1 minute on the Manual or Pressure Cook button. Quickly remove pressure until the float valve drops, then unlock the lid. Allow quinoa to cool slightly before serving.

Nutritional facts

Calories: 132| Carbohydrates: 17 g| Protein: 3 g| Fat: 5 g| Sodium 138 mg |

13. Meyer Lemon Poppy Seed Individual Baked Oatmeal Cups

Preparation time: 5 minutes

Cooking Time: 5 minute

Servings: 4

Ingredients

- 2 cups of rolled oats
- 1 teaspoon of baking powder
- 2 tablespoons of erythritol
- 1 tablespoon of poppy seeds
- ¼ teaspoon of salt
- 1 egg
- Juice from 1 Meyer lemon
- 1 cup of unsweetened vanilla almond milk

Instructions

Grease four (8-ounce) ramekins. Dispose of. The oats, baking powder, erythritol, poppy seeds, salt Stir in the egg, lemon juice and zest, and almond milk. Soak the oats in water for 30 minutes and put 12 cups of water into the Instant Pot® inner pot. Place the ramekins on top of the steam rack inside the inner pot. Fix the lid. Set the timer to 5 minutes on the Manual or Pressure Cook button. Quickly remove pressure until the float valve drops, then unlock the lid. The ramekins will be hot when you open the lid, so use little oven mitts to remove them and cool them before serving.

Nutritional facts

Calories: 250| Carbohydrates: 47 g| Protein: 3 g| Fat: 2 g| Sodium 122 mg |

14. Apple Cinnamon Steel Cut Oats

Preparation time: 10 minutes

Cooking Time: 4 minute

Servings: 6

Ingredients

- 2 cups of steel-cut oats
- 3 cups of unsweetened vanilla almond milk
- 3 cups of water
- 3 small apples, cut into 1"-thick chunks
- 2 teaspoons of ground cinnamon

- ¼ cup of date syrup
- ¼ teaspoon of salt

Instructions

Stir in the steel-cut oats, almond milk, water, apple pieces, cinnamon, date syrup, and salt. Fix the lid. Set the timer to 4 minutes on the Manual or Pressure Cook button. After 15 minutes, quick-release any leftover pressure until the float valve lowers, then open the lid.

Nutritional facts

Calories: 112 | Carbohydrates: 22 g | Protein: 3 g | Fat: 5 g | Sodium 146 mg |

15. Triple Berry Steel Cut Oats

Preparation time: 5 minutes

Cooking Time: 4 minute

Servings: 6

Ingredients

- 2 cups of steel-cut oats
- 3 cups of unsweetened almond milk
- 3 cups of water
- 1 teaspoon of vanilla extract
- ⅓ cup of monk fruit sweetener
- ¼ teaspoon of salt
- 1½ cups of frozen berry blend with strawberries, blackberries, and raspberries

Instructions

Stir in the steel-cut oats, almond milk, water, vanilla, sweetener, and salt. Add the frozen berries. Fix the lid. Set the Instant Pot® to Manual or Pressure Cook for 4 minutes. After 15 minutes, quick-release any leftover pressure until the float valve lowers, then open the lid. Warm-up.

Nutritional Facts

Calories: 224 | Carbohydrates 42g | Protein 7g | Fat 3g | Sodium 130 mg |

16. Banana Pancake Bites

Preparation time: 10 minutes

Cooking Time: 6 minute

Servings: 3

Ingredients

- 1¾ cups of rolled oats
- 3 small bananas
- 3 eggs
- 2 tablespoons of erythritol

- 1 teaspoon of ground cinnamon
- 1 teaspoon of pure vanilla extract
- 1 teaspoon of baking powder

Instructions

In a big, strong blender, combine the oats, bananas, eggs, erythritol, cinnamon, vanilla, and baking powder. Fill a silicone mold with seven wells. Cover with a paper towel, then aluminum foil. Tighten the edges to keep moisture out. Place the mold on top of the steam rack. 1 cup of water in the inner saucepan. Insert the steam rack and mold. Fix the lid. Set the timer to 6 minutes on the Manual or Pressure Cook button. Quickly remove pressure until the float valve drops, then unlock the lid. Remove the Instant Pot® steam rack, mold, aluminum foil, and paper towel. Allow the pancake bits to cool fully before removing them from the mold with a knife. Press the bottom of the mold to release the pancake bits.

Nutritional Facts

Calories: 204 | Carbohydrates 33 g | Protein 5 g | Fat 8 g | Sodium 120 mg |

17. Cinnamon Flaxseed Breakfast Loaf

Preparation time: 10 minutes

Cooking Time: 30 minute

Servings: 6

Ingredients

- ½ cup of ground golden flaxseed meal
- ½ cup of almond flour
- 1 tablespoon of ground cinnamon
- 2 teaspoons of baking powder
- ½ teaspoon of salt
- ⅔ cup of xylitol
- 4 eggs
- ½ cup of coconut oil

Instructions

Mix flaxseed meal, flour, cinnamon, baking powder, salt, and xylitol. Separately, mix the eggs and cooled coconut oil. Mix the wet and dry ingredients. Pour the mixture into a 6" cake pan and cover with aluminum foil. Fill the inner pot with 112 cups of water and add the steam rack with handles. The cake pan on the steam rack fixes the lid. Set the timer to 30 minutes in Manual or Pressure Cook mode. Quickly remove pressure until the float valve drops, then unlock the lid. Remove the pan from the Instant Pot® and allow the bread to cool completely before removing the loaf. Serve sliced.

Nutritional Facts

Calories: 124 | Carbohydrates 55 g | Protein 6 g | Fat 8 g | Sodium 120 mg |

18. Vegetable Breakfast Bowls

Preparation time: 10 minutes

Cooking Time: 16 minute

Servings: 2

Ingredients

* 2 tablespoons of avocado oil
* 3 leeks of white and light green portion thinly sliced
* 8 ounces sliced mushrooms
* ½ teaspoon of salt
* ¼ teaspoon of black pepper
* 2 carrots, peeled and sliced
* 5 kale leaves, finely chopped
* Juice from ½ lemon

Instructions

Pour the oil into the inner pot and press Sauté. After 2 minutes, add the leeks, mushrooms, salt, and pepper. 10 minutes sauté onions and mushrooms. Stir in the carrots, kale, and lemon juice. Fix the lid, Select Manual or Pressure Cook and set the timer to 4 minutes. Quickly remove pressure until the float valve drops, then unlock the lid. Instantly serve

Nutritional Facts

Calories: 200| Carbohydrates 27 g| Protein 17 g| Fat 8 g | Sodium 150 mg |

19. Root Vegetable Egg Casserole

Preparation time: 10 minutes

Cooking Time: 29 minute

Servings: 4

Ingredients

* 1 tablespoon of avocado oil
* 1 small onion, peeled and diced nicely
* 1 small turnip, peeled and diced nicely
* 1 medium parsnip, peeled and diced nicely
* 2 small carrots, peeled and diced nicely
* 1 teaspoon of kosher salt
* 8 eggs
* 1 tablespoon of lemon juice
* 1 tablespoon of fresh thyme leaves

Instructions

Press the Sauté button after adding the oil. After 1 minute, add the onion, turnip, parsnip, carrots, and salt. 10 minutes until the veggies are tender. Click Cancel. Whisk eggs and lemon juice in a medium bowl. Stir in the thyme and vegetable combination. Coat the interior of a 7-cup glass dish. Pour the egg mixture in. Add 1 cup of water and the steam rack to the inner pot. Assemble a dish on the steam rack. Fix the lid. Set the timer to 18 minutes on the Manual or Pressure Cooker. Release pressure until float valve lowers and then unlock lid when timer whistles. Allow it cool for 5 minutes before slicing and serving.

Nutritional Facts

Calories: 204| Carbohydrates 55 g| Protein 8 g| Fat 6 g | Sodium 175 mg |

20. Strawberries and Cream Quinoa Porridge

Preparation time: 2 minutes

Cooking Time: 1 minute

Servings: 6

Ingredients

* 1½ cups of dry quinoa
* 1½ cups of water
* 1 (13.66-ounce) can of unsweetened full-fat coconut milk
* ½ teaspoon of stevia powder
* 1 teaspoon of vanilla extract
* 1 cup of sliced strawberries
* ⅓ cup of unsweetened shredded coconut

Instructions

Rinse the quinoa well in a fine-mesh sieve. Pour in the quinoa, water, coconut milk, stevia, and vanilla. Mix well. Fix the lid. Select Manual or Pressure Cook and set a timer to 1 minute. Quickly release pressure, then unlock the lid. Add strawberries. Allow quinoa to cool slightly before serving. Top each dish with some coconut.

Nutritional Facts

Calories: 174| Carbohydrates 22 g| Protein 29 g| Fat 8 g | Sodium 125 mg |

21. Soft-Boiled Eggs with Asparagus

Preparation time: 2 minutes

Cooking Time: 3 minute

Servings: 1

Ingredients

* 2 eggs
* 5 asparagus spears, woody ends removed

Instructions

Put the entire eggs and asparagus in the steamer basket. Fill the inner pot with 1 cup of water and the steam rack. Arrange the steamer basket with the eggs and asparagus. Fix the lid. Select Manual or Pressure Cook and set the timer to 3 minutes. Fill a big dish with cold water and ice. Remove the float valve and unlock the lid when the timer sounds. Carefully remove the inner pot's steamer basket. In an ice bath, chill the eggs until they can be handled. Serve the eggs with the asparagus.

Nutritional Facts

Calories: 124| Carbohydrates 29 g| Protein 17 g| Fat 10 g | Sodium 100 mg |

22. Fruit-And-Seed Breakfast Bars

Preparation time: 15 minutes

Cooking Time: 30 minute

Servings: 6

Ingredients

- ½ cup of rutted dates
- ¾ cup of browned sunflower seeds
- ¾ cup heated pumpkin seeds
- ¾ cup of white sesame seeds
- ½ cup of dried blueberries
- ½ cup of dried cherries
- ¼ cup of flaxseed
- ½ cup of almond butter

Instructions

Preheat the oven to 325F. Parchment paper is an 8x8-inch baking dish. Pulse dates in a food processor until paste forms. Pulse in the sunflower, pumpkin, sesame, blueberry, cherry, and flaxseed. Pour the ingredients into a bowl. Add almond butter. Immediately press the mixture into the prepared dish. Minutes or until firm and golden brown. Let it cool for an hour to room temperature. Then cut into 12 squares. Refrigerate for up to 1 week. Substitute any dried fruit for the blueberries or cherries as long as it is sugar-free and preservative-free. Try apple, mango, currants, or papaya.

Nutritional Facts

Calories: 144| Carbohydrates 28 g| Protein 17 g| Fat 30 g | Sodium 120 mg |

23. Chia-Coconut Porridge

Preparation time: 5 minutes

Cooking Time: 30 minute

Servings: 4

Ingredients

- ¾ cup of water

- ¾ cup of unsweetened almond milk
- 1 teaspoon of vanilla extract
- ¼ cup of chia seeds
- ¼ cup of unsweetened shredded coconut
- 2 tablespoons of honey
- ½ cup of sliced strawberries

Instructions

Combine the water, almond milk, and vanilla in a medium bowl. Stir in the chia seeds, cover, and chill for 30 minutes overnight. Mix in the coconut and honey. And 4 bowls of porridge. Garnish with strawberries.

Nutritional Facts

Calories: 124| Carbohydrates 12 g| Protein 8 g| Fat 7 g | Sodium 120 mg |

24. Golden Coconut Pancakes

Preparation time: 10 minutes

Cooking Time: 10 minute

Servings: 4

Ingredients

- ½ cup of almond flour
- ¼ cup of coconut flour
- 1 teaspoon of baking soda
- 3 eggs must be beaten
- 2 mashed bananas
- 1 teaspoon of pure vanilla extract
- 1 tablespoon of coconut oil
- Maple syrup, for serving (optional)
- Fruit, for serving (optional)

Instructions

Combine almond flour, coconut flour, and baking soda in a larger basin. Add the eggs, bananas, and vanilla to the well. Beat until smooth. Heat the coconut oil in a large pan over medium heat. Pour 14 cups of batter into the skillet four times. 3 minutes, or until the bottom is golden and the surface bubbles explode. Cook for 2 minutes longer on the other side until golden. Repeat with the remaining batter. Drizzle with maple syrup or top with fresh fruit.

Nutritional Facts

Calories: 204| Carbohydrates 25 g| Protein 15 g| Fat 11 g | Sodium 102 mg |

25. Mini Broccoli Frittatas

Preparation time: 10 minutes

Cooking Time: 20 minute

Servings: 4

Ingredients

- Olive oil for greasing muffin cups
- 8 eggs
- ¼ cup of unsweetened almond milk
- ½ teaspoon of chopped fresh basil
- ½ cup of chopped broccoli
- ½ cup of shredded fresh spinach
- 1 scallion, white and green parts, chopped
- Squeeze sea salt
- Squeeze freshly ground black pepper

Instructions

350°F Oven Preheat. Set a 6-cup muffin tray aside. Whisk eggs, almond milk, and basil until foamy.12 c. broccoli and scallion. Put the egg mixture in muffin cups. Bake for 20 minutes, until puffed, golden, and cooked through. Serve with sea salt and pepper.

Nutritional Facts

Calories: 204| Carbohydrates 45 g| Protein 8 g| Fat 5 g | Sodium 144 mg |

26. Egg Casserole with Sweet Potato and Kale

Preparation time: 15 minutes

Cooking Time: 30 minute

Servings: 4

Ingredients

- Olive oil for greasing the baking plate
- 1 cup of diced cooked sweet potato
- 1 cup of chopped lightened cauliflower
- 1 cup of shredded kale
- 1 chopped scallion, white and green parts
- 1 teaspoon of chopped fresh basil
- 8 eggs
- ¼ cup of unsweetened almond milk
- 1 teaspoon of ground cumin
- 1 teaspoon of ground coriander
- Pinch salt
- Pinch black pepper

Instructions

Oven 375F. Olive oil in a 9-by-13-inch baking dish.

Arrange the sweet potato, cauliflower, kale, and basil in the dish. Eggs, almond milk, cumin, coriander, sea salt, and pepper. After pouring the egg mixture into the baking dish, softly tap it on the counter to spread the eggs. Bake for 30 minutes until the eggs are set and the top is brown.

Nutritional Facts

Calories: 124| Carbohydrates 25 g| Protein 17 g| Fat 5 g | Sodium 122 mg |

27. Sweet Potato–Ground Turkey Hash

Preparation time: 10 minutes

Cooking Time: 26 minute

Servings: 4

Ingredients

- 1½ pounds of extra-lean ground turkey
- 1 chopped sweet onion
- 2 teaspoons of bottled minced garlic
- 1 teaspoon of ground ginger
- 2 pounds of sweet potatoes (peeled, cooked, and diced)
- sea salt
- Pinch ground black pepper
- Squeeze ground cloves
- 1 cup of chopped kale

Instructions

Cook the turkey for 10 minutes in a large pan over medium-high heat. Set aside. 3 minutes sauté. Add the sweet potatoes, cloves, and salt. Reduce to medium heat. Pour in the sweet potato and stir for 10 minutes. Add the kale. 3 minutes, constantly tossing, until wilted. Serve the hash in four bowls.

Nutritional Facts

Calories: 204| Carbohydrates 44 g| Protein 6 g| Fat 5 g | Sodium 128 mg |

28. Ground Beef Breakfast Skillet

Preparation time: 20 minutes

Cooking Time: 20 minute

Servings: 4

Ingredients

- 1 tablespoon of olive oil
- 1 pound of lean ground beef
- 2 teaspoons of minced garlic

- 2 cups of chopped cauliflower
- 1 cup of cubed carrots
- 1 zucchini, cubed
- chopped white and green parts of 2 scallions
- Salt
- ground black pepper
- 2 tablespoons of chopped fresh parsley

Instructions

Heat the olive oil in a large pan over medium heat. Add meat and garlic. Cook for 8 minutes or until done. Be sure to mix in the veggies. About 10 minutes till tender. Add the scallions and sauté 1 minute. Salt and pepper the mixture. Garnish with parsley.

Nutritional Facts

Calories: 264 | Carbohydrates 45 g | Protein 8 g | Fat 4 g | Sodium 120 mg |

29. Turmeric Oven Scrambled Eggs

Preparation time: 10 minutes

Cooking Time: 15 minute

Servings: 6

Ingredients

- 8 to 10 eggs, pasture-raised
- ½ cup of unsweetened almond or coconut milk
- ½ teaspoon of turmeric powder
- 1 teaspoon of cut cilantro
- ¼ teaspoon of black pepper
- Salt

Instructions

Oven 3500F preheat. Grease a Carroll or a baked dish, Egg, milk, turmeric powder, black pepper, and salt; pour in the egg mixture and bake for 15 minutes. Remove and decorate with cilantro.

Nutritional Facts

Calories: 154 | Carbohydrates 26 g | Protein 4 g | Fat 8 g | Sodium 125 mg |

30. Breakfast Oatmeal

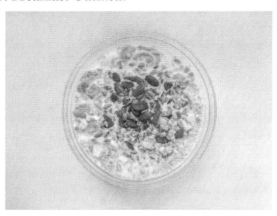

Preparation time: 10 minutes

Cooking Time: 15 minute

Servings: 6

Ingredients

- 2/3 cup of coconut milk
- 1 egg white
- ½ cup of gluten-free quick-cooking oats
- ½ teaspoon of turmeric powder
- ½ teaspoon of cinnamon
- ¼ teaspoon of ginger

Instructions

Heat non-dairy milk in a saucepan over medium heat. Whisk in the egg white and continue whisking until smooth. Add the other ingredients and simmer for 3 minutes.

Nutritional Facts

Calories: 184 | Carbohydrates 22 g | Protein 5 g | Fat 8 g | Sodium 138 mg |

31. Breakfast Porridge

Preparation time: 15 minutes

Cooking Time: 0 minute

Servings: 1

Ingredients

- 6 tablespoons of organic cheese
- 3 tablespoons of flax seed
- 3 tablespoons of flax oil
- 2 tablespoons of almond butter
- 1 tablespoon of organic coconut meat
- 1 tablespoon of raw honey
- ¼ cup water

Instructions

In a bowl, mix everything. Mix thoroughly. Serve in a chilled bowl.

Nutritional facts

Calories 180| Carbohydrates 8 g| Proteins 5 g| Fats 5 g| Sodium 100 mg |

32. Quinoa and Asparagus Mushroom Frittata

Preparation time: 5 minutes

Cooking Time: 30 minute

Servings: 3

Ingredients

- 2 tablespoons of olive oil
- 1 cup of carved mushrooms
- 1 cup of asparagus
- ½ cup of tomato
- 6 eggs
- 2 egg whites
- ¼ cup of milk
- 1 cup of quinoa
- 3 tablespoons chopped basil
- 1 tablespoon chopped parsley
- Salt and pepper

Instructions

Oven 3500F preheat in a skillet and heat the olive oil. Mix in the mushrooms and asparagus, seasoning to taste. Broil mushrooms and asparagus for 7 minutes. Cook for 3 minutes with the tomatoes. Dispose of. Meanwhile, combine the eggs, egg white, and milk. Dispose of. Top the quinoa with the veggie mixture and bake. The egg mixture is baked for 20 minutes or until the eggs are set.

Nutritional facts

Calories 170| Carbohydrates 5 g| Proteins 18 g| Fats 5 g| Sodium 144 mg |

33. Golden Milk Chia Pudding

Preparation time: 6 minutes

Cooking Time: 30 minute

Servings: 4

Ingredients

- 4 cups coconut milk
- 3 tablespoons honey

- 1 teaspoon of vanilla extract
- 1 teaspoon of ground turmeric
- ½ teaspoon of ground cinnamon
- ½ teaspoon of ground ginger
- ¾ cup coconut yogurt
- ½ cup of chia seeds
- 1 cup of mixed berry
- ¼ cup of toasted coconut chips

Instructions

A bowl of coconut milk, honey, vanilla, turmeric, cinnamon, and ginger. Leaky guts? Chia seeds, berries, and coconut chips. Pour in the milk. Refrigerate for 6 hours to set.

Nutritional facts

Calories 120| Carbohydrates 5 g| Proteins 18 g| Fats 6 g| Sodium 154 mg |

34. No-Bake Turmeric Protein Donuts

Preparation time: 50 minutes

Cooking Time: 0 minute

Servings: 8

Ingredients

- 1 ½ cups of cashews
- ½ cup of Medjool dates rutted
- 1 tablespoon vanilla protein powder
- ½ cup torn coconut
- 2 tablespoons of maple syrup
- ¼ teaspoon of vanilla extract
- 1 teaspoon of turmeric powder
- ¼ cup of dark chocolate

Instructions

In a food processor, combine everything except the chocolate. Until smooth. 8) Press the batter into a silicone donut mold. Set in 30 minutes. Melt the chocolate in a double boiler for the chocolate topping. Remove the donuts from the mold and sprinkle them with chocolate.

Nutritional facts

Calories 151| Carbohydrates 8 g| Proteins 9 g| Fats 4 g| Sodium 143 mg |

35. Choco-Nana Pancakes

Preparation time: 5 minutes

Cooking Time: 6 minute

Servings: 2

Ingredients

- 2 peeled and mashed bananas
- 2 eggs, pasture-raised
- 3 tablespoons of cacao powder
- 2 tablespoons of almond butter
- 1 teaspoon of vanilla extract
- 1/8 of a teaspoon of salt
- Coconut oil for oiling

Instructions

Melt coconut oil in a large skillet over medium heat. In a food processor, combine all ingredients and pulse. A pancake is formed by pouring 14 cups of batter onto the griddle. 3 minutes per side.

Nutritional facts

Calories 142 | Carbohydrates 8 g | Proteins 19 g | Fats 5 g | Sodium 133 mg |

36. Sweet Potato Cranberry Breakfast bars

Preparation time: 10 minutes

Cooking Time: 40 minute

Servings: 8

Ingredients

- 1 ½ cup of sweet potato puree
- 2 tablespoons of coconut oil, melted
- 2 tablespoons of maple syrup
- 2 pasture-raised eggs
- 1 cup of almond meal
- 1/3 cup of coconut flour
- 1 ½ teaspoon of baking soda
- 1 cup of fresh pitted and chopped cranberry
- ¼ of a cup of water

Instructions

Oven 3500F preheat Coconut oil in a baking pan. Dispose of. A bowl with sweet potato puree, eggs, and coconut oil. Sift almond, coconut, and baking soda. Join the dry and wet fixings. Mix. Press the cranberries on top. A toothpick put in the center comes out clean after 40 minutes. Remove from pan and cool.

Nutritional facts

Calories 147 | Carbohydrates 5 g | Proteins 19 g | Fats 6 g | Sodium 174 mg |

37. Savory Breakfast Pancakes

Preparation time: 5 minutes

Cooking Time: 6 minutes

Servings: 4

Ingredients

- ½ cup of almond flour
- ½ cup of tapioca flour
- 1 cup of coconut milk
- ½ teaspoon of chili powder
- ¼ teaspoon of turmeric powder
- ½ onion, chopped
- 1 handful of cilantro leaves, chopped
- ½ inch of ginger, aggravated
- 1 teaspoon of salt
- ¼ teaspoon of ground black pepper

Instructions

In a bowl, add all the fixings. Grease a pan on low-medium heat. 14 cup batter into the pan and spread into a pancake. 3 minutes per side.

Nutritional facts

Calories 198 | Carbohydrates 8 g | Proteins 18 g | Fats 6 g | Sodium 174 mg |

38. Scrambled Eggs with Smoked Salmon

Preparation time: 10 minutes

Cooking Time: 10 minutes

Servings: 2

Ingredients

- 4 eggs
- 2 tablespoons of coconut milk
- chives, chopped
- 4 slices of wild-caught smoked salmon
- salt

Instructions

An egg, coconut milk, and chives. Heat the skillet with the oil over medium heat. Cook the egg batter while scrambling it. Cook for 2 minutes longer when the eggs have settled.

Nutritional facts

Calories 177 | Carbohydrates 9 g | Proteins 18 g | Fats 5 g | Sodium 174 mg |

39. Breakfast Burgers with Avocado Buns

Preparation time: 10 minutes

Cooking Time: 5 minutes

Servings: 1

Ingredients

- 1 ripe avocado
- 1 pasture-raised egg
- 1 red slice
- 1 tomato
- 1 lettuce leaf
- Sesame seed for garnish
- salt

Instructions

Half the avocado. It'll be the bun. Dispose of. Cook the egg sunny-side up for 5 minutes or until set. Place the egg, red onion, tomato, and lettuce leaf on one avocado half. Then the avocado bun. Garnish with sesame seeds and salt to taste.

Nutritional facts

Calories 147| Carbohydrates 9 g| Proteins 22 g| Fats 7 g| Sodium 104 mg |

40. Spinach Mushroom Omelet

Preparation time: 3 minutes

Cooking Time: 15 minutes

Servings: 2

Ingredients

- Olive oil, one tablespoon + one tablespoon
- Spinach, chopped, 1.5 cup
- Green onion, one cubed
- Three Eggs
- One ounce of Feta cheese
- Mushrooms, button, five sliced
- Red onion, a diced, quarter cup

Instructions

Set aside the mushrooms, onions, and spinach in 1 tablespoon olive oil after three minutes. Beat the eggs thoroughly and fry in the remaining tablespoon of olive oil for 3–4 minutes until the edges are golden. Sprinkle the rest of the ingredients over half of the omelet and fold over the sautéed veggies. 1 minute on each side.

Nutritional facts

Calories 149| Carbohydrates 8 g| Proteins 25 g| Fats

9 g| Sodium 128 mg |

41. Weekend Breakfast Salad

Preparation time: 30 minutes

Cooking Time: 0 minutes

Servings: 4

Ingredients

- four full boiled eggs
- One Lemon
- ten cups Arugula
- one cup of cooked and cooled Quinoa
- two tablespoons of Olive oil
- one-half cup chopped dill
- One cup of chopped Almonds
- one large sliced thin Avocado
- one-half cup chopped Cucumber
- one large tomato cut into wedges

Instructions

Quinoa, tomatoes, and arugula tossed with olive oil, salt, and pepper. Place the egg and avocado on top. Garnish with almonds and herbs. Drizzle with lemon juice.

Nutritional facts

Calories 182| Carbohydrates 7 g| Proteins 19 g| Fats 20 g| Sodium 154 mg |

42. Kale Turmeric Scramble

Preparation time: 5 minutes

Cooking Time: 10 minutes

Servings: 1

Ingredients

- Olive oil, two tablespoon
- one-half cup of Kale, shredded,
- one-half cup of Sprouts
- Garlic, minced, one tablespoon
- one quarter teaspoon Black pepper,
- one tablespoon Turmeric, ground,
- Two Eggs

Instructions

Add turmeric, black pepper, and garlic to the eggs. After five minutes of sautéing the kale in the olive oil, throw in the egg batter. Cook, often stirring, until the eggs are done. Serve with raw sprouts.

Nutritional facts

Calories 166| Carbohydrates 8 g| Proteins 18 g| Fats 5 g| Sodium 155 mg |

43. Poached Salmon Egg Toast

Preparation time: 10 minutes

Cooking Time: 4 minutes

Servings: 2

Ingredients

- Bread or two slices of rye
- one-quarter teaspoon of Lemon juice
- Avocado, two tablespoons mashed
- one-quarter teaspoon of Black pepper
- two poached Eggs
- Salmon, burned, four ounces
- Scallions, one tablespoon sliced thin
- one-eighth teaspoon of Salt

Instructions

Lemon juice, pepper, and salt to avocado. Spread the avocado mixture on the toasted bread. Add smoked salmon and a poached egg on toast. Served with scallions.

Nutritional facts

Calories 177| Carbohydrates 15 g| Proteins 19 g| Fats 8 g| Sodium 174 mg |

44. Egg Muffins with Feta and Quinoa

Preparation time: 15 minutes

Cooking Time: 30 minutes

Servings: 12

Ingredients

- Eight Eggs
- One Cup of Tomatoes, chopped
- one-quarter teaspoon of salt
- One cup of Feta cheese
- one cup of cooked quinoa
- two teaspoons of olive oil
- one tablespoon Oregano, fresh chop
- one-quarter cup Black olives, chopped
- one quarter cup Onion, chopped
- Two cups of Baby spinach, chopped.

Instructions

Praise the Lord! Spray a 12-cup muffin tin with oil. 5 minutes in olive oil with spinach, oregano, olives, onion, and tomatoes. Eggs, beaten. Mix the cooked vegetables with the eggs, cheese, and salt. Fill muffin tins. Bake 30 min. These keep for two days in the fridge. Wrap in a paper towel and microwave for 30 seconds to consume.

Nutritional facts

Calories 166| Carbohydrates 37 g| Proteins 22 g| Fats 5 g| Sodium 104 mg |

45. Peaches with Honey Almond Ricotta

Preparation time: 15 minutes

Cooking Time: 0 minutes

Servings: 6

Ingredients

- Spread
- one cup Ricotta, skim milk
- one teaspoon Honey
- one half cup Almonds, thin slices
- one-quarter teaspoon of Almond extract

To Serve

- one cup of Peaches, sliced
- Bread, a whole-grain bagel

Instructions

Honey, ricotta and almond extract cover toasted bread with 1 tablespoon of this mix and peaches.

Nutritional Facts:

Calories: 252.8| Carbohydrates: 19.8g| Protein: 25.6g |Fats: 8g | Sodium 111 mg |

46. Quinoa Breakfast Bowl

Preparation time: 30 minutes

Cooking Time: 0 minutes

Servings: 6

Ingredients

- Quinoa, two cups cooked
- Eggs, twelve
- Greek yogurt, plain, one quarter cup
- Salt, one half teaspoon
- Feta cheese, one cup
- Cherry tomatoes, one pint cut in halves
- Black pepper, one teaspoon

- Garlic, minced, one teaspoon

- Baby spinach, chopped, one cup

- Olive oil, one teaspoon

Instructions

Make an egg mixture with yogurt and seasonings. Cook the spinach and tomatoes in olive oil for 5 minutes. Pour in the egg mixture and whisk until the desired doneness. Heat quinoa and feta till heated. It keeps for 2–3 days in the fridge.

Nutritional Facts:

Calories: 272| Carbohydrates: 38 g| Protein: 18 g |Fats: 10 g | Sodium 133 mg |

47. Cream Cheese Salmon Toast

Preparation time: 10 minutes

Cooking Time: 2 minutes

Servings: 2

Ingredients

- two slices of whole-grain or rye toast

- two tablespoons of Red onion chopped fine,

- two tablespoons of Cream cheese, low fat,

- one half teaspoon Basil flakes

- one half cup Arugula or spinach, chopped,

- two ounces of Smoked salmon,

Instructions

Toast the wheat bread. Mix cream cheese and basil and spread this mixture on the toast. Add salmon, arugula, and onion.

Nutritional Facts:

Calories: 295 | Carbohydrates: 49 g| Protein: 33 g |Fats: 18 g | Sodium 141 mg |

48. Carrot Cake Overnight Oats

Preparation time: overnight

Cooking Time: 1 minute

Servings: 2

Ingredients

- one cup Coconut or almond milk,

- one tablespoon of Chia seeds,

- one teaspoon Cinnamon, ground,

- one-half cup of Raisins,

- two tablespoons of Cream cheese, low fat,

- One Carrot, peel, and shred

- two tablespoons of Honey

- one teaspoon Vanilla

Instructions

Mix all ingredients and refrigerate overnight. Eat cold first thing. Pre-warm in the microwave for one minute, stirring well before eating.

Nutritional Facts:

Calories: 262| Carbohydrates: 25 g| Protein: 22 g |Fats: 11 g | Sodium 161 mg |

49. Mediterranean Frittata

Preparation time: 5 minutes

Cooking Time: 20 minutes

Servings: 6

Ingredients

- Six Eggs

- One quarter cup Feta cheese, crumbled

- one-quarter teaspoon of Black pepper

- Olive Oil

- One teaspoon Oregano

- one quarter cup Milk, almond or coconut

- one teaspoon of Sea salt

- one-quarter cup of Black olives

- one quarter cup Green olives, chopped

- one-quarter cup of Tomatoes, diced

Instruction

400°F oven 8x8-inch baking dish, oiled. Add the milk to the eggs, then the rest. Bake for 20 minutes with the rest of the ingredients.

Nutritional Facts:

Calories: 288| Carbohydrates: 49 g| Protein: 32 g |Fats: 14 g | Sodium 152 mg |

50. Maple Oatmeal

Preparation time: 5 minutes

Cooking Time: 20 minutes

Servings: 4

Ingredients

- One teaspoon of maple flavoring

- One teaspoon Cinnamon

- three tablespoons of Sunflower seeds

- one-half cup chopped Pecans

- one quarter cup Coconut flakes, unsweetened
- one-half cup chopped Walnuts
- one half cup milk, almond or coconut
- four tablespoons of Chia seeds

Instructions

In a food processor, crush sunflower seeds, walnuts, and pecans. Or put the nuts in a plastic bag, cover it in a towel, place it on a flat surface, and pound the cloth until the nuts shatter. Pour the crushed nuts and the rest of the ingredients into a big saucepan. 30 minutes on low heat with this combination. Stir often to prevent settling. Garnish with fresh fruit or cinnamon if preferred.

Nutritional Facts:

Calories: 182| Carbohydrates: 25 g| Protein: 27 g |Fats: 8 g | Sodium 181 mg |

51. Tomato Omelet

Preparation time: 20 minutes

Cooking Time: 8 minutes

Servings: 1

Ingredients

- two Eggs,
- one half cup Basil, fresh,
- one-half cup of Cherry tomatoes,
- one teaspoon Black pepper,
- one-quarter cup shredded Cheese, any type,
- one half teaspoon Salt,
- two tablespoons of Olive oil,

Instructions

Quarter the tomatoes. 3 minutes in olive oil. Set the tomatoes aside. Beat the eggs with salt and pepper in a small bowl. Pour the beaten egg mixture into the pan and carefully work the edges beneath the omelet for three minutes. Add the basil, tomatoes, and cheese while the egg mixture is still runny. Fold half the omelet over the other. Finished in 2 minutes.

Nutritional Facts:

Calories: 212| Carbohydrates: 26 g| Protein: 22 g |Fats: 11 g | Sodium 141 mg |

52. Chia Breakfast Pudding

Preparation time: 20 minutes

Cooking Time: 8 minutes

Servings: 1

Ingredients

- four tablespoons of Chia seeds
- one tablespoon of Almond butter,
- three-fourths cup Coconut milk,
- one teaspoon Cinnamon,
- one teaspoon Vanilla,
- three-fourths cup Cold coffee,

Instructions

Pour the ingredients into a refrigerator-safe container. Cover and chill overnight.

Nutritional Facts:

Calories: 220| Carbohydrates: 18 g| Protein: 26 g |Fats: 8 g | Sodium 161 mg |

53. Slow Cooker French toast Casserole

Preparation time: 15 minutes

Cooking Time: 4 minutes

Servings: 9

Ingredients

- eggs 2
- egg whites 2
- 1 ½ almond milk
- 2 tablespoons of honey
- 1/2 teaspoon cinnamon
- 1 teaspoon of vanilla extract
- 9 slices of bread

For filling:

- 3 cups of apples (diced)
- 2 tablespoons of raw honey
- 1 tablespoon of lemon juice
- 1/2 tsp of cinnamon
- 1/3 cup of pecans

Instructions

Mix the first six ingredients. Spray nonstick cooking spray on the slow cooker. Set aside a small dish with all the filling ingredients. Coat the apple slices properly. Place three apple slices on the bottom of each triangle and some filing on top. Stack the bread and filling in the same way. Egg batter on the bread and filling layers. Set the cooker for 2 12 hours on high or 4 hours low.

Nutritional Facts:

Calories: 252| Carbohydrates: 25 g| Protein: 47.6g |Fats: 6 g | Sodium 155 mg |

54. Crackpot Banana Foster

Preparation time: 15 minutes

Cooking Time: 2 minutes

Servings: 3

Ingredients

- 1 tablespoon of melted coconut oil (unrefined)
- 3 tablespoons of honey
- 1/4 teaspoon of cinnamon
- Juice ½ medium-sized lemon
- 5 bananas

For Garnish:

- Sliced nuts
- Greek Yogurt

Instructions

Mix the first four ingredients. Cut the bananas in halves and add to the slow cooker mixture. Cook on low heat for 12–2 hours. Toppings: Chopped nuts or simple Greek yogurt

Nutritional Facts:

Calories: 152| Carbohydrates: 79 g| Protein: 36 g |Fats: 13 g | Sodium 141 mg |

55. Chicken and Quinoa Burrito Bowl

Preparation time: 10 minutes

Cooking Time: 5 minutes

Servings: 6

Ingredients

- 1 lb. chicken thighs (skinless, boneless)
- 1 cup chicken broth
- 1 can of diced tomatoes (14.5oz)
- 1 medium onion (chopped)
- 3 cloves garlic (chopped)
- 2 teaspoon of chili powder
- ½ teaspoon of coriander
- ½ teaspoon of garlic powder
- 1 bell pepper chopped
- 15oz of pinto beans (drained)
- 1 ½ cup of cheddar cheese (grated)

Instructions

Then add the chicken and season with salt and pepper. Turn the cooker to low. With a fork and knife, shred the chicken. Reheat the chicken with quinoa and pinto beans for 2 hours. Cook and stir gently until the cheese melts. Serve.

Nutritional Facts:

Calories: 298| Carbohydrates: 29 g| Protein: 28 g |Fats: 13 g | Sodium 141 mg |

56. Nutty Blueberry Banana Oatmeal

Preparation time: 10 minutes

Cooking Time: 2 minutes

Servings: 6

Ingredients

- 2 cups of rolled eats
- 1/4 cup of almonds (toasted)
- 1/4 cup of walnuts
- 1/4 cup of pecans
- 2 tablespoons of ground flax seeds
- 1 teaspoon of ground ginger
- 1 teaspoon of cinnamon
- 1/4 teaspoon of sea salt
- 2 tablespoons of coconut sugar
- ½ teaspoon of baking powder
- 2 cups milk
- 2 bananas
- 1 cup of fresh blueberries
- 1 tablespoon of maple syrup
- 1 teaspoon of vanilla extract
- 1 tablespoon of melted butter
- Yogurt

Instructions

Mix nuts, flax seeds, baking powder, spices, and coconut sugar. Eggs, milk, maple syrup, and vanilla essence Layer half bananas and blueberries in the slow cooker pot. Pour the milk mixture over the oats mixture. Melting butter drizzle Cook on low for 4 hours or high for 4 hours. Soak oats in liquid till golden brown. Warm it up and top with plain Greek yogurt

Nutritional Facts:

Calories: 213| Carbohydrates: 29 g| Protein: 22 g |Fats: 5 g | Sodium 100 mg |

57. Slow Cooker Steamed Cinnamon Apples

Preparation time: 15 minutes

Cooking Time: 4 minutes

Servings: 6

Ingredients

- 8 apples (peeled, cored)
- 2 teaspoon of lemon juice
- 2 teaspoon of cinnamon
- ½ teaspoon of nutmeg
- ¼ cup of coconut sugar

Instructions

Put everything in the slow cooker. Set the slow cooker on low for 3-4 hours. Cook until the apple is soft. Serve.

Nutritional Facts:

Calories: 278| Carbohydrates: 22 g| Protein: 2 g |Fats: 9 g | Sodium 81 mg |

58. Carrot Rice with Scrambled Eggs

Preparation time: 15 minutes

Cooking Time: 3 minutes

Servings: 3

Ingredients

For Sweet Tamari Soy Sauce

- 3 tablespoons of tamari sauce
- 1 tablespoon of water
- 2-3 tablespoon molasses

For Spicy Mix-ins

- 3 cloves of garlic
- 1 shallot
- 2 red chilies
- Pinch ground ginger

For the Carrot Rice:

- 2 tablespoons of sesame oil
- 5 eggs
- 4 large carrots
- 8 ounces of sausage
- 1 tablespoon of sweet soy sauce
- 1 cup of bean sprouts
- 1/2 cup of fined diced broccoli
- salt and pepper

For Garnish:

- Cilantro
- Asian chili sauce
- Sesame seeds

Instructions

Boil molasses, water, and tamari in a heavy pot. After the sauce boils, reduce the heat and simmer until the molasses is dissolved. Keep the sauce separate. Mix ginger, garlic, onion, and red chilies in a bowl. Spiralized the carrots to create carrot rice. In a food processor, spiralize the carrots. Cut broccoli into tiny cubes. Sauté the sausage, carrots, and broccoli in the onion, ginger, garlic, and chilies dish. In the slow cooker, combine the spicy veggies and tamari sauce. Set the cooker for 3 hours on high or 6 hours on low. 2 eggs scrambled in a nonstick skillet top the carrot rice with scrambled eggs. Garnish with sesame seeds and cilantro.

Nutritional Facts:

Calories: 218| Carbohydrates: 28 g| Protein: 42 g |Fats: 15 g | Sodium 101 mg |

59. Breakfast Tofu

Preparation time: 40 minutes

Cooking Time: 20 minutes

Servings: 4

Ingredients

- 2 teaspoons of toasted sesame oil
- 1 teaspoon of rice vinegar
- 2 tablespoons of soy sauce
- ½ teaspoon of onion powder
- 1 teaspoon of garlic powder
- 1 block of tofu
- 1 tablespoon of potato starch

Instructions

All ingredients except tofu and potato starch are in a bowl. Blend well. Tofu in the bowl 30 min marinade

Potato starch tofu. Then add tofu. 20 minutes at 370°F, shaking midway.

Nutritional Facts:

Calories: 226| Carbohydrates: 18 g| Protein: 22 g |Fats: 11 g | Sodium 133 mg |

60. Breakfast Frittata

Preparation time: 15 minutes

Cooking Time: 20 minutes

Servings: 2

Ingredients

* 1 onion, chopped
* 2 tablespoons red bell pepper, chopped
* ¼ lb. breakfast turkey sausage, cooked and crumbled
* 3 eggs, beaten
* Pinch cayenne pepper

Instructions

Mix in a bowl. Pour into a baking dish. Bake pan in air fryer basket. 20 minutes in the air fryer

Nutritional Facts:

Calories: 200| Carbohydrates: 19 g| Protein: 25 g |Fats: 5 g | Sodium 151 mg |

61. Breakfast Potatoes

Preparation time: 5 minutes

Cooking Time: 15 minutes

Servings: 2

Ingredients

* 5 potatoes sliced
* 1 tablespoon of oil
* ½ teaspoon of garlic powder
* ¼ teaspoon of pepper
* ½ teaspoon of smoked paprika

Instructions

5 minutes at 400°F to warm your air fryer. Oil potatoes, Garlic, pepper, and paprika. Make sure the potatoes are

cooked for15 minutes.

Nutritional Facts:

Calories: 282| Carbohydrates: 39.8 g| Protein: 32.6g |Fats: 10.2 g | Sodium 141 mg |

62. Breakfast Omelet

Preparation time: 5 minutes

Cooking Time: 10 minutes

Servings: 2

Ingredients

* 2 beaten eggs
* 1 stalk of green onion, sliced
* ½ cup of mushrooms, sliced
* 1 red bell pepper, cubed
* 1 teaspoon of herb seasoning

Instructions

Put eggs in a dish. Add the remaining ingredients. Into a small baking pan. Place in the basket.10 minutes 350°F in an oven.

Nutritional facts

Calories 48| Carbohydrates 5 g| Proteins 4 g| Fats 1 g| Sodium 23 mg |

63. Breakfast Stuffed Biscuits

Preparation time: 35 minutes

Cooking Time: 30 minutes

Servings: 10

Ingredients

* 1 tablespoon of vegetable oil
* ¼ lb. of turkey sausage
* 2 beaten eggs
* Pepper
* 10 oz. frozen biscuits
* Cooking spray

Instructions

Cook sausage for 5 minutes in hot oil in a medium skillet. Set aside a bowl. Peppered eggs in a pan. Pour eggs into the sausage dish. Air fryer cookie dough Egg and sausage combination on top Seal the folds. Oil spray for 8 minutes at 325°F in an air fryer. Cook for 7 minutes more. Serve.

Nutritional facts

Calories 28| Carbohydrates 8 g| Proteins 6 g| Fats 5 g| Sodium 27 mg |

64. Breakfast Avocado Boat

Preparation time: 40 minutes

Cooking Time: 7 minutes

Servings: 2

Ingredients

- 2 avocados, sliced in half and rutted
- ¼ onion, sliced
- 2 tomatoes, sliced
- 1 bell pepper, sliced
- 2 tablespoons cilantro, sliced
- Pepper
- Eggs 4

Instructions

Cut the avocado into a dish. Combine all ingredients except the eggs. 30 min refrigerate. The egg on the avocado shell. Preheat your air fryer to 350°F. 7-minute air fry Avocado salsa on top.

Nutritional facts

Calories 37| Carbohydrates 7 g| Proteins 3 g| Fats 3 g| Sodium 20 mg |

65. Breakfast Casserole

Preparation time: 10 minutes

Cooking Time: 10 minutes

Servings: 4

Ingredients

- 1 lb. of hash browns
- 1 lb. of lean breakfast sausage, crumbled
- 1 yellow onion, sliced
- 1 red bell pepper, sliced
- 1 yellow bell pepper, sliced
- 1 green bell pepper, sliced
- Pepper

Instructions

Arrange hash browns, Sausage and vegetables for 10 minutes at 355°F. Add pepper and stir till it is completely cooked.

Nutritional facts

Calories 40| Carbohydrates 2 g| Proteins 4 g| Fats 3 g| Sodium 21 mg |

66. Sweet Potato Hash

Preparation time: 10 minutes

Cooking Time: 15 minutes

Servings: 6

Ingredients

- 2 sweet potatoes, cut into cubes
- 2 tablespoons of olive oil
- 1 tablespoon of paprika
- 1 teaspoon of dried dill weed
- Pepper

Instructions

Preheat your air fryer to 400°F. In a bowl, mix everything. Pour your air fryer. Cook for 15 minutes, stirring for 5 minutes.

Nutritional facts

Calories 22| Carbohydrates 2 g| Proteins 3 g| Fats 2 g| Sodium 23 mg |

67. Green Shakshuka

Preparation time: 20 minutes

Cooking Time: 25 minutes

Servings: 4

Ingredients

- 2 tablespoons of extra-virgin olive oil
- 1 onion (minced)
- 2 garlic cloves (minced)
- 1 jalapeño, seeded, minced
- 1-pound spinach
- 1 teaspoon of dried cumin
- ¾ teaspoon of coriander
- Salt and black pepper
- 2 tablespoons of harissa
- ½ cup of vegetable broth
- 8 eggs
- Sliced fresh parsley, as needed for serving
- Sliced fresh cilantro, as needed for serving
- Flakes of red pepper, as needed for serving

Instructions

Preheat the oven to 350°F. In a large oven-safe skillet, heat the olive oil. Sauté the onion for 4–5 minutes. Stir in the garlic and jalapeno and sauté for 1 minute. Add the spinach and simmer for 4–5 minutes until wilted. Cumin, coriander, salt, and harissa for 1 minute until aromatic. Puree the contents in a food processor or blender until gritty. Purée the broth until smooth and thick. Clean the skillet and coat it with nonstick spray. With a wooden spoon, form eight circular wells in the spinach mixture. Softly crack eggs in pipes. Cook in the oven for 20–25 minutes until the egg whites are set, but the yolks are still jiggly. Shakshuka with parsley, cilantro, and red pepper flakes to taste. Immediately serve.

Nutritional facts

Calories 38| Carbohydrates 2 g| Proteins 7 g| Fats 4 g| Sodium 50 mg |

68. Steel Cut Oats with Kefir and Berries

Preparation time: 15 minutes

Cooking Time: 30 minutes

Servings: 4

Ingredients

For the oats:

- 1 cup of steel-cut oats

- 3 cups water

- pinch salt

For the topping, Optional:

- nuts

- a sprinkle of maple syrup, a sprinkling of coconut sugar, a few

   Drops of stevia, or any other sweetener you like, to taste

Instructions

Oats in a small saucepan over medium heat. For 2-3 minutes, shake or swirl the pan. Bring the water to a boil. Cook for approximately 25 minutes or until the oats are soft enough to please you. Serve with fruit, nuts/seeds, kefir, and sweetener.

Nutritional facts

Calories 28| Carbohydrates 8 g| Proteins 4 g| Fats 1 g| Sodium 13 mg |

69. Rhubarb, Apple Plus Ginger Muffin Recipe

Preparation time: 15 minutes

Cooking Time: 30 minutes

Servings: 8

Ingredients

- 1/2 teaspoon of ground cinnamon

- 1/2 teaspoon of ground ginger

- pinch salt

- 1/2 cup of almond meal (ground almonds)

- 1/4 cup of unrefined raw sugar

- 2 tablespoons of finely chopped crystallized ginger

- 1 tablespoon of ground linseed meal

- 1/2 cup of buckwheat flour

- 1/4 cup fine of brown rice flour

- 1/4 cup of (60ml) olive oil

- 1 egg

- 1 teaspoon of vanilla extract

- 2 tablespoons of organic corn flour or true arrowroot

- 2 teaspoons of gluten-free baking powder

- 1 cup of finely sliced rhubarb

- 1 apple, peeled and finely diced

- 95ml (1/3 cup + 1 tablespoon) of rice or almond milk

Instructions

180/350°F oven preheating Grease or line 8 1/3 cup (80ml) muffin pans. Mix almonds meal, ginger, sugar, and linseed in a bowl. Mix in baking powder, flour, and spices equally. Coat rhubarb and apple in a flour mixture. Pour the milk, sugar, egg, and vanilla into the dry ingredients and whisk until incorporated. Bake for 20-25 minutes or until it rises and is brown around the edges. Remove, cool for 5 minutes, and then transfer to a wire rack to cool. Eat warm or cold.

Nutritional facts

Calories 45| Carbohydrates 2 g| Proteins 6 g| Fats 5 g| Sodium 22 mg |

70. Mushroom and Spinach Frittata

Preparation time: 15 minutes

Cooking Time: 30 minutes

Servings: 4

Ingredients

- Eggs 6

- 1/4 cup of milk

- 3 tablespoons of butter

- 2 cups of baby spinach

- Salt & pepper

- 1 cup of grated cheddar cheese

- 1 onion, finely sliced

- 4 oz. of mushrooms, sliced

Instructions

Preheat oven to 180°C with rack in center. Butter a 20 cm square baking dish. Dispose of Whisk the eggs and milk in a large bowl. Add cheese. Add pepper and salt. Discard dish. In a large nonstick pan, sauté the onion and mushrooms in butter. Add pepper and salt. Stir in the spinach and simmer for 1 minute. Pour mushroom mixture into egg mixture. Pour into a baking dish. Bake for 25 minutes or until golden and puffy. Remove the frittata from the plate using a spatula. Put them on a dish and serve warm or cold.

Nutritional facts

Calories 46| Carbohydrates 3 g| Proteins 1 g| Fats 1 g| Sodium 21 mg |

71. Gluten-Free Crepes

Preparation time: 15 minutes

Cooking Time: 30 minutes

Servings: 10

Ingredients

Option 1

- Making crepes by using waffle and pancake mix
- 3 tablespoons of sugar
- 1 1/2 cups of gluten-free pancake mix
- 1 cup of cold water
- Eggs 2
- 2 tablespoons of butter, melted

Option 2

- Make crepes by using your favorite gluten-free and gum-free

    Flour blend:
- 2 tablespoons of butter, melted
- 3 tablespoons of sugar
- 1 cup of cold water
- 2 tablespoons of cold water
- Eggs 2
- 1 1/2 cups of gluten-free flour
- 1/2 teaspoon of gluten-free baking powder or mix baking soda and cream

    Of tartar in equal parts
- 1/2 teaspoon of vanilla extract

Instructions

Whisk all crepe ingredients in a large bowl until the lumps dissolve. Let the mixture settle for 15 minutes at room temperature. After 15 minutes, it thickens. Pour a little quantity of batter into the frying pan using a soup spoon or 1/4 measuring cup as you roll the pan from side to side. Allow this thin layer of crepe batter to cook for 1, 2, or 3 minutes, then flip the crepe and cook for 1 minute more.

Nutritional facts

Calories 47| Carbohydrates 5 g| Proteins 3 g| Fats 1 g| Sodium 20 mg |

72. Amaranth Porridge with Roasted Pears

Preparation time: 10 minutes

Cooking Time: 30 minutes

Servings: 2

Ingredients

- ¼ teaspoon of salt
- 2 tablespoons of pecan pieces
- 1 teaspoon of pure maple syrup
- 1 cup of Greek yogurt for serving
- Pears
- Porridge
- ½ cup of uncooked amaranth
- 1/2 cup of water
- 1 cup of 2% milk
- 1 teaspoon of maple syrup
- 1 pear
- 1/2 tsp of ground cinnamon
- 1/4 tsp of ground ginger
- 1/8 tsp of ground nutmeg
- 1/8 tsp of ground clove
- Pear Topping

Instructions

Preheat oven to 400C. Rinse and drain the amaranth. 1 cup milk and 1 teaspoon salt heat the amaranth, then lower to a simmer. Cover and cook for 25 minutes until the amaranth is mushy but still has some liquid. Continue to thicken for 5–10 minutes after removing from heat. Apply extra milk to smooth the texture if required. 1 tablespoon maple syrup, chopped pecans. Toasted pecans and dried maple syrup take 10 to 15 minutes to roast. They may become rather aromatic when cooked. Pecans are crunchy after cooling. Ditto for the pears, pecans, and spices. 15 minutes until pears are cooked in a roasting pan 3/4 roasted pears in porridge. Coat yogurt with oatmeal, toasted nuts, and pears' leftovers.

Nutritional facts

Calories 48| Carbohydrates 5 g| Proteins 4 g| Fats 1 g| Sodium 23 mg |

73. Turkey Apple Breakfast Hash

Preparation time: 15 minutes

Cooking Time: 10 minutes

Servings: 5

Ingredients

For the meat:

- 1 lb. ground turkey
- 1 tablespoon of coconut oil
- ½ teaspoon of dried thyme
- ½ teaspoon of cinnamon
- sea salt, as per taste

For the hash:

- 1 tablespoon of coconut oil
- 1 medium onion
- 1 apple, peeled, cored, and chopped
- 2 cups of spinach
- ½ teaspoon of turmeric
- ½ teaspoon of dried thyme
- Salt as per taste
- 1 large zucchini
- ½ cup of carrots
- 2 cups of butternut squash
- 1 teaspoon of cinnamon
- ¾ teaspoon of powdered ginger
- ½ teaspoon of garlic powder

Instructions

There is a teaspoon of coconut oil on medium/high heat. Cook turkey on the ground till crispy. Thyme, cinnamon, and sea salt. Take the plate. Cook onion for 2-3 minutes with the remaining coconut oil in the same pan. Cook for 4-5 minutes, or until the courgette, apple, carrots, and frozen squash soften. Add spinach and stir until wilted. Add cooked turkey, spice, and salt. Enjoy this hot hash or chill it and refrigerate it for a week. Refrigerate the hash in a sealed jar for 5-6 days.

Nutritional facts

Calories 45| Carbohydrates 7 g| Proteins 1 g| Fats 1.2

g| Sodium 21 mg |

74. No-Bake Chocolate Chia Energy Bars

Preparation time: 15 minutes

Cooking Time: 0 minutes

Servings: 14

Ingredients

- 1 ½ cups of dates
- 1/cup of coconut
- 1 cup of raw walnut pieces
- 1/4 cup of natural cocoa powder
- 1/2 cup of whole chia seeds
- 1/2 cup of chopped dark chocolate
- 1/2 cup of oats
- 1 teaspoon of pure vanilla extract
- 1/4 teaspoon of salt

Instructions

Blend the dates until thick paste forms. Blend in the walnuts. Mix in the rest of the fixings until a thick dough forms. Line a rectangular baking pan. Fill the pan to the corners with the mixture. Place in the freezer until midnight, if not longer. Raise and cut into 14 strips. Refrigerate or seal in an airtight container.

Nutritional Facts

Calories: 264| Carbohydrates: 39 g| Protein: 6 g| Fat: 9 g| Sodium 236 mg |

75. Buckwheat Cinnamon and Ginger Granola

Preparation time: 15 minutes

Cooking Time: 40 minutes

Servings: 5

Ingredients

- ¼ cup of Chia seeds
- ½ Cup of Coconut Flakes
- 1 ½ Cup of mixed Raw nuts
- 2 cups gluten-free oats
- 1 cup buckwheat groats
- 2 tablespoons of nut butter
- 4 tablespoons of coconut oil
- 1 cup sunflower seeds
- ½ cup pumpkin seeds
- 1 ½ - 2 inches piece of ginger
- 1 teaspoon of Ground Cinnamon
- 1/3 cup of Rice Malt Syrup
- 4 tablespoons of raw cacao powder

Instructions

Preheat the oven to 180°C. In a food processor, blitz the nuts to a rough chop. Mix the chopped nuts and the other dry ingredients in a large basin. Melt the coconut oil with oats, coconut, cinnamon, buckwheat, seeds, and salt. Blend in the cacao powder (if using). Pour the wet batter over the dry ingredients and stir thoroughly. Move the mixture to a large baking sheet coated with coconut oil. For 35-40 minutes, evenly divide the ingredients, turning them halfway. Bake until granola is golden! You may also add your favorite super foods like goji berries, flax seeds, and bee pollen. Every day is different.

Nutritional facts

Calories 50| Carbohydrates 6 g| Proteins 1 g| Fats 4 g| Sodium 24 mg |

76. Fruity Flaxseed Breakfast Bowl

Preparation time: 8 minutes

Cooking Time: 5 minutes

Servings: 1

Ingredients

For the Porridge:

- ¼-cup of flaxseeds, freshly ground
- ¼-tsp of cinnamon, ground
- 1-cup of almond or coconut milk
- 1 banana, mashed
- A pinch of sea salt

For the Toppings:

- Blueberries
- Walnuts
- maple syrup

Instructions

Combine all porridge ingredients in a medium saucepan over medium heat. The porridge will thicken and come to a low boil in 5 minutes. Serve the prepared porridge in a bowl. Garnish with toppings and drizzle with maple syrup for a sweeter taste.

Nutritional facts

Calories 33| Carbohydrates 6 g| Proteins 5 g| Fats 2 g| Sodium 22 mg |

77. Perky Paleo Potato & Protein Powder

Preparation time: 8 minutes

Cooking Time: 0 minutes

Servings: 1

Ingredients

- 1 sweet potato, pre-baked and fleshed out
- 1-Tablespoon of protein powder
- 1 banana, sliced

- ¼-cup of blue berries
- ¼-cup of raspberries
- Choice of toppings: cacao nibs/ chia seeds/ hemp hearts
- Nut or seed butter (optional)

Instructions

Fork-mash the sweet potato in a small serving dish. Mix thoroughly. Top with banana slices, blueberries, and raspberries. Garnish as desired. This morning dish is delicious cold or hot.

Nutritional facts

Calories 55| Carbohydrates 9 g| Proteins 5 g| Fats 5 g| Sodium 26 mg |

78. Spicy Shakshuka

Preparation time: 12 minutes

Cooking Time: 37 minutes

Servings: 4

Ingredients

- 2-Tablespoon s of extra-virgin olive oil
- 1-bulb onion, crushed
- 1 jalapeño, seeded and crushed
- 2-cloves of garlic, minced
- 1-lb spinach
- Salt black pepper
- ¾-tsp of coriander
- 1-tsp of dried cumin
- 2-Tablespoon s of harissa paste
- ½-cup of vegetable broth
- 8-pcs of large eggs
- Red pepper flakes, serving
- Cilantro, chopped serving
- Parsley, chopped serving

Instructions

Preheat the oven to 350F. Preheat an oven-safe skillet over medium heat. 5 minutes with the onion stirred in Sauté the jalapeno and garlic for a minute or until aromatic. Cook for 5 minutes to wilt the spinach. Salt, pepper, coriander, cumin, and harissa

Cook for 1 minute. Transfer to a food processor and purée until thick. Pour in the broth and purée until smooth. Clean and re-grease the same skillet. Pour the purée. Form 8 round wells using a wooden spoon. Gently place each egg in the wells. Bake for 25 minutes, or poach the eggs until completely set. Serve with red pepper flakes, cilantro, and parsley to taste.

Nutritional facts

Calories 58| Carbohydrates 2 g| Proteins 1 g| Fats 4 g| Sodium 29 mg |

79. Choco Chia Banana Bowl

Preparation time: 4 hours & 5 minutes

Cooking Time: 0 minutes

Servings: 3

Ingredients

- ½-cup of chia seeds
- 1 banana, very ripe
- ½-tsp of vanilla extract
- 2-cups of almond milk, unsweetened
- 1-Tablespoon of cacao powder
- 2-Tablespoon s of raw honey or maple syrup
- 2-Tablespoon s of cacao nibs for mixing in
- 2-Tablespoon s of chocolate chips for mixing in
- 1 banana, sliced for mixing

Instructions

Mix chia seeds and bananas in a dish. With a fork, crush the banana and stir completely. Add vanilla and almond milk. Whisk until no lumps remain. Cover half of the mix in a glass container. Then add the cacao and syrup to the remaining half. Mix thoroughly. Cover the mixture in another glass container. Chill for 4 hours. Pour the cooled chia puddings into three serving dishes. Alternate the layers with the mixing ingredients.

Nutritional facts

Calories 52| Carbohydrates 5 g| Proteins 1 g| Fats 4 g| Sodium 29 mg |

80. Power Protein Porridge

Preparation time: 15 minutes

Cooking Time: 8 minutes

Servings: 2

Ingredients

- ¼-cup of walnut or pecan halves, roughly chopped
- ¼-cup of toasted coconut, unsweetened
- 2-Tablespoon s of hemp seeds
- 2-Tablespoon s of whole chia seeds
- ¾-cup of almond milk, unsweetened

- ¼-cup of coconut milk
- ¼-cup of almond butter, roasted
- ½-tsp of turmeric, ground
- 1-Tablespoon of extra virgin coconut oil or MCT oil
- 2-Tablespoon s of erythritol or 5-10 drops of liquid stevia (optional)
- A pinch of ground black pepper
- ½-tsp of cinnamon or ½-tsp of vanilla powder

Instructions

Heat the walnuts, flaked coconut, and hemp seeds. For 2 minutes until aromatic. Stir to avoid scorching. Set aside the roasted mix. Dispose of. In a small saucepan, combine almond and coco milk. Warm the mix. Please turn off the heat when it reaches a boil. Then the rest. Mix thoroughly. Wait 10 minutes. 1/2 roasted mix with porridge. Divides the porridge into two bowls. Sprinkle with the leftover roasted mixture and cinnamon powder. Immediately serve porridge.

Nutritional facts

Calories 40| Carbohydrates 5 g| Proteins 8 g| Fats 3 g| Sodium 29 mg |

81. Avo Toast with Egg

Preparation time: 15 minutes

Cooking Time: 0 minutes

Servings: 3

Ingredients

- 1½-tsp of ghee
- 1-slice of bread, gluten-free and toasted
- ½ avocado, finely sliced
- some spinach
- 1 egg scrambled/poached
- A scatter of red pepper flakes

Instructions

Ghee the toasted bread. Avocado slices and spinach leaves on top with scrambled or poached eggs. Garnish with red pepper flakes.

Nutritional facts

Calories 40| Carbohydrates 4 g| Proteins 1 g| Fats 2 g| Sodium 17 mg |

82. Quick Quinoa with Cinnamon & Chia

Preparation time: 15 minutes

Cooking Time: 3 minutes

Servings: 2

Ingredients

- 2-cups of quinoa, pre-cooked
- 1-cup of cashew milk
- ½-tsp of ground cinnamon
- 1-cup of fresh blueberries
- ¼-cup of walnuts, toasted
- 2-tsp of raw honey
- 1-Tablespoon of chia seeds

Instructions

In a saucepan, combine the quinoa and cashew milk. Add the blueberries and walnuts. Cook for 3 minutes. Turn off the heat. Add honey. Before serving, garnish with chia seeds.

Nutritional facts

Calories 45 | Carbohydrates 7 g | Proteins 1 g | Fats 1.2 g | Sodium 21 mg |

83. Plum, Pear & Berry-Baked Brown Rice Recipe

Preparation time: 12 minutes

Cooking Time: 30 minutes

Servings: 2

Ingredients

- 1-cup of water
- ½-cup of brown rice
- A pinch cinnamon
- ½-tsp of pure vanilla extract
- 2-Tablespoon s of pure maple syrup (divided)
- Sliced berries, pears, or plums
- Salt (optional)

Instructions

Preheat the oven to 400F. Bring the water and brown rice to a boil in a medium saucepan. Mix in cinnamon and vanilla. Lower the heat to medium. After 18 minutes, the brown rice is ready. Divide the rice into two oven-safe dishes. 1 tablespoon maple syrup in each. Add the sliced fruits and a dash of salt to the dishes if desired. Bake for 12 minutes or until the fruit caramelizes and the syrup bubbles.

Nutritional facts

Calories 105 | Carbohydrates 22 g | Proteins 4 g | Fats 8 g | Sodium 129 mg |

84. Swift & Spicy Energy Eggs

Preparation time: 2 minutes

Cooking Time: 3 minutes

Servings: 1

Ingredients

- 1-Tablespoon of milk
- 1-tsp of melted butter
- 2-pcs of eggs
- A peppering of herbs and spices: dried dill, dried oregano, dried
- parsley, dried thyme, and garlic powder

Instructions

A325°F preheated oven. Meanwhile, butter and milk are on a baking tray. Gently crack eggs over milk and butter. Dry herbs and garlic powder on the eggs. Bake the tray. 3 minutes, or until the eggs are cooked.

Nutritional facts

Calories 135 | Carbohydrates 49 g | Proteins 4 g | Fats 4 g | Sodium 139 mg |

85. Banana Bread Overnight Oats

Preparation time: 6 hours & 20 minutes

Cooking Time: 0 minutes

Servings: 3

Ingredients

- ¼-cup of plain Greek yogurt
- ¼-tsp of flaked sea salt
- 1½-cups of nonfat milk
- 1-cup of old-fashioned rolled oats
- 1-Tablespoon of chia seeds
- 2-pcs of medium bananas, very ripe and mashed
- 2-Tablespoon s of coconut flakes, unsweetened and toasted
- 2-Tablespoon s of honey
- 2-teaspoon of vanilla extract
- roasted pecans, pomegranate seeds, and honey for serving
- fig halves, and banana cuts

Instructions

In a mixing dish, combine all ingredients except the toppings. Mix well. Divide between two serving dishes. Cover and chill for 6 hours. Stir and serve with toppings.

Nutritional facts

Calories 185| Carbohydrates 28 g| Proteins 5 g| Fats 2 g| Sodium 129 mg |

86. Good Grains with Cranberries & Cinnamon

Preparation time: 8 minutes

Cooking Time: 35 minutes

Servings: 2

Ingredients

- 1-cup grains
- 2½-cups of coconut water or almond milk
- 1-stick of cinnamon
- 2-pcs of whole cloves
- 1-star anise pod (optional)
- apples, blackberries, cranberries, pears
- Maple syrup

Instructions

In a saucepan, combine the grains, coconut water, and spices. Cover and reduce heat to medium. Cook for 25 minutes. Discard seasonings and serve with fruit slices. Drizzle with maple syrup if desired.

Nutritional facts

Calories 125| Carbohydrates 20 g| Proteins 5 g| Fats 4 g| Sodium 149 mg |

87. Fresh & Fruity Perky Parfait

Preparation time: 20 minutes

Cooking Time: 0 minutes

Servings: 2

Ingredients

- ½-cup of fresh raspberries
- A pinch of cinnamon
- 1-tsp of maple syrup
- 2-Tablespoon s of chia seeds
- 16-oz. plain yogurt
- sliced blackberries, nectarines, or strawberries

Instructions

In a mixing bowl, crush raspberries until they form a jam-like consistency. Chia seeds, cinnamon, and syrup Mash until all elements are incorporated. Dispose of. Alternate layers of yogurt and ingredients in two glasses. Fruit slices for garnish

Nutritional facts

Calories 175| Carbohydrates 27 g| Proteins 4 g| Fats 5 g| Sodium 139 mg |

88. Seared Syrupy Sage Pork Patties

Preparation time: 12 minutes

Cooking Time: 10 minutes

Servings: 4

Ingredients

- 2-lbs of ground pork, pastured
- 3-Tablespoon s of maple syrup, grade B
- 3-Tablespoon s of minced fresh sage
- ¾-tsp of sea salt
- ½ teaspoon of garlic powder
- 1-teaspoon of solid cooking fat

Instructions

In a large mixing basin, break up the ground pork. Drizzle with maple syrup. Add the spices. Mix well. Patty the mixture into eight. Dispose of. Heated cast-iron skillet with grease over medium heat. Brown the patties for 10 minutes on each side.

Nutritional facts

Calories 195| Carbohydrates 29 g| Proteins 5 g| Fats 7.0 g| Sodium 159 mg |

89. Creamy Cinnamon Banana Bowl

Preparation time: 5 minutes

Cooking Time: 3 minutes

Servings: 1

Ingredients

- 1 banana, ripe
- ¼ teaspoon of cinnamon, ground
- Celtic sea salt pinch
- 2 tablespoons of coconut butter, melted
- fruit, seed, or nut for topping

Instructions

In a bowl, mash the banana with 1 teaspoon cinnamon. Heat the coconut butter in a small saucepan. Mix in the heated butter. Garnish with your favorite fruit, seed, or nut

Nutritional facts

Calories 240| Carbohydrates 32 g| Proteins 6 g| Fats 6 g| Sodium 123 mg |

90. Turkey with Thyme & Sage Sausage

Preparation time: 40 minutes

Cooking Time: 25 minutes

Servings: 4

Ingredients

- 1-lb of ground turkey
- ½-teaspoon of cinnamon
- ½-teaspoon of garlic powder
- 1-teaspoon of fresh rosemary
- 1-teaspoon of fresh thyme
- 1-teaspoon of sea salt
- 2-teaspoon of fresh sage
- 2-tablespoon s of coconut oil

Instructions

In a mixing dish, combine all ingredients except the oil. Refrigerate for 30 minutes. Pour the oil in. Patties the mixture into four. Cook the patties for 5 minutes on each side or until the middles are no longer pink. You may alternatively bake them for 25 minutes at 400°F.

Nutritional facts

Calories 260| Carbohydrates 42 g| Proteins 6 g| Fats 8.1 g| Sodium 153 mg |

91. Vegan High-Protein Pancakes

Preparation time: 5 minutes

Cooking Time: 10 minutes

Servings: 6

Ingredients

- 1 cup of water
- 1 tablespoon of baking powder
- 2 tablespoons of maple syrup
- ¼ cup of vegan protein powder
- ½ teaspoon of sea salt
- 1 cup of all-purpose flour

Instructions

Large mixing bowl - combine baking powder, all-purpose flour, protein powder and sea salt. Stir in the maple syrup to the dry ingredients. Slowly add the water until everything is mixed. If the batter looks too thick, add extra water. Heat a large skillet over medium heat. Add the butter to the heated skillet using a spoon. 3 minutes or until bubbles emerge. Cook for 2 minutes on the opposite side. Choose your preferred topping.

Nutritional facts

Calories 167| Carbohydrates 11 g| Proteins 3 g| Fats 2 g| Sodium 96 mg |

92. Quinoa Porridge

Preparation time: 5 minutes

Cooking Time: 20 minutes

Servings: Makes 1 bowl

Ingredients

- ½ cup of quinoa washed
- 1 tea bag
- 1 cup of almond milk, unsweetened
- 3 tablespoons of walnuts or your favorite alternative nut, chopped

Instructions

In a small saucepan, combine quinoa, almond milk, and teabag. Bring to a boil. Remove the tea bag once it boils. Reduce the heat and simmer the quinoa for 10–15 minutes until done. Remove the saucepan from the heat and cool. After cooling, the quinoa should absorb all residual liquid. In a serving dish, add hot milk to soften the porridge. Enjoy hot.

Nutritional facts

Calories 125| Carbohydrates 5 g| Proteins 3 g| Fats 5 g| Sodium 106 mg |

93. Pumpkin Seed Granola

Preparation time: 10 minutes

Cooking Time: 30 minutes

Servings: 14

Ingredients

- ¼ cup of chia seeds
- ¼ cup of coconut oil, melted
- 3 cups of rolled oats
- A pinch of salt
- ½ cup of whole wheat flour
- ½ teaspoon cinnamon
- ½ cup of maple syrup
- 2/3 cup of pumpkin seeds
- ¼ cup of coconut palm sugar
- ½ cup of dried coconut flakes, unsweetened
- 1 cup of split red lentils, cooked
- 2/3 cup of buckwheat groats

Instructions

Preheat the oven at 375F. Combine the oats with cinnamon and flour. Step 3: Combine the buckwheat grains, chia seeds, and coconut. Then add maple syrup, melted coconut oil, coconut sugar, and red lentils. Stir until completely blended. Spread the nut-groats mixture equally on a greased and coated baking sheet. Bake for 5–8 minutes until toasted. Remove the sheet from the oven and cool for 8-10 minutes. Cluster the cooked granola mixture. Bake for 6 minutes longer, then cool for 10 minutes. Bake for 5 minutes longer or until evenly toasted. Refrigerate the granola entirely before storing it.

Nutritional facts

Calories 145| Carbohydrates 12 g| Proteins 5 g| Fats 6 g| Sodium 106 mg |

94. Pumpkin Spice Oatmeal

Preparation time: 5 minutes

Cooking Time: 5 minutes

Servings: 1

Ingredients

- ½ tablespoon of maple syrup
- 2 tablespoons of steel-cut oats
- 1 tablespoon pecans, chopped
- 1 tablespoon of chia seeds
- ½ teaspoon of ginger, ground
- 1 cup of water, hot
- 1 scoop of vegan protein
- 3 tablespoons of pumpkin puree
- ¼ teaspoon of nutmeg, ground

Instructions

In a large mixing basin, combine the oats, water, chia seeds, ginger, pumpkin puree, nutmeg, and cinnamon. Microwave the mixture for 2 minutes on high. Mix in the protein powder with the heated oatmeal. If required, add extra water. Stir until all protein powder is dissolved. Finally, serve the oatmeal with chopped pecans and maple syrup.

Nutritional facts

Calories 160| Carbohydrates 25 g| Proteins 5 g| Fats 8 g| Sodium 106 mg |

95. Breakfast Burritos

Preparation time: 10 minutes

Cooking Time: 25 minutes

Servings: 4

Ingredients

- 1 cubed avocado,

- 1 cup of new potatoes, thinly sliced
- ½ cup of salsa
- 1 cup of roasted green chili, sliced into strips
- 4 burrito wraps
- 1 cup of black beans, washed and drained
- Sea salt and black pepper, as required
- Garden-fresh cilantro leaves, chopped
- 12 oz. Extra-firm tofu
- 1 teaspoon cumin, ground
- 1 clove of garlic, minced

Instructions

In a large saucepan, heat the oil over medium heat. Add the potatoes and roasted green chili strips once the oil is heated. 3–4 minutes till cooked and golden brown. After removing the potato mixture, add the tofu to the pan. Next, crush the tofu and heat for 4–5 minutes until browned. Tip: The tofu should now resemble ground beef. Re-add the potato green chili combination and stir well. Add cumin, salt, pepper, and garlic. Cook for 5 minutes more. Finale: reheat salsa and burritos. Spread salsa on wraps. Wrap the tortilla with the tofu potato mixture, avocado, and cilantro. Enjoy hot.

Nutritional facts

Calories 165| Carbohydrates 15 g| Proteins 3 g| Fats 10.1 g| Sodium 116 mg |

96. Chocolate Chia Seed Pudding

Preparation time: 5minutes

Cooking Time: 15 minutes

Servings: 1

Ingredients

- 1 tablespoon of maple syrup
- 2 tablespoons of chia seeds
- 1/3 cup of coconut milk
- 1 scoop of chocolate protein powder
- 1/3 cup of almond milk

Instructions

In a medium-sized mixing bowl, combine all the chia seed pudding ingredients. Refrigerate the medium basin for 4–5 minutes. Add your favorite toppings. Add fresh fruit or chocolate nibs for extra flavor.

Nutritional facts

Calories 120| Carbohydrates 27 g| Proteins 5 g| Fats 1.9 g| Sodium 100 mg |

97. Avocado Walnut Sandwich

Preparation time: 10minutes

Cooking Time: 10 minutes

Servings: 4

Ingredients

For the spread:

- 1 cup of walnuts
- 1 clove of garlic, minced
- 2 tablespoons. lemon juice, fresh
- ½ teaspoon of dill, dried
- ¼ cup of water
- 2 tablespoons of carrot, minced
- 2 tablespoons nutritional yeast
- 2 tablespoons of red bell pepper, minced
- ¼ teaspoon sea salt
- 2 tablespoons of sundried tomatoes, chopped
- 1/8 teaspoon of black pepper

For the sandwich:

- 1 cup of carrot, shredded
- 1 large avocado, sliced
- 8 grown grain bread slices
- 1 large tomato, sliced
- 2 cups mixed greens

Instructions

Combine the nutritional yeast, walnuts, lemon juice, salt, water, and pepper in a food processor. Add the rest of the ingredients and mix well. Well, toss. Next, spread the walnut paste on the bread pieces. Reassemble the sandwich on the bread. Enjoy.

Nutritional facts

Calories: 135| Carbohydrates: 22 g| Proteins: 4 g| Fats: 3 g| Sodium 150 mg |

98. Breakfast Rice Porridge

Preparation time: 10minutes

Cooking Time: 25 minutes

Servings: 2

Ingredients

- 2 dates, chopped
- 1 oz. of protein powder, unflavored
- 1 ½ cup of almond milk, unsweetened

- ½ cup of short grain brown rice
- 1 medium-sized banana, sliced
- 1 tablespoon of tahini
- 1 apple, chopped
- 1 teaspoon of sesame seeds, toasted

Instructions

Rice, almond milk, and protein powder in a large pot. Cook for 20–25 minutes or until the rice is done. Stir often. Serve the rice porridge with the fruits and dates. Garnish with sesame seeds and tahini.

Nutritional facts

Calories: 140| Carbohydrates: 28 g| Proteins: 8 g| Fats: 2 g| Sodium 120 mg |

99. Warm Maple and Cinnamon Quinoa

Preparation time: 5 minutes

Cooking Time: 15 minutes

Servings: 4

Ingredients

- 1 cup of unsweetened nondairy milk
- 1 cup of water
- 1 cup of quinoa, rinsed
- 1 teaspoon of cinnamon
- ¼ Cup of chopped pecans or other nuts or seeds, such as chia, sunflower seeds / almonds
- 2 tablespoons of pure maple syrup or agave

Instructions

Bring almond milk, water, and quinoa to a boil in a medium saucepan. Cover and reduce heat to medium. Simmer for 15 minutes to absorb most of the liquid and soften the quinoa. Allow to cool for 5 minutes, covered. Cinnamon, pecans, and hot syrup served

Nutritional facts

Calories: 145| Carbohydrates: 28 g| Proteins: 4 g| Fats: 2.1 g| Sodium 170 mg |

100. Warm Quinoa Breakfast Bowl

Preparation time: 5 minutes

Cooking Time: 0 minutes

Servings: 4

Ingredients

- 3 cups of freshly cooked quinoa
- 1⅓ cups of unsweetened soy or almond milk
- 2 bananas (sliced)

- 1 cup of raspberries
- 1 cup of blueberries
- ½ Cup of chopped raw walnuts
- ¼ Cup of maple syrup

Instructions

Prepare 4 bowls with 34 cups quinoa, 13 cups milk, 12 banana, 14 cups raspberries, 14 cups blueberries, and 2 tablespoons walnuts. 1 tablespoon of maple syrup over each bowl.

Nutritional facts

Calories 105| Carbohydrates 4 g| Proteins 8 g| Fats 6.2 g| Sodium 127 mg |

101. Banana Bread Rice Pudding

Preparation time: 5 minutes

Cooking Time: 50 minutes

Servings: 4

Ingredients

- 1cup of brown rice
- 1½ cups of water
- 1½ cups of nondairy milk
- 3 tablespoons of sugar (omit if using sweetened nondairy milk)
- 2 teaspoons of pumpkin pie spice or ground cinnamon
- 2 bananas
- 3 tablespoons of chopped walnuts or sunflower seeds (optional)

Instructions

Rice, water, sugar, milk, and pumpkin pie spice. Bring to a boil over high heat, then lower heat and cover. Soak the rice in the liquid, stirring intermittently, until tender. 50 minutes as opposed to twenty minutes for white rice. Combine the cooked rice and bananas. Finish with walnuts (if using). Refrigerate leftovers for up to five days.

Nutritional facts

Calories: 215| Carbohydrates: 44 g| Proteins: 4 g| Fats: 2.4 g| Sodium 94 mg

102. Apple and cinnamon oatmeal

Preparation time: 10 minutes

Cooking Time: 10 minutes

Servings: 2

Ingredients

- 1¼ cup of apple cider
- 1 apple
- ⅔ Cup of rolled oats
- 1 teaspoon of ground cinnamon
- 1 tablespoon of pure maple syrup or agave (optional)

Instructions

Bring the apple cider to a boil in a medium saucepan. Add apples, oats, and cinnamon. Bring the cereal to a boil, then reduce the heat. 3–4 minutes until the oatmeal thickens. If using maple syrup, divide it between two bowls.

Nutritional facts

Calories 45| Carbohydrates 7 g| Proteins 1 g| Fats 1.2 g| Sodium 21 mg |

103. Spiced orange breakfast couscous

Preparation time: 5 minutes

Cooking Time: 10 minutes

Servings: 4

Ingredients

- 3 cups of orange juice
- 1½ cups of couscous
- 1 teaspoon of ground cinnamon
- ¼ Teaspoon of ground cloves
- ½ Cup of dried fruit, such as raisins or apricots
- ½ Cup of chopped almonds or other nuts or seeds

Instructions

Boil the orange juice in a small pot. Remove the couscous, cinnamon, and cloves. Cover the pan and let it rest for 5 minutes to soften the couscous. Toss the couscous with the dried fruit and nuts.

Nutritional facts

Calories 165| Carbohydrates 15 g| Proteins 3 g| Fats 10.1 g| Sodium 116 mg |

104. Breakfast Parfaits

Preparation time: 15 minutes

Cooking Time: 0 minutes

Servings: 2

Ingredients

- One 14-ounce of can coconut milk, refrigerated overnight
- 1 cup of granola

- ½ Cup of walnuts
- 1 cup of sliced strawberries or other seasonal berries

Instructions

Pour out the liquid and save the solids. Layer granola, walnuts, and strawberries in two parfait glasses. Instantly serve

Nutritional facts

Calories 120| Carbohydrates 27 g| Proteins 5 g| Fats 1.9 g| Sodium 100 mg |

105. Sweet potato and kale hash

Preparation time: 10 minutes

Cooking Time: 15 minutes

Servings: 2

Ingredients

- 1 sweet potato
- 2 tablespoons of olive oil
- ½ Onion, sliced
- 1 peeled and chopped carrot
- 2 cloves of garlic minced
- ½ teaspoon of dried thyme
- 1 cup of chopped kale
- Sea salt
- Ground black pepper

Instructions

Microwave the sweet potato for 5 minutes on high and pierce with a fork. Remove and cut into 14-inch cubes. Heat the olive oil in a large nonstick sauté pan over high heat. Cook for 5 minutes until softened. Cook for 30 seconds until the garlic is aromatic. Cook for 7 minutes until the sweet potatoes start to brown. Cook for 1–2 minutes to wilt the kale. Add salt and pepper. Instantly serve

Nutritional facts

Calories: 145| Carbohydrates: 28 g| Proteins: 4 g| Fats: 2.1 g| Sodium 170 mg |

106. Delicious Oat Meal

Preparation time: 10 minutes

Cooking Time: 6 minutes

Servings: 4

Ingredients

- 3 cups of water
- 3 cups of almond milk

- 1 and ½ cups of steel oats
- 4 pitted and chopped dates
- 1 teaspoon of cinnamon, ground
- 2 tablespoons of coconut sugar
- ½ Teaspoon of ginger powder
- A pinch of nutmeg
- A pinch of cloves
- 1 teaspoon of vanilla extract

Instructions

Stir water and milk in the slow cooker. Cover and cook on low for 6 hours. Serve in breakfast dishes.

Nutritional facts

Calories 105| Carbohydrates 4 g| Proteins 8 g| Fats 6.2 g| Sodium 127 mg |

107. Breakfast Cherry Delight

Preparation time: 10 minutes

Cooking Time: 8 hours and 10 minutes

Servings: 4

Ingredients

- 2 cups almond milk
- 2 cups water
- 1 cup steel-cut oats
- 2 tablespoons cocoa powder
- 1/3 cup cherries, pitted
- ¼ Cup maple syrup
- ½ teaspoon almond extract

For the sauce:

- 2 tablespoons water
- 1 cup cherries
- ¼ Teaspoon almond

Instructions

Add almond milk to the slow cooker. 2 cups water, 1 cup oats, 1/3 cup cherries, maple syrup, and almond extract Cook on low for 8 hours. 2 tablespoons water, 12 cups cherries, 14 teaspoon almond essence, whisk well and bring to a boil over medium heat for 10 minutes until thickened. Serve the oats in breakfast dishes with cherry sauce.

Nutritional facts

Calories: 215| Carbohydrates: 44 g| Proteins: 4 g| Fats: 2.4 g| Sodium 94 mg |

108. Sweet Potato Home Fries

Preparation time: 15 minutes

Cooking Time: 6 minutes

Servings: 4

Ingredients

- 3 tablespoons of extra-virgin olive oil, plus more for coating the slow cooker
- 2 pounds of sweet potatoes, diced
- 1 red bell pepper, seeded and diced
- 1/2 onion, finely diced
- garlic powder 1 teaspoon
- Sea salt 1 teaspoon
- dried rosemary, minced 1 teaspoon
- freshly ground black pepper 1/2 teaspoon

Instructions

Olive oil in the slow cooker. Put the sweet potatoes, red bell pepper, and onion in the slow cooker. Distribute the olive oil evenly over the veggies. Garlic powder, salt, rosemary, and pepper toss coat the oil and spices. Set the cooker to low. 6–8 hours later, serve.

Nutritional facts

Calories 430| Carbohydrates 65 g| Proteins 4 g| Fats 18.2 g| Sodium 21 mg |

109. Perfect Hard-boiled Eggs

Preparation time: 15 minutes

Cooking Time: 2.5 minutes

Servings: 6

Ingredients

- 6 large eggs
- 1 tablespoon distilled white vinegar

Instructions

Place the eggs in the slow cooker, not stacked. Just cover the eggs with water in the slow cooker. Vinegar. Set the stove on high for 2 1/2 hours. Serve chilled.

Nutritional facts

Calories 45| Carbohydrates 7 g| Proteins 1 g| Fats 1.2 g| Sodium 21 mg |

110. Chicken-Apple Breakfast Sausage

Preparation time: 15 minutes

Cooking Time: 6 minutes

Servings: 4

Ingredients

- 1 pound ground chicken
- 1/2 apple, peeled and minced
- 1 teaspoon salt
- 1/2 teaspoon ground black pepper
- 1/2 teaspoon of dried parsley flakes
- 1/2 teaspoon of garlic powder
- 1/2 teaspoon of dried basil leaves
- 1/4 teaspoon of ground cinnamon

Instructions

Mix the chicken, apple, parsley flakes, garlic powder, basil, and cinnamon. Blend well. Press the chicken mixture into the slow cooker's bottom in a thin layer. Set the cooker to low. Cook for 6–8 hours or until the meat is tender. Loosen the chicken from the edges and move it to a chopping board. Serve in preferred forms (sticks or circles).

Nutritional facts

Calories 90| Carbohydrates 9 g| Proteins 1 g| Fats 6.4 g| Sodium 8 mg |

111. Golden Beet & Spinach Frittata

Preparation time: 15 minutes

Cooking Time: 5 minutes

Servings: 4

Ingredients

- 1 tablespoon of extra-virgin olive oil
- 8 eggs
- 1 cup fresh spinach leaves, chopped
- 1 cup of diced peeled golden beets
- ½ onion, diced
- 1/4 cup of unsweetened almond milk
- 3/4 teaspoon of salt
- 1/2 teaspoon of garlic powder
- 1/2 teaspoon of dried basil leaves Freshly ground black pepper

Instructions

Olive oil in the slow cooker. Salt, garlic powder and basil, and the eggs and spinach are combined in a large bowl. Pour the custard into the slow cooker. Set the cooker to low. Cook for 5–7 hours or until the eggs are fully set.

Nutritional facts

Calories 230| Carbohydrates 13 g| Proteins 5 g| Fats

19.1 g| Sodium 128 mg |

112. Sour Cherry & Pumpkin Seed Granola

Preparation time: 10 minutes

Cooking Time: 5 minutes

Servings: 4

Ingredients

- 5 tablespoons of melted coconut oil, divided
- 1 cup of unsweetened shredded coconut
- 1 cup of rolled oats
- 1 cup of pecans
- 1/2 cup of pumpkin seeds
- 1 banana
- 1 tablespoon of vanilla extract
- 1/2 teaspoon of sea salt
- 1/2 teaspoon of ground cinnamon
- 1/2 teaspoon of ground ginger
- 1 cup of dried sour cherries

Instructions

Combine coconut, oats, pecans, and pumpkin seeds with 1 tablespoon of coconut oil in a slow cooker. The banana is mashed with vanilla, salt, cinnamon, and ginger in a small bowl. Add the liquid components to the granola mixture while stirring. Reduce the heat on the stove to low. Five to six hours to cook. Add the cherries after the cooking process. Spread the granola on a flat surface or baking sheet to cool completely before storing it. This may be stored for six months if refrigerated.

Nutritional facts

Calories 380| Carbohydrates 78 g| Proteins 4 g| Fats 7.2 g| Sodium 142 mg |

113. Morning Millet

Preparation time: 15 minutes

Cooking Time: 7 minutes

Servings: 4

Ingredients

- 1 cup of millet
- 2 cups of water
- 2 cups of full-fat coconut milk
- 1/2 teaspoon of sea salt
- 1/2 teaspoon of ground cinnamon
- 1/2 teaspoon of ground ginger

- 1/4 teaspoon of vanilla extract
- 1/2 cup of fresh blueberries

Instructions

Pour millet, water and coconut milk into a slow cooker. Well, mix. Cover and cook on low. 7–8 hours cook time; finally, stir in the blueberries and serve.

Nutritional Facts

Calories 61| Carbohydrates 9g| Protein 2g| Fats 2g| Sodium 95 mg |

114. Caramel-Apple Oats

Preparation time: 15 minutes

Cooking Time: 6 minutes

Servings: 4

Ingredients

- 1 tablespoon of coconut oil
- 3 apples, such as Fuji or Gala
- 2 tablespoons of coconut sugar
- 1/4 teaspoon of sea salt
- 1 teaspoon of ground ginger
- 1 teaspoon of ground cinnamon
- 1 teaspoon of vanilla extract
- 2 cups of rolled oats
- 1 cup unsweetened applesauce
- 3 cups of unsweetened almond milk
- 1/2 cup of water

Instructions

Pour coconut oil into the slow cooker. Arrange the sliced apples in a layer on the slow cooker's bottom. Layer the oats, applesauce, almond milk, and water in this sequence. Cover and cook on low. 6–8 hours later, serve.

Nutritional Facts

Calories 33|Carbohydrates 4g|Protein 1g|Fats 2g|| Sodium 22 mg | Potassium 167 mg | Phosphorus 30 mg|

115. Carrot & Fennel Quinoa Breakfast Casserole

Preparation time: 15 minutes

Cooking Time: 5 minutes

Servings: 4

Ingredients

- 6 large eggs
- 1/2 cup of quinoa, rinsed well (see Tip)

- 1 ½ cups of unsweetened almond milk
- 1/2 teaspoon of sea salt
- 1/2 teaspoon of garlic powder
- 1/4 teaspoon of dried oregano Freshly ground black pepper
- 1 fennel bulb, sliced
- 3 carrots, diced
- 1 tablespoon of extra-virgin olive oil

Instructions

Whisk the eggs. Season with salt, garlic powder, oregano, and almond milk. Whisk well to integrate all components. Add fennel and carrots. In the slow cooker, coat the egg mixture with olive oil. Cover and cook on low. Cook for 5–7 hours.

Nutritional Facts

Calories 126 | Carbohydrate 12.1g | Protein 6.2g | Fat 7.4g | Sodium 251 mg |

116. Simple Steel-Cut Oats

Preparation time: 15 minutes

Cooking Time: 6 minutes

Servings: 4

Ingredients

- 1 tablespoon of coconut oil
- 4 cups of boiling water
- 1/2 teaspoon of sea salt
- 1 cup of steel-cut oats

Instructions

Coconut oil in the slow cooker. Boil the water, salt, and

oats in your slow cooker. Set the stove to warm. 6–8 hours later, serve.

Nutritional Facts:

Calories 123 | Carbohydrates 19g | Protein 5g | Fats 3g | Sodium 157 mg |

117. Grain-Free Savory Breakfast Casserole

Preparation time: 15 minutes

Cooking Time: 4 minutes

Servings: 4

Ingredients

- 1 tablespoon of coconut oil
- 6 eggs

- 1/2 cup of unsweetened almond milk
- 1 teaspoon of Dijon mustard
- 1 teaspoon of sea salt
- 1 teaspoon of garlic powder
- ground black pepper
- 1 cup of broccoli florets
- 1/2 onion, cubed
- 1 peeled and diced small sweet potato
- 1 cup diced Chicken-Apple

Instructions

Coconut oil in the slow cooker. Whisk the eggs, almond milk, mustard, salt, and garlic powder. Pour the egg mixture over the broccoli, onion, sweet potato, and sausage. Set the cooker to low. Serve after 4–5 hours, when the eggs have been set and the veggies are soft.

Nutritional facts

Calories 123 | Carbohydrates 19g | Protein 5g | Fats 3g | Sodium 78 mg |

118. German Chocolate Cake Protein Oats

Preparation time: 15 minutes

Cooking Time: 6 minutes

Servings: 4

Ingredients

- 1 tablespoon of coconut oil
- 2 cups of rolled oats
- 2 1/2 cups of water
- 2 cups of full-fat coconut milk
- 1/4 cup of unsweetened cacao powder
- 2 tablespoons of collagen peptides
- 1/4 teaspoon of sea salt
- 2 tablespoons of pecans
- 2 tablespoons of unsweetened
- tattered coconut

Instructions

Coconut oil in the slow cooker. Combine oats, coconut milk, cacao powder, collagen peptides, and salt in the slow cooker. Mix well. Set the cooker to low. Cook for 6–8 hours. Serve with pecans and coconut.

Nutritional Facts:

Calories 123 | Carbohydrates 19g | Protein 5g | Fats 3g | Sodium 157 mg |

119. Avocado Toast with Greens

Preparation time: 5 minutes

Cooking Time: 5 minutes

Servings: 4

Ingredients

- 1 teaspoon of anchovy paste
- 1 teaspoon of lemon juice
- ½ teaspoon of kosher salt
- ¼ teaspoon of ground pepper
- slices of your favorite bread
- 1-2 pitted, peeled and diced avocados
- ½ cucumber, sliced
- Olive oil
- Lemon wedges
- 2 garlic cloves
- 4 oz. feta cheese
- 1 cup of basil
- ¼ cup of chopped chives
- ¼ cup of tarragon leaves
- 2 tablespoons of Greek yogurt

Instructions

In a food processor, pulse the garlic, tarragon, chives, basil, pepper, and salt until finely chopped and combined. Add Greek yogurt for added decadence. The spread may be prepared and refrigerated one day in advance. Toast little pieces of naan or bread. Top the feta with the greens. Avocado and cucumber slices are atop the salad Sprinkle with olive oil, pepper, and salt.

Nutritional facts

Calories 123 |Carbohydrates 19g |Protein 5g| Fats 3g | Sodium 78 mg |

120. Maple -Tahini Oatmeal

Preparation time: 5 minutes

Cooking Time: 6 minutes

Servings: 2

Ingredients

- 1 cup of old-fashioned rolled oats
- 1 cup of vanilla unsweetened Almond Milk
- water 1 cup
- for topping, Blueberries and strawberries

Drizzle:

- 2 Tablespoons of tahini
- ½ tablespoon of maple syrup
- 2 Tablespoons of water

Instructions

Oats may be prepared on the stovetop or in the microwave. Cook the oats, almond milk, and water in the microwave for three to five minutes. Cover and cook oats, almond milk, and water over low heat until cooked. After cooking, allow the mixture to cool for 5 minutes to thicken. Your preferred condiments Pour the ingredients for the drizzle into a small bowl and whisk well.

Whisk together the ingredients for the dressing in a small dish. It will first separate and seem odd, but if you continue to mix it, you should be able to get a creamy dressing.

Nutritional Facts:

Calories 164 |Carbohydrates 25.6 g |Protein 8.1 g |Fat 3.8 g | Sodium 124 mg

121. Blueberry -Millet Breakfast Bake

Preparation time: 30 minutes

Cooking time: 35 minutes

Servings: 4

Ingredients

- 3 cups of water
- 1 cup of uncooked millet
- ½ teaspoon of salt
- ½ teaspoon of ground cinnamon
- ¼ teaspoon of ground nutmeg
- 1 cup of frozen blueberries
- ¼ cup of chopped walnuts
- Brown sugar (optional)

Instructions

Bring water, nutmeg, millet, salt, and cinnamon to a boil. Simmer for 20–25 minutes, stirring regularly, until the millet is soft and has absorbed almost all of the water. Turn the heat off. Stir in the frozen blueberries, cover, and allow stand for about three minutes, until warm and the water has been absorbed. Pour millet into four separate bowls. Almonds and brown sugar on the top.

Nutritional Facts:

Calories: 252.8| Carbohydrates: 19.8g| Protein: 25.6g |Fats: 8g | Sodium 111 mg

122. Savory Quinoa Breakfast Stew

Preparation time: 15 minutes

Cooking time: 30 minutes

Servings: 3

Ingredients

- 1 stalk celery, chopped
- 2 sliced carrots
- 1 teaspoon of ground turmeric
- 1 teaspoon of lime juice
- salt
- 1 small minced
- 1 garlic clove, minced
- 1 cup of vegetable stock
- ½ cup of uncooked quinoa, rinsed
- ¼ teaspoon of dried basil

Instructions

Heat the olive oil in a medium-sized saucepan. Then, add the onion and celery. Bake and toss the onion for 5 minutes, until it is soft and transparent. Mix turmeric, quinoa, and basil into the dish. Cook for 25 to 30 minutes, or until the quinoa is soft and has absorbed all of the liquid. Serve with salt and lime juice to taste.

Nutritional Facts:

Calories: 122.4 |Carbohydrates: 7.5g|Protein: 13.7g|Fats: 1.2g| Sodium 75 mg

123. Maple-Cinnamon Granola

Preparation time: 10 minutes

Cook time: 45 minutes

Servings: 20

Ingredients

- 10 cups of rolled oats
- 1 cup of raw hulled sunflower seeds
- ½ cup of unsweetened flaked coconut
- 1 ½ teaspoon of ground cinnamon
- 3 tablespoons of water
- ½ teaspoon of salt
- 1 cup of maple syrup
- 1/3 cup of vegetable oil
- 1 teaspoon of vanilla extract
- 2 cups of raisins
- 2 cups of roasted nuts

Instructions

Preheating the oven to 3000F while 2 pans. Set the ingredients aside. In boiling water, dissolve the salt. In the syrup and boil, simmer. Mix in the vanilla extract. Add the coconut, sunflower seeds, and oats. For 45 minutes, stir 3 times. Set aside to cool.

Nutritional Facts:

Calories 218| Carbohydrates 220 g| Protein 2 g| Fat 15g| Sodium 76 mg

124. Quick Greens and Cauliflower Bowl

Preparation time: 10 minutes

Cook time: 5 minutes

Servings: 2

Ingredients

- 1 cup of coarsely chopped fresh cilantro leaves and stems
- ½ cup of coarsely chopped white onion
- 1 clove of garlic
- 1 jalapeno seeded
- 2 tablespoons of olive oil
- 1 pound of fresh cauliflower
- 1 teaspoon of fresh lime juice
- 3/8 teaspoon kosher salt

Instructions

Fresh cilantro leaves and stems, garlic clove, white onion, and seeded jalapeno are processed in a little food processor until they resemble a paste. In a big skillet, heat olive oil to a high temperature. 3 minutes for cauliflower crumbles or cauliflower rice. Stir in the cilantro mixture; bake for 2 minutes while stirring intermittently. Add then lime juice and salt.

Nutritional Facts:

Calories 318| Carbohydrates 60 g| Protein 1.7 g |Fat 97 g | Sodium 50 mg

125. Avocado toast with Greens

Preparation time: 5 minutes

Cook time: 4 minutes

Servings: 1

Ingredients

- 2 slices of gluten-free bread
- 1 ripe avocado
- 1½ tablespoons of lemon juice
- ⅛ teaspoon of salt
- 2 cups of spinach leaves

Instructions

Toasted bread in a steamer basket and 2 inches of water in a medium saucepan. Bring the water to a rolling boil. Scoop the avocado flesh off the skin into a small basin. Lemon juice with salt Fork-mash together. If needed, add extra lemon juice or salt to taste. When the water boils, add the spinach. Cover and steam for 3–4 minutes until wilted. Distribute the avocado mixture between the two toasts. Half the wilted greens on each.

Nutritional Facts:

Calories 300| Carbohydrates 50 g| Protein 1 g |Fat 82 g | Sodium 35 mg

126. Maple-Tahini Oatmeal

Preparation time: 5 minutes

Cook time: 15 minutes

Servings: 2

Ingredients

- 2 cups of water
- 1 cup of gluten-free rolled oats
- ⅛ teaspoon of salt
- ⅓ cup of tahini
- 2 tablespoons of maple syrup, divided

Instructions

Stir the water, oats, and salt in a medium saucepan over medium heat. Boil. Cover and reduce heat to low. 10 minutes, occasionally stirring, until soft. Stir in the tahini, letting it melt. 3–4 minutes longer, or until the oatmeal is done. Pour the oatmeal into two dishes. Put 1 tablespoon maple syrup on each.

Nutritional Facts:

Calories 318| Carbohydrates 60 g| Protein 1.7 g |Fat 97 g | Sodium 40 mg

127. Blueberry-Millet Breakfast Bake

Preparation time: 10 minutes

Cook time: 55 minutes

Servings: 8

Ingredients

- 2 cups of millet, soaked in water overnight
- 2 cups of blueberries
- 1¾ cups of unsweetened applesauce
- ⅓ cup of melted coconut oil
- 2 teaspoons of grated fresh ginger
- 1½ teaspoons of ground cinnamon

Instructions

Oven at 350 degrees Fahrenheit, heat for 1–2 minutes of rinsing and draining the millet. A large dish is the best option. The blueberries should not be mashed. A 9x9-inch casserole dish should be used for this recipe. Wrap it up with foil. For 40 minutes, preheat the oven to 400 degrees F. Continue baking for 10–15 minutes to get the desired crispness.

Nutritional Facts:

Calories 74| Carbohydrate 9.8g | Protein 6g| Fat 9.4g | Sodium 129 mg

128. Savory Quinoa Breakfast Stew

Preparation time: 5 minutes

Cook time: 17 minutes

Servings: 1

Ingredients

- ¼ cup of quinoa
- ¾ cup of water, plus additional as needed
- ½ broccoli head, chopped
- 1 carrot, grated
- ¼ teaspoon of salt
- 1 tablespoon of chopped fresh dill

Instructions

Rinse the quinoa in a fine-mesh sieve. Stir quinoa and water in a small saucepan over high heat. Boil. Turn down the heat. Cook covered for 5 min. Salt, broccoli, and carrot. Cook for 10-12 minutes or longer, or until quinoa is soft. Make sure the stew is moist enough. It should be more liquid than a pilaf. Serve with dill.

Nutritional Facts:

Calories: 307 |Fat: 1g |Carbohydrates 56g |Protein 20g | Sodium 145 mg

129. Chia Breakfast Pudding

Preparation time: 5 minutes

Cook time: 0 minutes

Servings: 4

Ingredients

- ¾ cup of chia seeds
- ½ cup of hemp seeds
- 2¼ cups of coconut milk
- ½ cup of dried cranberries
- ¼ cup of maple syrup

Instructions

Combine chia seeds, hemp seeds, coconut milk, cranberries, and maple syrup in a medium bowl. Refrigerate the bowl overnight. Wake up, stir, and eat.

Nutritional Facts

Calories 92| Carbohydrates 4 g| Protein 5 g| Fats 8 g| Sodium 25 mg

130. Quick Greens and Cauliflower Bowl

Preparation time: 5 minutes

Cook time: 5 minutes

Servings: 1

Ingredients

- 4 kale leaves
- 1 cup of cauliflower florets
- ½ avocado
- 1 teaspoon of lemon juice
- 1 teaspoon of olive oil
- Salt

Instructions

Medium saucepan with a steamer basket and two inches of water, Bring to a vigorous boil. Add the cauliflower and kale. 5 minutes are simmering while covered. Place the vegetables in an avocado, lemon juice, olive oil, and salt bowl.

Nutritional Facts

Calories 97| Carbohydrates 5g| Protein 2g| Fats 8g| Sodium 23 mg |

131. Maple-Cinnamon Granola

Preparation time: 15 minutes

Cook time: 35 minutes

Servings: 8

Ingredients

- 4 cups of gluten-free rolled oats
- 1½ cups of sunflower seeds
- ½ cup of maple syrup
- ½ cup of coconut oil
- 1½ teaspoons of ground cinnamon

Instructions

A 325°F, preheat the oven. Parchment paper on two baking sheets. Mix oats, sunflower seeds, maple syrup, coconut oil, and cinnamon. Stir thoroughly to cover oats and seeds with syrup, oil, and cinnamon. Distribute the granola between the two sheets. Bake for 35-40 minutes, stirring every 10 minutes to ensure uniform browning.

Refrigerate in big glass jars with tight-fitting lids

Nutritional Facts

Calories 91| Carbohydrates 15g| Protein 5g| Fats 6g| Sodium 676 mg |

132. Coconut Rice *with* Berries

Preparation time: 10 minutes

Cook time: 30 minutes

Servings: 4

Ingredients

- 1 cup of brown basmati rice
- 1 cup of water
- 1 cup of coconut milk
- 1 teaspoon of salt
- 2 pitted and chopped dates
- 1 cup of fresh blueberries or raspberries
- ¼ cup of toasted slivered almonds, divided
- ½ cup of shaved coconut, divided

Instructions

Combine the basmati rice, water, coconut milk, salt, and date bits in a medium saucepan. Stir until the mixture boils. Cook for 20-30 minutes, without stirring, until the rice is tender. 4 bowls of rice, 14 cups blueberries, 1 tablespoon almonds, and 2 teaspoons coconut.

Nutritional Facts

Calories 92| Protein 4g| Carbohydrates 10g| Fats 4g| Sodium 184 mg |

133. Overnight Muesli

Preparation time: 10 minutes

Servings: 4

Ingredients

- 2 cups of gluten-free rolled oats
- 1¾ cups of coconut milk
- ¼ cup of no-added-sugar apple juice
- 1 tablespoon of apple cider vinegar (optional)
- 1 cored and chopped apple
- ground cinnamon

Instructions

Mix oats, coconut milk, apple juice, and vinegar in a medium bowl (if using). Cover and chill overnight. Add the diced apple and cinnamon the following morning.

Nutritional Facts

Calories 202| Carbohydrates 22g| Protein 14g| Fats 6g| Sodium 52 mg |

134. Spicy Quinoa

Preparation time: 10 minutes

Cooking time: 20

Servings: 4

Ingredients

- 1 cup quinoa rinsed well
- 2 cups of water
- ½ cup of shredded coconut
- ¼ cup of hemp seeds
- 2 tablespoons of flaxseed
- 1 teaspoon of ground cinnamon
- 1 teaspoon of vanilla extract
- salt
- 1 cup of fresh berries of your choice, divided
- ¼ cup of chopped hazelnuts

Instructions

Quinoa and water in a medium saucepan over high heat. Then decrease the heat to a simmer for 15–20 minutes, or until the quinoa is cooked (it should double or triple in bulk, similar to couscous, and be slightly translucent). Coat with a thin layer of coconut oil. 14 cups berries and 1 tablespoon of hazelnuts on each dish of quinoa.

Nutritional Facts

Calories 87| Carbohydrates 7g|Protein 4g| Fat 5g| Sodium 241 mg |

135. Buckwheat Crêpes *with* Berries

Preparation time: 15 minutes

Cooking time: 5

Servings: 4

Ingredients

- 1 cup of buckwheat flour
- ½ teaspoon of salt
- 2 tablespoons of coconut oil (1 tablespoon melted)
- 1½ cups of almond milk
- 1 egg
- 1 teaspoon of vanilla extract
- 3 cups of fresh berries, divided
- 6 tablespoons of Chia Jam

Instructions

Then add the almond milk, egg and vanilla and stir until smooth. Melt the remaining 1 tablespoon of coconut oil in a 12-inch nonstick pan over medium heat. Tilt the pan to coat it with the melted oil. 14 cup batter into the skillet. Tilt the skillet to coat everything evenly for 2 minutes or until the edges curl. Flip the crêpe and cook for 1 minute on the other side. Place on a platter. Make more crêpes using the leftover batter. 4–6 crêpes, 12 cup berries, and 1 tablespoon Chia Jam on 1 crêpe overfilling. Serve with the leftover crêpes.

Nutritional facts

Calories 245| Carbohydrates 22g| Protein 3g| Fat 16g| Sodium 164 mg |

136. Warm Chia-Berry Non-dairy Yogurt

Preparation time: 10 minutes

Cooking time: 5

Servings: 4

Ingredients

- 1 (10-ounce) mixed berries, thawed
- 2 tablespoons of maple syrup
- 2 tablespoons of freshly squeezed lemon juice
- ½ vanilla bean
- 1 tablespoon of chia seeds
- 4 cups of unsweetened almond yogurt or coconut yogurt

Instructions

Combine the berries, maple syrup, lemon juice, and vanilla bean in a medium saucepan. Bring to a boil, continually stirring. Cook for 3 minutes at a simmer. Turn off the heat. Remove and discard the vanilla bean. Add the chia seeds. Allow 5-10 minutes for the seeds to thicken. Pour 1 cup of yogurt over each dish of fruit.

Nutritional Facts

Calories 208 | Carbohydrates 18g| Protein 4.2g| Fats 13g| Sodium 5 mg |

137. Buckwheat Waffles

Preparation time: 15 minutes

Cooking time: 6

Servings: 4

Ingredients

- 1½ cups of buckwheat flour
- ½ cup of brown rice flour
- 2 teaspoons of baking powder
- 1 teaspoon of baking soda

- ½ teaspoon of salt

- 1 egg

- 1 tablespoon of maple syrup

- 2 teaspoons of vanilla extract

- 1 cup of water

- 1½ cups of almond milk

- Coconut oil

Instructions

Buckwheat flour, rice flour, baking powder, baking soda, and salt. Add egg, maple syrup, and vanilla to dry the ingredients. Whisk in the water and almond milk until the batter is smooth. Allow 10 minutes for the batter to thicken. The buckwheat may sink to the bottom during resting, so mix thoroughly before serving. Brush the waffle iron with coconut oil. Cook the waffle iron according to the manufacturer's instructions.

Nutritional Facts

Calories 173 |Carbohydrates 24g| Protein 3.7g| Fats 7.1g | Sodium 20 mg |

138. Coconut Pancakes

Preparation time: 10 minutes

Cooking time: 5

Servings: 4

Ingredients

- 4 eggs

- 1 cup of coconut or almond milk

- 1 tablespoon of melted coconut oil

- 1 tablespoon of maple syrup

- 1 teaspoon of vanilla extract

- ½ cup of coconut flour

- 1 teaspoon of baking soda

- ½ teaspoon of salt

Instructions

Mix the eggs, coconut milk, coconut oil, maple syrup, and vanilla in a medium bowl. Coconut flour, baking soda, and salt beat in the dry ingredients until smooth and lump-free. If the mixture is too thick, add more liquid to make it like pancake batter. Coconut oil in a big skillet. Heat it to medium-high. Cook for 3 minutes or until golden brown on the bottom. Cook for 2 minutes more. Stack the pancakes on a dish and fry the rest of the batter. It makes 8 pancakes.

Nutritional Facts

Calories 223| Carbohydrates 20g| Protein3 g| Fats 0 g| Sodium 6 mg |

139. Spinach Muffins

Preparation time: 15 minutes

Cooking time: 15

Servings: 12 muffins

Ingredients

- Cooking spray

- 2 cups of packed spinach

- 2 large eggs

- ¼ cup of raw honey

- 3 tablespoons of extra-virgin olive oil

- 1 teaspoon of vanilla extract

- 1 cup of oat flour

- 1 cup of almond flour

- 2 teaspoons of baking powder

- 1 teaspoon of baking soda

- ½ teaspoon of salt

- Black pepper as per taste

Instructions

350°F Oven Preheat 12 muffin cups sprayed with cooking spray. Blend spinach, eggs, honey, olive oil, and vanilla. Blitz to a paste. Mix oat flour, almond flour, baking powder, baking soda, salt, and pepper. Add the spinach mixture and stir thoroughly. Fill each cup 2/3 full. Bake for 15 minutes, or until gently browned and the centers are firm to the touch. Let cool for 10 minutes before removing the muffins from the tin.

Nutritional Facts

Calories 203| Carbohydrates 24g| Protein3.7g| Fats 0.7g| Sodium 8 mg |

140. Herb Scramble with Sautéed Cherry Tomatoes

Preparation time: 5 minutes

Cooking time: 10 minutes

Servings: 2 muffins

Ingredients

- 4 normal size eggs

- 2 teaspoons of chopped fresh oregano

- 1 tablespoon of extra-virgin olive oil

- 1 cup cherry tomatoes, split

- ½ garlic clove, divided

- ½ avocado

Instructions

Whisk the eggs and oregano together in a medium bowl. Melt butter in a large skillet. Add the olive oil once it's heated. Pour the eggs into the skillet and scramble using a heat-resistant spatula or a wooden spoon. Place the eggs on a plate. Sauté the cherry tomatoes and garlic for 2 minutes. Add the tomatoes and avocado slices to the eggs.

Nutritional Facts

Calories 42| Carbohydrates 8g| Protein 1g| Fats 0g| Sodium 77 mg |

141. Mushroom "Frittata"

Preparation time: 15 minutes

Cooking time: 20

Servings: 6 muffins

Ingredients

- 1½ cups of chickpea flour
- 1½ cups of water
- 1 teaspoon of salt
- 2 tablespoons of extra-virgin olive oil
- 1 small red onion, cubed
- 2 pints of sliced mushrooms
- 1 teaspoon of ground turmeric
- ½ teaspoon of ground cumin
- 1 teaspoon of salt
- ½ teaspoon of freshly ground black pepper
- 2 tablespoons of chopped fresh parsley

Instructions

350°F Oven Preheat In a small bowl, combine the chickpea flour, water, and salt. Big cast iron or oven-safe pan with olive oil. Add the onion to the heated oil. 3–5 minutes until the onion is cooked and transparent. Sauté mushrooms for 5 minutes. Sauté for 1 minute with turmeric, cumin, salt, and pepper. Pour the batter over the veggies and parsley. Bake for 20–25 minutes in a preheated oven. Serve warm or cold.

Nutritional Facts

Calories 62| Carbohydrates 4g| Protein 4g| Fats 2g| Sodium 72 mg |

142. Cucumber and Smoked-Salmon Lettuce Wraps

Preparation time: 10 minutes

Cook time: o minutes

Servings: 4

Ingredients

- 8 large butter lettuce leaves
- ½ English cucumber, sliced
- 8 ounces smoked salmon, divided
- 1 tablespoon of chopped fresh chives
- 4 tablespoons of Almost Caesar Salad Dressing, divided

Instructions

Arrange the lettuce in a single layer on a serving plate. Distribute cucumber slices among lettuce leaves. 2 oz. Smoked salmon per leaf. Drizzle each wrap with 1 tablespoon of chives. Almost Caesar Salad Dressing.

Nutritional Facts

Calories 42| Carbohydrates 8g| Protein 1g| Fats 0g| Sodium 77 mg |

143. Sweet Potato Hash

Preparation time: 15 minutes

Cooking time: 15 muffins

Servings: 4

Ingredients

- 2 tablespoons of coconut oil
- ½ onion, sliced
- 1 cup of sliced mushrooms
- 1 garlic clove, sliced
- 2 sweet potatoes, cooked and cut into ½-inch cubes
- 1 cup of chopped Swiss chard
- ½ cup of vegetable broth
- 1 teaspoon of salt
- ¼ teaspoon of freshly ground pepper
- 1 tablespoon of chopped fresh thyme
- 1 tablespoon of chopped fresh sage

Instructions

Melt 2 tablespoon of coconut oil in a large pan over high heat. Add onion, mushrooms, garlic. Allow the onions and mushrooms to cook for 8 minutes. Add the sweet potatoes and Swiss chard. 5 min. Salt, pepper, thyme, and sage

Nutritional Facts

Calories 15| Carbohydrates 5g| Protein 3g| Fats 0g| Sodium 142 mg |

144. Yogurt, Berry, and Walnut Parfait

Preparation time: 10 minutes

Cook time: 0 minutes

Servings: 2

Ingredients

- 2 cups plain unsweetened yogurt, or plain unsweetened coconut yogurt or almond yogurt
- 2 tablespoons honey
- 1 cup fresh blueberries
- 1 cup fresh raspberries
- ½ cup walnut pieces

Instructions

Mix yogurt and honey in a medium bowl. 2 serving bowls 12 cup blueberries, 12 cup raspberries, 14 cup walnut bits

Nutritional Facts

Calories 25| Carbohydrates 9g| Protein 1g| Fats 0g| Sodium 102 mg |

145. Oatmeal and Cinnamon with Dried Cranberries

Preparation time: 10 minutes

Cook time: 8 minutes

Servings: 2

Ingredients

- 1 cup of water
- 1 cup of almond milk
- Sea salt
- 1 cup of old-fashioned oats
- ½ cup of dried cranberries
- 1 teaspoon of ground cinnamon

Instructions

Bring the water, almond milk, and salt to a boil in a medium saucepan. Then add the cranberries and cinnamon. Cook for 5 minutes, stirring periodically, over medium heat. Turn off the heat. Cover the pot and wait 3 minutes. Serve with a mix.

Nutritional Facts

Calories 45| Carbohydrates 6g| Protein 1g| Fats 0g| Sodium 112 mg |

146. Spinach Frittata

Preparation time: 10 minutes

Cook time: 12 minutes

Servings: 4

Ingredients

- 2 tablespoons oil
- 2 cups of fresh baby spinach
- 8 medium eggs, beaten
- 1 teaspoon of garlic powder
- ½ teaspoon of sea salt
- ⅛ teaspoon of freshly ground black pepper
- 2 tablespoons of grated parmesan cheese

Instructions

Preheat high broiler. Heat the olive oil until it shimmers in a large ovenproof skillet (seasoned cast iron works great). Cook for 3 minutes, stirring periodically. Eggs, garlic powder, salt, and pepper; pour the egg mixture over the spinach and heat for 3 minutes until the edges are firm. Pull the eggs away from the pan's edges using a rubber spatula. Uncooked egg flows into the pan's edges. 2–3 minutes until the edges are firm. Sprinkle with Parmesan and broil under the broiler. 3 minutes are broiling until the top puffs. Serve in wedges.

Nutritional Facts

Calories 30| Carbohydrates 6g| Protein 3g| Fats 0g| Sodium 122 mg |

147. Mushroom and Bell Pepper Omelet

Preparation time: 10 minutes

Cook time: 10 minutes

Servings: 2

Ingredients

- 2 tablespoons of virgin olive oil
- 1 red bell pepper, sliced
- 1 cup of mushrooms, sliced
- 6 eggs
- ½ teaspoon of salt
- ⅛ teaspoon of freshly ground black pepper

Instructions

Heat the olive oil until it shimmers in a large nonstick skillet. Peppers with mushrooms. Stir periodically for 4 minutes until tender. Eggs, salt, and pepper in a medium bowl. In a nonstick pan, fry the eggs over the veggies for approximately 3 minutes, without stirring. Pull the eggs away from the pan's edges using a rubber spatula. Lingering raw egg flows to the pan's edges. Cook for 2–3 minutes until the eggs are set. Invert the omelet using a spatula. Serve in wedges.

Nutritional Facts

Calories 43| Carbohydrates 7g| Protein 1g| Fats 0g| Sodium 132 mg |

148. Smoked Salmon Scrambled Eggs

Preparation time: 5 minutes

Cook time: 8 minutes

Servings: 4

Ingredients

- 2 tablespoons of extra-virgin olive oil
- 6 ounces of smoked salmon, flaked
- 8 eggs
- ¼ teaspoon of black pepper

Instructions

Heat the olive oil until it shimmers in a large nonstick skillet for 3 minutes with the fish, stirring. Whisk the eggs and pepper in a bowl. Cook for 5 minutes, stirring gently until done.

Nutritional Facts

Calories 45| Carbohydrates 9g| Protein 1g| Fats 0g| Sodium 152 mg |

149. Five-Minute Breakfast

Preparation time: 5 minutes

Cook time: 2 minutes

Servings: 4

Ingredients

- 1 cup of leftover cooked brown rice
- ¼ teaspoon of cinnamon powder
- 1/8 cup of raisins
- ¼ cup of chopped walnuts
- ¼ cup of sunflower seeds
- ½ cup of rice milk or other alternative milk
- ¼ teaspoon of carob powder (optional)
- ½ teaspoon of maple syrup (optional)

Instructions

In a saucepan, combine all ingredients. Pour milk over rice for a cereal consistency. Warm to the desired temperature and serve.

Nutritional Facts

Calories 372|Carbohydrates 55g| Proteins 13.7g|Fats 2g| Sodium 371 mg |

150. Broccoli and Olive Frittata

Preparation time: 30 minutes

Cook time: 45 minutes

Servings: 4

Ingredients

- 1 yellow bell pepper
- 1 red bell pepper
- 2 broccoli crowns, cut into bite-size pieces
- ½ cup of pitted ripe olives halved
- 6 eggs, beaten
- ½ cup of soy milk
- 2 tablespoons of chopped fresh sweet basil or 1 teaspoon of dried basil
- 1 teaspoon of dried oregano
- salt and pepper
- ¼ cup of cashews, ground fine for garnish

Instructions

Broil peppers for 5–10 minutes until lightly browned. Cool for 5 minutes in a closed brown paper bag. Peel and shave. (Leave the peel on and slice the roasted peppers thinly.) Bake at 400°F. 9-inch circular cake pan Arrange the broccoli, peppers, and olives in the pan equally. Pour the remaining ingredients over the veggies. 35–40 minutes, or until set in the middle. Broil for 2 minutes to brown the top. Serve warm or cold, garnished with ground cashews (in place of Parmesan cheese).

Nutritional Facts

Calories 149| Carbohydrates 10g| Protein 8.1g| Fats 2g| Sodium 128 mg |

151. Mexican Morning Eggs

Preparation time: 15 minutes

Cook time: 5 minutes

Servings: 3

Ingredients

- 4 eggs, cooked any way you like
- 1 cup leftover cooked brown rice
- ¾ cup of black beans
- a can (rinse first to remove excess salt)
- ½ teaspoon of cumin
- ½ teaspoon of paprika
- ½ teaspoon of chili powder
- ½ teaspoon of sea salt

- 1 avocado, diced

Instructions

In a pan, combine rice, beans, and spices. Prepare eggs as desired in a separate skillet. Serve the eggs, rice, and beans together in a dish. Avocado sliced on top.

Nutritional Facts

Calories 273|Carbohydrates 7g| Protein 1g| Fats 27g| Sodium 61 mg |

152. Protein Power Breakfast

Preparation time: 10 minutes

Cook time: 10 minutes

Servings: 1

Ingredients

- 1 tablespoon of flaxseeds
- 2 tablespoons of sesame seeds
- 2 tablespoons of sunflower seeds
- 1 teaspoon of honey
- ½ banana, sliced

Instructions

In a pan, combine rice, beans, and spices. Prepare eggs

as desired in a separate skillet. Serve the eggs, rice, and beans together in a dish. Avocado sliced on top.

Nutritional Facts:

Calories 84 | Fat 7.9g |Carbohydrates 2.4g |Protein 2g| Sodium 824 mg |

153. Quickest Oatmeal You'll Ever Eat

Preparation time: 5 minutes

Cook time: 0 minutes

Servings: 1

Ingredients

- 1 cup of nut-and-fruit muesli (natural with no additives)
- ½–1 cup of boiling water
- ½ teaspoon of maple syrup (optional; the fruit in the cereal adds
- sweetness)

Instructions

In a cereal bowl, mix all ingredients. Wait 1 minute before eating.

Nutritional Facts:

Calories 194 | Fat 6g| Protein 20g| Carbohydrates 15g | Sodium 368 mg |

154. Tofu Scramble

Preparation time: 10 minutes

Cook time: 5 minutes

Servings: 6

Ingredients

- 1 pound of firm tofu
- 2 tablespoons of spelled flour (or any type of non-wheat flour)
- 1 tablespoon of olive oil
- 4–5 cups of chopped mixed vegetables
- 1 teaspoon of onion powder
- 1 teaspoon of paprika
- 2 teaspoons powder of garlic
- ½ teaspoon of sea salt
- ½ teaspoon of turmeric
- 1 teaspoon of curry powder
- Black pepper
- Dash cayenne
- ½ cup of filtered water

Instructions

Drain excess water from tofu and slab it. In a small bowl, mix spices and flour. Sauté garlic and onions in a large pan over medium heat until tender. Continue sautéing additional veggies until partly cooked. Crumble tofu to mimic scrambled eggs. Water and spice/flour combination Sauté until veggies are cooked to your preference. (Cook flour for 2 minutes to remove raw starch flavor.) Instantly serve

Nutritional Facts:

Calories 56 | Fat 6 g| Protein 1 g| Carbohydrates 6 g | Sodium 258 mg |

155. Dr. Fisel's Tofu Scramble

Preparation time: 15 minutes

Cook time: 10 minutes

Servings: 4

Ingredients

- 1 tablespoon of olive oil
- ½ onion, sliced
- 1 clove garlic
- 5 mushrooms, cut
- 1 cup of chopped broccoli

- 1 1-pound of tofu
- 2 teaspoons of herbs
- 1 tablespoon of yeast powder
- 2 teaspoons of kelp powder
- 1 teaspoon of cumin powder
- ¼ teaspoon of cayenne powder
- 1 tablespoon of tamari
- Pepper to taste
- Salt to taste

Instructions

Add the onions, garlic, mushrooms, and broccoli to the hot oil. Sauté until the onions are transparent. Tofu crumbles to the pan. Sauté the remaining ingredients for 10 minutes or until moisture has evaporated and the veggies are soft.

Nutritional Facts:

Calories 60 | Fat 2 g| Protein 2 g| Carbohydrates 6 g | Sodium 258 mg |

156. Wheat-Free Pancakes

Preparation time: 10 minutes

Cook time: 10 minutes

Servings: 6

Ingredients

- ½ cup of walnuts, ground in the food processor to a fine powder
- ¾ cup of spelled flour
- ¾ cup of rice flour
- 1 teaspoon of cream of tartar
- 1 teaspoon of baking soda
- ¾ teaspoon of sea salt
- 11/3 cup of water
- 1 tablespoon of olive oil

Instructions

An equal amount of each of the following ingredients should be combined in a medium-sized mixing bowl: 1 cup water whisked into dry ingredients, then remaining water to desired consistency. If the batter is too thick, add water. Add optional items and mix well. Lightly oil a big pan or skillet. Set aside. Large spoon batters onto hot frying surface. Cook until bubbles appear on top; flip. Brown the second side.

Nutritional Facts:

Calories 62 | Fat 4g| Protein 1g| Carbohydrates 7g | Sodium 238 mg |

157. Easy Pancakes

Preparation time: 10 minutes

Servings: 2

Ingredients

- 3 tablespoons of raw sunflower seeds, ground fine
- 3 tablespoons of raw pumpkin seeds, ground fine
- 3 eggs
- ¼ cup of no gluten oat flour
- ¼ cup of rice milk
- ¼ cup of blueberries (optional)

Instructions

Mix all ingredients thoroughly in a medium-sized basin until clumps dissolve. Preheat a lightly greased skillet or griddle pan. Pour batter into 3-inch rounds. When pancakes begin to bubble, flip and cook on the other side for a short time until lightly browned.

Nutritional Facts:

Calories 66 | Fat 4g| Protein 1g| Carbohydrates 7g | Sodium 338 mg |

158. Breakfast Eggnog

Preparation time: 5 minutes

Servings: 1

Ingredients

- 2 eggs
- 1 cup of rice milk, cold
- 1 tablespoon of vanilla extract
- Sprint cinnamon
- Sprint nutmeg

Instructions

Mix all ingredients in a large cup or bowl until completely combined. Serve with a tiny strainer into a serving glass.

Nutritional Facts:

Calories 126| Fats 2g| Protein 4g| Carbohydrates 24g| Sodium 7 mg |

159. Ginger Apple Muffins

Preparation time: 10 minutes

Cooking Time: 15 minutes

Servings: 4

Ingredients

- All-purpose flour (2 cups)

- Sugar (2/3 cup)

- Baking powder 1 tablespoon

- Salt 1/2 tsp

- Ground cinnamon 1 tsp

- Ground ginger 1 tsp

- (3/4 cup Unsweetened almond milk) - To make almond milk, you'll need to soak

- Almonds in water for 1 – 2 days, channel and rinse them, then grind them with fresh water in a blender.

- Tattered apple (1 cup)

- Mashed banana (1/2 cup)

- Apple (1 tablespoon)

Instructions

Preheat the oven to 400°F. Grease or line the muffin pan molds with parchment paper. In a large mixing basin, combine flour, sugar, baking powder, salt, cinnamon, and ginger. Add almond milk, shredded apples, mashed banana, and apple cider vinegar to another dish. Stir in the flour mixture until the milk mixture is incorporated. Fill the muffin tins 2/3 full with batter. Bake the muffins for 15–20 minutes at 400°F. A toothpick inserted into a muffin should come out clean. The ginger apple muffins make 12 servings, each one weighing around.

Nutritional Facts:

Calories 70 |Fat 1g| Protein: 1g| Carbohydrates 16g| Sodium 118 mg |

160. Spinach and Mushroom Frittatas

Preparation time: 10 minutes

Cooking Time: 15 minutes

Servings: 4

Ingredients

- (1 lb.) Sliced button mushrooms

- (1 pc.) Chopped large onion

- (1 tablespoon .) Chopped garlic

- (1 lb.) Spinach

- (1/4 cup) Water

- (6 pcs.) Egg whites

- (4 pcs.) Eggs

- (6 oz.) Firm tofu

- (1/2 tsp.) Ground turmeric

- (1/2 tsp.) Kosher salt

- (1/2 tsp.) Cracked or powdered black pepper

Instructions

350°F preheated oven Sauté the button mushrooms in a nonstick skillet over medium-high heat. Sauté chopped onions for 3 minutes or until tender. Water it. Then add spinach and heat for 2 minutes with the lid on, or until wilted. Cook until all water is gone. Dispose of. Blend eggs, turmeric, salt, pepper, tofu, and egg whites on high until creamy. Then gently pour it in. Bake the sauté pan at 350°F for 25-30 minutes. Remove the pan, transfer the frittata onto a platter, and let it rest for 10 minutes. After that, cut the frittata into wedges and serve.

Nutritional Facts:

Calories: 226|Fat 12g| Protein 9g| Carbohydrates 23g| Sodium 61.1 mg |

161. Gluten-Free Strawberry Crepes

Preparation time: 10 minutes

Cooking Time: 15 minutes

Servings: 4

Ingredients

- 6 cups sliced strawberries

- 2 tablespoons Sugar or honey

- Large eggs 4 pcs

- 1 cup unsweetened almond milk

- Olive oil 2 tablespoon

- 1 teaspoon Vanilla extract

- 1 teaspoon Light brown sugar

- 1 teaspoon salt

- 3/4 cup Gluten-free flour baking mix

Instructions

Mix sugar and strawberries until covered. 30 minutes at room temperature, add the eggs, almond milk, olive oil, vanilla extract, brown sugar, and salt to a large mixing bowl. Mix in the gluten-free four until the batter is smooth. Preheat a nonstick skillet or crepe pan on medium heat. 14 cup butter in the skillet, coat evenly. Cook for 45 seconds or until the crepe becomes golden. Cook for 10 seconds on the opposite side, then transfer to a serving platter.12 cups of sugared strawberries spooned on top of the crepe. Fold the crepe in half as you cover the strawberries. Serve the crepe with syrup or drink.

Nutritional Facts:

Calories 135 | Fat 9g| Protein 2g| Carbohydrates 13g| Sodium 308 mg |

162. Cherry Quinoa Porridge

Preparation time: 12 minutes

Cooking Time: 13 minutes

Servings: 4

Ingredients

- 1 cup Water
- ½ cup Dry quinoa
- ½ cup Dried unsweetened cherries
- ½ teaspoon Vanilla extract
- ¼ teaspoon Ground cinnamon
- 1 tsp. Honey

Instructions

Combine water, quinoa, cherries, vanilla, and cinnamon in a medium saucepan. On medium-high heat, bring to a boil. Cover the pot and simmer for 15 minutes. A soft porridge and all the water absorbed are signs of cooked quinoa. Serve with a honey drizzle.

Nutritional Facts

Calories 224| Fat 14g|Protein 3g| Carbohydrates: 25g

| Sodium 254 mg |

163. Buckwheat and Quinoa Granola

Preparation time: 15 minutes

Cooking Time: 13 minutes

Servings: 6

Ingredients

- 3 tablespoon Honey
- 3 tablespoon liquid coconut oil
- 1 teaspoon Vanilla extract
- 1/4 teaspoon ground cinnamon
- 1/4 teaspoon ground ginger
- 1 cup Buckwheat oats
- 1 cup of quinoa cooked quinoa
- 1/2 cup Regular oats
- 1/2 cup dried unsweetened cranberries

Instructions

Prepare a baking sheet with parchment paper or a silicone baking mat, or gently oil it. Preheat the oven to 325°F. Combine coconut oil, vanilla, honey, ginger, and cinnamon in a small mixing dish. In a large mixing dish, combine buckwheat, quinoa, and oats. Stir in the honey mixture until all ingredients are incorporated. Spread

evenly in a pan and bake at 325°F for 40–45 minutes, or until golden. Pour in the cranberries. Stir thoroughly and cool entirely on a cooling rack. Keep the granola airtight.

Nutritional Facts:

Calories: 313 | Fat: 10g|Protein 14g| Carbohydrates 41g | Sodium 468 mg |

164. Cherry Quinoa Porridge

Preparation time: 2 minutes

Cooking Time: 5 minutes

Servings: 2

Ingredients

- Water 1 cup
- Dry quinoa 1 cup
- Dried unsweetened cherries 1 cup
- Vanilla extract 1/2 teaspoon
- Ground cinnamon ¼ teaspoon
- Honey ¼ teaspoon

Instructions

In a medium saucepan, combine all ingredients (except honey). Bring to a boil over medium heat. Reduce the heat, cover and simmer. Tend to the quinoa for 15 minutes or until it is soft. Drizzle with honey before serving.

Nutritional Facts:

Calories 149| Fat 5g| Proteins 5g| Carbohydrates 22g | Sodium 350 mg |

165. Gingerbread Oatmeal

Preparation time: 10 minutes

Servings: 1

Ingredients

- (1 cup)Water
- (½ cup)Old-fashioned oats
- (¼ cup) Dried, unsweetened cranberries or cherries
- (1 teaspoon) Ground ginger
- (½ teaspoon) Ground cinnamon
- (¼ teaspoon) Ground nutmeg
- (1 tablespoon) Flaxseeds
- (1 tablespoon) Molasses

Instructions

Combine the water, oats, ginger, cinnamon, and nutmeg in a small saucepan. Bring to a boil, then lower the heat. Simmer for 5 minutes or until water is practically absorbed. Cover the flaxseeds. Let it sit for 5 minutes. Before serving, drizzle with molasses.

Nutritional Facts:

Calories 316 | Fat 10g| Protein 9g| Carbohydrates 45g | Sodium 400 mg |

166. Spanish Frittata

Preparation time: 10 minutes

Servings: 4 to 6

Ingredients

- (1 dozen) Large organic eggs

- (½ cup) Coconut milk

- (½ tsp, or more to taste) Sea salt

- (2 tablespoons) Extra-virgin olive oil or coconut oil

- (1 pc) Small, finely chopped red onion

- (½ cup) Sautéed mushrooms or vegetable of your choice

- (1 cup) Spinach or arugula

Instructions

Preheat the oven to 375oF. Set aside the coconut milk and eggs with two pinches of salt. Heat coconut oil in a pan over medium heat. 3 minutes until the onions are transparent. Sauté the mushrooms or veggies until softened. Fold in the spinach until it wilts. Set aside the vegetables from the pan. Reduce the heat to low and add extra coconut oil as needed. Shake the eggs in the same skillet to spread the mixture evenly. Cook for a few minutes longer over medium heat. Collect the eggs around the borders with a spatula and combine them in the middle. Do this until the edges are dry. Distribute the vegetable mix equally. Return the casserole to the oven for 5 minutes or until firm and browned. Turn off the heat and remove the dish from the oven using oven mitts first. Finish by transferring the cooked frittata to a large serving platter. Place a plate on top. Invert the pan and plate so the frittata falls on the platter. Please return it to the pan with the slightly cooked side up. Return the casserole to the oven for 3-4 minutes. Serve with a simple citrus vinaigrette salad.

Nutritional Facts:

Calories: 204 |Fat 9g|Protein 2g| Carbohydrates 28g | Sodium 9 mg |

167. Orange Apple Breakfast Shake

Preparation time: 10 minutes

Cooking time: 15 minutes

Servings: 4 to 6

Ingredients

- (2 tablespoons.) Almonds

- (1/2 cup) Apple slices

- (1/2 cup) Orange sections

- (1 cup) 2% milk

- (14g) Zone Protein Powder

Instructions

Blend all ingredients. Mix until smooth and well-incorporated. Pour the mixture into a large glass. Enjoy!

Nutritional Facts:

Calories 222|Fat 7g |Protein 4g| Carbohydrates 7g | Sodium 141 mg |

168. Oatmeal Spiced with Apple Pie

Preparation time: 45 minutes

Servings: 4

Ingredients

- (3 cups) Water

- (3/4 cup) Steel Cut Oats

- (2 tsp) Pumpkin Spice - Pumpkin Pie Spice

- (70 grams) Zone Protein Powder

- (1 cup) Applesauce

- (1 tsp, to taste) Stevia Extract

- (16 pcs – halves) 16 Pecans or walnuts

Instructions

Stir in the pumpkin pie spice and steel-cut oats after boiling. After 5 minutes, turn off the heat. Simmer for 30 min. Stir in the protein powder when the dish cools. (Prepare the night before, chill, and microwave the next morning.) Add the remainder of the ingredients just before eating. Take the dish out of the refrigerator and divide it into 4 bowls. Distribute the remaining ingredients among the 4 bowls and microwave for 2 12 minutes on high. Stir halfway.

Nutritional Facts:

Calories 242|Fat 9g |Protein 4g| Carbohydrates 37g | Sodium 141 mg |

169. Eggs and Fruit Salad

Preparation time: 20 minutes

Servings: 1

Ingredients

- (1/2 cup) Strawberries, sliced

- (1/2 cup) Mandarin orange sections,

unsweetened or fresh

- (1/2 cup) Blueberries
- (6 hardboiled eggs, discard yolks) Egg whites
- (1/2 cup) Avocado
- (3 tablespoons) Salsa

Instructions

Make the fruit salad in a bowl. Strawberries, blueberries, and mandarin slices are gently mixed. Allow eggs to cool after boiling for 10 minutes. Remove the yolks from the eggs. Separately dice the hardboiled egg whites and avocado. Add the salsa. Serve with fruit salad sidings.

Nutritional Facts

Calories: 224| Carbohydrates 42g| Protein 7g| Fat 3g | Sodium 130 mg |

170. Ham & Onion Frittata

Preparation time: 30 minutes

Servings: 4

Ingredients

- (olive oil) Cooking spray
- (1 pc) Onion, chopped
- (4 oz.) Canadian bacon, cut into bite-sized pieces
- (2 cups) Egg whites
- (1 tablespoon .) Olive oil
- (1/4 cup) 1% milk
- (1 tablespoon or 3 tablespoons of fresh) Dried dill
- Salt and pepper
- (3/4 cup) Mozzarella cheese, shredded
- (1/4 cup) Parmesan cheese, grated
- (1 cup, divided) Blueberries
- (3 tablespoons) Freshly squeezed lemon juice
- Vanilla 1 1/2 tsps.
- (1 ½ tablespoon .) Agave nectar
- (1 pc) Peach, sliced
- (1pc) Pear, sliced
- (1 ½ cups) Strawberries, sliced

Instructions

Oil a big ovenproof skillet. Sauté ham and onion till browned. Discard them. 2. Preheat the broiler oven. Combine them with the salt and pepper in a medium

bowl to make the egg whites. Mix in the cheeses. Fill the pan with the chilled ham and onion. Add the egg mixture. Cook until the bottom settles on medium heat. Cook under the broiler until the eggs are set, and the top is golden brown. Remove the skillet from the oven and cool completely. Combine 14 cups of blueberries, vanilla, agave nectar, and lemon juice in a small dish. Set aside the mix. A large dish of cut fruits and blueberries. Pour the sauce over the fruits and stir well. Enjoy the frittata.

Nutritional Facts:

Calories 77| Carbohydrates 0g |Proteins 2g|Fats 5g | Sodium 28 mg |

171. Grapefruit Breakfast

Preparation time: 5 minutes

Servings: 1

Ingredients

- (1 pc) Canadian bacon Grapefruit
- (1/2 cup) 0%-fat Greek yogurt
- (1/3 cup) Blueberries
- (3 1/2 tablespoon .) Sliced almonds

Instructions

Cut the Canadian bacon into smaller pieces. Warm in the microwave. Cut the grapefruit in half, then slice each half. Could you put them in a basin? Add the bacon. Next, combine the almonds and blueberries with the yogurt. Mix the contents of the two dishes thoroughly. Enjoy!

Nutritional Facts:

Calories 207|Carbohydrates 27g | Proteins 3g| Fats 10g| Sodium 90 mg |

172. Scrambled Eggs with Turmeric

Preparation time: 5 minutes

Cook time: 10 minutes

Servings: 1

Ingredients

- (shredded) 2 kale leaves
- (grated) 2 radishes
- (pastured) 2 eggs
- 2 tablespoons of coconut oil
- 1 tablespoon of turmeric
- 1 small clove of garlic (minced)
- 1 pinch of cayenne pepper
- clover and radish sprouts

Instructions

Heat coconut oil in a pan over medium heat. Sauté garlic. Pour the eggs in. Stir to scramble the eggs. Add the kale, cayenne, and turmeric just before the scrambled eggs are done. Stir. Move to a dish. Sprouts and radishes on top Serve.

Nutritional Facts

Calories 120| Carbohydrates 13g | Proteins 2g | Fats 7g | Sodium 87 mg |

173. Chia Seed and Milk Pudding

Preparation time: 10 minutes

Cook time: 10 minutes

Servings: 4

Ingredients

- (full-fat) 4 cups coconut milk
- 1 cup mixed berries for garnishing
- 3/4 cup coconut yogurt
- 1/2 cup chia seeds
- 1/4 cup coconut chips)
- 3 tablespoons honey
- 1 teaspoon of turmeric (ground)
- 1 teaspoon of vanilla extract
- 1/2 teaspoon of ginger (ground)
- 1/2 teaspoon of cinnamon (ground)

Instructions

Combine ginger, cinnamon, turmeric, vanilla, honey, and coconut milk. Mix till the mixture becomes yellowish. Add the chia seeds to the mix. Mix thoroughly. Wait 5 minutes before stirring the mixture. Stir the mixture again after 5 minutes. Cover it. Refrigerate it for 6 hours or overnight. The chia seeds will swell up and form a pudding-like texture. 4 glasses of pudding Mix berries into each glass of pudding. Serve.

Nutritional Facts:

Calories 95| Carbohydrates 10g | Proteins 5g| Fats 5g | Sodium 122 mg |

174. Protein-Rich Turmeric Donuts

Preparation time: 10 minutes

Cook time: 5 minutes

Servings: 8 mini donuts

Ingredients

- (pitted) 7 Medjool dates
- (raw) 1 1/2 cups cashews
- (shredded) 1/4 cup coconut

- (for topping) 1/4 cup dark chocolate
- 1 tablespoon of vanilla protein powder
- 2 teaspoons of maple syrup
- 1 teaspoon of turmeric powder
- 1/4 teaspoon vanilla essence

Instructions

Add all ingredients except dark chocolate to a food processor. Blend on high until it becomes a dough. Make 8 balls of dough. Place each ball in a doughnut mold. Mask the mold. Freeze the doughnuts for 30 minutes. 1 cup water in a medium saucepan. Boil the water. Dark chocolate in a smaller pot. Place the smaller saucepan on top of the larger one. Stir in the melted chocolate. Take the frozen doughnuts out. Chocolate glaze the doughnuts. Serve.

Nutritional Facts:

Calories 161| Carbohydrates 6g| Protein 18g| Fats 7g| Sodium 23 mg |

175. Nutty Choco-Nana Pancakes

Preparation time: 15 minutes

Servings: 10 pancakes

Ingredients

Sauce:

- 4 tablespoons of cacao powder (raw)
- 1/4 cup of coconut oil

Pancakes:

- 2 bananas
- 2 eggs
- 2 tablespoons of creamy almond butter
- 2 tablespoons of cacao powder (raw)
- 1/8 teaspoon of salt
- 1 teaspoon of pure vanilla extract
- Coconut oil (greasing)

Instructions

Put the coconut oil in a pot on low heat. Mix cacao powder and oil thoroughly. Get out of the sun. Dispose of.

A warm skillet is required. Grease the pan with 1 tablespoon of coconut oil. Put all pancake ingredients in a food processor. Pulse on high until the batter is smooth. To prepare one pancake, pour 1/4 cup of batter onto the hot skillet. 5 minutes on each side for each pancake. Carefully flip the pancake for 2 minutes on the opposite side. Repeat until the batter is gone. Serve the pancakes with or without the sauce.

Nutritional facts

Calories 179 | Carbohydrates 34g | Proteins 2.4g | Fats 5g | Sodium 75 mg |

176. Cranberry and Sweet Potato Bars

Preparation time: 15 minutes

Servings: 16 bars

Ingredients

- 1 1/2 cups of sweet potato purée
- 1 cup of almond meal
- 1 cup of cranberries (fresh)
- 1/4 cup of water
- 1/3 cup of coconut flour
- 2 eggs
- 2 tablespoons of maple syrup
- 2 tablespoons of coconut oil (melted)
- 1 1/2 teaspoon of baking soda

Instructions

Preheat the oven to 350°F. Water, sweet potato puree, maple syrup, eggs, and melted coconut oil Mix thoroughly. Sift coconut flour, almond meal, and baking soda. Mix thoroughly. Mix the dry and liquid mixtures. Mix thoroughly. Grease a 9" square pan of Parchment paper too. Place batter on a lined pan. Use a damp spatula to spread the batter. Stack cranberries on top of the batter. 35 minutes or until done. After it cools, cut it into 16 bars.

Nutritional facts

Calories 255 | Carbohydrates 21g | Proteins 2.5g | Fats 19g | Sodium 99 mg |

177. Turmeric Scones

Preparation time: 10 minutes

Servings: 6 scones

Ingredients

- 1 cup almonds (chopped)
- 1 1/3 cup of almond flour
- 1/4 cup of red palm oil
- 1/4 cup of arrowroot flour
- 3 tablespoons of maple syrup
- 1 tablespoon of coconut flour
- 1 teaspoon of vanilla extract
- 1 teaspoon turmeric
- 1/2 teaspoon of black pepper

- 1 egg
- salt

Instructions

Preheat the oven to 350°F. Mix the dry ingredients in a large bowl. Fork-fluff them. Combine vanilla, maple syrup, red palm oil, and egg in a separate dish. Whisk them. Pour the wet mixture in. They should form a dough. Flatten the dough into an inch-thick spherical shape. 6 scones from the dough. Preheat the oven to 375°F. 15 minutes or until cooked

Nutritional facts

Calories 191 | Carbohydrates 5g | Proteins 17g | Fats 11g | Sodium 348 mg |

178. Blueberry Avocado Chocolate Muffins

Preparation time: 10 minutes

Servings: 9 muffins

Ingredients

- 1 cup of almond flour
- 1/2 cup of almond milk (unsweetened)
- 1/3 cup of coconut sugar
- 1/4 cup of blueberries (fresh)
- 1/4 cup of cacao powder + 1 tablespoon (raw)
- 2 eggs (room temperature)
- 1/4 of teaspoon salt
- 1 small avocado
- 2 tablespoons of coconut flour
- 2 tablespoons of dark chocolate chips
- 2 teaspoons of baking powder

Instructions

Preheat the oven to 375°F. Prepare muffin tin. Blend the eggs, sugar, avocado, salt, and cacao powder. Blend them on high until they form a smooth pudding. Pour the mixture into a bowl. Coconut flour, baking powder, almond flour, and cocoa powder. Mix thoroughly. Mix in the almond milk. Fold in the flour mixture until blended. Mix gently. Mix in the chocolate chips and blueberries. Fill the prepared muffin tray with the batter equally. Bake for 18 minutes or until done. Serve the muffins cool.

Nutritional facts

Calories 305 | Carbohydrates 24 g | Proteins 6 g | Fats 22.1 g | Sodium 185 mg |

179. Smoked Salmon in Scrambled Eggs

Preparation time: 5 minutes

Servings: 2

Ingredients

- 4 slices of smoked salmon (chopped)
- 4 eggs
- 3 stems of fresh chives (finely chopped)
- 2 tablespoons of coconut milk
- Pinch of salt
- Cooking fat
- black pepper

Instructions

Mix the coconut milk, eggs, and chives. Whisk them. Add salt and pepper. Cook the scrambled eggs in enough cooking grease in a pan over medium heat. Pour the egg mixture into the pan. Scramble the eggs. Scramble the eggs with the fish. Cook for 2 minutes more. Serve.

Nutritional facts

Calories 65| Carbohydrates 10 g| Proteins 3 g| Fats 2.0 g| Sodium 71 mg |

180. Tropical Smoothie Bowl

Preparation time: 10 minutes

Servings: 2 bowls

Ingredients

- 1 cup of pineapple (frozen)
- 1 cup of orange juice
- 1 cup of mango (frozen)
- 1 spoonful of chia
- 1/2 banana large
- 1/8 teaspoon of turmeric

Toppings:

- Coconut flakes
- Kiwis (carved)
- Strawberries (carved)
- Almonds (sliced)

Instructions

Blend all ingredients in a blender. Blend till creamy and smooth. If the mixture is too thick, add a dash of orange juice at a time. Divide the smoothie across two bowls. Add the toppings to each smoothie bowl. Serve.

Nutritional facts

Calories 95| Carbohydrates 9 g| Proteins 1 g| Fats 6.9 g| Sodium 13 mg |

181. Spinach and Potatoes with Smoked Salmon

Preparation time: 10 minutes

Servings: 4

Ingredients

- 4 eggs medium
- 2 russet potatoes (peeled and diced)
- 1/2 onion (carved)
- 8 ounces of smoked salmon (sliced)
- 2 cups of baby spinach (fresh)
- 1/2 cup of mushrooms (sliced)
- 1 garlic clove (minced)
- 2 tablespoons of olive oil
- 2 tablespoons of ghee
- 1/2 teaspoon of onion powder
- 1/2 teaspoon of garlic powder
- 1/4 teaspoon of paprika
- salt
- Black pepper

Instructions

Preheat the oven to 425°F. Parchment paper is a baking dish. Preheat the oven to 425°F. Olive oil, paprika, garlic powder, and onion powder on potatoes. Add salt and pepper. 30 minutes baking russet potatoes Halfway through baking, flip the potatoes. Add water to a hot pot. Boil the water. Boil the eggs. Stop the heat. Cook the eggs for 7 minutes in boiling water. Take the eggs out. Run cold water over the eggs. Egg peeling Melt the ghee in a saucepan over medium heat. Sauté onion and garlic for a few minutes. Add mushrooms. Add salt and pepper. Cook for 5 minutes more. Add spinach. For 2 minutes till wilted. 4 servings of russet potatoes. Top with spinach, smoked salmon, and an egg. Serve.

Nutritional facts

Calories 175| Carbohydrates 5 g| Proteins 16 g| Fats 10.5 g| Sodium 83 mg |

182. Bacon Avocado Burger

Preparation time: 5 minutes

Servings: 1

Ingredients

- 2 bacon rashers
- 1 ripe avocado
- 1 red onion
- 1 large egg

- 1 lettuce leaf
- 1 tomato
- 1 tablespoon of Paleo mayonnaise
- Sesame seeds (garnishing)
- Salt

Instructions

Fry the bacon rashers. Set stove to medium heat. Make bacon. When the bacon rashers curl, flip them with a fork. Cook until crispy. Set aside the bacon. Crack the egg on the same frying pan. Use bacon grease to fry the egg. The egg white should be firm, but the yolk liquid. Keep the cooked egg. Cut the avocado in half. Could you get rid of it? Spoon the meat from the skin. Fill the avocado hole with mayonnaise. Layer lettuce, onion, tomato, bacon, and egg on top of the avocado. Add salt. Top with the remaining avocado. Sesame seeds garnish. Serve

Nutritional facts

Calories 100| Carbohydrates 17 g| Proteins 3 g| Fat 2.6 g| Sodium 433 mg |

183. Bacon and Eggs in a Mushroom

Preparation time: 8 minutes

Servings: 4

Ingredients

- 4 pasture-raised eggs
- 4 Portobello mushroom caps
- 2 strips of thick-cut and pasture-raised bacon (cooked and chopped)
- 1 tomato (chopped)
- 1 cup of arugula
- Salt
- Pepper

Instructions

Preheat the oven to 350°F. A baking sheet Parchment paper it. Spoon out the gills from the mushrooms. Toss the gills. Place the mushrooms on the baking sheet. Fill each hat with arugula and tomato. Crack an egg on each mushroom cap. 20 minutes in the oven, center rack. Bacon, pepper, and salt, each mushroom. Serve.

Nutritional facts

Calories 155| Carbohydrates 7 g| Proteins 10 g| Fats 6 g| Sodium 174 mg |

184. Tomato Mushroom & Spinach Fry Up

Preparation time: 10 minutes

Servings: 2

Ingredients

- 6 button mushrooms
- 3 large handfuls of English spinach leaves (torn)
- A handful of cherry tomatoes
- 1/2 red onion
- 1 garlic clove
- 2 tablespoons of olive oil
- 1 teaspoon of ghee
- 1/2 teaspoon of lemon zest
- 1/2 teaspoon of sea salt
- Pinch nutmeg
- Pinch of black pepper
- Sprinkle with lemon juice

Instructions

Melt ghee and olive oil in a medium saucepan. Cooked onions with mushrooms, Tomatoes, garlic, and lemon zest: mix. Nutmeg, pepper, and salt Cook for 2 minutes more. Using the spatula, mix up the Add spinach leaves. Cook until wilted. Lemon juice drizzle. Serve.

Nutritional facts

Calories 140| Carbohydrates 6 g| Proteins 10 g| Fats 4 g| Sodium 124 mg |

185. Almond Sweet Cherry Chia Pudding

Preparation time: 10 minutes

Cooking time: 20 minutes

Servings: 4

Ingredients

- 2 cups of whole sweet cherries (pitted)
- 3/4 cup of chia seeds
- 1/2 cup of hemp seeds
- 1/4 cup of maple syrup
- 13.5 ounces of can coconut milk
- 1 teaspoon of vanilla extract
- 1 teaspoon of almond extract
- 1/8 teaspoon of salt

Topping:

- 4 cups of cherries

Instructions

Melt chocolate in a saucepan over low heat until melted. Blend them well. Add hemp and chia seeds. To combine, blend on low. Divide the mixture across 4 glasses. Refrigerate the pudding for an hour. Cherries on each pudding. Serve.

Nutritional facts

Calories 140| Carbohydrates 8 g| Proteins 13 g| Fats 6.0 g| Sodium 194 mg |

186. Shakshuka

Preparation time: 5 minutes

Cooking time: 5 minutes

Servings: 6

Ingredients

- 4 cups of tomatoes (diced)
- 6 eggs
- 1/2 onion (sliced)
- 1 red bell pepper (seeded and sliced)
- 1 clove of garlic (crushed)
- 2 tablespoons of tomato paste
- 1 tablespoon of cooking fat
- 1/2 tablespoon of fresh parsley (finely chopped)
- 1 teaspoon of paprika
- 1 teaspoon of chili powder
- Pinch of cayenne pepper
- Black pepper
- salt

Instructions

Cooking lard in a pan over medium heat. 2 minutes onion sauté. Add the garlic. Sauté until the onions are soft. Add the pepper. Cook until the peppers are done. Be sure to mix in the tomatoes and tomato paste. Add salt and pepper. Cool down. Simmer for a few minutes. Pour the eggs over the hot mixture. Distribute the eggs. Cover the pan. Simmer until the eggs are done. Parsley garnish. Serve.

Nutritional facts

Calories 145|Carbohydrates 12 g| Proteins 13 g| Fats 5.6 g | Sodium 252 mg |

187. Amaranth Porridge with Pears

Preparation time: 5 minutes

Cook time: 15 minutes

Servings: 2 bowls

Ingredients

Porridge:

- 1/2 cup of water
- 1/2 cup of amaranth (uncooked, drained, and rinsed)
- 1/4 teaspoon of salt
- 1 cup of 2% milk

Pears:

- 1 pear
- 1 teaspoon of maple syrup
- 1/2 teaspoon of cinnamon (ground)
- 1/8 teaspoon of nutmeg (ground)
- 1/4 teaspoon of ginger (ground)
- 1/8 teaspoon of clove (ground)

Topping:

- 2 tablespoons of pecan pieces
- 1 cup of 0% Greek yogurt (plain)
- 1 teaspoon of maple syrup (pure)

Instructions

Preheat the oven to 400°F. Parchment paper on a baking sheet. Put the porridge ingredients in a medium saucepan. Boil. Cool it down. Simmer for 25 minutes. Dispose of. Layout the pecans on the baking pan. Maple syrup them. Then arrange the chopped pears next to the pecans. Maple syrup, the pears. 15 minutes in the oven. Add pears to the cereal. There is no need for topping. 2 oat bowls Soup: divide it between the two bowls. Fill each bowl with porridge. Top with pecans and the remainder of the pears. Serve.

Nutritional facts

Calories: 212| Carbohydrates: 24 g| Protein: 3 g| Fat: 4 g| Sodium 196 mg |

188. Anti-Inflammatory Salad

Preparation time: 10 minutes

Cook time: 0 minutes

Servings: 6

Ingredients

Salad:

- 2 12-ounce bags of Trader Joe's Sweet Kale Salad Mix
- 16 ounces beets (cooked, peeled, and chopped)
- 1 1/2 cup blueberries (fresh)

Dressing:

- 1/3 cup extra virgin olive oil
- 1 clove of garlic (grated)

- 2 tablespoons apple cider vinegar
- 1 teaspoon turmeric
- 1 tablespoon lemon juice
- 1 teaspoon fresh ginger (grated)
- 1/4 teaspoon black pepper (freshly ground)
- 1/2 teaspoon sea salt

Instructions

Blend the dressing ingredients in a blender. Blend well with 6 salad dishes with salad components. Dress with dressing. Serve.

Nutritional facts

Calories 207| Carbohydrates: 14 g| Protein: 1 g| Fat: 2 g| Sodium 106 mg |

189. Sweet Potato Breakfast Bowl

Preparation time: 5 minutes

Cook time: 0 minutes

Servings: 1

Ingredients

- 1 banana (sliced)
- 1 sweet potato (pre-baked)
- 1/4 cup of raspberries
- 1 serving of protein powder
- 1/4 cup of blueberries

Toppings:

- Chia seeds
- Cacao nibs
- Favorite nuts
- Hemp hearts

Instructions

Sweet potato flesh is mashed in a bowl. Add protein powder. Mix. Bananas, blueberries, and raspberries, then the toppings. Serve.

Nutritional facts

Calories: 252| Carbohydrates: 27 g| Protein: 7 g| Fat: 6 g| Sodium 186 mg |

190. Overnight Oats with Almonds and Blueberries

Preparation time: 5 minutes

Cook time: 0 minutes

Servings: 1

Ingredients

Oats:

- 3/4 cup almond milk
- 3/4 cup old-fashioned oats
- 1 tablespoon maple syrup

Toppings:

- 1/3 cup yogurt
- 1/4 cup blueberries
- 3 tablespoons almonds (sliced)

Instructions

Mason jar oats (1-pint). In a bowl, combine maple syrup and almond milk. Mix in the milk mixture. Jar up. Refrigerate for 8 hours or overnight. Add the icing. Serve.

Nutritional facts

Calories: 172| Carbohydrates: 25 g| Protein: 5 g| Fat: 4 g| Sodium 96 mg |

191. Apple Turkey Hash

Preparation time: 10 minutes

Cook time: 20 minutes

Servings: 5

Ingredients

Meat

- 1 pound of ground turkey
- 1/2 teaspoon of thyme (dried)
- 1 tablespoon of coconut oil
- Salt
- 1/2 teaspoon of cinnamon

Hash:

- 2 cups of frozen butternut squash (cubed)
- 2 cups of spinach
- 1/2 cup of carrots (shredded)
- 1 onion medium
- 1 apple (peeled, cored, and chopped)
- 1 zucchini
- 1 tablespoon of coconut oil
- 1 teaspoon of cinnamon
- 1/2 teaspoon of garlic powder

- 3/4 teaspoon of powdered ginger
- 1/2 teaspoon of turmeric
- salt
- 1/2 teaspoon of thyme (dried)

Instructions

Heat coconut oil in a skillet over medium heat. Stir in cooked ground turkey. Thyme, cinnamon, and salt Dispose. In the same skillet, melt the coconut oil. Soften the onions. Be sure to include the apple and carrots. Cook until softened. Add the spinach. Wilt the spinach. Mix in the turkey and the remaining ingredients. Serve.

Nutritional facts

Calories: 199| Carbohydrates: 45 g| Protein: 3 g| Fat: 5 g| Sodium 56 mg |

192. Chia Energy Bars with Chocolate

Preparation time: 20 minutes

Cook time; 0 minutes

Servings: 14

Ingredients

- 1 1/2 cups of pitted dates (packed)
- 1 cup of walnut pieces (raw)
- 1/3 cup of cacao powder (raw)
- 1/2 cup of shredded coconut (unsweetened)
- 1/2 cup of whole chia seeds
- 1/2 cup of oats
- 1/2 cup of dark chocolate (chopped)
- 1 teaspoon of pure vanilla extract
- 1/4 teaspoon of sea salt (unrefined)

Instructions

Put dates in a food processor. Process until thick paste forms. Could you put it in a mixing basin? Add the walnuts. Mix thoroughly. Pour in the rest. Mix well until dough forms. Oftener UN tabloid. Parchment paper it. Place the dough on the pan. Spread the dough into the pan. Freeze for many hours or overnight. 14 bars Serve.

Nutritional facts

Calories: 200| Carbohydrates: 34 g| Protein: 3 g| Fat: 4 g| Sodium 176 mg |

193. Banana Chia Pudding

Preparation time: 10 minutes

Cook time: 0 minutes

Servings: 3 glasses

Ingredients

- 2 cups of almond milk (unsweetened)
- 1/2 cup of chia seeds
- 1 banana
- 2 tablespoons of maple syrup
- 1/2 teaspoon of pure vanilla extract
- 1 tablespoon of cacao powder

Mix-ins:

- 2 tablespoons of cacao nibs
- 2 tablespoons of chocolate chips
- 1 banana (sliced)

Instructions

Mix the chia seeds and bananas in a bowl. Mix them thoroughly. Add vanilla and milk. Whisk until no lumps remain. Prepare two re-sealable bags, one jar with half the chia seeds combination. 1/2 chia seed combination with cacao powder and maple syrup. Blend well. Into the second container. Cover. Refrigerate for a few hours or overnight. Divide the chia pudding across 3 glasses and top with the mix-ins. Serve.

Nutritional facts

Calories: 112| Carbohydrates: 27 g| Protein: 6 g| Fat: 5 g| Sodium 96 mg |

194. Baked Rice Porridge with Maple and Fruit

Preparation time: 10 minutes

Cook time: 15 minutes

Servings: 2 bowls

Ingredients

- 1/2 cup of brown rice
- 2 tablespoons of pure maple syrup
- 1/2 teaspoon of pure vanilla extract
- Sliced fruits
- cinnamon Pinch
- Pinch of salt

Instructions

Preheat the oven to 400°F. 1 cup water and 1 cup brown rice in a medium saucepan Boil. Mix in cinnamon and vanilla. Cover. Cool it down. Cook the rice until done. Need to stir the rice? 2 oven-safe bowls. Rice evenly between dishes. Fruit cut and maple syrup on the rice. Add salt. Bake 15 min. Serve.

Nutritional facts

Calories: 200| Carbohydrates: 20 g| Protein: 3 g| Fat: 4 g| Sodium 146 mg |

195. Baked Eggs with Herbs

Preparation time: 5 minutes

Cook time: 10 minutes

Servings: 1

Ingredients

- 2 eggs large
- 1 tablespoon of milk
- 1 teaspoon of butter (melted)
- Scattering of dried thyme, garlic powder, dried parsley, dried oregano, and dried dill

Instructions

Preheat oven to low broil. Pour the milk and butter into a baking dish. Blend well. Buttermilk the baking dish. Fill the baking dish with eggs. Add herbs and garlic. Bake for a few minutes to cook the eggs.

Nutritional facts

Calories: 152 | Carbohydrates: 24 g | Protein: 5 g | Fat: 8 g | Sodium 126 mg |

196. Cinnamon Granola with Fruits

Preparation time: 30 minutes

Cooking time: 25 minutes

Servings: 3 cups

Ingredients

- 2 cups of old-fashioned rolled oats
- 1/4 cup of walnuts (chopped)
- 1/4 cup of shredded coconut (unsweetened)
- 1/4 cup of honey
- 1/4 cup of dried apricots (chopped)
- 1/4 cup of raisins
- 1/4 cup of dried cranberries
- 4 tablespoons of unsalted butter (melted)
- 2 tablespoons of pumpkin seeds

- 1/2 teaspoon of ground cinnamon
- 1/4 teaspoon of ground nutmeg
- 1/4 teaspoon of ground cloves

Instructions

Preheat the oven to 300°F. Parchment paper on a baking tray. A mixing dish with the coconuts and oats. Dispose of. Butter and honey in another dish. Blend well. Pour into the oat mixture. Blend well. Place the oat mixture on a lined baking sheet. Assembled Bake 25 min. Cool it down. Granola crumbles Combine crumbled granola and dried fruit. Keep airtight.

Nutritional facts

Calories: 152 | Carbohydrates: 24 g | Protein: 5 g | Fat: 8 g | Sodium 126 mg |

197. Banana Bread Pecan Overnight Oats

Preparation time: 10 minutes

Cook time: 0 minutes

Servings: 2 bowls

Ingredients

- 1 1/2 cups of milk
- 1 cup of old-fashioned rolled oats
- 1/4 cup of Greek yogurt (plain)
- 2 bananas
- 2 tablespoons of honey
- 2 tablespoons of coconut flakes (unsweetened, toasted)
- 1 tablespoon of chia seeds
- 1/4 teaspoon of salt (flaked)
- 2 teaspoons of vanilla extract

Topping

- Roasted pecans
- Banana slices
- Honey
- Fig halves
- Pomegranate seeds

Instructions

Mix oats, bananas, milk, coconut flakes, yogurt, chia seeds, honey, sea salt, and vanilla essence. Mix thoroughly. 2 bowls of the oat mixture Cover. Refrigerate for 6 hours or overnight. Mix thoroughly. Then top each dish with oats. Serve.

Nutritional facts

Calories: 112 | Carbohydrates: 22 g | Protein: 3 g | Fat:

5 g| Sodium 146 mg |

198. Yogurt Parfait with Chia Seeds and Raspberries

Preparation time: 10 minutes

Cook time: 0 minutes

Servings: 2 glasses

Ingredients

- 1/2 cup raspberries (fresh)

- 16 ounces yogurt (plain, divided into 4 portions)

- 2 tablespoons chia seeds

- Pinch of cinnamon

- 1 teaspoon maple syrup

Topping:

- Blackberries (sliced)

- Strawberries (sliced)

- Nectarines (sliced)

Instructions

Put raspberries in a basin. Make a jam out of them. The chia seeds and cinnamon. Mix them all thoroughly. Divide in half. Get two. Each glass has a layer of yogurt at the bottom. The raspberry concoction follows. The last layer is yogurt leftovers. Add the icing. Serve.

Nutritional facts

Calories: 212| Carbohydrates: 26 g| Protein: 5 g| Fat: 4 g| Sodium 186 mg |

199. Winter Morning Breakfast Bowl

Preparation time: 10 minutes

Cook time: 25 minutes

Servings: 2 bowls

Ingredients

- 2 1/2 cups of coconut water

- 1 cup of quinoa

- 2 whole cloves

- 1 cinnamon stick

- 1-star anise pod

Fresh Fruits:

- Apples

- Blackberries

- Cranberries

- Pears

- Persimmons

Instructions

Heat quinoa, coconut water, and spices in a saucepan. Boil them. Cover it. Cool it down. Cook for 25 minutes. Partially fill two bowls with quinoa. Discard whole spices. Fresh fruit in each dish. Serve.

Nutritional facts

Calories: 210| Carbohydrates: 22 g| Protein: 3 g| Fat: 4 g| Sodium 196 mg |

200. Avocado Toast with Egg

Preparation time: 10 minutes

Cook time: 2 minutes

Servings: 1

Ingredients

- 1 1/2 teaspoon of ghee

- 1 slice of gluten-free bread (toasted)

- 1 egg (scrambled)

- 1/2 avocado (shared)

- Red pepper flakes

- Handful spinach leaves

Instructions

Ghee the toasted bread. Avo-slices on the bread. Add spinach leaves. Scrambled egg on top with Red pepper flakes. Serve.

Nutritional facts

Calories: 212| Carbohydrates: 24 g| Protein: 3 g| Fat: 4 g| Sodium 196 mg |

Chapter 3: Lunch and Brunch Recipes

1. Low-phosphorus Biscuits

Preparation time: 10 minutes

Cooking time: 12 minutes

Serving: 10

Ingredients

- 2 cups all-purpose flour
- 1 tablespoon baking powder
- 2 teaspoon sugar
- ½ cup unsalted butter (melted)
- 1 cup non-dairy creamer
- 1/8 teaspoon salt

Instructions

Preheat the oven to 450 degrees Fahrenheit. Mix flour, sugar, salt, and baking powder in a mixing basin. Stir in the melted butter, add the non-dairy creamer and stir until well combined. Using a tablespoon, drop the batter onto a lightly prepared cookie sheet.

8-12 minutes in a preheated oven until brown on the edges. Warm the dish before serving.

Nutritional facts

Calories: 212| Carbohydrates: 24 g| Protein: 3 g| Fat: 4 g| Sodium 196 mg

2. Sesame of Vermicelli

Preparation time: 10 minutes

Cooking time: 5 minutes

Serving: 9

Ingredients

- 3 cups cooked vermicelli
- ½ cup sliced scallions
- 3 tablespoon sesame oil
- ½ cup frozen green peas
- 1 clove garlic
- ½ cup onion (finely chopped)
- 2 tablespoons lemon juice
- 2 tablespoons vegetable oil
- 2 tablespoons honey

Instructions

Set aside a mixture of sesame oil, lemon juice, and honey. Sauté garlic and onions in vegetable oil until slightly brown. Combine vermicelli, peas, and scallions in a large mixing basin. Combine the onions and sesame oil mixture in a mixing bowl. In a large mixing bowl, combine all ingredients and toss thoroughly. Serve at room temperature.

Nutritional facts

Calories: 192| Carbohydrates: 20 g| Protein: 1 g| Fat: 2 g| Sodium 16 mg

3. Crunchy Chicken Salad

Preparation time: 10 minutes

Cooking time: 0 minutes

Serving: 6

Ingredients

- 2 cups cooked chicken
- 1 large hard-boiled egg
- 1/4 cup low-fat mayonnaise
- 2 tablespoon onion
- 1/4 cup celery
- 1 teaspoon lemon juice
- 1/3 teaspoon sugar or Splenda
- Pepper to taste

Instructions

Combine the chicken, onion, celery, and egg in a large mixing basin. Combine mayonnaise, lemon juice, sugar, and pepper in a mixing bowl. Combine all ingredients in a mixing bowl. Before serving, cover it and refrigerate for at least 2 hours or overnight. If wanted, top with leaf lettuce and serve on bread, roll, or pita.

Nutritional facts

Calories: 125| Carbohydrates: 2 g| Protein: 16 g| Fat: 18 g| Sodium 96 mg

4. Summer Grilled Veggie Sandwich

Preparation time: 15 minutes

Cooking time: 3 minutes

Serving: 4

Ingredients

- 1 eggplant
- 1 red bell pepper
- 4 oz. Swiss cheese
- 4 teaspoon dried tarragon
- 1 medium onion
- 2 tablespoons olive oil
- 2 tablespoons balsamic vinegar
- 2 submarine rolls

Instructions

Cut four equal slices of eggplant, pepper, and onion. Combine the tarragon, olive oil, and vinegar in a mixing bowl. Allow at least 15 minutes for the veggies to marinate. Preheat the grill to medium. Cook the veggies on the grill for 2-3 minutes or until they are cooked. On rolls, layer one slice of eggplant, one slice of onion, and one slice of pepper. Put a slice of cheese on each roll (on top). If desired, add a little more vinegar.

Nutritional facts

Calories: 441| Carbohydrates: 51 g| Protein: 16 g| Fat: 18 g| Sodium 546 mg

5. Barley-Rice Pilaf

Preparation time: 10 minutes

Cooking time: 6 minutes

Serving: 4

Ingredients

- 1 small yellow onion
- 1/3 cup barley
- 1/3 cup white rice
- 1 tablespoon margarine
- 1/2 teaspoon dried thyme
- 2 cups low-sodium chicken broth
- 1 carrot (peeled and chopped fine)
- 1 stalk celery (chopped fine)
- 1/8 teaspoon pepper

Instructions

Melt margarine in a pan, then adds onion over medium

heat. Cook for approximately 5 minutes or until the onion is tender. Cook, constantly stirring, for 1 minute after adding the barley and rice. Bring the remaining ingredients to a boil. Then reduce the heat to low, cover for 15 minutes, or until the liquid has been absorbed.

Nutritional facts

Calories: 171| Carbohydrates: 30 g| Protein: 4 g| Fat: 4 g| Sodium 98 mg

6. Egg Fried Rice

Preparation time: 10 minutes

Cooking time: 5 minutes

Serving: 6

Ingredients

- 3 tablespoons oil
- 2 cloves garlic (minced)
- 1/4 cup chopped green onion
- 1/2 cup cooked chopped pork
- 4 cups cooked rice
- 1 teaspoon low-sodium soy sauce
- 1/2 cup frozen green peas
- 1/4 teaspoon dry mustard
- 6 eggs or 1 1/2 cups low-cholesterol egg substitute (scrambled and chopped)

Instructions

In a pan, heat the oil over medium heat. Cook until the garlic is tender. Cook for 2 minutes after adding the onion. Toss in the meat, rice, and soy sauce. Cook for 3 minutes, stirring occasionally. Cook until all of the ingredients are fully heated.

Nutritional facts

Calories: 270| Carbohydrates: 38 g| Protein: 12 g| Fat: 8 g| Sodium 238 mg

7. Herbed Rice Dressing

Preparation time: 10 minutes

Cooking time: 60 minutes

Serving: 12

Ingredients

- 5 cups cooked rice
- 3/4 cup margarine
- 1/2 cup chopped onion
- 1 cup diced celery
- 1/2 teaspoon sage
- 1/2 teaspoon celery seed
- 1/2 teaspoon thyme
- 1/2 teaspoon poultry seasoning
- 1/4 cup chopped fresh parsley

- 1/4 teaspoon pepper

Instructions

Melt margarine in a pot, then adds onion over medium heat. Cook for 6 minutes or until the onion and celery are soft. Toss in the remaining ingredients to combine. Stuff a 10 to 12-pound turkey or bake for 1 hour in a covered casserole dish at 325°F.

Nutritional facts

Calories: 202| Carbohydrates: 22 g| Protein: 2 g| Fat: 12 g| Sodium 13 mg

8. Moroccan Couscous

Preparation time: 10 minutes

Cooking time: 3 minutes

Serving: 4

Ingredients

- 2 tablespoons chopped onion
- 1 cup water
- 1/2 tablespoon margarine or olive oil
- 2/3 cup dry couscous

Instructions

In a pan with margarine or olive oil, sauté the chopped onion until soft. Bring water to a boil in a medium saucepan. Combine the couscous and onion in a mixing bowl. Allow for a 5-minute rest period. Before serving, softly fluff with a fork.

Nutritional facts

Calories: 115| Carbohydrates: 21 g| Protein: 3.5 g| Fat: 2 g| Sodium 5.6 mg

9. Orzo Pasta

Preparation time: 10 minutes

Cooking time: 15 minutes

Serving: 6

Ingredients

- 1 1/3 cups (8 oz.) dry orzo pasta
- 3 quarts water
- 2 teaspoons olive oil
- 1/2 teaspoon Italian seasoning (blend of marjoram, thyme, rosemary, savory, sage, oregano, and basil)
- 1 tablespoon grated
- 1/2 teaspoon garlic powder
- Parmesan cheese as required

Instructions

Bring the amount, as mentioned earlier, of water to a boil. Stir orzo pasta into the water. Return to a boil and simmer for 9 to 11 minutes, uncovered. Avoid overcooking for the best results. Drain it well in a colander. Drain the pasta, then place it in a serving dish. Combine the olive oil, garlic powder, Italian seasoning, and Parmesan cheese in a mixing bowl. As with any other pasta, toss lightly and serve as a side dish complement.

Nutritional facts

Calories: 137| Carbohydrates: 27 g| Protein: 6.5 g| Fat: 3 g| Sodium 193 mg

10. Pasta with Pesto

Preparation time: 10 minutes

Cooking time: 10 minutes

Serving: 8

Ingredients

- 1/4 cup olive oil
- 1/4 cup chopped fresh parsley
- 1/4 cup grated Parmesan cheese
- 2 tablespoons dried basil
- 1 clove of garlic (minced)
- 1 lb. pasta (uncooked)

Instructions

In a blender, put all ingredients except pasta. Blend or process until the mixture is completely smooth. Cook pasta according to package guidelines in unsalted boiling water. Toss the pasta with the sauce once it has been drained. Serve immediately.

Nutritional facts

Calories: 283| Carbohydrates: 45 g| Protein: 8 g| Fat: 8 g| Sodium 47 mg

11. Chicken and Mushroom Stew

Preparation time: 10 minutes

Cooking time: 35 minutes

Serving: 4

Ingredients

- 2 chicken breast halves
- 1 pound mushrooms (sliced) (5-6 cups)
- 1 bunch spring onion (chopped)
- 4 tablespoons olive oil
- 1 teaspoon thyme
- Salt and pepper as needed

Instructions

In a large pan, heat the oil over medium to high flame. The chicken should then be added and cooked for 4-5 minutes on each side until lightly browned. Add the spring onions and mushrooms at this time, and season with salt and pepper to taste. After that, stir well, cover, and bring to a boil. Reduce the heat to low, and cook for 25 minutes. Serve.

Nutritional facts

Calories: 850.36| Carbohydrates: 10.79 g| Protein: 72.49 g| Fat: 58.04 g

12. Roasted Carrot Soup

Preparation time: 10 minutes

Cooking time: 45 minutes

Serving: 4

Ingredients

- 8 large carrots (washed and peeled)
- 6 tablespoons olive oil
- 1-quart broth
- Cayenne pepper to taste
- Salt and pepper to taste

Instructions

Preheat the oven to 425 degrees Fahrenheit. The carrots should then be placed on a baking pan and drizzled with olive oil. Cook the carrots for 30-45 minutes in the oven.

Place the carrots in a blender with the broth once cooked. Blend until smooth, then reduce to a puree. Season the puree with salt, pepper, and cayenne in a saucepan. Serve with a drizzle of olive oil.

Nutritional facts

Calories: 510.8| Carbohydrates: 29.55 g| Protein: 3.81 g| Fat: 43.92 g| Sodium 486.4 mg

13. Healthy Garlic and Butter flavored cod

Preparation time: 10 minutes

Cooking time: 20 minutes

Serving: 3

Ingredients

- 3 Cod fillets (8 ounces each)
- 3/4 pound baby choy halved
- 1/3 cup almond butter (thinly sliced)
- 1 1/2 tablespoons garlic (minced)
- Salt and pepper to taste

Instructions

Preheat the oven to 400 degrees Fahrenheit. Cut three sheets of aluminum foil (big enough to accommodate the fillet). Place a fish fillet on each sheet, then cover it with butter and garlic. Season it with pepper and salt after adding the book choy. Fold the aluminum foil in half and set them on a baking pan to make pouches. Bake for 20 minutes; set the bags containing the cod on a cooling rack to cool. Serve.

Nutritional facts

Calories: 554.78| Carbohydrates: 14.72 g| Protein: 72.46 g| Fat: 25.53 g| Sodium 281 mg

14. Healthy Tilapia Broccoli Platter

Preparation time: 5 minutes

Cooking time: 25 minutes

Serving: 4

Ingredients

- 6 ounces of tilapia (frozen)
- 1 tablespoon of almond butter
- 1 cup of broccoli florets (fresh)
- 1 teaspoon of lemon pepper seasoning
- 1 tablespoon of garlic (minced)

Instructions

Preheat the oven to 350 degrees Fahrenheit. After that, place the fish in foil packets and surround them with broccoli. After that, season with lemon pepper and tightly seal the containers. Allow for 15 minutes of cooking time. Meanwhile, combine the garlic and butter in a bowl, stir well, and set away. Transfer the packets to a serving plate after removing them from the oven. Serve the fish and broccoli with the butter on top, and enjoy!

Nutritional facts

Calories: 146.99| Carbohydrates: 2 g| Protein: 19.72 g| Fat: 5.92 g| Sodium 315.2 mg

15. Parsley Scallops

Preparation time: 5 minutes

Cooking time: 15 minutes

Serving: 2

Ingredients

- 16 large sea scallops
- Salt and pepper to taste
- 8 tablespoons almond butter
- 1 1/2 tablespoons olive oil
- 2 garlic cloves (minced)

Instructions

Add the oil to a pot and heat it over medium heat. Season the scallops with salt and pepper in the meanwhile. When the oil is heated, sear the scallops for 2 minutes on each side, then continue with the remaining scallops. When the scallops are done, take them from the pan and add the butter to melt. Cook for 15 minutes after adding the garlic. Return the scallops to the pan and coat them with the sauce. Serve and have fun!

Nutritional facts

Calories: 409| Carbohydrates: 13.36 g| Protein: 34 g| Fat: 24.91 g| Sodium 290 mg

16. Blackened Chicken

Preparation time: 10 minutes

Cooking time: 10 minutes

Serving: 4

Ingredients

- 1/2 teaspoon paprika
- ¼ teaspoon pepper
- 1/4 teaspoon ground cumin
- 1/8 teaspoon ground white pepper
- 1/8 teaspoon onion powder
- 1/4 teaspoon dried thyme
- 2 chicken breasts (boneless and skinless)
- 2 teaspoon olive oil
- 1/8 teaspoon salt

Instructions

Butter a baking sheet and preheat the oven to 350 degrees Fahrenheit. Heat 12 teaspoons of oil in a pan over high heat for 5 minutes. Meanwhile, combine salt, paprika, cumin, white pepper, cayenne, thyme, and onion powder in a small bowl. Then, oil both sides of the chicken breast and coat it with the spice mixture. Cook the chicken for 1 minute on each side in the heated pan. Bake for 5 minutes after transferring to the prepared baking sheet. Serve and have fun.

Nutritional facts

Calories: 136| Carbohydrates: 1 g| Protein: 44 g| Fat: 5 g| Sodium 134 mg

17. Spicy Paprika Lamb Chops

Preparation time: 10 minutes

Cooking time: 10 minutes

Serving: 4

Ingredients

- 0.5 lb. lamb racks (cut into chops)
- 3/4 cup cumin powder
- 3 tablespoons paprika
- 1 teaspoon chili powder
- Salt and pepper to taste

Instructions

Combine the paprika, cumin, chili, salt, and pepper in a bowl. Allow the spice mixture to cling to the lamb chops before serving. Heat the grill at medium, place the lamb chops on it, and cook for 5 minutes. Change the side and cook for another 5 minutes. Serve and have fun.

Nutritional facts

Calories: 529.25| Carbohydrates: 22.7 g| Protein: 108.72 g| Fat: 37.34 g| Sodium 236 mg

18. Healthy Mushroom and Olive Sirloin Steak

Preparation time: 10 minutes

Cooking time: 14 minutes

Serving: 4

Ingredients

- 1 cup mushrooms
- 1 pound boneless beef sirloin steak
- 1 large red onion (chopped)
- 4 garlic cloves (thinly sliced)
- 1 cup parsley leaves (finely cut)
- 4 tablespoons olive oil

Instructions

Heat only 2 tablespoons of oil in a large pot over medium-high heat. Cook until the meat is browned on all sides; remove the steak from the pan and discard the fat. Add the remaining oil to the skillet and heat it at this stage. Cook, often stirring, for 2-3 minutes after adding the onions and garlic. Reduce the heat to low, and add the steak back to the skillet. With the cover on, cook for 3-4 minutes. Serve with parsley as a garnish. Serve and have fun.

Nutritional facts

Calories: 754.46 Carbohydrates: 8.09 g| Protein: 49.58 g| Fat: 57.82 g| Sodium 90 mg

19. Healthy Parsley and Chicken Breast

Preparation time: 10 minutes

Cooking time: 30 minutes

Serving: 4

Ingredients

- 1 tablespoon dry parsley
- 1 tablespoon dry basil
- 4 chicken breast halves (boneless and skinless)
- 1 garlic clove (sliced)
- 1/2 teaspoon red pepper flakes (crushed)
- 1/2 teaspoon salt

Instructions

Heat the oven to about 350 degrees Fahrenheit and grease a 9x13-inch baking dish with cooking spray. Arrange the chicken breast halves on the baking sheet with one teaspoon parsley and one teaspoon basil, then distribute the garlic slices on top. Combine one teaspoon of parsley, basil, salt, and red pepper in a small mixing dish. Pour the mixture over the chicken breasts. Heat oven to about 350°F and bake for 30 minutes. Serve and have fun.

Nutritional facts

Calories: 560.55| Carbohydrates: 0.4 g| Protein: 80.38 g| Fat: 8 g| Sodium 66 mg

20. Simple Mustard Chicken

Preparation time: 10 minutes

Cooking time: 35 minutes

Serving: 4

Ingredients

- 3 chicken breasts
- 1/2 cup chicken broth
- 2 tablespoons olive oil
- 3-4 tablespoons mustard
- 1 teaspoon paprika
- 1 teaspoon garlic powder
- 1 teaspoon chili powder

Instructions

To make an emulsion, whisk together the mustard, olive oil, paprika, chicken broth, garlic powder, and chili powder in a small bowl. Pour the emulsion over the chicken breasts and set aside for 30 minutes to marinate. Arrange the chicken on a large baking sheet lined with parchment paper. Preheat the oven to about 375°F and bake for 35 minutes. Serve and have fun.

Nutritional facts

Calories: 750| Carbohydrates: 2 g| Protein: 130 g| Fat: 80 g| Sodium 224 mg

21. Healthy Golden Eggplant Fries

Preparation time: 10 minutes

Cooking time: 15 minutes

Serving: 8

Ingredients

- 2 eggs
- Sunflower seeds and pepper as required
- 2 cups almond flour
- 2 tablespoons coconut oil (for spray)
- 2 eggplants (peeled and cut thinly)

Instructions

Preheat the oven to 400 degrees Fahrenheit. Combine the almond flour, sunflower seeds, and black pepper in a mixing dish. In a separate dish, whisk the eggs until foamy. Put the eggplant slices in the flour mixture after dipping them in the eggs. After that, dip the eggplant in the egg, then in the flour. Arrange the eggplants on a baking sheet that has been greased with coconut oil on top. Preheat the oven to about 350°F and bake for 15 minutes. Serve.

Nutritional facts

Calories: 855.72| Carbohydrates: 42.55 g| Protein: 30.63 g| Fat: 69.01 g| Sodium 86 mg

22. Very Wild Mushroom Pilaf

Preparation time: 10 minutes

Cooking time: 3 hours

Serving: 4

Ingredients

- 1 cup wild rice
- 2 garlic cloves (minced)
- 6 green onions (chopped)
- 1/2 pound baby Bella mushrooms
- 2 cups water
- 2 tablespoons olive oil

Instructions

Combine the rice, garlic, onion, oil, mushrooms, and water in your Slow Cooker. Stir until everything is completely combined. Cook on LOW for 3 hours with the lid on. Toss the pilaf with a fork and distribute it across serving dishes. Enjoy.

Using other Pots:

In a saucepan, heat the oil and add the garlic and onion. Add the mushrooms and simmer for a few minutes after the onion has been beautifully browned. Add the rice at this stage and let it blanch. Meanwhile, preheat the water in a separate small saucepan. Once the rice has begun to brown, slowly pour in the boiling water, constantly stirring, until the rice is thoroughly cooked. It will take about 30 minutes to complete this task. Serve.

Nutritional facts

Calories: 210| Carbohydrates: 16 g| Protein: 4 g| Fat: 6 g| Sodium 312 mg

23. Sporty Baby Carrots

Preparation time: 5 minutes

Cooking time: 5 minutes

Serving: 4

Ingredients

- 1-pound baby carrots
- 1 cup water
- 1 tablespoon chopped up fresh mint leaves
- 1 tablespoon clarified ghee
- Sea flavored vinegar as needed

Instructions

Place the carrots on a steamer rack on top of your cooker. Fill the container halfway with water. Cook for at least 2 minutes at HIGH pressure with the lid closed. Carry out a rapid release. Drain the carrots by straining them through a filter. Clean the insert with a damp cloth. Set the pot to Sauté mode and place the insert in the saucepan. Allow the clarified butter to melt before adding it. Sauté for 30 seconds after adding the mint. Add the carrots to the insert and cook until they are soft. Please remove them and top them with a dash of seasoned vinegar. Enjoy.

Nutritional facts

Calories: 131| Carbohydrates: 11 g| Protein: 1 g| Fat: 10 g| Sodium 286 mg

24. Saucy Garlic Greens

Preparation time: 5 minutes

Cooking time: 20 minutes

Serving: 4

Ingredients

- 1/2 cup cashews
- 1/4 cup water
- 1 tablespoon lemon juice
- 1 clove peeled the whole clove
- 1 teaspoon coconut amino
- 1/8 teaspoon of flavored vinegar
- 1 bunch of leafy greens lite Sauce

Instructions

Drain the soaking water of the cashews before blending them to create the sauce. Freshwater, lemon juice, flavored vinegar, coconut amino, and garlic are added to the mixture. Blend until a creamy cream forms, then transfer to a bowl. Place a steamer basket on top of 1/2 cup of water in the pot. Fill the basket with the greens. Steam for 1 minute with the lid closed. Release the pressure as soon as possible. Drain the excess water from the steamed greens in a sieve. In a mixing basin, combine the greens. Toss in the lemon, garlic, and sauce. Serve.

Nutritional facts

Calories: 196.63| Carbohydrates: 11.2 g| Protein: 5.25 g| Fat: 15.88 g| Sodium 176 mg

25. Pasta with Creamy Broccoli Sauce

Preparation time: 15 minutes

Cooking time: 40 minutes

Serving: 2

Ingredients

- 1 tablespoon olive oil
- 0.25 lb. broccoli florets
- 1 1/2 garlic cloves (halved)
- 1/2 cup low-sodium vegetable broth
- 1/4 cup whole-wheat spaghetti pasta
- 1/2 teaspoon dried basil leaves
- 2 tablespoon cream cheese

Instructions

To cook your pasta, fill a pot halfway with water and bring it to a boil. Meanwhile, heat the olive oil and sauté the broccoli and garlic for 3 minutes in a large pan. Then, in the same pot, add the broth and bring it to a simmer. Reduce the heat to low, and cook for 5–6 minutes until the broccoli is soft. Cook the pasta for 12-14 minutes or according to the package recommendations. Drain the pasta reserving 1 cup of the cooking water. When the broccoli is soft, combine it with the cream cheese and basil in an immersion blender and puree until smooth. Half of the mixture should be placed in a food processor and puréed until smooth; return the sauce to the skillet. Combine the cooked pasta with the broccoli sauce in a large mixing bowl. Toss with enough pasta water to completely cover the pasta with sauce. Serve.

Nutritional facts

Calories: 410| Carbohydrates: 35 g| Protein: 11 g| Fat: 26 g| Sodium 286 mg

26. Delicious Vegetarian Lasagna

Preparation time: 10 minutes

Cooking time: 1 hour 15 minutes

Serving: 4

Ingredients

- 1 teaspoon basil
- 1 cup sliced eggplant
- 1 tablespoon olive oil
- 1/2 sliced red pepper
- 2 lasagna sheets
- 1/4 teaspoon black pepper
- 1 cup rice milk
- 1/2 diced red onion
- 1 minced garlic clove
- 1/2 sliced zucchini
- 1/2 pack soft tofu
- 1 teaspoon oregano

Instructions

If using a gas oven, preheat the oven to 325 degrees Fahrenheit or 325 degrees Fahrenheit. Vertically slice the zucchini, eggplant, and pepper. Blitz the rice milk and tofu together in a food processor until smooth. Remove from the equation. Heat the oil, add the garlic and onions, and cook for 3-4 minutes, until tender. Stir in the herbs (oregano) and pepper for 5-6 minutes or until the mixture is heated. Layer 1 lasagna sheet, 1/3 eggplant, 1/3 zucchini, 1/3 pepper, and 1/3 white tofu sauce into a lasagna or similar oven dish. Continue with the following two layers, ending with the white sauce. Bake for 40-50 minutes until the vegetables are tender and easily cut into portions.

Nutritional facts

Calories: 235| Carbohydrates: 10 g| Protein: 5 g| Fat: 9 g| Sodium 86 mg

27. Pesto Pasta with Cream

Preparation time: 10 minutes

Cooking time: 20 minutes

Serving: 4

Ingredients

- 4 ounces linguine noodles
- 2 cups packed arugula leaves
- 2 cups packed basil leaves
- 1/ 3 cup walnut pieces
- 3 tablespoon extra-virgin olive oil
- 3 garlic cloves
- Freshly ground black pepper

Instructions

Bring a medium stockpot halfway full of water to a boil. Cook the noodles until they are well boiled, approximately 10-12 minutes, then drain. Combine the basil, arugula, walnuts, and garlic in a food processor. Process until the mixture is coarsely ground. Slowly drizzle olive oil while the food processor runs, and blend until smooth. Season with salt and pepper. Combine the noodles and pesto in a bowl and serve.

Nutritional facts

Calories: 394| Carbohydrates: 0 g| Protein: 10 g| Fat: 21 g| Sodium 236 mg

28. Garden Salad

Preparation time: 10 minutes

Cooking time: 20 minutes

Serving: 4

Ingredients

- 5 oz. raw peanuts in the shell
- 1 bay leaf
- 1 medium-sized chopped up Red bell peppers
- 5 tablespoons + 1 teaspoon diced up green pepper
- 0.5 teaspoon flavored vinegar
- 5 tablespoons +1 teaspoon diced a sweet onion
- 2 tablespoons +2 teaspoons finely diced hot pepper
- 2 tablespoons + 2 teaspoons diced up celery
- 1 tablespoon + 1 teaspoon olive oil
- ¼ teaspoon freshly ground black pepper

Instructions

Bring a medium stockpot halfway full of water to a boil. Cook the noodles until they are well boiled, approximately 10-12 minutes, then drain. Combine the basil, arugula, walnuts, and garlic in a food processor. Process until the mixture is coarsely ground. Slowly drizzle olive oil while the food processor runs, and blend until smooth. Season with salt and pepper. Combine the noodles and pesto in a bowl and serve.

Nutritional facts

Calories: 240| Carbohydrates: 24 g| Protein: 5 g| Fat: 4 g| Sodium 136 mg

29. Zucchini Pasta

Preparation time: 15 minutes

Cooking time: 30 minutes

Serving: 4

Ingredients

- 3 Tablespoons of olive oil
- 2 cloves garlic (minced)
- 3 Zucchini (large and diced)
- 1/2 Cup of 2% milk
- 1/4 Teaspoon of nutmeg
- 1 Tablespoon of lemon juice (fresh)
- 1/2 Cup of cheddar (grated)
- 8 Ounces uncooked farfalle pasta
- Sea salt and black pepper to taste

Instructions

Get a skillet out and heat it over medium heat before adding the oil. Cook for a minute after adding your garlic. Stir often to avoid burning. Season with salt and pepper, then toss in the zucchini. Cook for fifteen minutes, covered, after thoroughly stirring. It would help if you whisked the mixture twice throughout this time.

Heat the milk in a microwave-safe bowl for thirty seconds. Pour it into the skillet after stirring in the nutmeg. Cook for five minutes with the lid off. To avoid scorching, stir periodically. Prepare your pasta in a stockpot according to the package directions. Save two tablespoons of pasta water after draining the noodles. Combine all ingredients in a mixing bowl, and add the cheese, lemon juice, and pasta water.

Nutritional facts

Calories: 813.76| Carbohydrates: 99.71 g| Protein: 27.15 g| Fat: 34.79 g| Sodium 136 mg

30. Spicy Cabbage Dish (Healthy)

Preparation time: 10 minutes

Cooking time: 4 hours

Serving: 4

Ingredients

- 2 yellow onions (chopped)
- 10 cups red cabbage (shredded)
- 1 cup plums (pitted and chopped)
- 1 garlic clove (minced)
- 1 teaspoon cumin seeds
- 1 teaspoon coriander seeds
- 1 teaspoon cinnamon powder
- 1/4 teaspoon cloves (ground)
- 2 tablespoons red wine vinegar
- 1/2 cup water

Instructions

Combine the cabbage, garlic, cumin, coriander, water, and other ingredients in your Slow Cooker. Stir everything together well. Cook on for 4 hours with the lid on. Serve on individual serving dishes. Serve.

Nutritional facts

Calories: 219.48| Carbohydrates: 51.05 g| Protein: 3 g| Fat: 1.38 g| Sodium 146 mg

31. Extreme Balsamic Chicken (Healthy)

Preparation time: 10 minutes

Cooking time: 25 minutes

Serving: 2

Ingredients

- 3 boneless chicken breasts (skinless)
- 2 tablespoon almond flour
- 1 teaspoon arrowroot
- 1/3 cup low-fat chicken broth
- 1/4 cup low sugar raspberry preserve
- 1 tablespoon balsamic vinegar

Instructions

Chicken breasts should be sliced into bite-sized pieces and seasoned with seeds. Using flour, dredge the chicken pieces and brush off any excess. Preheat a nonstick skillet over medium-high heat. Put the chicken in the pot and cook for 10 minutes, turning halfway through. Remove the chicken from the pan and place it on a serving plate. Stir in the arrowroot, broth, and raspberry preserves in the skillet. Reduce heat to low and whisk for a few minutes after adding the balsamic vinegar. Return the chicken to the sauce and simmer for another 10 minutes. Serve.

Nutritional facts

Calories: 546| Carbohydrates: 11 g| Protein: 44 g| Fat: 35 g| Sodium 186 mg

32. Enjoyable Green Lettuce and Bean Medley

Preparation time: 10 minutes

Cooking time: 4 hours

Serving: 2

Ingredients

- 3 carrots (sliced)
- 1 cup great northern beans (dried)
- 1 garlic clove (minced)
- 1/2 yellow onion (chopped)
- 1/4 teaspoon oregano (dried)
- 2.5 ounces baby green lettuce
- 2 1/2 cups low sodium veggie stock
- 1 teaspoon lemon peel (grated)
- 1 ½ tablespoon lemon juice
- Pepper to taste

Instructions

Combine the beans, onion, carrots, garlic, oregano, and stock in Cooker. Stir everything together well. Cook for 4 hours on HIGH with the lid on. Combine the ingredients in a mixing bowl. Allow for an 8-minute rest period after stirring. Serve by dividing the mixture between serving dishes.

Nutritional facts

Calories: 570.63| Carbohydrates: 110.17 g| Protein: 33.13 g| Fat: 2.17 g| Sodium 186 mg

33. Cauliflower and Dill Mash

Preparation time: 10 minutes

Cooking time: 5 hours

Serving: 3

Ingredients

- 1/2 cauliflower head (florets separated)
- 2 tablespoon + 2 teaspoon cup dill (chopped)
- 3 garlic cloves
- 1 tablespoon olive oil
- Pinch of black pepper

Instructions

Add cauliflower to the Slow Cooker. Cover them with dill, garlic, and enough water to cover them. Cook for 5 hours on HIGH with the lid on. Remove the flowers and drain them. Season it with salt and pepper, then add the oil and mash with a potato masher. Serve with a whisk.

Nutritional facts

Calories: 42.74| Carbohydrates: 3.55 g| Protein: 1.26 g| Fat: 3.03 g| Sodium 146 mg

34. Peas Soup

Preparation time: 10 minutes

Cooking time: 10 minutes

Serving: 2

Ingredients

- 1 egg
- 1 cup peas
- 1/2 white onion (chopped)
- 1/2 teaspoon olive oil
- 1/2 quart veggie stock
- 1 1/2 tablespoons lemon juice
- 1 tablespoons parmesan (grated)
- Salt and black pepper to the taste

Instructions

1 teaspoon oil, heated in a saucepan over medium-high heat. After that, add the onion and cook for another 4 minutes. Bring the other ingredients, except the eggs, to a simmer, and cook for another 4 minutes. Stir in the whisked eggs, simmer for another 2 minutes, then divide into dishes and serve.

Nutritional facts

Calories: 264| Carbohydrates: 33 g| Protein: 17 g| Fat: 7.2 g| Sodium 126 mg

35. Basil Zucchini Spaghetti

Preparation time: 1 hour 10 minutes

Cooking time: 10 minutes

Serving: 4

Ingredients

- 1/3 cup coconut oil (melted)
- 4 zucchinis (cut with a spiralizer)
- 1/4 cup basil (chopped)
- 0.25 cup walnuts (chopped)
- 2 garlic cloves (minced)
- A pinch of sea salt
- Black pepper to taste

Instructions

Mix zucchini spaghetti with salt and pepper in a mixing basin, tossing to coat, set aside for 1 hour, drain thoroughly, and place in a bowl. Warm the oil in a pan over medium-high heat, add the zucchini spaghetti and garlic, swirl to combine, and cook for 5 minutes. Stir in the basil, walnuts, and black pepper, and simmer for another 3 minutes. Serve as a side dish by dividing the mixture across plates. Enjoy.

Nutritional facts

Calories: 287| Carbohydrates: 8 g| Protein: 4 g| Fat: 27 g| Sodium 186 mg

36. Cauliflower Rice and Coconut

Preparation time: 20 minutes

Cooking time: 15 minutes

Serving: 4

Ingredients

- 3 cups cauliflower (riced)
- 1-2 teaspoons sriracha paste
- 2/3 cup full-fat coconut milk
- 1/4- 1/2 teaspoon onion powder
- Salt as needed
- Fresh basil for garnish

Instructions

Place a pan on the stovetop over medium-low heat. Combine the ingredients mentioned above in a mixing bowl and whisk well to combine. Allow for 5-10 minutes of cooking time with the cover on. Remove the cover and continue to cook until there is no more liquid. Serve the rice after it has turned creamy.

Nutritional facts

Calories: 225| Carbohydrates: 4 g| Protein: 5 g| Fat: 19 g| Sodium 196 mg

37. Kale and Garlic Platter

Preparation time: 5 minutes

Cooking time: 12 minutes

Serving: 2

Ingredients

- 1/2 bunch kale
- 1 tablespoon olive oil
- 2 garlic cloves (minced)

Instructions

Remove the stems from the kale and chop them into bite-sized pieces. Heat the olive oil over medium heat in a big, heavy-bottomed saucepan. Stir in the garlic for 2 minutes. Cook for 5-10 minutes with the kale. Serve.

Nutritional facts

Calories: 121| Carbohydrates: 6 g| Protein: 4 g| Fat: 8 g| Sodium 129 mg

38. Healthy, Blistered Beans and Almond

Preparation time: 10 minutes

Cooking time: 20 minutes

Serving: 2

Ingredients

- 1/2 pound of fresh green beans (ends trimmed)
- 1 tablespoon olive oil
- 1 tablespoon fresh dill (minced)
- Juice of 1/2 lemon
- 1/8 cup crushed almonds
- 1/8 teaspoon salt
- Salt as needed

Instructions

Preheat the oven to 400 degrees Fahrenheit. Combine the green beans, olive oil, and salt in a bowl. After that, lay them out on a broadsheet pan. Roast for 10 minutes, then mix well and roast for another 8-10 minutes. Please remove it from the oven and continue to whisk in the lemon juice and dill. Serve with crushed almonds and a pinch of sea salt on top.

Nutritional facts

Calories: 271| Carbohydrates: 9 g| Protein: 7.57 g| Fat: 1.86 g| Sodium 182 mg

39. Cucumber Soup (Low Caloric)

Preparation time: 10 minutes

Cooking time: 0 minutes

Serving: 2

Ingredients

- 1 tablespoon garlic (minced)
- 1/2 tablespoon lemon juice
- 2 cups English cucumbers (peeled and diced)
- 1/4 cup onions (diced)
- 1 cup vegetable broth
- 1/8 teaspoon red pepper flakes
- 1/8 cup parsley (diced)
- 1/4 teaspoon salt
- 1/4 cup Greek yogurt (plain)

Instructions

Combine all ingredients in a blender (except 1/4 cup of

sliced cucumbers). Blend until completely smooth. Serve the soup in four bowls, garnished with additional cucumbers. Serve.

Nutritional facts

Calories: 55| Carbohydrates: 8.77 g| Protein: 2.33 g| Fat: 1.26 g| Sodium 436 mg

40. Eggplant Salad

Preparation time: 10 minutes

Cooking time: 50 minutes

Serving: 3

Ingredients

- 2 eggplants (peeled and sliced)
- 2 garlic cloves
- 1/2 cup egg-free mayonnaise
- 2 green bell pepper (sliced and remove seeds)
- 1/2 cup fresh parsley
- Salt and black pepper

Instructions

Preheat the oven to 480 degrees Fahrenheit. After that, put the eggplants and bell pepper on a baking pan. Bake the veggies for approximately 30 minutes, flipping halfway through. Then, combine the cooked veggies with the other ingredients in a mixing dish. Mix thoroughly. Serve.

Nutritional facts

Calories: 196| Carbohydrates: 13.4 g| Protein: 14.6 g| Fat: 10.8 g| Sodium 156 mg

41. Cajun Crab (Low Caloric)

Preparation time: 10 minutes

Cooking time: 10 minutes

Serving: 2

Ingredients

- 1 lemon (fresh and quartered)
- 3 tablespoons Cajun seasoning
- 2 bay leaves
- 4 snow crab legs (precooked and defrosted)
- 1 teaspoon golden ghee

Instructions

Fill half a saucepan with water and salt and set it aside. Bring the water to a boil after that. Squeeze the lemon juice into the kettle and throw in the remaining lemon quarters once the water has reached a boil. Add cay leaves and Cajun seasoning now. After that, season them for one minute. Add the crab legs and cook for 8 minutes (keeping them submerged the whole time). Use ghee as a dipping sauce by melting it in the microwave. Serve.

Nutritional facts

Calories: 49.71| Carbohydrates: 0.65 g| Protein: 10.39 g| Fat: 0.39 g| Sodium 186 mg

42. Mushroom Pork Chops

Preparation time: 10 minutes

Cooking time: 40 minutes

Serving: 3

Ingredients

- 8 ounces of mushrooms (sliced)
- 1 teaspoon garlic
- 1 onion (peeled and chopped)
- 1 cup egg-free mayonnaise
- 3 pork loins
- 1 teaspoon ground nutmeg
- 1 tablespoon balsamic vinegar
- 1/2 cup of coconut oil

Instructions

Put the coconut oil in a pan and heat it over medium heat. After that, add the mushrooms and onions and mix thoroughly. Cook for 4 minutes in the oven, and then season pork loins with nutmeg and garlic powder and brown on both sides. Heat the oven to about 350 F and bake the pan for 30 minutes. Place the pork loins on dishes and cover them with aluminum foil to keep them warm. Place the same pan on a medium heat setting. Over the mushroom mixture, pour the vinegar and mayonnaise and swirl for a few minutes. Pour the sauce over the pork loins. Serve.

Nutritional facts

Calories: 400| Carbohydrates: 1.4 g| Protein: 30 g| Fat: 18.39 g| Sodium 186 mg

43. Caramelized Pork Chops

Preparation time: 5 minutes

Cooking time: 30 minutes

Serving: 2

Ingredients

- 2 pounds of pork chops
- 1 teaspoon salt
- 1 teaspoon pepper
- 2 tablespoons chili powder
- ½ teaspoon olive oil
- 2 ounces green chili (chopped)
- 1/4 teaspoon dried oregano
- 1/4 teaspoon ground cumin
- 1 garlic clove (minced)
- 1 onion (sliced)
- ½ glass of water

Instructions

Sprinkle 1/2 teaspoon pepper, 1/2 teaspoon seasoned salt, chili powder, oregano, and cumin over the pork chops. Then, heat 1/2 teaspoon of oil and the garlic over medium heat in a pan. Cook the pork chops on both sides. Toss in the onion and water in the skillet. Cover and reduce the heat to low, and cook for approximately 20 minutes. Turn the loins over and season with the remaining pepper and salt. Cover and cook until the liquid has evaporated and the onions are medium brown. Remove the chops from the pan. Serve with a sprinkling of onions on top.

Nutritional facts

Calories: 500| Carbohydrates: 4 g| Protein: 27 g| Fat: 19 g| Sodium 86 mg

44. Mediterranean Pork

Preparation time: 10 minutes

Cooking time: 35 minutes

Serving: 2

Ingredients

- 2 pork chops (bone-in)
- 1/2 teaspoon salt pepper to taste
- 1 1/2 garlic cloves (peeled and minced)
- 1/2 teaspoon dried rosemary

Instructions

Preheat the oven to 425 degrees Fahrenheit. Sprinkle on the pork chops with salt and pepper. Add rosemary and garlic to them in a roasting pan. Cook for 10 minutes in the oven and then reduce the heat to 350 F and roast for another 25 minutes. Pork chops should be sliced and served on plates. Drizzle the pan liquid all over the place. Serve.

Nutritional facts

Calories: 335| Carbohydrates: 1.52 g| Protein: 40.48 g| Fat: 17.42 g| Sodium 126 mg

45. Ground Beef and Bell Peppers

Preparation time: 10 minutes

Cooking time: 10 minutes

Serving: 2

Ingredients

- 1 cup spinach (chopped)
- 1 onion (chopped)
- 1 tablespoon coconut oil
- 0.5-pound ground beef
- 1 red bell pepper (diced)
- 1/4 teaspoon salt
- 1/4 teaspoon black pepper

Instructions

Combine the onion and coconut oil in a pan, and sauté over medium-high heat until the onion is gently browned. Add the spinach, salt, and ground meat after that. Stir fry until everything is done. Meanwhile, remove all of the seeds from the interior of the red bell pepper. After that, remove the mixture from the pan and spoon it into the bell pepper. Serve.

Nutritional facts

Calories: 357| Carbohydrates: 7.89 g| Protein: 31.68 g| Fat: 19.61 g| Sodium 136 mg

46. Spiced Up Pork Chops

Preparation time: 4 minutes

Cooking time: 14 minutes

Serving: 4

Ingredients

- 1/4 cup lime juice
- 1 Mango (sliced)
- 4 pork rib chops
- 2 teaspoons cumin
- 1 tablespoon coconut oil (melted)
- 2 garlic cloves (peeled and minced)

- 1 tablespoon chili powder
- 1 teaspoon ground cinnamon
- Salt and pepper to taste
- 1/2 teaspoon hot pepper sauce

Instructions

In a mixing bowl, stir together lime juice, oil, garlic, cumin, cinnamon, chili powder, salt, pepper, and hot pepper sauce. Then put in the pork chops. Refrigerate for 4 hours if kept on the side. Preheat your grill to medium and place the pork chops on it. Give 7 minutes for each side on the grill. Serve with mango pieces, divided amongst serving dishes.

Nutritional facts

Calories: 400| Carbohydrates: 3 g| Protein: 35 g| Fat: 8 g| Sodium 136 mg

47. Healthy, Juicy Salmon Dish

Preparation time: 5 minutes

Cooking time: 13 minutes

Serving: 1

Ingredients

- 1/4 cup of water
- Few sprigs of parsley, basil, and tarragon
- 0.5 pounds of salmon (skin on)
- 1 teaspoon of ghee
- 1 tablespoon + 1 teaspoon of salt
- 2 tablespoon + 2 teaspoons of pepper
- 1/4 of lemon (thinly sliced)
- 0.5 whole carrot (julienned)

Instructions

Add water and herbs to your pot and set it to Sauté mode. Place the salmon on a steamer rack inside your pot. Season the salmon with salt and pepper and drizzle with ghee. Place the slices of lemon on top. Cook for at least 3 minutes on HIGH pressure with the cover locked on the pot. Allow 10 minutes for the pressure to dissipate naturally. Place it on a serving plate and serve. Add carrots, parsley, basil, and tarragon to your pot in Sauté mode. Cook for 1-2 minutes before serving the salmon on a dish. Serve.

Nutritional facts

Calories: 464| Carbohydrates: 3 g| Protein: 34 g| Fat: 34 g| Sodium 266 mg

48. Platter-o- Brussels

Preparation time: 10 minutes

Cooking time: 25 minutes

Serving: 2

Ingredients

- 1 tablespoon olive oil
- 1/2 yellow onion (chopped)
- 1 pound Brussels sprouts (trimmed and halved)
- 2 cups chicken stock
- 1/2 teaspoon black pepper
- 1/8 cup coconut cream

Instructions

Put the oil in a saucepan and heat it over medium heat. Stir in the onion and simmer for 3 minutes. Stir in the Brussels sprouts and simmer for 2 minutes. After that, add the stock and black pepper, mix to combine, and bring to a low boil. Cook for another 20 minutes. Make the soup creamy using an immersion blender now. Stir in the coconut cream well. Serve soup in soup bowls.

Nutritional facts

Calories: 621.97| Carbohydrates: 78.24 g| Protein: 28.23 g| Fat: 26.29 g| Sodium 276 mg

49. Almond Chicken

Preparation time: 15 minutes

Cooking time: 15 minutes

Serving: 3

Ingredients

- 2 large chicken breasts (boneless and skinless)
- 1/3 cup lemon juice
- 1 1/2 cups seasoned almond meal
- 2 tablespoons coconut oil
- Lemon pepper (to taste)
- Parsley for decoration

Instructions

Chicken breasts should be cut in half and sliced till 1/4 inch thick on each side. Heat the oil in a pan over medium flame. Allow each chicken breast slice to soak in lemon juice for 2 minutes. Turn the chicken over and let it marinate for another 2 minutes. After that, cover both sides with an almond meal. Place the coated chicken in the oil and cook for 4 minutes on each side, being careful to generously sprinkle with lemon pepper. Repeat with the remaining chicken on a paper-lined baking sheet. Serve garnished with parsley.

Nutritional facts

Calories: 360| Carbohydrates: 3 g| Protein: 44 g| Fat: 24 g| Sodium 176 mg

50. Blackberry Chicken Wings

Preparation time: 35 minutes

Cooking time: 45 minutes

Serving: 2

Ingredients

- 0.75 pounds of chicken wings (about 20 pieces)
- 1/4 cup blackberry chipotle jam
- 1/4 cup of water
- Salt and pepper to taste

Instructions

To prepare the marinade, combine the water and jam in a mixing dish. Place two-thirds of the marinade in a zip bag with the chicken wings. Season with salt and pepper after that. Allow 30 minutes for marinating. Preheat the oven to about 400 degrees Fahrenheit in the meanwhile. Bake for 15 minutes after preparing a baking sheet and placing chicken wings on it. After that, spray the leftover marinade on top and bake for another 30 minutes. Serve.

Nutritional facts

Calories: 702| Carbohydrates: 1.8 g| Protein: 45 g| Fat: 29 g| Sodium 336 mg

51. Fennel and Figs Lamb

Preparation time: 10 minutes

Cooking time: 40 minutes

Serving: 2

Ingredients

- 6 ounces lamb racks
- 2 figs (cut in half)
- 1 fennel bulb (sliced)
- Salt and pepper to taste
- 1/8 cup apple cider vinegar
- 1/2 tablespoon swerve
- 1 tablespoon olive oil

Instructions

Toss the fennel, figs, vinegar, swerve, and oil together in a mixing dish. Sprinkle salt and pepper before transferring to a baking dish. Preheat the oven to 400 degrees Fahrenheit and bake for 15 minutes. Meanwhile, sprinkle the lamb with salt and pepper and place it in a hot skillet. Cook for about 5 minutes. Bake for 20 minutes with the lamb and fennel in the baking dish. Serve by dividing the mixture across plates.

Nutritional facts

Calories: 456.76| Carbohydrates: 28.63 g| Protein: 23.02 g| Fat: 31.02g| Sodium 88 mg

52. Herbed Butter Pork Chops

Preparation time: 10 minutes

Cooking time: 25 minutes

Serving: 2

Ingredients

- 1 tablespoon almond butter (divided)
- 2 boneless pork chops
- 1 tablespoon olive oil
- Salt and pepper to taste
- 1 tablespoon dried
- Italian seasoning to taste

Instructions

Preheat the oven to 350 degrees Fahrenheit. Take out the pork chops from the pan and dry them with a paper towel. After that, put them on a baking dish. Add salt, pepper, and Italian seasoning as per taste. Drizzle olive oil over pork chops and smear 1/2 tablespoon of butter on each chop. Preheat the oven to about 350°F and bake for 25 minutes. Place the pork chops on two plates and drizzle with the butter juice. Serve.

Nutritional facts

Calories: 333| Carbohydrates: 1 g| Protein: 31 g| Fat: 23 g| Sodium 242 mg

53. Simple Rice Mushroom Risotto

Preparation time: 5 minutes

Cooking time: 15 minutes

Serving: 2

Ingredients

- 2 1/2 cups cauliflower (riced)
- 1 shallot (diced)
- Salt and pepper according to taste
- 1/8 cup organic vegetable broth
- 1 1/2 tablespoon coconut oil
- 1/2 pound of Portobello mushrooms (thinly sliced)
- 1/2 pound white mushrooms (thinly sliced)
- 1 1/2 tablespoons chives (chopped)
- 2 tablespoons almond butter

Instructions

Blend cauliflower florets until riced in a food processor. Then, in a big saucepan over medium-high heat, melt 1/2 tablespoon of coconut oil. Add the mushrooms and cook for 3 minutes, or until they are soft. Remove the mushrooms, together with the liquid, from the pot and set them aside. Allow the remaining 1 tablespoon of coconut oil to heat in the skillet.

Cook for 60 seconds after tossing the shallot. Stir in the cauliflower rice for 2 minutes or until it is well covered in oil. Stir in the broth with the riced cauliflower for 5 minutes. Remove the skillet from the heat and stir in the liquid and mushrooms. Season with salt and pepper, and add the chives and butter. Serve.

Nutritional facts

Calories: 555| Carbohydrates: 38.14 g| Protein: 26.16 g| Fat: 39.91 g| Sodium 296 mg

54. Zucchini Bowl

Preparation time: 10 minutes

Cooking time: 25 minutes

Serving: 2

Ingredients

- 1/2 onion (chopped)
- 2 zucchini (cut into medium chunks)
- 1 tablespoon coconut milk
- 1 garlic clove (minced)
- 2 cups chicken stock
- 1 tablespoon coconut oil
- Pinch of salt
- Black pepper to taste

Instructions

Put the oil in a saucepan and heat it over medium heat. Stir in the zucchini, garlic, and onion, and cook for 5 minutes. Stir in the stock, salt, and pepper. Bring to a boil, then reduce the heat. Cook for 20 minutes on low heat. Remove the pan from the heat and stir in the coconut milk. Using an immersion blender, mix until completely smooth. Fill soup bowls with the mixture and serve.

Nutritional facts

Calories: 404.35| Carbohydrates: 33.37 g| Protein: 16.84 g| Fat: 23.86 g| Sodium 186 mg

55. Nice Coconut Haddock (Healthy, Low Caloric)

Preparation time: 10 minutes

Cooking time: 12 minutes

Serving: 3

Ingredients

- 4 haddock fillets (5 ounces each, boneless)

- 2 tablespoons coconut oil (melted)
- 1 cup coconut (shredded and unsweetened)
- 1/4 cup hazelnuts (ground)
- Salt to taste

Instructions

Preheat the oven to 400 degrees Fahrenheit. Then, using parchment paper, line a baking sheet and set it aside. In a mixing dish, combine the hazelnuts and shredded coconut.

Then, blot the fish fillets dry with a paper towel, season with salt, and dredge them in the coconut mixture until completely coated. Brush the fish fillets with coconut oil and place them on the baking sheet. Preheat the oven to 350°F and bake for 12 minutes, or until flaky. Serve.

Nutritional facts

Calories: 194| Carbohydrates: 4.85 g| Protein: 8.43 g| Fat: 16.24 g| Sodium 187 mg

56. Baked Halibut

Preparation time: 10 minutes

Cooking time: 15 minutes

Serving: 7

Ingredients

- 1 1/2 lb. halibut steaks
- 3/4 cup bread crumbs
- 1/4 cup mayonnaise
- Lemon slices dipped in paprika

Instructions

Preheat the oven to 400 degrees Fahrenheit. Cut the steaks into serving-size pieces, keeping the bone in the middle. Mayonnaise should cover the whole surface. Use the bread crumbs to coat the meat. Place in a baking pan that has been greased. Bake for 15 minutes in a preheated oven or until fish flakes easily when examined with a fork. Serve on a hot serving dish. Serve with lemon slices as a garnish.

Nutritional facts

Calories: 205| Carbohydrates: 8 g| Protein: 33 g| Fat: 9 g| Sodium 236 mg

57. Broiled Garlic Shrimp

Preparation time: 10 minutes

Cooking time: 10 minutes

Serving: 5

Ingredients

- 1 lb. shrimp in shells

- 1/2 cup unsalted margarine (melted)
- 2 teaspoons lemon juice
- 1/8 teaspoon pepper
- 2 tablespoons chopped onion
- 1 clove of garlic (minced)
- 1 tablespoon fresh parsley (chopped)

Instructions

Preheat the oven to broil. Shrimp should be washed, peeled, and dried. Melt margarine in a shallow baking pan and add lemon juice, onion, garlic, and pepper. Toss in the shrimp to coat. 5 minutes under the broiler Broil for another 5 minutes on the other side. Serve with drained pan juices on a plate. Serve with a parsley garnish.

Nutritional facts

Calories: 264| Carbohydrates: 2 g| Protein: 19 g| Fat: 20 g| Sodium 96 mg

58. Cajun Pork Chops

Preparation time: 10 minutes

Cooking time: 36 minutes

Serving: 4

Ingredients

- 1/4 teaspoon paprika
- 1/4 teaspoon thyme
- 1/4 teaspoon dry mustard
- 1/4 teaspoon ground sage
- 1/4 teaspoon ground cumin
- 1/4 teaspoon garlic powder
- 4 pork chops cut 1/2-inch thick (4 oz each)
- 1 small onion (sliced)
- 1/8 teaspoon pepper
- 1 tablespoon margarine
- 1 teaspoon parsley flakes
- 1/8 teaspoon garlic powder
- 2 to 3 drops of hot pepper sauce

Instructions

Combine 1/4 teaspoon garlic powder, paprika, thyme, mustard, sage, cumin, and pepper on waxed paper. Coat the pork chops on both sides with the mixture. Place chops on an 8"-inch square microwave-safe dish in a single layer. Place the onion slices place on top of each chop. Use the waxed paper to cover the dish. Microwave for 5 minutes on high. Microwave on low (30%) for 25 to

30 minutes or until vegetables are soft, turning once throughout this time. Allow resting while you prepare the sauce. Combine margarine, parsley, 1/8 teaspoon garlic powder, and pepper sauce in a small glass bowl. Microwave for 30 to 40 seconds on high, or until melted. Before serving, drizzle the sauce over the chops.

Nutritional facts

Calories: 243| Carbohydrates: 3 g| Protein: 22 g| Fat: 16 g| Sodium 116 mg

59. Chicken Veronique

Preparation time: 10 minutes

Cooking time: 27 minutes

Serving: 5

Ingredients

- 1 tablespoon flour
- 1 bay leaf
- 1/4 teaspoon pepper
- 1/2 cup water
- 1 lb. chicken breast meat
- 6 tablespoons unsalted margarine
- 1/4 cup white wine
- 1 teaspoon parsley
- 1/4 teaspoon pepper
- 2 tablespoons orange marmalade
- 1 cup halved white grapes

Instructions

Combine flour and 1/4 teaspoon pepper in a mixing bowl. Dust the chicken with a light coating of flour. In a large pan, cook the chicken in margarine until golden brown on both sides. Except for the grapes, combine the remaining ingredients. Cover and cook for 25 minutes or until the vegetables are soft. Place the chicken on a serving plate. Cook for 2 minutes, stirring regularly, after adding the grapes to the gravy. Pour the sauce over the chicken.

Nutritional facts

Calories: 274| Carbohydrates: 13 g| Protein: 22 g| Fat: 13 g| Sodium 86 mg

60. Fish with Peppers

Preparation time: 10 minutes

Cooking time: 20 minutes

Serving: 5

Ingredients

- 1 1/2 lb. fish fillets

- 1 teaspoon garlic powder
- 1/2 cup low-sodium chicken broth
- 1/4 cup no-salt-added tomato sauce
- 1 teaspoon capers
- 2 tablespoons oil
- 1/2 teaspoon lemon pepper
- 1/2 medium green pepper (cut into rings)
- 1/2 medium red pepper (cut into rings)

Instructions

Cut the fish into 4-inch chunks. In a large pan, cook the salmon in oil for 5 minutes over medium heat, flipping often. Combine the broth, tomato sauce, and capers in a large mixing bowl. Reduce the heat to low, cover, and cook for 10 minutes. Cook for another 5 minutes, or until the fish flakes easily with a fork and soft peppers.

Nutritional facts

Calories: 205| Carbohydrates: 8 g| Protein: 23 g| Fat: 11 g| Sodium 136 mg

61. Grilled Chicken Sesame

Preparation time: 10 minutes

Cooking time: 10 minutes

Serving: 4

Ingredients

- Vegetable cooking spray
- 1 tablespoon sesame seeds (toasted)
- 1 tablespoon sherry
- 2 teaspoons ginger (grated)
- 4 4 oz. skinned chicken breast (into halves)
- 2 tablespoons honey
- 1 tablespoon (reduced) sodium soy sauce

Instructions

In a small mixing dish, combine the first five ingredients. Remove from the equation. Using a mallet or rolling pin, flatten the chicken pieces to ¼ inch thickness. Use the cooking spray on the grill. Grill the chicken for 4 minutes on each side over medium to hot coals, regularly basting the soy sauce mixture. Place on a serving dish.

Nutritional facts

Calories: 179| Carbohydrates: 11 g| Protein: 27 g| Fat: 3 g| Sodium 116 mg

62. Grilled Marinated Beef Steak

Preparation time: 10 minutes + 8 hours to marinate

Cooking time: 20 minutes

Serving: 6

Ingredients

- 1 1/2 lb. chuck steak
- 1 can (12 oz.) beer
- 2 tablespoons sugar
- 1/2 cup sliced green onion
- 2 tablespoons vinegar
- 1/4 cup chopped green pepper
- 1 tablespoon teriyaki sauce
- 2 cloves garlic (minced)
- 1/4 teaspoon pepper

Instructions

In a big shallow dish, place the steak. Pour the remaining ingredients over the meat. Refrigerate for 6 to 8 hours, flipping at least once to allow flavors to permeate. Remove the meat from the marinade and set it aside. Broil steak for 15 to 20 minutes over medium coals or until the desired doneness is reached, brushing meat periodically with remaining marinade.

Nutritional facts

Calories: 201| Carbohydrates: 12 g| Protein: 25 g| Fat: 6 g| Sodium 126 mg

63. Herb Topped Fish

Preparation time: 10 minutes

Cooking time: 20 minutes

Serving: 8

Ingredients

- 8 1-1/2 inch thick pieces of salmon, halibut or other white fish (24 oz.)
- 1/2 cup mayonnaise
- 1/4 cup grated Parmesan cheese
- 4 tablespoons chives (chopped)
- 1/2 cup sour cream
- 2 tablespoons parsley (chopped)
- 1/2 teaspoon onion powder
- 1/2 teaspoon dry mustard
- Fresh ground pepper to taste
- 1/2 teaspoon dried dill

Instructions

In a greased shallow baking pan, place uncooked fish fillets. By hand, combine the remaining ingredients. Apply the mixture to the tops of the fillets. Preheat the oven to 350°F and bake for 20 minutes or fish flakes.

Nutritional facts

Calories: 244| Carbohydrates: 1 g| Protein: 19 g| Fat: 18 g| Sodium 126 mg

64. Lemon Tarragon Chicken

Preparation time: 10 minutes

Cooking time: 15 minutes

Serving: 12

Ingredients

- 2 tablespoons margarine
- 8 medium skinless, boneless chicken breast halves
- 2 cups fresh mushrooms (halved)
- 1/3 cup flour
- 2 cloves garlic (minced)
- 3 tablespoons dry sherry
- 1/2 teaspoon dried tarragon (crushed)
- 1/2 teaspoon lemon pepper seasoning
- 1 3/4 cups salt-free chicken broth
- 1/4 cup cream
- Hot cooked noodles

Instructions

Melt margarine in a 12-inch pan over medium heat. Combine the chicken, garlic, sherry, tarragon, mushrooms, and lemon pepper spice in a large mixing bowl. Cook for 10 to 12 minutes, rotating once or until the chicken becomes white. Using a slotted spoon, remove the chicken and mushrooms. Mix chicken broth and flour in a screw-top container and mix well to combine. Fill the skillet with the mixture. Cook, constantly stirring, until the sauce is thick and bubbling. Remove 1/2 cup of the mixture from the skillet and whisk it into the sour cream. Return the chicken and mushrooms to the skillet. Bring to a boil (do not boil). Over hot cooked noodles, serve. Noodles may be used as a starch substitute.

Nutritional facts

Calories: 151| Carbohydrates: 5 g| Protein: 20 g| Fat: 5 g| Sodium 96 mg

65. Meat Loaf

Preparation time: 10 minutes

Cooking time: 1 hour

Serving: 8

Ingredients

- 2 beaten eggs
- 3/4 cup milk
- 2/3 cup bread crumbs
- 1/2 teaspoon sage
- 2 tablespoons onions
- 1 1/2 lb. ground beef
- 1/2 cup fresh sliced mushrooms

Topping:

- 1/4 cup salt-free ketchup
- 1 teaspoon dry mustard
- 2 tablespoons brown sugar
- 1/4 teaspoon nutmeg
- 1/4 cup shredded cheddar cheese

Instructions

Combine all of the ingredients for the beef loaf and pat it in a loaf pan. Preheat the oven to 350°F and bake for 1 hour. Remove the pan from the oven and drain the fat. Combine the first four topping ingredients and place them on the meatloaf. Sprinkle cheese on top. Bake until the cheese has melted.

Nutritional facts

Calories: 335| Carbohydrates: 14 g| Protein: 26 g| Fat: 19 g| Sodium 136 mg

66. Onion Smothered Steak

Preparation time: 10 minutes

Cooking time: 15 minutes

Serving: 8

Ingredients

- 1/4 cup flour
- 1/8 teaspoon pepper
- 1 1/2 lb. round steak
- 1 cup water
- 1 tablespoon vinegar
- 1 clove of garlic (minced)
- 2 tablespoons oil
- 1 bay leaf
- 1/4 teaspoon dried thyme (crushed)
- 3 medium onions (sliced)

Instructions

Cut the meat into 8 portions. Mix the flour and pepper and pound it into the meat. Heat the oil and brown the meat on both sides in a skillet. Remove the pan from the heat and put it aside. Combine the water, vinegar, garlic, bay leaf, and thyme in a pan. Bring the water to a boil. Place the meat in the center of the mixture and top with sliced onions. Cook for 1 hour with the lid on.

Nutritional facts

Calories: 271| Carbohydrates: 6 g| Protein: 18 g| Fat: 19 g| Sodium 136 mg

67. Oven Fried Chicken

Preparation time: 10 minutes

Cooking time: 60 minutes

Serving: 14

Ingredients

- 1 3-lb broiled-fryer chicken (cut up)
- 1/2 cup flour
- 1/4 cup shortening
- 1/4 cup margarine
- 1 teaspoon paprika
- 1/2 teaspoon pepper
- 1/2 teaspoon onion powder

Instructions

Preheat the oven to 425 degrees Fahrenheit. Rinse the chicken and pat it dry. Melt shortening and margarine in a 13 x 9 x 2-inch baking pan in the oven. Combine flour, paprika, pepper, and onion powder in a medium mixing basin. Coat the chicken pieces in the flour mixture completely. Place the skin side of the chicken in the melted shortening. Cook for 30 minutes, uncovered. Cook for another 30 minutes or until the thickest parts are fork-tender.

Nutritional facts

Calories: 184| Carbohydrates: 2 g| Protein: 21 g| Fat: 10 g| Sodium 136 mg

68. Pork with Julienne Vegetables

Preparation time: 10 minutes

Cooking time: 60 minutes

Serving: 14

Ingredients

- 4 pork cutlets (4 oz. each, 1/2-inch thick)
- 2 tablespoons flour
- 2 tablespoons lemon juice
- 1/2 teaspoon salt-free seasoning
- 3 tablespoons + 1 teaspoon margarine
- 1/3 cup dry white wine
- 2 cups julienne zucchini strips
- 1 cup julienne summer squash strips
- 1/2 cup red bell pepper strips
- 1 clove of garlic (minced)
- 1/4 teaspoon basil
- 1/8 teaspoon pepper

Instructions

Pounded each cutlet to a thickness of 1/4 inch. Combine flour and salt-free seasoning in a mixing bowl. Cutlets should be dredged in the flour mixture. In a large pan, brown cutlets in 2 tablespoons of margarine for 5 minutes on each side over medium-high heat. Transfer to a serving plate and keep it heated. Toss in the wine and lemon juice with the pan juices. Heat until the liquid is reduced to 1/4 cup. 1 teaspoon margarine; the melted sauce should be poured over the cutlets. Keep yourself warm. In a pan, combine the veggies and 1 tablespoon of margarine. Garlic, basil, and pepper to taste. Over high heat, cook and stir for 3 to 4 minutes. Serve with meat on a plate.

Nutritional facts

Calories: 403| Carbohydrates: 9 g| Protein: 20 g| Fat: 32 g| Sodium 136 mg

69. Salt-Free Pizza

Preparation time: 10 minutes

Cooking time: 60 minutes

Serving: 35

Ingredients

For the Dough:

- 1 tablespoon oil
- 2 cups of flour
- 1 cup of warm water
- ½ pack of dry yeast
- 1 tablespoon sugar

For Sauce:

- 1/4 teaspoon garlic powder
- 1 tablespoon oil
- 3 oz. no-salt tomato paste
- 1/2 cup water
- 1 tablespoon sugar
- 1/4 cup onion
- 1/2 teaspoon oregano

- 1/4 cup chopped green pepper
- 1/2 lb. beef
- 6 oz. mozzarella cheese (shredded)

Instructions

In a bowl of warm water, dissolve the yeast, add oil, flour and sugar to produce a soft dough are combined in a mixing bowl. 20 strokes of the whisk Place in a greased mixing bowl, turn to wet all sides, cover, and set aside in a warm location. In a small saucepan, combine tomato paste, 1/2 cup water, oregano, 1 tablespoon of sugar, and 1 tablespoon of oil. Cook for 5 minutes. Grease a 17 × 14-inch baking sheet. Overlap the dough to the edges of the sheet. Cover with a layer of sauce. Onion, green pepper, steak, and cheese go on top. Preheat the oven to 400°F and bake for 20 to 30 minutes, or until the dough and cheese are golden brown. Cut the cake into 12 pieces.

Nutritional facts

Calories: 201| Carbohydrates: 19 g| Protein: 11 g| Fat: 9 g| Sodium 256 mg

70. Scampi Linguini

Preparation time: 10 minutes

Cooking time: 5 minutes

Serving: 4

Ingredients

- 1 tablespoon olive oil
- 1/2 teaspoon basil
- 1/4 cup dry white wine
- 1 clove of garlic (minced)
- 1/2 lb. shrimp
- 1 tablespoon lemon juice
- 1 tablespoon chopped fresh parsley
- 4 oz. dry linguini

Instructions

In a large skillet, heat the oil. Toss in the garlic and shrimp. Cook, constantly stirring, until the shrimp becomes pink. Combine the wine, lemon juice, basil, and parsley in a mixing bowl. Cook for a further 5 minutes. Meanwhile, cook linguini till soft in unsalted water.

Drain. Serve the linguini with the shrimp and any leftover liquid on top.

Nutritional facts

Calories: 208| Carbohydrates: 26 g| Protein: 15 g| Fat: 5 g| Sodium 166 mg

71. Spanish Paella

Preparation time: 10 minutes

Cooking time: 10 minutes

Serving: 8

Ingredients

- 1/2 lb. boned
- 1/4 cup water
- 1/4 teaspoon pepper
- 1 10-1/2-oz chicken broth
- 1/2 lb. shrimp
- 1/2 cup frozen green peas
- 1/3 cup chopped red bell pepper
- 1/3 cup thinly sliced green onion
- 2 cloves garlic (minced)
- 1 cup uncooked instant white rice
- Dash ground saffron

Instructions

In a 2-quart casserole, combine the first three ingredients and cover with the lid. Microwave for 4 to 5 minutes on high. Combine the shrimp and the following six ingredients in a large mixing bowl. Microwave for 3 to 4minutes on high, or until shrimp becomes pink. Add the rice and mix well. Cover and set aside for 5 minutes, or until rice is cooked through.

Nutritional facts

Calories: 163| Carbohydrates: 24 g| Protein: 15 g| Fat: 1 g| Sodium 124 mg

72. Sweet and Sour Chicken

Preparation time: 10 minutes

Cooking time: 7 minutes

Serving: 6

Ingredients

- 1/2 cup sugar
- 2 tablespoons orange marmalade
- 1/2 cup vinegar
- 1/4 cup margarine
- 1 green pepper (sliced)
- 1 (20 oz.) can of pineapple chunks (juice pack)
- 1 lb. boned (skinned chicken breasts, cut into 1/2-inch cubes)
- 1 medium onion, thinly sliced and separated into rings
- 2 tablespoons cornstarch

- 3 cups hot cooked white rice

Instructions

Drain the pineapple, keeping 1/3 cup of the liquid. Combine the sugar and cornstarch in a mixing bowl. Combine the pineapple, reserved juice, vinegar, and orange marmalade in a mixing bowl. Remove from the equation. In a wok or big pan, melt margarine. Cook, often stirring, for 5 minutes after adding the chicken. Cook for 2 minutes after adding the green pepper and onion. Toss in the pineapple mixture. Bring to a boil, stirring now and again. Over rice, if desired. Rice may be used as a starch substitute.

Nutritional facts

Calories: 433| Carbohydrates: 67 g| Protein: 21 g| Fat: 9 g| Sodium 212 mg

73. Turkey Fajitas

Preparation time: 10 minutes + 4 hours to marinate

Cooking time: 30 minutes

Serving: 10

Ingredients

- 1 lb. boneless turkey breast
- 1/4 teaspoon pepper
- 1 clove of garlic (minced)
- 1 teaspoon chili powder
- 1 cup chopped tomato
- 2 tablespoons lime juice
- 1 tablespoon chopped fresh cilantro (coriander)
- 1 tablespoon oil
- 3 cups shredded lettuce
- 2 tablespoons chopped fresh cilantro
- 1 tablespoon chopped red onion
- 1/4 teaspoon minced garlic
- 10 7-inch flour tortillas
- 1/2 cup light sour cream

Instructions

Pepper, 1 minced garlic clove, chili powder, lime juice, 1 tablespoon cilantro, and oil are sprinkled over the turkey. Coat on the other side. Cover and marinate for 3 hours or longer in the refrigerator. Mix the tomato, 2 tablespoons cilantro, onion, and 1/4 teaspoon garlic in a small bowl to create the salsa. Allow 1 hour for cooling. Broil the turkey for 10 minutes on each side, 6 inches from the flame. Make strips out of it. Wrap tortillas in aluminum foil and reheat them in the oven for 8 minutes while the turkey cooks. Wrap warm tortillas around turkey, salsa, lettuce, and sour cream to serve.

Nutritional facts

Calories: 208| Carbohydrates: 19 g| Protein: 13 g| Fat: 17 g| Sodium 126 mg

74. Broccoli-Cauliflower-Carrot Bake

Preparation time: 10 minutes

Cooking time: 40 minutes

Serving: 12

Ingredients

- 3 cups broccoli (raw)
- 1 cup carrots
- 2 cups cauliflower (raw)
- 1 cup frozen whole small onions / 3 medium onions quartered
- 4 tablespoons butter
- 2 tablespoons flour
- 1 cup milk
- 1 package (3 oz) cream cheese (softened)
- Dash pepper
- 1/2 cup sharp cheddar cheese (shredded)
- 1/2 cup soft bread crumbs

Instructions

Vegetables should be washed and sliced before steaming till crisp yet soft. Drain. Melt 2 tablespoons butter in a skillet; stir in flour and pepper. Pour in the milk. Cook, constantly stirring, until the sauce is thick and bubbling. Reduce the heat to low and stir in the cream cheese until smooth. Fill a 1 1/2-quart casserole dish halfway with veggies. Pour the sauce over the top and toss gently. Shredded cheese is sprinkled on top. Preheat the oven to 350°F and bake for 15 minutes. Combine the bread crumbs and the remaining butter in a bowl and sprinkle over the dish. Bake for another 25 minutes.

Nutritional facts

Calories: 114| Carbohydrates: 7 g| Protein: 3.9 g| Fat: 9 g| Sodium 126 mg

75. Broccoli Blossom

Preparation time: 10 minutes

Cooking time: 10 minutes

Serving: 2

Ingredients

- 1/4 cup onion
- 1 cup chopped red cabbage
- 1/2 cup chopped broccoli

- 2 to 3 tablespoons of water
- 1/4 teaspoon tarragon
- 1 tablespoon oil
- 1/4 teaspoon garlic powder
- 1/4 teaspoon onion powder
- Black pepper per taste
- Red pepper as required
- 1 English muffin (split and toasted)
- 2 tablespoons grated Parmesan cheese

Instructions

In a large pan or wok, stir-fry veggies in oil for 2 to 3 minutes. Cover and add water. Steam for 5 minutes. During the final 2 minutes of cooking, add the spices.

Serve with English muffin halves on the side. Sprinkle parmesan cheese on top.

Nutritional facts

Calories: 174| Carbohydrates: 17 g| Protein: 6 g| Fat: 9 g| Sodium 126 mg

76. Crispy Fried Okra

Preparation time: 10 minutes

Cooking time: 10 minutes

Serving: 2

Ingredients

- 1 pint fresh okra (cut into 1-inch segments) / 1 16-oz package frozen okra
- 1/2 cup flour
- 2 tablespoons margarine
- 1/2 cup cornmeal
- 1/4 teaspoon pepper
- 1 cup beer or water

Instructions

If you have frozen okra, it will need to be thawed. Combine flour, cornmeal, and pepper in a medium mixing basin. Mix in the margarine until it crumbles. After dipping the okra in beer or water, roll it in the cornmeal mixture to coat it. Place on a baking sheet that has been buttered. Preheat the oven to 350°F and bake for 20 minutes or golden brown. Serve with toothpicks and low-sodium ketchup while still hot.

Nutritional facts

Calories: 215| Carbohydrates: 36 g| Protein: 4 g| Fat: 6 g| Sodium 296 mg

77. Hot German Cabbage

Preparation time: 10 minutes

Cooking time: 10 minutes

Serving: 6

Ingredients

- 2 tablespoons sugar
- 1/2 teaspoon caraway seed
- 1/4 teaspoon pepper
- 1 tablespoon minced onion
- 3 tablespoons vinegar
- 1/2 teaspoon dry mustard
- 2 tablespoons margarine
- 4 cups shredded red cabbage
- 1 cup unpeeled diced green apple

Instructions

Combine the sugar, onion, caraway seed, dry mustard, pepper, and vinegar in a mixing dish. Set aside after thoroughly mixing. In a large skillet, melt the margarine. In a pan, sauté the cabbage and apple for 3 minutes. Stir in the vinegar mixture and cook, stirring periodically, for 5 minutes, or until the cabbage is soft.

Nutritional facts

Calories: 77| Carbohydrates: 9 g| Protein: 1 g| Fat: 4 g| Sodium 136 mg

78. Steamed Green Beans

Preparation time: 10 minutes

Cooking time: 15 minutes

Serving: 4

Ingredients

- 1 pound of green beans (trimmed)
- 1/2 cup diced sweet red pepper
- 1/2 teaspoon basil
- 1 tablespoon vegetable oil
- 2 tablespoons water
- 1/4 teaspoon pepper
- 1 tablespoon lemon juice

Instructions

Place all ingredients, except lemon juice, in a 12-inch heavy skillet with a tight-fitting cover. Cook, covered, over medium heat for 15 minutes or until tender-crisp, shaking the pan regularly to avoid sticking. Toss with a squeeze of lemon juice.

Nutritional facts

Calories: 47| Carbohydrates: 6 g| Protein: 1.5 g| Fat: 2 g| Sodium 228 mg

79. Summer Vegetable Sauté

Preparation time: 10 minutes

Cooking time: 15 minutes

Serving: 6

Ingredients

- 2 tablespoons margarine
- 2 cups sliced zucchini
- 1/8 teaspoon garlic powder
- 1/2 cup diced green pepper
- 1 10-oz package of frozen corn (thawed)
- 2 tablespoons chopped pimiento
- 1/8 teaspoon pepper

Instructions

In a large skillet, melt margarine. Add the other ingredients and cook for approximately 15 minutes or until the vegetables are soft.

Nutritional facts

Calories: 81| Carbohydrates: 9 g| Protein: 2 g| Fat: 4 g| Sodium 312 mg

80. Sunshine Carrots

Preparation time: 10 minutes

Cooking time: 10 minutes

Serving: 6

Ingredients

- 3 cups sliced carrots
- 2 tablespoons margarine
- 1 tablespoon lemon juice
- 1 tablespoon sugar
- 1/4 teaspoon grated lemon peel
- 1 teaspoon fresh parsley (chopped)

Instructions

Cook carrots until tender in boiling water; drain thoroughly. Combine the sugar, margarine, lemon juice, and lemon peel in a mixing bowl. Heat, constantly stirring, until the margarine is completely melted. Add the parsley and mix well.

Nutritional facts

Calories: 66| Carbohydrates: 7 g| Protein: 0.5 g| Fat: 2 g| Sodium 199 mg

81. Spicy Garlic Bread

Preparation time: 10 minutes

Cooking time: 20 minutes

Serving: 16

Ingredients

- 3 tablespoons vegetable oil
- 1 teaspoon Italian herbs
- 4 cloves garlic (minced)
- 2 teaspoons paprika
- 1 teaspoon lemon juice
- 2 tablespoons grated Parmesan cheese
- Dash of cayenne pepper
- 3/4 cup mayonnaise
- 1 loaf (1 lb.) French bread

Instructions

Fill a small dish halfway with oil. Allow the garlic to sit in the oil overnight. Drain garlic from the oil the next day, retaining the oil. Garlic should be discarded. Toss in paprika, cayenne, lemon juice, and Parmesan cheese. Mix thoroughly. Mix in the mayonnaise. Half the loaf of bread lengthwise. Spread a liberal amount of garlic spread on each side. Preheat the broiler and broil both sides until golden brown. Serve immediately.

Nutritional facts

Calories: 175| Carbohydrates: 14 g| Protein: 3 g| Fat: 9 g| Sodium 186 mg

82. Pineapple Bread

Preparation time: 10 minutes

Cooking time: 60 minutes

Serving: 20

Ingredients

- 1/3 cup sugar
- 2 cups flour
- 2 eggs
- 1/3 cup margarine
- 3 teaspoons baking powder
- 1 cup crushed pineapple in juice (undrained)
- 6 maraschino cherries (chopped)

Instructions

Combine the sugar and margarine in a mixing bowl and

beat until light and fluffy. Mix in the eggs well. Combine the flour and baking powder in a mixing bowl. Combine the sugar and flour ingredients in a mixing bowl. Blend. Mix in the pineapple and cherries until everything is well combined. Fill a greased 9 x 5-inch baking pan halfway with the batter. Preheat the oven to 350°F and bake for 1 hour. Cut the cake into 20 wedges.

Nutritional facts

Calories: 103| Carbohydrates: 15 g| Protein: 2 g| Fat: 4 g| Sodium 116 mg

83. Beef and Barley Stew

Preparation time: 15 minutes

Cooking time: 2 hours

Serving: 6

Ingredients

- 1 cup pearl barley (uncooked)
- 1 lb. lean beef stew meat (cut into 1 ½- inch cubes)
- 2 tablespoon all-purpose flour water
- ½ cup onion (diced)
- 1 large stalk of celery (sliced)
- 1 clove of garlic (minced)
- 2 carrots (sliced ¼ - inch thick)
- ¼ teaspoon pepper
- 2 bay leaves
- 2 tablespoon canola oil
- 1 teaspoon onion herb seasoning

Instructions

Soak barley for 1 hour in 2 cups of water. In a plastic bag, combine the flour, pepper, and meat. Dust the stew meat with flour by shaking it. Brown the meat in a heavy big saucepan with oil. Take the meat out of the pot. In the meat drippings, sauté the onion, celery, and garlic for 2 minutes. Bring 8 cups of water to a boil in a separate pot. Put the meat back in the pot. Toss in the bay leaves. Reduce the heat to a low setting. After draining and rinsing the barley, add it to the saucepan. Cook for 1 hour with the lid on. Every 15 minutes, give it another stir. Add the carrots and spices after 1 hour. Continue to cook for another hour. If necessary, add more water to avoid sticking.

Nutritional facts

Calories: 260| Carbohydrates: 13 g| Protein: 26 g| Fat: 28 g| Sodium 310 mg

84. Broiled Maple Salmon

Preparation time: 10 minutes

Cooking time: 15 minutes

Serving: 4

Ingredients

- 1 tablespoon ginger root (grated)
- 1 clove of garlic (minced)
- ¼ cup maple-flavored pancake syrup
- 1 lb. (about 4) salmon fillet portions (fresh, skinless)
- 1 tablespoon hot pepper sauce

Instructions

Heat a nonstick frying pan over medium heat, spraying it with veggie spray. Cook, occasionally stirring, for 3-5 minutes with the ginger and garlic. Turn off the heat in the pan. Combine the syrup and hot pepper sauce in a mixing bowl. Preheat the oven to broil. Spray a baking pan with cooking spray and line it with foil. Place the fillets on the baking sheet that has been prepared. Brush the tops and sides of the fillets with the sauce. Broil salmon 4 inches beneath the broiler for 10 minutes or until it readily flakes when poked with a fork. Serve right away. With boiling rice or pasta, this recipe is wonderful.

Nutritional facts

Calories: 282| Carbohydrates: 13 g| Protein: 25 g| Fat: 27 g| Sodium 196 mg

85. Chicken Curry

Preparation time: 10 minutes

Cooking time: 11 minutes

Serving: 4

Ingredients

- 1 lb. (454 g) chicken (skinless, diced)
- 1 tablespoon curry powder
- 1 clove of garlic (crushed or garlic powder to taste)
- 1 medium onion (chopped)
- 1 teaspoon cornstarch
- 1 teaspoon canola oil water as required
- ¼ teaspoon pepper
- 1 oz. non-hydrogenated unsalted margarine

Instructions

Brown the onion and garlic in a skillet. In a tiny quantity of oil, add diced chicken and sauté slowly. Melt the margarine in a separate pan and stir in the cornstarch. To make a paste, add a little amount of water. Whisk in the water (up to 1 cup), curry powder, and pepper. Add the sauce to the chicken and cook until it thickens and reduces. Reduce the heat to low, cover, and cook until the chicken is done. If necessary, add extra water to avoid scorching. With boiling rice or pasta, this recipe is wonderful.

Nutritional facts

Calories: 268| Carbohydrates: 36 g| Protein: 4 g| Fat: 38 g| Sodium 196 mg

86. Chicken Fingers with Honey Dill Dipping Sauce

Preparation time: 15 minutes

Cooking time: 20 minutes

Serving: 4

Ingredients

Chicken:

- ¾ cup breadcrumbs
- ¼ teaspoon pepper
- 2 tablespoon Parmesan cheese (to taste)
- 1 ½ teaspoon dried thyme
- ¾ teaspoon garlic powder
- ¾ teaspoon onion powder

Sauce:

- ½ cup light mayonnaise
- ½ teaspoon dried dill weed
- 4 chicken breast halves (boneless, skinless, cut into 1" strips)
- ¼ cup liquid honey
- ¼ cup non-hydrogenated unsalted margarine (melted)

Instructions

Refrigerate for 30 minutes after combining mayonnaise, honey, and dill weed. Preheat the oven to 400 degrees Fahrenheit. Combine the first six ingredients in a bowl. Dip the chicken in melted margarine before coating it with the other ingredients. Place on a cookie sheet on a lightly oiled oven rack. Bake for 10 minutes, then flip and bake for another 10 minutes.

Nutritional facts

Calories: 290| Carbohydrates: 15 g| Protein: 28 g| Fat: 30 g| Sodium 136 mg

87. Turkey Meatloaf

Preparation time: 15 minutes

Cooking time: 1 hour 10 minutes

Serving: 6

Ingredients

- 1 ½ lb. ground turkey breast
- 1 tablespoon olive oil
- 1 bay leaf
- 1 medium onion (diced)
- ¼ cup red bell pepper (diced)
- 2 eggs (lightly beaten)
- 1 teaspoon dried thyme
- 2 tablespoon Worcestershire Sauce
- 1/3 cup bread crumbs
- ¼ cup low-sodium ketchup

Instructions

Preheat the oven to 325 degrees Fahrenheit. In a medium-sized pan, heat the olive oil over medium heat. Sauté for 2-3 minutes with the onions and bell pepper. Add the bay leaf and thyme. Sauté for approximately 6-7 minutes or until the onions are transparent. Remove the bay leaf before setting aside the onion combination and allowing it to cool to room temperature. Combine the turkey, bread crumbs, eggs, Worcestershire sauce, and onion in a medium mixing bowl. Fill a loaf pan halfway with the mixture. Serve with ketchup on the side. Bake for 1 to 12 hours or until the meatloaf temperature reaches 160 degrees Fahrenheit.

Nutritional facts

Calories: 283| Carbohydrates: 10 g| Protein: 26 g| Fat: 28 g| Sodium 196 mg

88. Chicken and Dumplings

Preparation time: 15 minutes

Cooking time: 1 hour 20 minutes

Serving: 6

Ingredients

- 2 ½ lb. chicken (whole)
- 2-liter water
- ½ teaspoon pepper
- 3 tablespoon shortening
- 2 cups all-purpose flour
- ½ teaspoon baking soda
- ¾ cup unsalted buttermilk

Instructions

Fill a big saucepan halfway with water and add the chicken. Bring to a boil, then decrease the heat to low and cook for 1 hour. Remove the chicken and set it aside to cool somewhat. Remove the flesh from the bones and chop it into bite-size pieces. Remove any extra foam or fat from the top of the chicken stock in the pot. Bring to a boil, season with pepper, and put the chicken pieces back in the pot. Combine the flour, baking soda, and shortening, then cut in until the mixture resembles a coarse meal. Stir in the buttermilk with a fork until all dry ingredients are moistened.

Knead the dough gently 4 or 5 times on a well-floured surface. Flatten the dough to a thickness of 1/2 inch. Pinch off 12-inch pieces of dough and dip them into boiling soup. Reduce heat to low-medium and simmer, stirring regularly, for 8-10 minutes, or until firm dumplings. Serve with chicken.

Nutritional facts

Calories: 430| Carbohydrates: 33 g| Protein: 20 g| Fat: 22 g| Sodium 126 mg

89. Bruce's Homemade Sausage

Preparation time: 15 minutes

Cooking time: 20 minutes

Serving: 15

Ingredients

- 2 ½ lb. ground pork
- ½ lb. lean ground beef
- 2 tablespoon ground coriander
- 2 teaspoon allspice
- ½ cup warm water
- 1/8 teaspoon pepper
- Sausage casings (optional)

Instructions

Mix all of the ingredients well. Form patties or put in casings. Cook sausage in batches in a large pan over medium heat for 15-20 minutes or until uniformly browned on both sides. Freeze for up to three months in advance.

Nutritional facts

Calories: 264| Carbohydrates: 1 g| Protein: 23 g| Fat: 26 g| Sodium 336 mg

90. Fish Cakes

Preparation time: 15 minutes

Cooking time: 15 minutes

Serving: 6

Ingredients

- 1 lb. haddock (cooked and flaked)
- 1-2 teaspoon lemon juice
- ½ cup plain bread crumbs
- 2 eggs (beaten)

- 3 cups mashed potatoes
- Pepper and paprika to taste

Instructions

Toss flaked fish with lemon juice. In a mixing dish, combine all of the ingredients. Make 6 cakes that are about 1 inch thick. Roll in bread crumbs after dipping in beaten egg. Bake until cooked through on a cookie sheet at 375°F. Double boil or soak peeled and chopped potatoes for low potassium diets.

Nutritional facts

Calories: 152| Carbohydrates: 16 g| Protein: 20 g| Fat: 22 g| Sodium 186 mg

91. Low Salt Pizza

Preparation time: 15 minutes

Cooking time: 60 minutes

Serving: 12

Ingredients

Dough:

- 2 cups all-purpose flour
- 1 cup of warm water
- 1 teaspoon instant yeast
- 1 tablespoon sugar
- 1 tablespoon canola oil

Sauce:

- 6 oz. mozzarella cheese (shredded)
- ½ teaspoon oregano
- ½ lb. ground beef (cooked, well-drained)
- ¼ cup green pepper (chopped)
- ½ cup water
- ¼ cup onion (chopped)
- 1 tablespoon canola oil
- 1/3 teaspoon garlic powder
- 75 ml. unsalted tomato sauce

Instructions

Preheat the oven to 400 degrees Fahrenheit. In a bowl of warm water, dissolve the yeast. To produce a soft dough, combine the oil, sugar, and flour. Gradually add the flour since not all of it may be required. Cover and set aside for approximately 15 minutes in a greased basin. Combine tomato sauce, water, garlic powder, oregano, and oil in a small saucepan. Cook for 5 minutes on low heat. A 17 × 14-inch baking sheet should be greased. The dough should be pressed onto the sheet and over the edges. Cover with a layer of sauce. Onion, green pepper, steak, and cheese go on top. Bake for 20-30 minutes in the center of the oven until the dough and cheese are golden brown. Serve by slicing into 12 pieces.

Nutritional facts

Calories: 204| Carbohydrates: 19 g| Protein: 11 g| Fat: 21 g| Sodium 196 mg

92. Slow Cooker Kabocha Barley Risotto

Preparation time: 10 minutes

Cooking time: 6 hours

Serving: 6

Ingredients

- 2 teaspoons avocado/olive oil
- ½ small yellow onion (diced)
- 2 garlic cloves (minced)
- 8 ounces of mushrooms (thinly sliced)
- 1 ½ cups pearl barley (rinsed)
- 3 cups kabocha squash (peeled, seeded, and cut into ¼-inch cubes)
- 4 cups low-sodium / no-salt-added vegetable broth
- 1 cup frozen shelled edamame (thawed)
- Pinch freshly ground black pepper

Instructions

Heat the oil in a medium skillet or pan over medium-high heat. Combine the onion, garlic, and pepper in a mixing bowl. Cook, stirring periodically, for 5 minutes or until the onions are transparent. Cook for approximately 2 minutes or until the mushrooms are slightly brown and tender. Cook for approximately 2 minutes or until the barley is slightly brown.

Fill a 6-quart slow cooker halfway with the ingredients. Combine the squash and broth in a large mixing bowl. To blend, stir everything together. Cook for 5 to 6 hours on low heat until the liquid has been absorbed and the squash is fork-tender. Add the edamame and serve right away. Refrigerate for up to 5 days or freeze for 6 months if stored in an airtight container or re-sealable bag. If freezing, we suggest using a re-sealable bag and freezing it flat to make storage easy.

Nutritional facts

Calories: 222| Carbohydrates: 38 g| Protein: 8.4 g| Fat: 3 g| Sodium 313 mg

93. Chickpea Shawarma Wraps

Preparation time: 5 minutes

Cooking time: 10 minutes

Serving: 4

Ingredients

For The Chickpea Shawarma

- 1 (15-ounce) can of no-salt-added or low-sodium chickpeas (drained, rinsed, and patted dry)
- ½ teaspoon ground cumin
- 1 garlic clove (minced)
- ½ teaspoon salt
- ¼ teaspoon paprika
- ⅛ teaspoon ground cinnamon
- ¼ teaspoon ground coriander
- ⅛ teaspoon ground cayenne pepper
- 1 tablespoon olive or avocado oil
- black pepper to taste

For The Sauce

- ½ cup cucumber (seeded, peeled, and finely chopped)
- 1 tablespoon freshly squeezed lemon juice
- 1 cup plain nonfat Greek yogurt
- 1 garlic clove (minced)
- 1 teaspoon ground cumin

For The Wraps

- 4 medium (6-inch) whole-wheat pita pockets
- 8 leaves of romaine lettuce
- 1 small tomato (cut into 8 thin rounds)
- ¼ medium red onion (thinly sliced) (optional)

Instructions

For Shawarma:

In a medium mixing basin, combine the chickpeas, cumin, salt, coriander, paprika, cinnamon and cayenne. Mix everything until the chickpeas are evenly covered. Heat the oil in a pan over medium heat. Add the garlic and the seasoned chickpeas. Cook, turning periodically, for approximately 10 minutes, or until the chickpeas are warm and crispy. Toss in a pinch of black pepper to taste.

For sauce:

Meanwhile, mix the yogurt, cucumber, lemon juice, garlic, and cumin in a small bowl.

For Wraps:

After toasting the pitas in the toaster oven, put the pita pockets together. 2 lettuce leaves, 2 tomato slices, one-quarter of the chickpea mixture, and a drizzle of sauce to each pita pocket. If using, garnish with red onion. The leftover chickpea mixture may be kept in the refrigerator for 5 days or frozen for 3 months.

Nutritional facts

Calories: 216| Carbohydrates: 29 g| Protein: 13.4 g| Fat: 6 g| Sodium 186 mg

94. Roasted Vegetable and Tofu Fried Rice

Preparation time: 15 minutes

Cooking time: 45 minutes

Serving: 6

Ingredients

- 1 medium eggplant (cubed)
- 1 medium red bell pepper (sliced)
- 1 medium unpeeled sweet potato (diced)
- 14 ounces firm tofu (diced)
- 1 medium zucchini (diced)
- 2 tablespoons coconut amino
- 1 tablespoon rice vinegar
- 2 cups cooked brown rice
- 1 tablespoon light brown sugar
- 1 tablespoon minced fresh ginger
- 2 garlic cloves (minced)
- 2 large eggs (beaten)
- 1 tablespoon sesame oil
- 2 cups cauliflower rice (thawed)
- Avocado or olive oil cooking spray

Instructions

Preheat the oven to 400 degrees Fahrenheit and line two baking pans with parchment paper. On one baking sheet, arrange the eggplant, zucchini, bell pepper, and sweet potato in a single layer; on the other baking sheet, arrange the tofu in a single layer. On top of everything, spray with oil. Toss to coat evenly. Bake for 30 minutes, or until the veggies are roasted and the tofu is crisp and golden brown around the edges.

Whisk the coconut amino, rice vinegar, brown sugar, and ginger in a small bowl. Heat the sesame oil in a large wok or pan over medium heat. Sauté for 30 to 45 seconds or until the garlic is aromatic.

Scramble the eggs until they are fully cooked, approximately 5 minutes. If using packaged rice, heat it to the appropriate temperature in the microwave. Cook, constantly stirring, for 2 minutes after adding the cooked brown rice and cauliflower rice. Drizzle the coconut amino sauce over the roasted veggies. Cook for 3 minutes after gently mixing everything. Remove the pan from the heat and divide the mixture into six portions. Serve immediately with the tofu on top. Leftovers may be stored

in an airtight container for up to 3 days in the refrigerator and up to 3 months in the freezer.

Nutritional facts

Calories: 276| Carbohydrates: 36 g| Protein: 11.5 g| Fat: 10 g| Sodium 339 mg

95. Vegetarian Garam Masala Burritos

Preparation time: 15 minutes

Cooking time: 30 minutes

Serving: 6

Ingredients

- 1 tablespoon olive or avocado oil
- 2 cups yellow potatoes (cubed)
- 1 cup low-sodium / no-salt-added vegetable broth
- 1 medium tomato (diced)
- ¼ cup chopped fresh cilantro
- 2 garlic cloves (minced)
- 2 teaspoons minced fresh ginger
- 1 teaspoon ground cumin
- 14 ounces firm tofu (drained and patted dry)
- ½ teaspoon ground coriander
- 1 cup plain frozen mixed vegetables
- ½ teaspoon ground turmeric
- ½ teaspoon garam masala
- 6 (10-inch) whole-grain tortillas

Instructions

Heat the oil in a large skillet over medium heat. Cook for 1 minute or until the potatoes are gently browned. Cover the vegetable stock and boil until the potatoes are cooked approximately 15 minutes. Stir once in a while. Combine the tomato, garlic, ginger, cumin, coriander, and turmeric in a large mixing bowl. Cook for a total of 2 to 3 minutes. Cook for a further 4 minutes after crumbling in the tofu. Combine the mixed veggies, cilantro, and garam masala in a large mixing bowl. Cook, stirring gently, for 3 minutes, or until the veggies and mixture are heated.

Remove from the heat and set aside to cool. Assemble the burritos as follows: Place approximately a third of a cup of the filling in the center of the tortilla. Wrap the tortilla securely by tucking in the ends and folding it up. Rep with the remaining burritos. Leftover burritos may be wrapped in foil and stored in the refrigerator for up to 5 days or frozen for 6 months in an airtight resealable bag.

Nutritional facts

Calories: 294| Carbohydrates: 43 g| Protein: 10.4 g| Fat: 12 g| Sodium 316 mg

96. "Cheesy" Pasta with Broccoli

Preparation time: 10 minutes

Cooking time: 30 minutes

Serving: 4

Ingredients

- 12 ounces whole-wheat pasta
- 1 tablespoon avocado oil
- 2 garlic cloves (minced)
- 1 tablespoon white vinegar or lemon juice
- 1 small carrot (peeled and diced)
- ½ cup minced white onion
- 2 rounded tablespoons of nutritional yeast
- 1 (15-ounce) can of no-salt-added or low-sodium white beans (drained and rinsed)
- 1 cup low-sodium or no-salt-added vegetable broth (plus more as needed)
- ½ teaspoon salt
- ½ teaspoon freshly ground black pepper
- 4 cups broccoli florets

Instructions

Bring a large pot of water to a boil, then add the pasta and cook according to package directions. Meanwhile, heat the oil and garlic in a big pan over medium heat. Cook for 5 minutes, or until the carrot and onion are tender. Remove the pan from the heat and transfer the contents to a food processor or blender.

Combine the beans, broth, nutritional yeast, vinegar, salt, and pepper in a blender. Puree until the mixture is creamy and smooth, with a sauce-like consistency. Set aside. Add the broccoli to the saucepan after the pasta has been cooking for around 3 minutes. Drain the water from the saucepan and combine the pasta and broccoli with the sauce.

To blend, stir everything together. If the sauce needs to be thinned, add additional vegetable broth or save some pasta water. Serve. Keep leftovers refrigerated for up to 5 days in an airtight container.

Nutritional facts

Calories: 307| Carbohydrates: 52 g| Protein: 14.9 g| Fat: 7 g| Sodium 176 mg

97. Tangy Kale Orzo with Tempeh Sausage

Preparation time: 10 minutes

Cooking time: 15 minutes

Serving: 4

Ingredients

- 16 ounces whole-wheat orzo pasta
- 1 tablespoon avocado or olive oil
- 8 ounces tempeh (crumbled)
- 2 garlic cloves (minced)
- ½ teaspoon Italian Seasoning Blend or store-bought
- ½ teaspoon onion powder
- 3 cups roughly chopped fresh kale
- Juice of 3 medium lemons
- ½ teaspoon dried parsley
- ¼ teaspoon salt
- ¼ teaspoon smoked paprika
- ¼ teaspoon black pepper

Instructions

Cook the orzo pasta according to the package directions in a medium saucepan of water and bring it to a boil. Meanwhile, heat the oil in a big pan over medium to high heat. Combine the tempeh and garlic in a mixing bowl. Mix with a spoon, stir parsley, Italian seasoning, onion powder, and paprika continuously until the tempeh is well coated. Cook, occasionally stirring, for 5 to 6 minutes or until browned. Add the kale and cook for 2 minutes, or until it has wilted. Lemon juice should be squeezed all over the pan. Drain the water and return the orzo to the pan after cooking. Toss the orzo with the tempeh and greens to incorporate. Serve immediately after seasoning with salt and pepper. Refrigerate leftovers for up to 5 days and freeze them for 6 months in an airtight container.

Nutritional facts

Calories: 314| Carbohydrates: 44 g| Protein: 18.6 g| Fat: 9 g| Sodium 206 mg

98. Spicy Black Bean Power Bowls

Preparation time: 5 minutes

Cooking time: 15 minutes

Serving: 4

Ingredients

- 1 cup fresh Pico de Gallo
- 1 tablespoon olive oil or avocado oil
- 1 (15-ounce) can of no-salt-added or low-sodium black beans (drained and rinsed)
- ½ teaspoon ground cumin
- ½ teaspoon ground cayenne pepper or chili powder
- 4 cups finely chopped mustard greens

- 2 cups cooked brown rice
- 2 garlic cloves (minced)
- ½ cup low-sodium salsa
- 4 tablespoons crumbled feta cheese

Instructions

Sauté the Pico de Gallo in a large pan or skillet over medium heat for 2 to 3 minutes, until tender. Stir in the black beans, cumin, and cayenne, gently crushing some of the beans. Cook for 5 minutes, or until heated and slightly thickened. Remove the pan from the heat and put it aside.

Heat the oil and garlic in the same pan over medium heat. Cook for 45 seconds or until the garlic smells good. Cook for 4 to 5 minutes until the mustard greens are soft. If you're using readymade or bagged rice, cook it to the proper temperature in the microwave. Assemble the bowls as follows: 12 cups cooked brown rice, a quarter of the mustard greens, a quarter of the black beans, 2 tablespoons salsa, and 1 tablespoon feta cheese in each dish. Refrigerate leftovers for up to 5 days or freeze them for 3 months in an airtight container.

Nutritional facts

Calories: 271| Carbohydrates: 54 g| Protein: 12.7 g| Fat: 7 g| Sodium 136 mg

99. Vegetarian Enchiladas

Preparation time: 5 minutes

Cooking time: 35 minutes

Serving: 8

Ingredients

- Avocado or olive oil cooking spray
- 2 tablespoons avocado or olive oil
- 1 small red onion (diced)
- 2 cups diced zucchini
- 1 (10-ounce) package of frozen corn
- 1 (15-ounce) can of no-salt-added or low-sodium black beans (drained and rinsed)
- 3 cups Enchilada Sauce or store-bought (divided)
- 8 (10-inch) whole-wheat tortillas
- 2 cups shredded low-sodium mozzarella or Mexican-blend cheese
- Handful chopped cilantro (for garnish) (optional)

Instructions

Preheat the oven to 350 degrees Fahrenheit. Set aside a 13-by-9-inch baking dish that has been sprayed with cooking spray. Heat the oil in a big skillet or pan over medium-high heat. Sauté the zucchini, corn, and onion

for approximately 5 minutes or until the veggies are tender. Cook for 1 to 2 minutes after adding the beans, stirring gently. Turn off the heat. 1 cup of enchilada sauce should be spread on the bottom of the baking dish. Take one tortilla and distribute approximately 12 cups of the bean mixture along the middle. Roll up the tortilla with roughly 2 tablespoons of cheese on top. Place the tortilla in the baking dish seam-side down. Rep with the remaining tortillas.

Top with the remaining 14 cups of cheese and the rest of the enchilada sauce. Bake for 20 minutes, covered with foil. Remove the lid and bake for another 10 minutes. Serve garnished with cilantro (if using). Refrigerate leftovers for up to 5 days or freeze them for 3 months in an airtight container.

Nutritional facts

Calories: 314| Carbohydrates: 32 g| Protein: 15.3 g| Fat: 13 g| Sodium 176 mg

100. Pressure Cooker Lentil Sloppy Joes with Coleslaw

Preparation time: 5 minutes

Cooking time: 35 minutes

Serving: 8

Ingredients

- 1 medium onion (diced)
- 1 medium red bell pepper (diced)
- 2 garlic cloves (minced)
- 1 teaspoon avocado oil
- 2 cups low-sodium or no-salt-added vegetable broth
- 1 (15-ounce) can of low-sodium or no-salt-added diced tomatoes
- 2 tablespoons low-sodium or no-salt-added tomato paste
- 1 tablespoon maple syrup
- 1 teaspoon coconut amino
- 1 tablespoon Low-Sodium Dijon Mustard or store-bought
- 1 teaspoon (smoked) paprika
- 1 teaspoon chili powder
- 1 cup dry lentils (green or brown), rinsed
- 1 teaspoon ground cumin
- 1 teaspoon freshly squeezed lemon juice
- 6 whole-wheat hamburger buns

For Coleslaw

- 2 tablespoons Low-Sodium Dijon Mustard or store-bought
- 2 tablespoons apple cider vinegar
- 4 cups bagged coleslaw mix
- ¼ teaspoon black pepper

Instructions

Select the sauté setting on high in the pressure cooker. For 3 minutes, sauté the oil, onion, bell pepper, and garlic until the veggies are tender. Combine the broth, tomatoes and juices, lentils, tomato paste, maple syrup, mustard, paprika, chili powder, cumin, lemon juice, and coconut amino in a large mixing bowl. Stir continuously and combine well. Close the cover and cook for 15 minutes under high pressure.

For Coleslaw

Meanwhile, whisk the mustard, vinegar, and black pepper in a medium mixing bowl. Toss in the coleslaw lightly. Allow 15 minutes for the pressure to relax naturally. Release any residual pressure manually. Distribute the lentil mixture between the buns. Coleslaw may be served on the side or on top of the sloppy joes.

Refrigerate the remaining lentil mixture for up to 1 week or freeze it for 3 months in an airtight container.

Nutritional facts

Calories: 320| Carbohydrates: 51 g| Protein: 15.5 g| Fat: 5 g| Sodium 286 mg

101. Tofu Spring Rolls

Preparation time: 10 minutes

Cooking time: 15 minutes

Serving: 3

Ingredients

- 6 cups water
- 12 rice paper wrappers
- 14 ounces firm tofu (drained and patted dry)
- ½ tablespoon ground cumin
- ½ teaspoon freshly ground black pepper
- ½ tablespoon garlic powder
- 1 tablespoon olive or avocado oil
- 12 leaves romaine lettuce (washed, and each leaf halved lengthwise)
- 2 medium carrots (peeled and thinly sliced)
- 2 medium red bell peppers (thinly sliced)
- 1 medium cucumber (thinly sliced)
- ¼ teaspoon salt

Instructions

Boil the water in a medium saucepan and leave it aside to cool somewhat. This water will be used to soak the rice sheets later. Cut the tofu lengthwise into 12 uniform pieces and distribute them evenly on a platter. Combine the cumin, garlic powder, black pepper, and salt in a small bowl. Season both sides of the tofu with the spice mixture. Heat the oil in a medium pan or skillet over medium heat. Arrange the tofu strips on the pan in a single layer. Cook for 1 to 2 minutes on each side, or until lightly browned. Remove the tofu from the pan and place it on a cooling rack.

Fill a small pan halfway with gently chilled water. 5 seconds in the water, immerse a piece of rice paper. The paper may be a little stiff at this point, but it will soften while you make the meal. Place the wet rice paper using a moist towel or a damp cutting board. Place two lettuce halves in the middle of the wrapper. Top the lettuce with carrots, bell peppers, and cucumbers. 1 tofu strip, cooled, should be placed on top of the veggies. Fold the rice paper in half and roll it up from the bottom. Make that the roll is tightly wound. Rep with the remaining rice paper pieces. Serve right away and enjoy.

Nutritional facts

Calories: 322| Carbohydrates: 41 g| Protein: 18 g| Fat: 11 g| Sodium 196 mg

102. Feta, Onion, and Pepper Pizza

Preparation time: 10 minutes

Cooking time: 15 minutes

Serving: 4

Ingredients

- 1 recipe Salt-Free Pizza Dough or store-bought
- 2 tablespoons avocado oil
- 1 cup sliced red onion
- 3 medium red bell peppers (diced)
- 2 garlic cloves (minced)
- ½ cup crumbled feta cheese
- 1 teaspoon Italian Seasoning Blend or store-bought
- ½ cup fresh basil leaves for garnish (optional)

Instructions

Preheat the oven to 450 degrees Fahrenheit. Place the pizza dough on a baking sheet or a pizza pan. Arrange the bell peppers, onions, and garlic on top of the oil-coated crust. Season with feta cheese and Italian spice. Bake the veggies for 10 to 12 minutes or until crispy and tender. Allow cooling for 2 to 3 minutes before cutting into 12 slices and garnishing with basil leaves (if using). Keep leftovers in an airtight jar in the refrigerator for up to 5 days

Nutritional facts

Calories: 425| Carbohydrates: 62 g| Protein: 11.1 g| Fat: 15 g| Sodium 286 mg

103. Shrimp Quesadillas

Preparation time: 10 minutes + 15 minutes to marinate

Cooking time: 10 minutes

Serving: 2

Ingredients

- 5 ounces raw shrimp (peeled and deveined)
- 2 tablespoons plain nonfat Greek yogurt
- 2 tablespoons chopped fresh cilantro (plus more for garnish)
- 1 tablespoon freshly squeezed lime juice
- ¼ teaspoon ground cumin
- 2 (10-inch) flour tortillas
- ⅛ teaspoon ground cayenne pepper
- 2 tablespoons shredded low-sodium mozzarella or Mexican-blend cheese
- Lime wedges, for garnish (optional)

Instructions

Cut the shrimp into bite-size pieces after rinsing them. Combine the cilantro, lime juice, cumin, and cayenne in a small dish or re-sealable bag. Mix in the shrimp well. Allow 15 minutes for the shrimp to marinate. Heat the shrimp in a medium sauté pan over medium heat. Cook for 2 minutes, often stirring, until the shrimp becomes orange. Take the pan off the flame and stir in the yogurt.

Heat 1 tortilla on all sides in a large pan over low-medium heat. Sprinkle 1 tablespoon of cheese over half of the shrimp mixture. Fold the tortilla in half and cook for 2 minutes on the other side in the skillet. Remove the pan from the heat. For the second quesadilla, repeat steps 4 and 5. Each quesadilla should be cut into four pieces. Before serving, garnish with more cilantro and lime wedges (if desired).

Nutritional facts

Calories: 221| Carbohydrates: 25 g| Protein: 17.7 g| Fat: 6 g| Sodium 176 mg

104. Baked Carb Cake with Corn and Roasted Broccoli

Preparation time: 10 minutes

Cooking time: 20 minutes

Serving: 4

Ingredients

- 1 large egg
- 8 ounces crabmeat
- 1 large egg white or 2 tablespoons liquid egg whites
- ¼ cup plain nonfat Greek yogurt
- 1 tablespoon Low-Sodium Dijon Mustard or store-bought
- 2 garlic cloves (minced)
- ½ teaspoon paprika
- ¼ teaspoon freshly ground black pepper
- ½ cup celery (finely chopped)
- ½ cup finely chopped sweet onion
- Juice of 1 medium lemon
- ½ cup red bell pepper (finely chopped)
- ¾ cup whole-wheat panko bread crumbs
- 2 teaspoons avocado or olive oil
- 2½ cups broccoli florets
- Avocado or olive oil cooking spray
- 1 tablespoon Trader Joe's 21 Seasoning Salute or no-sodium seasoning of choice
- 4 medium corn cobs (husks and silks removed)
- Lemon wedges (for garnish)
- Brand hot sauce (for dipping)

Instructions

Preheat the oven to 4 F and line two baking pans with parchment paper. In a large mixing basin, combine the egg, egg white, yogurt, lemon juice, mustard, paprika, and black pepper. Combine the crabmeat, celery, onion, bell pepper, and garlic in a large mixing bowl. Mix in the bread crumbs until they are evenly distributed. Form the mixture into 10 patties with your hands and place on one prepared baking pan. Set aside after lightly brushing the tops of each crab cake with oil. Place the broccoli on the second baking sheet that has been prepped. Spray with cooking spray and season with salt and pepper. Toss gently to coat, then set both baking sheets in the oven. Bake for 15-20 minutes, or until golden brown on top and broccoli is slightly caramelized and cooked through.

Meanwhile, fill a big stockpot halfway with water and set it over high heat. Bring the water to a boiling point before adding the corn to the cob. Cook for 5 to 7 minutes or until done. 12 cups broccoli and 1 corn cob should be served with 2 crab cakes. Serve with lemon wedges and spicy sauce on the side.

Nutritional facts

Calories: 309| Carbohydrates: 44 g| Protein: 20.7 g| Fat: 8 g| Sodium 136 mg

105. Zesty Tuna Salad Sandwiches with Carrot Sticks

Preparation time: 15 minutes

Cooking time: 0 minutes

Serving: 4

Ingredients

- 1 (5-ounce) can of no-salt-added albacore tuna (drained and rinsed)
- ½ cup plain nonfat yogurt
- 1 celery stalk (diced)
- 1 mini cucumber (diced)
- 1 small radish (diced)
- 1 scallion, green part only (diced)
- ¼ cup chopped fresh parsley or cilantro
- 4 tablespoons Low-Sodium Dijon Mustard or store-bought (optional)
- ¼ teaspoon freshly ground black pepper
- 8 Ezekiel 4:9 low-sodium sprouted whole-grain bread slices
- Juice of ½ lemon
- 4 ounces carrot sticks

Instructions

In a large mixing basin, combine the tuna, yogurt, parsley, celery, cucumber, radish, scallion, lemon juice, and pepper. Mix everything until it's completely smooth. Toast the bread until it's done to your liking, and put 1 tablespoon of mustard on one piece. Distribute the tuna salad evenly across 4 pieces of bread and top with the remaining toast slices. A 1-ounce carrot stick should be served with each sandwich.

Nutritional facts

Calories: 324| Carbohydrates: 34 g| Protein: 19.4 g| Fat: 14 g| Sodium 186 mg

106. Sheet Pan Teriyaki Salmon with Roasted Vegetables

Preparation time: 10 minutes + 2 hours to marinate

Cooking time: 30 minutes

Serving: 4

Ingredients

- 4 ounces of wild-caught salmon fillets
- 2 cups eggplant (cut into 1-inch pieces)
- ½ cup Mango Teriyaki Sauce
- 1 medium carrot (cut into ½-inch pieces)
- 1 medium turnip (cut into ½-inch pieces)
- 2 tablespoons sesame oil
- ½ teaspoon ground ginger
- ½ teaspoon garlic powder

Instructions

Marinate the salmon fillets in the mango teriyaki sauce for 2 hours in a gallon-size resealable bag. Preheat the oven to 400 degrees Fahrenheit. Spread the eggplant, carrot, and turnip out on a baking sheet lined with parchment paper. Season with ginger and garlic powder and a drizzle of sesame oil. Toss until all of the ingredients are evenly coated.

Roast for 15-20 minutes or until the vegetables are somewhat soft. Remove the veggies from the oven and turn them over. Place the marinated salmon on the same baking sheet and bake for another 10 minutes or until everything is done.

Nutritional facts

Calories: 374| Carbohydrates: 25 g| Protein: 19.7 g| Fat: 23 g| Sodium 296 mg

107. Rotisserie Chicken Noodle Soup

Preparation time: 10 minutes

Cooking time: 30 minutes

Serving: 6

Ingredients

- 8 cups of no-salt-added or low-sodium chicken broth
- 9 ounces rotisserie chicken (deboned and shredded)
- 1 cup chopped white onion
- 8 ounces elbow macaroni
- 1 cup chopped celery
- 1 cup chopped carrots
- ¼ teaspoon freshly ground black pepper

Instructions

Bring the chicken stock and onion to a boil in a large soup pot over high heat. Return the saucepan to a boil with the chicken, macaroni, celery, carrots, and pepper. Cook for approximately 15 minutes or until the noodles are done. Serve right away. You can store the leftovers by refrigerating them in an airtight container for up to 5 days. If you wish to freeze it, measure it into individual portions, place it in a big resealable bag, and set it flat in the freezer. Freeze for up to 3 months in advance.

Nutritional facts

Calories: 281| Carbohydrates: 34 g| Protein: 19.6 g| Fat: 7 g| Sodium 136 mg

108. Chicken and Veggie Soba Noodles

Preparation time: 10 minutes

Cooking time: 10 minutes

Serving: 4

Ingredients

- 6 ounces uncooked soba noodles
- 2 cups of no-salt-added or low-sodium chicken broth
- 1 medium red bell pepper (julienned)
- 1 cup julienned carrots
- 2 cups chopped green cabbage
- 1 cup frozen shelled edamame (thawed)
- 1 (5-ounce) can Wild Planet no-salt-added chicken (drained and rinsed)
- ½ cup Peanut Apple Sauce
- 1 to 2 tablespoons water (optional)

Instructions

Heat the soba noodles and broth in a large saucepan over high heat. Combine the cabbage, bell pepper, and carrots in a large mixing bowl. Bring it to a boil, then remove it from heat. Reduce the heat to medium-low and cook for 5 to 7 minutes, stirring periodically, until the noodles are mushy and the veggies are cooked through. Turn off the heat. Toss together the edamame, chicken, and peanut apple sauce until well combined and uniformly covered. If the sauce becomes too thick, you may need to add more water.

Nutritional facts

Calories: 369| Carbohydrates: 44 g| Protein: 19 g| Fat: 22 g| Sodium 286 mg

109. Jerk Chicken with Rice and Vegetables

Preparation time: 15 minutes + 3 hours to chill

Cooking time: 25 minutes

Serving: 6

Ingredients

- 1 small red onion (chopped)
- 6 scallions use both white and green parts (chopped)
- 2 habanero chili peppers (seeded and chopped)
- 2 tablespoons white vinegar or lemon juice
- 2 tablespoons brown sugar or honey
- 2 teaspoons chopped fresh thyme
- 1 tablespoon coconut amino

- 1 tablespoon minced fresh ginger
- 1 tablespoon avocado oil
- 2 garlic cloves (minced)
- 1 teaspoon ground allspice
- ½ teaspoon salt
- ¼ teaspoon ground nutmeg
- ⅛ teaspoon ground cinnamon
- ½ teaspoon freshly ground black pepper
- Avocado or olive oil cooking spray
- 12 ounces boneless, skinless chicken thighs
- 3 cups frozen mixed vegetables
- 3 cups cooked brown rice

Instructions

Combine the onion, scallions, habanero, vinegar, brown sugar, coconut amino, oil, ginger, garlic, thyme, allspice, nutmeg, salt, black pepper, and cinnamon in a food processor and pulse until smooth. Puree until completely smooth. Cover the chicken with the pureed sauce mixture in a big resealable bag. Refrigerate the bag for at least 3 hours or overnight. Preheat the grill to medium-high heat, coat the chicken thighs with cooking spray, and place them on it. Grill them until the chicken is cooked through and the internal temperature reaches 165 degrees Fahrenheit.

Meanwhile, cook the brown rice according to the package directions and steam the frozen veggies. Remove each thigh from the grill and serve with 12 cups brown rice and 12 cup steamed veggies.

Nutritional facts

Calories: 301| Carbohydrates: 45 g| Protein: 12 g| Fat: 18 g| Sodium 86 mg

110. Soy Chicken Stir-Fry

Preparation time: 1 minute

Cooking time: 20 minutes

Serving: 2

Ingredients

- 1/3 cup brown rice or 1 cup cooked brown rice
- 1 tablespoon coconut amino
- 1 tablespoon red pepper flakes
- 2 teaspoons honey
- 2 garlic cloves (minced)
- 2 teaspoons rice wine vinegar
- 1 teaspoon cornstarch (dissolved in about 2 teaspoons of water)

- 4 ounces boneless (skinless chicken breast, cut into ½-inch cubes)
- 1 tablespoon sesame oil (divided)
- 6 cups frozen stir-fry vegetable mix

Instructions

Set aside the brown rice once cooked according to the package directions. Whisk the coconut amino, red pepper flakes, honey, vinegar, cornstarch mixture, and garlic in a medium mixing bowl. Mix in the chicken until it is evenly covered.

Heat 12 tablespoons sesame oil in a large wok or skillet over medium-high heat. Cook for 5-7 minutes until the chicken is browned and cooked thoroughly. Combine the remaining 12 tablespoons of sesame oil and the vegetable mixture in a mixing bowl. Cook for 5–7 minutes. If you want the veggies to be softer, cook them for longer. 12 cups brown rice, 12 cups chicken and vegetable combination, Serve right away.

Nutritional facts

Calories: 362| Carbohydrates: 54 g| Protein: 18 g| Fat: 23 g| Sodium 136 mg

111. Turkey Flatbread Pizza

Preparation time: 5 minutes

Cooking time: 15 minutes

Serving: 1

Ingredients

- 1 package Astoria's Family Bakery lavish flatbread
- 1 tablespoon no-salt-added tomato paste
- 1 ounce no-salt-added or low-sodium sliced turkey
- 1 large mushroom (thinly sliced)
- 1 teaspoon Italian Seasoning Blend
- 1 small zucchini (thinly sliced)
- 1 mini red bell pepper (thinly sliced)
- ½ cup chopped fresh baby kale
- 2 tablespoons grated low-sodium mozzarella cheese

Instructions

Preheat the oven to 350 degrees Fahrenheit. On a baking sheet, place the flatbread. Spread the tomato paste over top and season with Italian spice. Combine the turkey, mushroom, zucchini, bell pepper, and kale in a large mixing bowl. Bake for approximately 16 minutes, or until the cheese has melted and the vegetables have softened and warmed.

Nutritional facts

Calories: 238| Carbohydrates: 31 g| Protein: 19.4 g| Fat: 4 g| Sodium 88 mg | Potassium 99 mg | Phosphorus 166 mg|

112. Spicy Turkey Burgers

Preparation time: 10 minutes

Cooking time: 30 minutes

Serving: 5

Ingredients

- Avocado or olive oil cooking spray
- 12 ounces lean ground turkey
- 1 cup minced yellow onion
- ¼ cup panko bread crumbs
- 1 large egg
- 1 cup shredded zucchini
- 1 jalapeño pepper (seeded and minced)
- 1 teaspoon red pepper flakes
- ½ teaspoon freshly ground black pepper
- 2 medium Poblano peppers (seeded and halved lengthwise)
- 5 teaspoons Low-Sodium Dijon Mustard or store-bought (optional)
- 5 whole-wheat hamburger buns
- ½ teaspoon garlic powder
- 5 romaine lettuce leaves

Instructions

Preheat the oven to 400 degrees Fahrenheit. Spray a baking sheet with cooking spray and line it with foil. Combine the turkey, zucchini, onion, bread crumbs, egg, jalapeno, red pepper flakes, black pepper, and garlic powder in a large mixing basin. Mix until everything is properly blended. Form the meat mixture into 4-5 burger patties by dividing it into 4 equal pieces. Place the patties and Poblano peppers on the baking sheet that has been prepared. Bake for 20-25 minutes, or until the patties are no longer pink and have reached a temperature of 165°F on the inside.

On the bottom bun, spread 1 teaspoon of mustard (if using). Before putting the top bread on, add 1 leaf of romaine, the turkey patties, and 12 Poblano peppers. Serve right away. Refrigerate any leftover patties in an airtight container for up to 5 days. Freeze for up to 3 months, sandwiched between parchment papers in an airtight container.

Nutritional facts

Calories: 279| Carbohydrates: 24 g| Protein: 23 g| Fat:

10 g| Sodium 216 mg

113. Turkey Nuggets with Roasted Vegetables

Preparation time: 10 minutes

Cooking time: 25 minutes

Serving: 2

Ingredients

- 1 small zucchini (cut into long strips)
- 1 small bunch of broccoli
- 1 medium carrot (cut into long strips)
- 1 small leek (cut into long strips)
- 1 medium-sized red bell pepper (cut into long strips)
- ½ small eggplant (cut into long strips)
- 8 asparagus spears (trimmed)
- Avocado or olive oil cooking spray
- ¼ cup whole-grain panko bread crumbs
- 1 tablespoon olive or avocado oil (divided)
- 5 ounces boneless, skinless turkey breast (diced)
- 1 teaspoon Italian Seasoning Blend
- ½ cup cooked brown lentils (if using canned lentils, be sure to rinse and drain before using)

Instructions

Preheat the oven to 400 degrees Fahrenheit. Using parchment paper, line a baking sheet.

Using cooking spray, gently coat the zucchini, carrots, leek, bell pepper, eggplant, broccoli, and asparagus on the baking sheet. Bake until the veggies are soft and gently browned, approximately 25 minutes. Meanwhile, combine the bread crumbs, Italian seasoning, and 12 tablespoons of oil in a medium mixing bowl. Set aside the turkey after coating it with the breadcrumb mixture.

Heat the remaining 12 tablespoons of oil in a medium skillet over medium-high heat. Lightly fry the turkey nuggets for 5 to 8 minutes on each side until golden brown and cooked, with an internal temperature of 165 degrees Fahrenheit. Add 14 cups of lentils, half of the roasted veggies, and half of the turkey nuggets to a large mixing bowl. Serve right away and enjoy. You can refrigerate the leftovers for up to 5 days and freeze them for 3 months in an airtight container.

Nutritional facts

Calories: 287| Carbohydrates: 22 g| Protein: 18 g| Fat: 21 g| Sodium 296 mg

114. Turkey-Stuffed Bell Peppers

Preparation time: 10 minutes

Cooking time: 40 minutes

Serving: 4

Ingredients

- 1 tablespoon avocado oil
- 8 ounces lean ground turkey
- ½ cup finely chopped yellow onion
- 1 cup grated carrots
- ½ teaspoon garlic powder
- ½ teaspoon Italian Seasoning Blend
- ¼ teaspoon paprika
- 2 cups cooked white rice
- 2 medium bell peppers, any color, halved lengthwise
- 2 tablespoons grated Parmesan cheese

Instructions

Preheat the oven to 400 degrees Fahrenheit. Heat the oil in a medium pan or skillet over medium heat. Toss together the turkey, onion, carrots, garlic powder, Italian seasoning, and paprika in a large mixing bowl. Cook for 4-5 minutes or until the meat is thoroughly cooked. Cook for another 2 minutes after adding the cooked rice. Fill a baking dish halfway with cut bell pepper halves. Fill each pepper half with one-quarter of the meat mixture (approximately 34 cups) and 12 tablespoons of Parmesan cheese. Bake until the peppers have softened, around 25 to 30 minutes. Serve right away and enjoy. Refrigerate cooled leftovers in an airtight jar for up to four days.

Nutritional facts

Calories: 307| Carbohydrates: 32 g| Protein: 19 g| Fat: 11 g| Sodium 86 mg

115. Chili with Flatbread Crackers

Preparation time: 5 minutes

Cooking time: 1 hour 10 minutes

Serving: 4

Ingredients

- 1 tablespoon avocado or olive oil
- 8 ounces extra-lean ground beef
- 1 large onion (diced)
- ¼ teaspoon ground cumin
- 1 tablespoon garlic powder
- 2 cups of no-salt-added or low-sodium beef broth
- 2 cups no-salt-added canned tomato sauce

- 1 medium red bell pepper (diced)

- 1 (4-ounce) can of green chili peppers (drained, rinsed, and diced)

- ½ teaspoon dried oregano

- 2 tablespoons chili powder

- 1 teaspoon dried basil

- ½ teaspoon dried thyme

- 16 Garlic and Herb Flatbread Crackers or store-bought

Instructions

Cook the ground beef in a big stockpot over medium heat for about 5 minutes or brown. Cook for about 2-3 minutes or until the onion is tender. Stir together the broth, tomato sauce, bell pepper, chili peppers, chili powder, garlic powder, basil, oregano, thyme, and cumin. Bring the saucepan to a boil, then reduce to medium-low heat. Cook for an hour. With 4 flatbread crackers, serve 1 cup of chili. You can refrigerate the leftovers for up to 5 days and freeze them for 3 months in an airtight container.

Nutritional facts

Calories: 303| Carbohydrates: 27 g| Protein: 20 g| Fat: 13 g| Sodium 126 mg

116. Beef Shish Kebabs with Grilled Corn

Preparation time: 10 minutes + 1 hour to marinate

Cooking time: 10 minutes

Serving: 6

Ingredients

- ½ cup apple cider vinegar

- ½ cup olive or avocado oil

- 1 pound beef sirloin (cut into 1½-inch cubes)

- ½ teaspoon freshly ground black pepper

- ½ teaspoon dried oregano

- ¼ teaspoon garlic powder

- 2 medium white onions (quartered)

- 2 medium green bell peppers, cut into 1½-inch squares

- 1 medium red bell pepper, cut into 1½-inch squares

- 6 medium corn cobs (husks and silks removed)

Instructions

Combine the vinegar, olive oil, black pepper, oregano, and garlic powder in a large mixing basin. In a large mixing basin, combine the sirloin, onions, and bell peppers and toss to coat evenly. Cover the bowl with plastic wrap and then place it in the fridge for 1 hour to marinate. Soak wooden skewers in water for 32 minutes before using them.

Alternate sirloin, bell peppers, and corn on the skewers with the meat and chopped veggies. Over medium heat, grill the kebabs and corn. Cook for 4 to 6 minutes on each side of the kebabs. Depending on how well you prefer your meat cooked, you may modify the cooking times. Cook for approximately 10 minutes, turning often. Serve immediately.

Nutritional facts

Calories: 381| Carbohydrates: 28 g| Protein: 31 g| Fat: 27 g| Sodium 136 mg

117. Taco-Seasoned Roast Beef Wraps

Preparation time: 10 minutes

Cooking time: 0 minutes

Serving: 2

Ingredients

- 2 tablespoons low-fat cream cheese

- 2 (10-inch) flour tortillas

- 4 ounces low-sodium roast beef

- ½ cup fresh spinach

- 1 teaspoon Taco Seasoning

- 2 tablespoons diced red onion

- 2 tablespoons pimento or cherry pepper (halved lengthwise)

Instructions

Put 1 tablespoon of cream cheese on one tortilla and top with taco seasoning. Top with 14 cups spinach, 1 tablespoon red onion, 1 tablespoon pimento pepper and 2 ounces roast meat.

Nutritional facts

Calories: 278| Carbohydrates: 27 g| Protein: 18 g| Fat: 11 g| Sodium 116 mg

118. Sweet and Sour Beef Meatballs

Preparation time: 10 minutes

Cooking time: 20 minutes

Serving: 10

Ingredients

For Meatballs:

- 2 pounds extra-lean ground beef

- ½ cup diced zucchini

- ½ cup diced carrots

- 1 garlic clove (minced)
- ½ cup diced yellow onion
- ¼ cup plain Unsweetened Almond Milk
- 1 tablespoon low-sodium soy sauce
- ½ cup diced orange bell pepper
- 1 tablespoon low-sodium Worcestershire sauce
- ¼ teaspoon ground cinnamon

For Sauce:

- 1 cup water
- 1/3 cup apple cider vinegar
- ¼ cup packed brown sugar
- ½ teaspoon sesame oil
- 6 tablespoons cornstarch
- 2 tablespoons low-sodium soy sauce
- 1 (40-ounce) can of pineapple chunks in 100 percent juice (reserve 1½ cups pineapple juice)
- 2 cups cooked white or brown rice (for serving)

Instructions

Preheat your oven to 375 degrees Fahrenheit and prepare a baking sheet with parchment paper. Remove from the equation. Mix the meat, zucchini, carrots, bell pepper, onion, almond milk, soy sauce, Worcestershire sauce, garlic, and cinnamon in a large mixing basin until everything is well blended. Overworking the meat will result in toughness.

Roll them into 1-inch balls and place them on the baking sheet that has been prepared. Bake for 15 minutes or until the meatballs are cooked through.

For Sauce:

Meanwhile, whisk the water, vinegar, brown sugar, cornstarch, soy sauce, and sesame oil in a large stockpot until well blended. Reduce the heat to low and cook, stirring periodically, until the sauce thickens, approximately 5 minutes. Toss in the pineapple chunks to coat. Add the meatballs to the sauce after cooking and toss to coat. Plate 12 cups of rice and 5 meatballs to serve. Refrigerate the leftovers for up to 5 days and freeze them for 3 months in an airtight container.

Nutritional facts

Calories: 294 | Carbohydrates: 46 g | Protein: 20 g | Fat: 4 g | Sodium 96 mg

119. Spiced Lamb Meatballs with Roasted Vegetables

Preparation time: 10 minutes

Cooking time: 40 minutes

Serving: 5

Ingredients

For Vegetables:

- 1 medium head cauliflower (cut into florets)
- 2 cups carrots, cut into medallions
- 1 teaspoon ground cumin
- 2 tablespoons avocado or olive oil
- ½ teaspoon paprika
- ½ teaspoon ground cinnamon
- ¼ teaspoon freshly ground black pepper
- 1¼ cup frozen corn

For Meatballs

- 1 pound ground lamb
- ¼ cup whole-wheat bread crumbs
- 1 teaspoon garlic powder/1 garlic clove (minced)
- ½ teaspoon ground coriander
- 1 large egg (lightly beaten)
- ½ teaspoon ground cumin
- ½ teaspoon ground cinnamon
- ½ teaspoon freshly ground black pepper
- ½ teaspoon paprika
- ½ teaspoon ground cayenne pepper (optional)

For Sauce

- ¼ cup tahini
- 2 tablespoons finely chopped fresh mint/1 tablespoon dried mint
- Freshly squeezed lemon juice
- 3 to 4 tablespoons of warm water

Instructions

Preheat the oven to 400 degrees Fahrenheit. Spread the carrots and cauliflower in a single layer on a baking tray lined with parchment paper. Drizzle with oil and toss to cover with cumin, cinnamon, paprika, and black pepper. Roast for 20–25 minutes or until golden brown.

To make Meatballs:

Meanwhile, add the lamb, bread crumbs, egg, garlic powder, coriander, cumin, paprika, cinnamon, black pepper, and cayenne (if using) in a large mixing bowl and stir until well blended. Overworking the flesh will result in toughness. Make 1-inch balls out of the dough. After 20 to 25 minutes of cooking, turn the veggies and add the meatballs to the pan. Put the meatballs in the middle of the veggies and return the pan to the oven. Bake for 15 minutes or until well done.

To make Mint Tahini Sauce:

Meanwhile, whisk the tahini, water, mint, and lemon juice to taste in a small bowl. Toss the corn with the vegetable and meatball combination after heating it according to package directions. When the dish is done, divide it into four equal parts and top with the sauce.

Refrigerate the leftovers for up to 5 days and freeze them for 3 months in an airtight container. The sauce can be kept in the refrigerator; however, freezing it is not recommended. Make the sauce when you're ready to reheat frozen meals.

Nutritional facts

Calories: 436| Carbohydrates: 26 g| Protein: 18 g| Fat: 19 g| Sodium 226 mg

120. Baked Apple Pork Chops with Wild Rice and Green Beans

Preparation time: 10 minutes

Cooking time: 1 hour Serving: 4

Ingredients

- ½ cup water
- Avocado or olive oil cooking spray
- 2 tablespoons avocado or olive oil
- 2 tablespoons brown sugar or honey
- 2 tablespoons apple cider vinegar
- 9 ounces center loin pork chops
- 2 medium apples (cored and sliced)
- 1 pound of green beans (trimmed)
- ½ teaspoon freshly ground black pepper
- 1 cup cooked wild rice
- ½ teaspoon salt

Instructions

Preheat the oven to 325 degrees Fahrenheit. Spray an oven-safe pan with cooking spray and line it with foil. Heat the oil in a skillet or pan over medium-high heat. Brown the pork chops for 2 to 3 minutes on each side. Remove the pan from heat and set it in the oven pan with the cut apples on top. Spray the green beans gently with cooking spray and arrange them in a single layer in the pan. Deglaze the skillet with the water, scraping up the browned bits from the bottom with a spatula. Over the pork chops and green beans, pour the sauce. Brown sugar, vinegar, salt, and pepper are sprinkled over the pork chops. Bake for 30 minutes with the pan covered with foil. Cook for a further 15 to 20 minutes after uncovering.

Meanwhile, microwave the wild rice until it is hot. Serve the pork with green beans, apples, and rice on the side. Refrigerate the leftovers for up to 5 days and freeze them for 3 months in an airtight container.

Nutritional facts

Calories: 304| Carbohydrates: 35 g| Protein: 10 g| Fat: 21 g| Sodium 116 mg

121. Lamb Chops with Redcurrant and Mint Sauce

Preparation time: 10 minutes

Cooking time: 40 minutes

Serving: 4

Ingredients

- 4 Lean lamb chops
- 4 tablespoon Redcurrant jelly
- 1 tablespoon Lemon juice
- 4 tablespoon Water
- 1 tablespoon Mint sauce

Instructions

Combine the redcurrant jelly, mint sauce, lemon juice, and water in an ovenproof dish.

Trim the chops and set them on the sauce-coated plate, rotating to coat each chop well.

Bake uncovered for 35-40 minutes at 180°C (Gas Mark 4) in a preheated oven until the lamb is cooked. Before serving, the sauce may need to be thinned with cornflour and a little water.

Nutritional facts

Calories: 352| Carbohydrates: 55 g| Protein: 41 g| Fat: 15 g| Sodium 166 mg

122. Lamb and Ginger Stir Fry

Preparation time: 10 minutes

Cooking time: 8 minutes

Serving: 2

Ingredients

- 225g Minced lamb
- 1 teaspoon Ginger root (chopped or grated)
- 1 tablespoon Cooked peas
- A little sunflower oil
- Pepper to taste

Instructions

Fry, the lamb for 3-4 minutes in the sunflower oil or until lightly browned. Add the ginger and continue to cook for another 2-3 minutes, stirring constantly. Season with pepper, and add the peas.

Nutritional facts

Calories: 177| Carbohydrates: 18 g| Protein: 13 g| Fat: 12 g| Sodium 126 mg

123. Spicy Chicken

Preparation time: 10 minutes

Cooking time: 18 minutes

Serving: 4

Ingredients

- 450g Chicken (cut into 2.5cm cubes)
- 1 medium onion (finely chopped)
- ½ teaspoon Ginger powder
- 300ml homemade chicken stock or water
- 2 tablespoons Cooking oil
- 2 tablespoon Mango chutney
- 1 teaspoon soft dark brown sugar
- 150ml Cream

Seasoning:

- 55g Plain flour
- 1 tablespoon hot curry powder
- 1 teaspoon Paprika
- 1 teaspoon Cayenne pepper
- 1 tablespoon Turmeric
- 1 teaspoon ground coriander
- 1 teaspoon Chili powder
- 1 teaspoon ground cumin

Instructions

Mix all of the seasoning ingredients and coat the chicken in it. In a big heavy-bottomed frying pan, heat the oil. Fry the chicken until it is completely sealed. Cook for 1-2 minutes after adding the onion and ginger. Combine the stock of water, chutney, and sugar in a mixing bowl. Bring to a boil, then reduce heat and cook for 15 minutes. Stir in the cream and heat until the sauce is warmed through. Be careful not to boil the sauce.

Nutritional facts

Calories: 394| Carbohydrates: 40 g| Protein: 10 g| Fat: 22 g| Sodium 236 mg

124. Chicken and Sweetcorn Stir fry

Preparation time: 10 minutes

Cooking time: 20 minutes

Serving: 2

Ingredients

- 200g Chicken breast (cut into strips)
- 2 small Shallots (chopped)
- 1 small can of sweetcorn (drained)
- 2 tablespoon half fat crème fraiche (heaped)
- 30g Frozen peas
- Black pepper to taste
- Oil for frying

Instructions

In a little oil, fry the shallots and chicken for around 15 minutes, stirring periodically until done. Add peas and sweetcorn and cook for another 5 minutes. Stir in the crème Fraiche and season with black pepper.

Nutritional facts

Calories: 390| Carbohydrates: 40 g| Protein: 19 g| Fat: 23 g| Sodium 136 mg

125. Spicy Barbeque Chicken

Preparation time: 10 minutes

Cooking time: 15 minutes

Serving: 4

Ingredients

- 4 chicken breasts (skinned)
- 25g Plain flour
- 2 tablespoons Sunflower oil
- 1 tablespoon Red wine vinegar
- 4 tablespoons Lemon juice
- 1 Garlic clove (skinned and crushed)
- 2 tablespoon Low-fat natural yogurt
- 1 teaspoon Ginger root (grated)
- 1 teaspoon Paprika
- 1 teaspoon crushed peppercorns

Instructions

Mix 2 tablespoons of lemon juice, yogurt, flour, vinegar, oil, garlic, paprika, and peppercorns.

Make 1cm-wide parallel incisions in the chicken and sprinkle with lemon juice. Cover the chicken with the yogurt better in a mixing dish. Chill for many hours, rotating now and then. Cook the chicken for about 10-13 minutes on each side on the grill or barbecue or until the juices flow clear.

Nutritional facts

Calories: 278| Carbohydrates: 42 g| Protein: 16 g| Fat: 21 g| Sodium 206 mg

126. Sweet and Sour Pork

Preparation time: 10 minutes

Cooking time: 12 minutes

Serving: 4

Ingredients

- 225g Lean pork (cut into 2.5cm cubes)
- 1 teaspoon Olive oil
- 1 teaspoon ground ginger
- Black pepper to taste
- Vegetable oil for frying

Batter

- 175g Plain flour
- 300ml Water
- ½ teaspoon Oil
- 1 small Egg

Sweet and sour sauce

- 2 tablespoons White sugar
- 6 tablespoon Vinegar
- 200ml Water
- 2 teaspoon Cornflour (heaped)
- 2 tablespoon Pineapple juice (can be drained from a tin)
- Black pepper to taste
- A few drops of red food coloring

Instructions

Make a well with a spoon in the center of the flour in a basin. Gradually beat in the water while adding the egg. Set aside for 20 minutes after adding the oil. In a saucepan, combine the sugar, pepper, vinegar, water, and pineapple juice and bring to a boil for 2 minutes. Maintain a high temperature.

Combine the pork cubes, olive oil, pepper, and ground ginger in a mixing dish. Mix thoroughly. Remove any extra flour from the pork after coating it in 2 tablespoons. In a mixing bowl, combine the meat and the batter. In a deep pot, heat the oil until it is hot but not smoking. Cook the battered pork for 8-9 minutes or until golden brown in the oil. Drain it on absorbent paper. Serve in a hot serving dish with the sauce on top.

Nutritional facts

Calories: 676| Carbohydrates: 22 g| Protein: 18 g| Fat: 24 g| Sodium 336 mg

127. Fried Pork with Noodles

Preparation time: 10 minutes

Cooking time: 15 minutes

Serving: 2

Ingredients

- 225g Lean pork fillet (chicken may also be used)
- 2 medium Carrots (pre-boiled and drained)
- ½ teaspoon Thai seven-spice powder
- 1 medium Courgette (pre-boiled and drained)
- 1 small Red pepper (pre-boiled and drained)
- Oil for frying

Instructions

Cut the pork into thin strips and cook them in a wok or frying pan with a tiny oil. Carrot, courgette, and pepper should be cut into strips and added to the pork. Stir in the Thai seven-spice powder and simmer, often stirring, until the meat is well cooked.

Nutritional facts

Calories: 280| Carbohydrates: 40 g| Protein: 39 g| Fat: 11 g| Sodium 136 mg

128. Texas Hash

Preparation time: 10 minutes

Cooking time: 45 minutes

Serving: 4

Ingredients

- 450g Minced beef
- 2 tablespoon Rice
- 1 large onion (chopped)
- 1 tin of Tomatoes
- 1 teaspoon Sugar

- 1 Green pepper (deseeded and thinly sliced)
- 1 tablespoon Worcestershire sauce
- Pepper to taste
- Oil for frying

Instructions

In a little amount of oil, fry the onion until golden. Stir in the mince until it is fully broken up. Toss in the pepper and whisk to combine. Add the Worcestershire sauce and rice to the tin of tomatoes (fruit and liquid) in the pan. Stir well and boil for a few minutes until part of the tomato juice has evaporated. Cook for about 45 minutes in a moderate oven at 180°C (Gas Mark 4) in a greased ovenproof dish.

Nutritional facts

Calories: 324| Carbohydrates: 30 g| Protein: 27 g| Fat: 17 g| Sodium 136 mg

129. Shepherd's Pie

Preparation time: 10 minutes

Cooking time: 40 minutes

Serving: 4

Ingredients

- 450g Minced lamb (or beef)
- 1 large onion (chopped)
- 1 tablespoon Oil
- 2 medium Carrots (chopped)
- 1 tablespoon Flour
- 1 Stock cube
- 300ml Boiling water
- 675g Potatoes
- 25g Grated cheese
- Knob of margarine
- Dash of milk
- Black pepper to taste

Instructions

In a large pot, heat the oil, then add the onion and sauté until golden. Brown the mince in a little amount of oil. Boil carrots, drain and add to the mince and onions in a separate pan. Combine 300ml boiling water with the stock cube, add to the meat and season with black pepper. Boil the potatoes until they become tender, then drain and mash with a splash of milk, a knob of margarine, and a pinch of black pepper. Place the mince in an ovenproof dish, top with mashed potatoes, and then cheese. Cook for 30-40 minutes at 190°C (Gas Mark 5) until the potato is golden brown.

Nutritional facts

Calories: 478| Carbohydrates: 35 g| Protein: 34 g| Fat: 22 g| Sodium 136 mg

130. Spicy Beef

Preparation time: 10 minutes

Cooking time: 10 minutes

Serving: 4

Ingredients

- 560g Sirloin/rump steak
- 4 small Tomatoes (peeled, de-seeded and sliced)
- 1-2 Garlic cloves (crushed)
- 4 Celery sticks
- 2 tablespoons clear honey
- 2-3 teaspoons Mild chili powder
- 2 tablespoon Paprika
- 1 Beef stock cube
- 4 Spring onions (thinly sliced)
- 300ml Water
- 2 tablespoons Red wine vinegar
- 2 tablespoons Sunflower oil
- 1 tablespoon Worcestershire sauce

Instructions

The steak should be cut into 1cm pieces. Mix in the paprika and chili powder until the steak is uniformly coated. Allow for an hour of marinating time. Celery should be cut into 5cm lengths and then 5mm thick strips. Add the stock cube to the water and the Worcestershire sauce, honey, and red wine vinegar to make the stock. Before adding the steak, heat the oil and sauté the celery and garlic for a minute. Fry for another 3-4 minutes on high heat. Cook until the meat is fully covered and sizzling hot before adding the sauce. Heat the tomatoes until they are hot. Serve right away.

Nutritional facts

Calories: 414| Carbohydrates: 38 g| Protein: 46 g| Fat: 21 g| Sodium 96 mg

131. Saffron and Coriander Rice

Preparation time: 10 minutes

Cooking time: 10 minutes

Serving: 2

Ingredients

- 100g Basmati rice

- 5 Cloves

- 2 tablespoons fresh coriander (chopped)

- 5 Whole cardamom pods (optional)

- Pinch of saffron threads

Instructions

Combine the rice, cloves, and cardamom in a pan of boiling water. Cook according to the package directions. Remove the spices and drain the rice. Toss the rice back into the pan.

Stir in the saffron threads, cover them, and set aside 5-10 minutes. Serve immediately after adding the chopped coriander.

Nutritional facts

Calories: 184 | Carbohydrates: 7 g | Protein: 4 g | Fat: 1 g | Sodium 116 mg

132. Tomato Pasta

Preparation time: 10 minutes

Cooking time: 15 minutes

Serving: 2

Ingredients

- 1 tablespoon Olive oil

- 1 small onion (chopped)

- Pinch Sugar

- 1 Garlic clove (chopped)

- A 400g Tin of chopped tomatoes (drained)

- Pinch Mixed herbs

- Pinch Black pepper

- 200g Dried pasta

Instructions

In a pot, brown the onion and garlic. Combine the tomato tin, black pepper, herbs, and sugar in a mixing bowl. Cook for 10 to 15 minutes. Meanwhile, cook the pasta until it is well-boiled. Drain and combine with the tomato sauce for a delicious meal.

Nutritional facts

Calories: 452 | Carbohydrates: 17 g | Protein: 14 g | Fat: 21 g | Sodium 336 mg

133. Salmon Pasta with Butter

Preparation time: 10 minutes

Cooking time: 15 minutes

Serving: 4

Ingredients

- 350g Salmon fillets

- 600ml Water

- 400g Dried pasta

- 15g Butter or margarine

- 2 tablespoons Plain flour

- 2 tablespoons fresh tarragon (chopped)

- 1 Bay leaf

- Black pepper to taste

Instructions

Poach the salmon fillets for 15 minutes or until cooked in the water with the bay leaf. Remove the fish from the water and save the cooking liquid (450ml). In a big pot of boiling water, cook the pasta. Flake the fish while the pasta is boiling, discarding the skin and any bones. In a small saucepan, melt the butter or margarine, add the flour and whisk for 1 minute. Remove the pot from the heat and slowly stir in the fish stock. Return the sauce to heat and whisk until it thickens. Stir in the tarragon after seasoning the sauce with black pepper. Drain the pasta and set it aside. Mix the pasta with the salmon and sauce and toss gently.

Nutritional facts

Calories: 394 | Carbohydrates: 30 g | Protein: 27 g | Fat: 15 g | Sodium 126 mg

134. Tuna and Potato Bake

Preparation time: 10 minutes

Cooking time: 40 minutes

Serving: 2

Ingredients

- 450g Boiled potatoes

- 1 medium Onion

- A 550g Tin of tuna (drained)

- ½ Lemon juice

- 2 pinches Nutmeg

- Black pepper to taste

- 4 Eggs (beaten)
- Butter/margarine as required

Instructions

Cook the onion for 10 minutes at a low temperature. Combine the onion and potato in a mixing bowl. Combine the pepper, lemon juice, nutmeg, and beaten eggs in a mixing bowl.

Toss the tuna with the potato mixture and flake it up. Brush the top of the mixture with melted butter or margarine and place it in an ovenproof dish that has been properly buttered. Preheat the oven to about 200°C (Gas Mark 6) and bake for 30 minutes until the top is well browned.

Nutritional facts

Calories: 521| Carbohydrates: 70 g| Protein: 76 g| Fat: 6 g| Sodium 146 mg

135. Lemon Sole with Ginger and Lime

Preparation time: 10 minutes

Cooking time: 15 minutes

Serving: 2

Ingredients

- 2 medium plaice fillets
- 1 teaspoon Ginger
- 2 tablespoons Sunflower oil
- ½ Lime
- Lime slices to garnish
- 2 metal skewers

Instructions

Each sole fillet should be cut in half along the middle. Each strip should be cut in half lengthwise. Roll the sole strips neatly on each skewer, and thread four rolls. Brush the remaining ingredients over the fish. Refrigerate for 10 minutes or up to 3 hours, covered. Grill over medium heat until done, flipping once and sprinkling with any residual marinade. Serve with lime slices as a garnish.

Nutritional facts

Calories: 245| Carbohydrates: 35 g| Protein: 31 g| Fat: 21 g| Sodium 176 mg

136. Root Vegetable Loaf

Preparation time: 20 minutes

Cooking time: 55 minutes

Serving: 6 to 8

Ingredients

- 1 onion

- 2 tablespoons of water
- 2 cups of grated carrots
- 1½ cups of sweet potatoes
- 1½ cups of gluten-free rolled oats
- ¾ cup of butternut squash purée
- 1 teaspoon of salt

Instructions

Preheat the oven to 350 degrees Fahrenheit. Using parchment paper, line a loaf pan. Sauté the onion in the water in a large saucepan over medium heat for approximately 5 minutes or until tender. Add the sweet potatoes and carrots. 2 minutes after cooking, Take the saucepan off the heat. Combine the oats, butternut squash purée, and salt in a mixing bowl. Mix thoroughly. Press the mixture evenly into the loaf pan that has been prepared. Bake for 50 to 55 minutes, uncovered, and in a preheated oven until the bread is firm and brown. Allow 10 minutes to cool before slicing.

Nutritional facts

Calories: 169| Carbohydrates: 34 g| Protein: 5 g| Fat: 2 g| Sodium 442 mg

137. Baked Falafel

Preparation time: 15 minutes

Cooking time: 30 minutes

Serving: 6 to 8

Ingredients

- 3 cups cooked chickpeas
- ⅓ Cup of tahini
- 1 tablespoon ground cumin
- 4 garlic cloves
- ½ teaspoon of salt
- 1 small bunch of basil
- Water (for thinning)

Instructions

Preheat the oven to 350 degrees Fahrenheit. Using parchment paper, line a baking sheet. Combine the chickpeas, cumin, tahini, garlic, and salt in a food processor. Blend until almost completely smooth. Toss in the basil. Pulse until fully combined. If required, add 1 or 2 tablespoons of water to assist the ingredients in forming a ball, but don't overdo it. Wet and pasty mixtures should be avoided. 2 tablespoons of dough, rolled into a ball, should go on the baking sheet. Press the ball into a 1-inch thick patty with the bottom of a glass or your palm. Repeat with the remaining chickpea mixture; 24 patties should result. Preheat the oven to 350°F and bake the patties for 30 minutes. The falafels will be mushy right out of the oven, but they will firm up as they cool.

Nutritional facts

Calories: 242| Carbohydrates: 24 g| Protein: 12 g| Fat: 12 g| Sodium 225 mg

139. Bean Burgers

Preparation time: 15 minutes

Cooking time: 35 minutes

Serving: 4 to 6

Ingredients

- 1 tablespoon of ginger
- 1 cup gluten-free rolled oats
- 3 cups cooked navy beans (1½ cups dried)
- 2 cups yam/sweet potato purée (about 2 yams/sweet potatoes, steamed and mashed)
- ½ cup sunflower seed butter or tahini
- ½ teaspoon of salt

Instructions

Pulse the oats a few times in a food processor until a rough meal forms. Combine the beans, yam purée, sunflower seed butter, ginger, and salt in a large mixing bowl. Blend until well combined. You may smooth it out entirely or leave it somewhat lumpy. Refrigerate for thirty minutes to firm up the mixture.

Preheat the oven to 350 degrees Fahrenheit. Use parchment paper or Silpat to line a baking sheet. Scoop the mixture onto the prepared sheet using a 13-cup or 12-cup measuring. (The scoop size is determined by the size of the burgers you desire.)

Gently pat the ingredients down to make 1-inch thick patties. This recipe makes around 12 patties. Preheat the oven to 350°F and bake the sheet for 35 minutes. Halfway through the cooking period, flip the burgers.

Nutritional facts

Calories: 581| Carbohydrates: 81 g| Protein: 27 g| Fat: 19 g| Sodium 355 mg

138. Black Bean Chili

Preparation time: 10 minutes

Cooking time: 60 minutes

Serving: 6

Ingredients

- 2 onions
- 2 tablespoons water
- 4 cups cooked black beans
- 1 (28-ounce) can of crushed tomatoes
- 4 teaspoons of chili powder

- 1½ teaspoons salt

Instructions

Sauté the onions in the water in a large saucepan over medium heat for approximately 5 minutes or until tender. Combine the black beans, tomatoes, chili powder, and salt in a bowl. Bring the water to a boil. Reduce heat to a low setting. Cook, stirring periodically, for 1 hour. Adjust the seasoning to taste if required.

Nutritional facts

Calories: 294| Carbohydrates: 55 g| Protein: 18 g| Fat: 1 g| Sodium 858 mg

140. Vegetable Spring Roll Wraps

Preparation time: 20 minutes

Cooking time: 0 minutes

Serving: 6

Ingredients

- 10 rice paper wrappers
- 2 cups of baby spinach
- 1 cup grated carrot
- 1 cucumber (cut into thin, 4-inch-long strips)
- 1 avocado (cut into thin strips)

Instructions

Place the veggies in front of you on a chopping board on a level surface. Fill a large, shallow basin halfway with heated water—hot enough to fry the wrappers but not too hot to touch.1 wrapper should be soaked in water before placing it on the cutting board. 14 cups spinach, 2 tablespoons shredded carrot, a few cucumber slices, and 1 or 2 avocado slices go into the wrapper's center. Fold the sides over the center, then burrito-style roll the wrapper from the bottom (the side closest to you). Continue with the rest of the wrappers and veggies. Serve right away.

Nutritional facts

Calories: 246| Carbohydrates: 36 g| Protein: 4 g| Fat: 10 g| Sodium 145 mg

141. Tahini-Kale Noodles

Preparation time: 5 minutes

Cooking time: 10 minutes

Serving: 4

Ingredient

- ½ cup tahini
- 8 ounces brown rice spaghetti or buckwheat noodles
- 4 cups of kale
- ¾ cup hot water

- ¼ teaspoon of salt
- ½ cup of chopped parsley

Instructions

Follow the package directions for cooking the noodles. Toss in the greens in the final 30 seconds of cooking time. Drain the noodles and greens in a colander. Place in a large mixing basin. Combine the tahini, boiling water, and salt in a medium mixing bowl. Add extra water if you want a thinner sauce. Toss the noodles with parsley and sauce. Toss to coat evenly. Adjust the seasoning to taste if required. Serve warm or chilled.

Nutritional facts

Calories: 404| Carbohydrates: 54g| Protein: 15 g| Fat: 18 g| Sodium 223 mg

Chapter 4: Dinner Recipes

1. Grilled Salmon with Papaya-Mint Salsa

Preparation time: 10 minutes

Cooking time: 40 minutes

Serving: 4

Ingredients

- 4 salmon steaks
- 1/4 cup papaya
- 1/4 cup bell pepper
- 1 teaspoon fresh ginger
- 1 tablespoon pimiento
- 1 tablespoon fresh mint
- 1 tablespoon rice wine or white vinegar
- 1 tablespoon fresh lime juice
- ¼ cup green onion
- 1 teaspoon jalapeño pepper
- Vegetable oil cooking spray

Instructions

In a bowl, add and mix all of the ingredients for the salsa, except the salmon. Refrigerate round about 30 minutes after covering. Cooking Oil the grill or broiler pan lightly. Sauté the salmon on both sides with pepper. 5 minutes on each side on the grill or under the broiler, or until done. 1/4 cup salsa on top of each salmon steak.

Nutritional facts

Calories: 194| Carbohydrates: 3 g| Protein: 25 g| Fat: 8.9 g| Sodium 116 mg |

2. Rosemary Sage Burger with Apple Slaw and Chive Mayo

Preparation time: 10 minutes

Cooking time: 20 minutes

Serving: 4

Ingredients

Burgers:

- 6 ounces 90 percent extra-lean ground round beef
- 4 whole-grain buns
- 6 ounces lean ground pork
- 1 tablespoon fresh rosemary (chopped)
- 1/4 teaspoon salt

- 1 cup baby spinach leaves
- 1 teaspoon ground sage

Chive mayo:

- 1/2 cup nonfat sour cream
- 2 tablespoons chives (chopped)
- 1 dash pepper
- 1 dash salt

Apple slaw:

- 3 medium green apples (peeled, cored and grated)
- 2 teaspoons extra-virgin olive oil
- 1 teaspoon fresh lemon juice

Instructions

Preheat the grill to medium-high temperature. In a medium-size mixing basin, combine the beef, pork, rosemary, sage, and salt; shape into 4 patties. Combine the ingredients for the chive mayo in a small bowl. Combine the slaw ingredients in a medium mixing basin. Patties should be grilled for 4 minutes on each side or until juices flow clear. Toast the buns and sprinkle the chive mayo on top of each one. Place the burger on the bread, then add the slaw and a few spinach leaves.

Nutritional facts

Calories: 284| Carbohydrates: 22 g| Protein: 19 g| Fat: 21 g| Sodium 144 mg | Potassium 166 mg | Phosphorus 61 mg|

3. Peach Pork Tenderloin

Preparation time: 10 minutes

Cooking time: 45 minutes

Serving: 8

Ingredients

- 2 pork tenderloins (1 pound each, trimmed)
- 3 medium peaches (firm but ripe, pitted, and wedged)
- Fresh ground black pepper per taste
- 1/2 teaspoon olive oil
- 1/2 cup white wine vinegar
- 1/3 cup packed light brown sugar
- 1/2 cup water
- 1 lemon (juiced)
- Salt (optional)
- 2 teaspoons whole-grain mustard
- 1/4 teaspoon pepper

- 1/4 teaspoon rosemary

Instructions

Preheat the grill to medium-high. Season the pork with pepper after patting it dry (and salt lightly, if you wish). Grill pork for roughly 10 minutes on each side on a lightly greased grill. In a saucepan, mix peaches, wine/vinegar, brown sugar, and water while cooking. Squeeze the juice from the lemon peel strips into the pan. Cook, covered, for 5 minutes on medium to high heat or until peaches are soft. With a slotted spoon, transfer solid ingredients to another bowl. To the juice in the pan, add mustard, a sprinkle of salt, and 1/4 teaspoon pepper. Transfer 1/3 cup of the fluid to a bowl, add the chopped rosemary, and brush over the pork; continue grilling for another 10 to 15 minutes. Allow pork to cool on a chopping board. Remove from heat and add peaches and rosemary sprigs to the remaining liquid in the saucepan. Simmer for a few minutes until it gets thick. Pork should be sliced and served with peach sauce.

Nutritional facts

Calories: 194| Carbohydrates: 15 g| Protein: 12 g| Fat: 19 g| Sodium 236 mg |

4. Salmon with Pineapple Salsa

Preparation time: 10 minutes

Cooking time: 25 minutes

Serving: 6

Ingredients

- 1 1/2 pounds salmon fillets

Marinade:

- 2 tablespoons low-sodium soy sauce
- 1/2 clove garlic (minced)
- 2 tablespoons brown sugar
- 1/4 cup unsweetened pineapple juice
- 1/4 teaspoon ground ginger
- 1 1/2 tablespoons apple cider vinegar

Pineapple salsa:

- 1/4 cup of red pepper (finely chopped)
- 2 tablespoons of red onion (finely chopped)
- 1 cup fresh pineapple (chopped)
- 2 tablespoons fresh cilantro (finely chopped)

Instructions

Combine soy sauce, garlic, ginger, brown sugar, pineapple juice, and apple cider vinegar in a small bowl to form a marinade. Measure out 2 tablespoons of pineapple salsa and keep aside. Fill a big resealable plastic bag or a glass dish halfway with fish. Turn to coat thoroughly with the remaining marinade, omitting 2 tablespoons (set aside). Refrigerate for at least 15 minutes for added taste. In a small bowl, combine 2 tablespoons of the marinade, pineapple, bell pepper, cilantro, and onion until thoroughly combined. Take the salmon out of the marinade. Remove and discard any leftover marinade. Grill the salmon for 6 to 7 minutes on each side over medium-high heat, or until it flakes easily with a fork, coating with the remaining 2 tablespoons of marinades halfway through. Serve the salmon with pineapple salsa on the side.

Nutritional facts

Calories: 185| Carbohydrates: 8 g| Protein: 22 g| Fat: 24 g| Sodium 136 mg |

5. Lamb Saag

Preparation time: 1 hour

Cooking time: 4 hours

Serving: 4

Ingredients

- 1 tablespoon coconut or rapeseed oil
- 1 medium onion, peeled and finely sliced
- 500 grams lamb neck fillets, trimmed and cut into roughly 3–4cm chunks
- 60g medium Indian curry paste
- 50 grams dried red split lentils
- 200 grams of frozen spinach

Instructions

Preheat the oven to 180 °C. Heat the oil in a flame-safe pan and gently sauté the onion for 5 minutes, or till it gets softened and golden brown. Season the lamb chunks with sea salt and ground black pepper and cook for 3 minutes, flipping frequently or until browned on all sides. Cook for 1 minute with the lamb and onion after adding the curry paste. Stir in 500ml water with the lentils and spinach. Bring to a boil, then cover and bake for 1–4 hours, or until the lamb is tender and the sauce has thickened.

Nutritional facts

Calories: 361| Carbohydrates: 29 g| Protein: 31.5 g| Fat: 24 g| Sodium 76 mg |

6. Spiced Lamb and Minted Yogurt

Preparation time: 1 hour

Cooking time: 2 hours

Serving: 2

Ingredients

- ½ teaspoon ground cumin
- ½ teaspoon ground coriander

- 2 boneless lamb leg steaks

- 2 tablespoon olive oil

- 1 medium onion skinned cut into 12 small portions

- 1 pepper cut into roughly 3cm portions

- 1 medium courgette halved lengthwise cut into roughly 1.5cm slices

- For the minted yogurt sauce

- 100g full-Fats live Greek yogurt

- ½ small garlic clove, peeled and crushed

- 2 tablespoon finely chopped fresh mint leaves

Instructions

Combine the cumin, coriander, a pinch of sea salt, and plenty of ground black pepper on a plate. Coat both sides of the lamb steaks with the spice mixture and set aside. Combine the yogurt, garlic, and mint in a small dish, then add enough cold water to produce a drizzling consistency. Take a nonstick frying pan, heat 1 tablespoon of the oil and gently cook the onion, pepper, and courgette for 4–5 minutes, stirring frequently. Push the veggies to one side of the pan, add the remaining 1 tablespoon oil, and cook the steaks for at least 3 to 4 minutes on each side, or until done to your liking, over medium heat. (To avoid burning the vegetables, turn them occasionally while the lamb is cooking.) Allow 5 minutes of resting time before dividing between two dishes and drizzle with yogurt sauce.

Nutritional facts

Calories: 24| Carbohydrates: 6 g| Protein: 1 g| Fat: 2 g| Sodium 146 mg |

7. Meatballs in Tomato Sauce

Preparation time: 45 minutes

Cooking time: 50 minutes

Serving: 4

Ingredients

- 300 grams small good-quality beef meatballs (around 20)

- 1 tablespoon olive oil

- 1 medium onion, peeled and finely chopped

- 2 garlic cloves, peeled and crushed

- 400g can of chopped tomatoes

- 1 teaspoon dried oregano

- ¼–½ teaspoon crushed dried chili flakes (optional)

Instructions

Preheat the oven to 200 °C. Heat the oil in a flame-safe pan and gently sauté the onion for 5 minutes, or till it gets softened and golden brown. Cook the meatballs for 10 minutes on a baking sheet. Meanwhile, in a large nonstick frying pan, heat the oil and gently cook the onion for 5 minutes, or till it gets soft and golden browned, stirring frequently. Cook for a few seconds longer, stirring constantly. Bring the tomatoes, 200ml water, oregano, and chili, if using, to a gentle simmer in the pan. Cook for 5 minutes, stirring occasionally. Place the meatballs in the tomato sauce when removed from the oven. Cook for another 5 minutes, or until the meatballs are thoroughly cooked, seasoning with sea salt and ground black pepper. If the sauce is too dense, add a drop of water to thin it down.

Nutritional facts

Calories: 272| Carbohydrates: 16 g| Protein: 20 g| Fat: 2 g| Sodium 246 mg |

8. Simple Steak and Salad

Preparation time: 30 minutes

Cooking time: 25 minutes

Serving: 2

Ingredients

- 225 grams lean sirloin beef steak, cut in half

- 1 tablespoon olive oil

- 150 grams button chestnut mushrooms sliced if large

For the salad

- 100g mixed leaves

- ½ yellow pepper, deseeded and sliced

- 10 cherry tomatoes, halved

- 1/3 cucumber (around 135g), sliced

- 2 spring onions, trimmed and finely sliced

For the balsamic dressing

- 2 tablespoon extra-virgin olive oil

- 2 teaspoon balsamic vinegar

Instructions

To make the salad, combine all ingredients in a large mixing basin. Season the beef with sea salt and a generous amount of ground black pepper. Take a large nonstick frying pan, heat the oil over medium-high heat and cook the steaks for a minimum of 5 minutes on both sides or until done to your liking. Place the steaks on two hot plates to rest for a few minutes. Cook, frequently stirring, for 2 to 4 minutes or until the mushrooms are browned. On top of the steaks, spoon the sauce. Toss the salad with a slight drizzle of oil and vinegar. Serve with the steak and mushrooms on the side.

Nutritional facts

Calories: 346 | Carbohydrates: 30 g | Protein: 22 g | Fat: 5 g | Sodium 178 mg |

9. Pie with Swede Mash

Preparation time: 30 minutes

Cooking time: 45 minutes

Serving: 5

Ingredients

- 2 tablespoon olive oil
- 500 grams of lean minced beef (around 10% Protein)
- 1 medium onion, peeled and finely chopped
- 200 grams carrots (around 2 medium), trimmed and cut into roughly 1cm chunks
- 1 beef stock cube
- 2 tablespoon tomato purée
- 1 tablespoon Worcestershire sauce
- 1 teaspoon dried mixed herbs
- 1.2kg swede (around 1 large or 2 small), peeled and cut into roughly 3cm chunks
- 150 grams of frozen peas

Instructions

Take a large nonstick saucepan, heat the oil and cook the mince, onion, and carrots for 6 to 10 minutes, or until the mince is browned and the onions have softened. Over the mince, crumble the stock cube and add 700ml water, tomato purée, Worcestershire sauce, and herbs. Season generously with sea salt and powdered black pepper and bring to a simmer. Cook, stirring regularly and adding a little more water if necessary, for about 25 minutes, covered loosely. The tender and saucy mince should be used. Preheat the oven to 220°C. Meanwhile, throw the swede in a large pot and cover it with cold water to prepare the swede mash. Bring to a boil, covered with a cap. Cook for 20 minutes or until the potatoes are tender. Drain the swede in a sieve, then return to the pan and mash till smooth as possible with a potato masher. Sprinkle the salt and black pepper.

Cook for 1 minute, stirring regularly, after adding the frozen peas to the mince. Pour into a 2-liter shallow ovenproof dish with care. Bake for 15 to 25minutes, or till the swede is tipped with brown and the filling is bubbling, or until the swede is tipped with brown and the filling is bubbling. (Unlike mashed potatoes, it will not get golden.)

Nutritional facts

Calories: 354 | Carbohydrates: 27 g | Protein: 19 g | Fat: 21 g | Sodium 136 mg |

10. Beef Stroganoff

Preparation time: 35 minutes

Cooking time: 50 minutes

Serving: 2

Ingredients

- 250 grams sirloin steak
- 2 tablespoon olive oil
- 1 medium onion, peeled and thinly sliced
- 150 grams button chestnut mushrooms, sliced
- 1 teaspoon paprika (not smoked)
- 175ml beef stock (made with ½ beef stock cube)
- 2 teaspoon cornflour
- 30 grams (around 2 tablespoons) full-Protein crème Fraiche
- Chopped fresh parsley to serve

Instructions

Remove any excess Protein from the steak and cut it into long, thin strips that are no more than 1cm broad on a slight diagonal. Season with salt and ground black pepper.

Take a nonstick frying pan, and heat 1 tablespoon of the oil over medium-high heat. Cook for 2–3 minutes, or until the steak is browned but not cooked through. Return the pan to heat and remove the steak to a platter.

Cook for 4–5 minutes, or until the onions are softened and lightly browned, using the remaining oil in the pan is onion and mushrooms.

Cook for a few more seconds after adding the paprika.

Bring the broth to a low fire in the pan. Cook, frequently stirring, for 2 minutes.

Mix the cornflour and 1 tablespoon of fresh water in a small dish, then stir into the pan. Put the steak in the pan with the crème Fraiche. Warm the meat in the sauce for 1–2 minutes, stirring frequently and adding a splash of water if necessary. To serve, garnish with chopped fresh parsley.

Nutritional facts

Calories: 394 | Carbohydrates: 33 g | Protein: 22 g | Fat: 11 g | Sodium 56 mg |

11. Classic Burger with Celeriac Chips

Preparation time: 30 minutes

Cooking time: 30 minutes

Serving: 4

Ingredients

- ½ onion peeled and coarsely grated
- 1 garlic clove, peeled and finely grated
- 100 grams carrot (around 1 medium), trimmed

and finely grated

- 400 grams of lean minced beef with around 10% Protein
- ½ teaspoon flaked sea salt
- ½ teaspoon dried mixed herbs
- For the celeriac chips
- 750 grams celeriac peeled around 600 grams peeled weight
- 1 tablespoon rapeseed oil

Instructions

Preheat the oven to 220 °C.

To create the celeriac chips:

1. Cut the celeriac into 1.5cm slices and then chips using a sharp knife.
2. Combine with the oil, a pinch of sea salt, and a generous amount of ground black pepper in a mixing bowl.
3. Toss everything together thoroughly.
4. Bake for 20 minutes after scattering onto a baking tray.
5. Return to the oven for another 5–10 minutes or until the chips are soft and gently browned.

Make the burgers in the meantime. Take a mixing bowl, add the onion, garlic, carrot, minced, salt, and dried mixed herbs, season with black pepper, and mix well with your hands. Make four balls out of the mixture and flatten them into burger shapes. Because they will shrink as they cook, make them a little flatter than you think they should be. Cook the burgers without any additional grease in a large nonstick frying pan over medium heat for 10 minutes or till it become lightly browned and cooked through, rotating periodically. With a spatula, press the burgers now and then to ensure equal cooking. Serve the chips on four hot plates with a burger on the side.

Nutritional facts

Calories: 394| Carbohydrates: 0 g| Protein: 10 g| Fat: 21 g| Sodium 236 mg |

12. Beef Rending

Preparation time: 40 minutes

Cooking time: 1 hour

Serving: 4

Ingredients

- 600-gram beef braising steak cut into roughly 4cm pieces
- 6 garlic cloves, peeled
- 50 grams fresh ginger roughly chopped

- 2 medium red onions, peeled and quartered
- 1 teaspoon crushed dried chili flakes
- 2 tablespoons coconut or rapeseed oil
- 400ml can of coconut milk
- 3 tablespoon soya sauce
- 1 beef stock cube
- ½ teaspoon cinnamon
- 2 lemongrass
- lime wedges, to serve

Instructions

Preheat the oven to 170 °C. Sea salt and black pepper should be used to season the beef. Pulse the garlic, ginger, onions, and chili flakes until very finely chopped in a food processor. Take a large nonstick frying pan, and heat 1 tablespoon of the oil over high heat. Transfer the meat to a flame-proof casserole dish in two batches and fry until lightly browned on all sides. Cook the garlic and onion combined in the same pan with the remaining oil for 5 minutes, stirring often. Stir in the coconut milk, soya sauce, and 200ml water to the casserole with the beef. Crumble the stock cube and stir in the cinnamon in a small bowl. Smash with a rolling pin before adding to the curry (this will release the flavor). Bring to a low simmer, stirring constantly. Cook for 234–314 hours in the oven, covered, or until the beef is meltingly soft.

Nutritional facts

Calories: 494| Carbohydrates: 36 g| Protein: 31.5 g| Fat: 12.5 g| Sodium 136 mg |

13. Speedy Pizza

Preparation time: 20 minutes

Cooking time: 20 minutes

Serving: 2

Ingredients

- 227 grams can of chopped tomatoes (400g can)
- 1 tablespoon tomato sauce
- ½ teaspoon dried oregano roughly chopped fresh oregano leaves
- 1 whole meal pitta bread, around 58 grams
- 2 roasted red peppers
- 2 chestnut mushrooms around
- 45 grams of very finely sliced mushrooms
- 35 grams grated mozzarella
- 1 tablespoon olive oil

Instructions

Preheat the grill to medium-high temperature. To make the pizza topping, strain the tomatoes over a strainer to eliminate extra liquid. (You don't have to press it.) Toss the tomato pulp with the tomato purée and oregano in a mixing dish. Season with a pinch of salt and a generous amount of freshly ground black pepper. Place the pita bread on a board and lightly toast it to warm it up, then gently cut it in half horizontally with a bread knife and separate the two oval pieces. Top with the peppers, mushrooms, and mozzarella after spreading the tomato sauce on the pita halves. Grilled for 4 to 5 minutes

Nutritional facts

Calories: 224| Carbohydrates: 9 g| Protein: 11.5 g| Fat: 18.5 g| Sodium 136 mg |

14. Smoked Haddock with Lentils

Preparation time: 25 minutes

Cooking time: 30 minutes

Serving: 2

Ingredients

- 2 tablespoon olive oil

- ½ medium onion, peeled and finely chopped

- 1 celery stick, trimmed and finely sliced

- 1 medium carrot, trimmed, halved lengthways and diagonally sliced

- 1 rosemary sprig or ¼ teaspoon dried rosemary

- 1 garlic clove very finely sliced

- 250 grams sachet of ready-cooked lentils

- 200ml vegetable stock (made with ½ stock cube)

- 140 grams smoked haddock or cod fillets, skinned

- A small handful of parsley leaves

Instructions

Heat the oil over low heat in a nonstick frying pan or a wide-based saucepan. Cook for 5 minutes, or till the onion becomes soft and carrots are tender but not browned. Cook for a few seconds more, constantly stirring, after adding the rosemary and garlic. Pour the stock over the lentils into the pan. Bring to a moderate simmer before adding the fish fillets. Season with freshly ground black pepper and, if desired, chopped parsley. Cook the fish for about 8 minutes or until it begins to flake. When probed with a knife, covered with a lid (or a heatproof plate). Top the lentils with the fish and serve on two warm plates or bowls.

Nutritional facts

Calories: 494| Carbohydrates: 0 g| Protein: 16 g| Fat: 21 g| Sodium 29 mg |

15. Pan-Fried Fish with Lemon and Parsley

Preparation time: 30 minutes

Cooking time: 20 minutes

Serving: 1

Ingredients

- 1 plaice fillet

- 15-gram butter

- 1 tablespoon extra-virgin olive oil

- 1 tablespoon fresh lemon juice

- Small bunch of fresh parsley

Instructions

Season the skinless side of the fish with salt and black pepper. Take a nonstick frying pan, and melt the butter with the oil over medium heat. Cook for 3 minutes with the place skin-side down. Turn carefully and cook for another 1–2 minutes on the other side, depending on the thickness of the fillet. (If you choose, you can carefully peel off the skin.) With a fish slice or spatula, lift the plaice onto a hot plate, skin side down. Return the pan to heat, add the lemon juice and parsley, and frequently whisk for a few seconds. To serve, pour the buttery liquids over the fish.

Nutritional facts

Calories: 367| Carbohydrates: 25 g| Protein: 33 g| Fat: 13 g| Sodium 125 mg |

16. Crunchy Fish Bites

Preparation time: 25 minutes

Cooking time: 30 minutes

Serving: 2

Ingredients

- 1 medium egg

- 40 grams quick-cook polenta (fine cornmeal)

- 20 grams of ground almonds

- 275 grams thick skinless white fish fillet (such as cod, haddock or Pollock), cut into roughly 3cm chunks

- 2 tablespoons olive or rapeseed oil

- Lemon wedges, to serve

Instructions

Use a small bowl, whisk the egg and season with salt and pepper. In a separate bowl, combine the polenta and almonds. Season with black pepper and sea salt. Turn the pieces of fish in the beaten egg one at a time until thoroughly coated, then toss in the polenta mixture. Place on a platter and set away. Place a big nonstick frying pan over medium heat and pour the oil. Fry the fish bites for

5–7 minutes, depending on thickness, until cooked through, golden brown, and crisp on all sides, flipping occasionally. Lemon is also served on the side for squeezing.

Nutritional facts

Calories: 384| Carbohydrates: 15 g| Protein: 33 g| Fat: 0 g| Sodium 99 mg |

17. Mediterranean Fish Bake

Preparation time: 20 minutes

Cooking time: 45 minutes

Serving: 2

Ingredients

- 1 medium red onion cut into 12 parts

- 1 red pepper cut into roughly 2cm chunks

- 1 courgette halved lengthways and cut into roughly 2cm chunks

- 2 medium tomatoes, quartered

- 1½ tablespoon olive oil

- 100 grams of sea bass or sea bream fillets

- 40 grams pitted black olives (preferably Kalamata), drained

- Juice ½ large lemon, plus extra wedges to serve

Instructions

Preheat the oven to 200 °C. Scatter the onion, pepper, courgette and tomato quarters on a large baking tray. Toss everything together with 1 tablespoon of oil drizzled on top. Roast for 20 minutes, seasoning with sea salt and freshly ground black pepper. Retrieve the dish from the oven and season the fish with pepper before placing it skin-side downwards amongst some vegetables. Sprinkle the olives on top after squeezing the lemon zest over the top. Return the dish to the oven for approximately 10 minutes until the vegetables are supple or the salmon is cooked through. Serve the fish and veggies on two hot plates with the remaining oil drizzled on top and lemon wedges on the side.

Nutritional facts

Calories: 274| Carbohydrates: 22 g| Protein: 11 g| Fat: 26 g| Sodium 146 mg |

18. Swedish Spicy Carrot with Cod

Preparation time: 30minutes

Cooking time: 35 minutes

Serving: 2

Ingredients
- 2 large carrots (around 300 grams), trimmed and thickly sliced

- 1 garlic clove, peeled

- 15 grams fresh root ginger, peeled

- 15 grams butter

- ½ tablespoon fresh lemon juice

- 150 grams thick, skinless cod fillets (or other white fish)

- 1 tablespoon olive oil

- Good pinch dried chili flakes

Instructions

Take a medium saucepan and add the carrots, garlic, and ginger to the water. Bring to a boil, then reduce to low heat and cook for 15 minutes, or until the vegetables are tender. Remove the carrot, garlic, and ginger from the pan, scoop out, set aside a ladleful of water (about 100ml), and drain. Return the potatoes to the pan with 3 tablespoons of the cooking liquid, the butter, and the lemon juice. Using a stick blender, blitz the carrots until they're a smooth, creamy purée, applying a little more boiling water if required. To taste, stir with salt and black pepper. Take it out of the equation. Coat the fish fillets on both sides with salt and black pepper. Heat the oil in a greased frying pan over medium heat. After adding the fish, cook for 4 minutes. Turn the fish over, sprinkle with a few chili flakes, and cook for 3–5 minutes more, depending on the thickness of each fillet. When the cod begins to flake into huge chunks, it is ready. Place the purée on two warmed plates and top with the fish.

Nutritional facts

Calories: 244| Carbohydrates: 33 g| Protein: 12 g| Fat: 19 g| Sodium 116 mg |

19. Ginger and Chili Baked Fish

Preparation time: 30 minutes

Cooking time: 40 minutes

Serving: 1

Ingredients

- 2 teaspoon olive oil

- 175 grams thick white fish fillet,

- 1 garlic clove, peeled and thinly sliced

- 15 grams of stem ginger

- 1 spring onion

- 1 red bird's eye chili,

- ½ small lime

- Handful fresh coriander leaves

Instructions

Preheat the oven to 200 °C. Drizzle the oil over a rectangle of kitchen foil on a baking tray. Place the fish on half of the foil, skin side down, with enough foil to cover it. Garlic, ginger, spring onion, and chili are sprinkled over the fish, and lime juice is squeezed over it. Toss the fish with salt and black pepper before folding the foil over it and rolling up the edges to seal it within. Because steam is required to cook the fish, make sure the package isn't too tight. Oven preheated to 350°F and bake the fish for approximately 20 minutes, or until a fork pierces the fish and it flakes into big pieces. Using a fish slice or spatula, carefully open the foil bundle and lift the fish onto a warming platter. Serve the fish with the cooking fluids, lots of fresh coriander, and lime wedges on the side.

Nutritional facts

Calories: 233 | Carbohydrates: 7 g | Protein: 31 g | Fat: 11 g | Sodium 346 mg |

20. Steak Tuna

Preparation time: 35 minutes

Cooking time: 50 minutes

Serving: 1

Ingredients

- 110 grams fresh tuna steak, cut into roughly 3cm chunks

- 1 tablespoon coconut or rapeseed oil

- 300–350 grams pack of stir-fry vegetables

- 2 tablespoon ready-made hoisin sauce

- Pinch crushed dried chili

Instructions

Sprinkle salt and black pepper on tuna. Heat the oil in a big nonstick frying pan or wok over high heat and stir fry the tuna and veggies for 3–4 minutes, or until the tuna is gently browned, or according to the package directions. Drizzle the hoisin sauce over the fish and veggies and toss for another 20– 30 seconds. If using, top with the chili flakes and serve right away.

Nutritional facts

Calories: 308 | Carbohydrates: 16 g | Protein: 31 g | Fat: 13 g | Sodium 224 mg |

21. Sesame Salmon with Broccoli and Tomatoes

Preparation time: 30 minutes

Cooking time: 25 minutes

Serving: 2

Ingredients

- 2 teaspoons rapeseed oil

- 2 pieces of salmon fillets

- 6 spring onions

- 12 tomatoes

- 200g broccoli, trimmed

- 1 tablespoon soya sauce

- 1 teaspoon Sesame oil

- ½ teaspoon crushed dried chili flakes

- 1 teaspoon sesame seeds

Instructions

Preheat the oven to 200 °C. Drizzle the oil over a baking tray. Place the salmon fillets down in the tray, spring onions and tomatoes, and season generously with ground black pepper. Heated the oven to 350°F and bake for 8 minutes. In the meantime, fill a pan halfway with water and bring it to a boil. Return the pot to a boil with the broccoli. Drain after 4 minutes of cooking. Place the broccoli on the baking tray after removing it from the oven. Soya sauce and sesame oil should be drizzled over the fish. Revert the salmon to the oven for the next 3 to 4 minutes, or until just done, then sprinkle with the chili powder and sesame seeds. Split it up between two heated plates to serve.

Nutritional facts

Calories: 224 | Carbohydrates: 20 g | Protein: 17 g | Fat: 21 g | Sodium 196 mg |

22. Thai Curry with Prawns

Preparation time: 20 minutes

Cooking time: 30 minutes

Serving: 2

Ingredients

- 1 tablespoon coconut oil

- 1 red pepper cut into roughly 2cm chunks

- 4 spring onions thickly sliced

- 20 grams root ginger, peeled and finely grated

- 3 tablespoon Thai red curry paste

- ½ Can use coconut milk of about 400ml

- 100g mange tout or sugar snap peas, halved

- 1 red chili, finely sliced

- 200 grams of cooked prawns

Instructions

Take a large nonstick frying pan, heat the oil over medium-high heat and stir-fry the pepper for 2 minutes. Cook for another minute, constantly stirring, after adding the spring onions, ginger, and curry paste. Fill the pan halfway with coconut milk and bring to a medium simmer. Add the mange tout or sugar snap peas and the chili if using. Return to low heat and cook for another 2 minutes, stirring occasionally. Heat for 1–2 minutes or until the prawns are heated. If the sauce becomes thick, too, add a drop of water. Serve with cauliflower rice that has just been cooked.

Nutritional facts

Calories: 374| Carbohydrates: 13.5 g| Protein: 9 g| Fat: 21 g| Sodium 352 mg |

23. Mussels with Creamy Tarragon Sauce

Preparation time: 20 minutes

Cooking time: 25 minutes

Serving: 2

Ingredients

- 1kg fresh, live mussels

- 1 tablespoon olive oil

- 1 medium leek, trimmed and thinly sliced (around 100 grams prepared weight)

- 2 garlic cloves, peeled and thinly sliced

- 100ml dry white wine

- 75g full-Protein crème fraiche

- 3–4 fresh tarragon stalks (around 5 grams), leaves picked and roughly chopped/1 teaspoon dried tarragon

Instructions

Remove the 'beards' by dumping the mussels into the sink and scrubbing them thoroughly under cold running water. Mussels with fractured shells or those that do not close when pounded on the sink's side should be discarded. Drain the ones that are good in a colander. Heat the oil over low heat in a deep, lidded, wide-based saucepan or shallow casserole. Gently sauté the leek and garlic for 2–3 minutes, or until softened but not browned. Season generously with salt and pepper after adding the white wine, crème Fraiche, and tarragon. Bring the wine to a simmer by increasing the heat under the pan. Cook for about 4 minutes, or until most of the mussels have steamed open, after stirring in the mussels and covering closely with a lid. Stir thoroughly, then cover and cook for another 1–2 minutes, or until the rest of the vegetables are done. Remove any mussels that haven't opened, divide the mussels between two bowls, and pour the tarragon broth over the top.

Nutritional facts

Calories: 381| Carbohydrates: 4 g| Protein: 27 g| Fat: 2 g| Sodium 236 mg |

24. Prawn Nasi Goreng

Preparation time: 20 minutes

Cooking time: 35 minutes

Serving: 2

Ingredients

- 2 tablespoon coconut

- 1 medium onion, peeled and diced

- 1 red pepper cut into roughly 2cm chunks

- ½ small Savoy cabbage leaves thinly sliced

- 2 garlic cloves, peeled and thinly sliced

- 20 grams root ginger, peeled and finely grated

- ½–1 teaspoon crushed dried chili flakes

- 200g cauliflower rice

- 2 tablespoon soya sauce

- 150 grams prawns

- Generous handful of fresh coriander leaves roughly chopped

- 20 grams roasted peanuts, roughly chopped

Instructions

Take a large nonstick frying pan or wok, and heat the oil over medium-high heat. 2–3 minutes, stirring constantly, stir-fry the onion, red pepper, and cabbage. Stir in the garlic, ginger, chili, and cauliflower rice for 2–3 minutes or until the cauliflower is heated. Cook for another 1–2 minutes, swirling and tossing until the prawns are heated, before adding the soy sauce, prawns, and half of the coriander if using. To taste:

1. Add extra soy sauce.

2. If using, top with the chopped nuts and the leftover coriander, and divide between bowls.

Nutritional facts

Calories: 354| Carbohydrates: 23 g| Protein: 21 g| Fat: 17 g| Sodium 86 mg |

25. Baked Salmon with Pea and Broccoli Mash

Preparation time: 30 minutes

Cooking time: 35 minutes

Serving: 2

Ingredients

- 15 grams butter, plus extra for greasing

- 225 grams of fresh salmon fillets

- 150 grams of frozen peas

- 150 grams broccoli cut into small florets and stalks thinly sliced

- 1 tablespoon finely chopped fresh mint (optional)

- Lemon wedges, to serve

Instructions

Preheat the oven to 200 °C. Line a small baking pan and lightly coat it with butter using foil. Season the salmon with a bit of salt and some ground black pepper and place it skin-side down on the foil. Depending on thickness, bake for 10–12 minutes. On the other hand, half-fill a pan with water and boil to prepare the pea and broccoli mash. Return the pot to a boil with the peas and broccoli. Cook, occasionally stirring, for 5 minutes or until the broccoli is cooked. Wash the veggies and return them to the pan with a tiny ladleful of the cooking water (about 75ml). Stir with a stick blender until almost smooth, adding the butter, mint if using, and 3 tablespoons of the conserved cooking water. Season to taste, and loosen with a splash of water if necessary. Split the mash among two heated plates and top with the seared salmon, which you can simply break open from the foil and discard. Serve with a lemon wedge. Serve with a wedge of lemon.

Nutritional facts

Calories: 440| Carbohydrates: 11 g| Protein: 34g| Fat: 7 g| Sodium 96 mg |

26. Baked Potato

- 1 medium potato
- 1/3 cup of flour
- 1 can of black beans
- 1/2 cup onion
- 3/4 teaspoon apple cider
- 1/2 teaspoon of chili powder
- 1 cup greens
- 1 cup panko for coating
- 1/4 cup olive oil
- 4 buns
- 1 teaspoon of garlic powder
- Pinch of salt

Toppings:

Avocado, mustard, greens, and tomato

Instructions

Cook the potato and combine it with the black beans in a mash. Continue to mash with a fork after adding the onion, vinegar, garlic powder, chili powder, salt, flour, and greens. Coat patties with panko and form them into four patties. Fry in a frying pan or saucepan and serve with your favorite toppings.

Nutritional facts

Calories: 365| Carbohydrates: 62 g| Protein: 15 g| Fat: 2 g| Sodium 146 mg |

27. Baked Salmon

Preparation time: 10 minutes

Cooking time: 1 hour 50 minutes

Serving: 4

Ingredients

- 4-ounce salmon fillets
- 2 cloves garlic
- 3 tablespoons of olive oil
- 1 teaspoon of basil leave
- 1/4 teaspoon of black pepper
- 1/2 tablespoon of lemon juice
- 1/2 tablespoon of parsley (chopped)
- Pinch of salt (optional)

Instructions

Prepare the marinade in a medium bowl by combining garlic, olive oil, basil leaves, salt, pepper, lemon juice, and parsley. Cover the salmon fillets with the marinade in a medium glass baking dish. Marinate for 1 hour in the refrigerator, rotating periodically. Preheat the oven to 375 degrees Fahrenheit. Fill the aluminum foil with fillets, top with marinade, and seal. Place the sealed salmon in the dish and bake for a minimum of 35 minutes or until fork-tender.

Nutritional facts

Calories: 244| Carbohydrates: 1 g| Protein: 21 g| Fat: 2 g| Sodium 56 mg |

28. Shrimp and Crab Gumbo

Preparation time: 10 minutes

Cooking time: 30 minutes

Serving: 6

Ingredients

- 1/4 cup olive oil
- 4 cups low-sodium chicken broth
- 1/3 cup all-purpose flour
- 1 cup bell pepper (chopped)
- 1 tablespoon celery leaves or diced celery
- 1 1/2 cups onion (diced)
- 1 clove of garlic (chopped)
- 1 cup green onion tops (diced)
- 4 cups water (divided use)
- 8 ounces uncooked fresh shrimp
- 6 ounces crab meat (can also use imitation crab meat)
- 1/4 cup fresh parsley (chopped)
- 1 teaspoon hot sauce (optional)
- 6 cups cooked white rice (1 cup mixed in; 5 cups

for serving gumbo over)

- Pepper to taste

Instructions

Heat the oil and flour over moderate heat in a large skillet to make a roux. Stir continually until the flour has taken on a pecan-colored hue. 1 cup water, bell pepper, onion, garlic, and celery leaves. Cook, covered, over low heat until the veggies are soft. Add 3 cups water and 4 cups low-sodium chicken broth to the pot on high heat. 5 minutes at a boil. Reduce the flame, and add the shrimp and crab meat. Cook for 10 minutes. Top with parsley and green onion tops. Reduce the heat of the stove setting and cook for 5 minutes. 1 cup cooked rice 1 cup cooked rice 1 cup cooked rice 1 cup cooked rice 1 cup cooked. Season with salt, pepper, and spicy sauce if desired. Gumbo should be served on overheated rice.

Nutritional facts

Calories: 415 | Carbohydrates: 60 g | Protein: 19 g | Fat: 12 g | Sodium 101 mg |

29. Chicken and Spanish rice

Preparation time: 5 minutes

Cooking time: 10 minutes

Serving: 5

Ingredients

- 1 cup onions
- 3/4 cup green pepper
- 5 cups cooked brown rice
- 1 tablespoon olive oil
- 1 can tomato sauce
- 1/2 teaspoon black pepper
- 1/4 teaspoon garlic
- 2 1/2 cups chicken breasts
- 1 teaspoon fresh parsley

Instructions

Cook onions and green peppers in oil in a large pan over medium heat for 5 minutes. Combine the tomato sauce, spices, salt, and pepper in a large mixing bowl. Bring to a boil and keep warm. Combine the chicken and cooked rice in a large mixing bowl. Bring to a boil and keep warm.

Nutritional facts

Calories: 394 | Carbohydrates: 9 g | Protein: 11 g | Fat: 21 g | Sodium 236 mg |

30. Grilled Malt Chicken with Peppers and Onion

Preparation time: 10 minutes

Cooking time: 55 minutes

Serving: 8

Ingredients

- 4 4-ounce chicken breasts (skinless)
- 1/2 teaspoon dried oregano
- 1 medium yellow bell pepper (sliced)
- 3 cloves garlic (minced)
- 1 medium red bell pepper (sliced)
- 1 medium onion (sliced)
- 4 ounces mushrooms, Cremini, or button (washed and sliced)
- Pinch salt and pepper to taste

Marinade:

- 1 shallot sliced
- 3 tablespoons malt vinegar
- 1/4 cup olive oil
- 1 teaspoon dried oregano
- 1/2 teaspoon salt
- 1/2 teaspoon black ground pepper

Instructions

Preheat the grill to medium-high. Mix all of the marinade ingredients well. In a resealable bag, combine the chicken and marinate. Allow 30 to 45 minutes for the chicken to marinate. Remove the chicken and set it aside to drain for a few minutes. To cook, place it on the grill. In a separate skillet, sauté the onion and pepper. Cook for 5 minutes before adding the mushrooms. Cook until all of the veggies are completely tender. Cook the chicken on the grill till it has cooked completely. Place the chicken first on the platter, then the veggies.

Nutritional facts

Calories: 155 | Carbohydrates: 40 g | Protein: 10 g | Fat: 21 g | Sodium 26 mg |

31. Satay Chicken

Preparation time: 40 minutes

Cooking time: 1 hour

Serving: 4

Ingredients

- 1 tablespoon. coconut or rapeseed oil
- Juice 1 lime (around 2 tablespoons.)
- ½ tsp. crushed dried chili flakes
- 2 tsp. dark soy sauce

- lime wedges, to serve

- 3 boneless, skinless chicken breasts (175g), cut into 16 long, thin strips

- 1 green chili (optional)

For the satay sauce

- 60g no-added-sugar crunchy peanut butter (around 4 tablespoons.)

- 1 tablespoon. dark soy sauce

- 15g root ginger (peeled and finely grated)

Instructions

If using coconut oil, slowly melt it in a small saucepan before pouring it into a medium mixing bowl. Add the lime juice, chili flakes, soy sauce, and black pepper to taste. Mix thoroughly. Toss in the chicken strips and thoroughly combine everything. Using the skewers, thread the chicken strips on. Working fast is necessary since the lime juice will begin to 'cook' the chicken. The coconut oil will start to harden. Cook the chicken for at least 3 to 5 minutes more on each side, depending on thickness, on a large, lightly greased griddle or nonstick frying pan over medium-high heat or until lightly browned and cooked through.

Meanwhile, make the satay sauce by combining the peanut butter, 4 tablespoons of water, soy sauce, and shredded ginger in a small saucepan. Heat on low heat, stirring regularly until the peanut butter softens and the mixture thickens and becomes glossy. If necessary, add a bit more soy sauce or water to taste. In individual dipping bowls or drizzled over the chicken, serve with lime wedges, chili, if using, and the warm sauce.

Nutritional facts

Calories: 155| Carbohydrates: 20 g| Protein: 10 g| Fat: 18 g| Sodium 276 mg |

32. Turkey fajitas

Preparation time: 50 minutes

Cooking time: 1 hour 30 minutes

Serving: 4

Ingredients

- 1 iceberg lettuce

- 1 tablespoon olive oil

- 400g thin turkey breast steaks finely sliced into thin strips

- 1 medium onion roughly chopped and cut into 12 small pieces

- 2 peppers, 1 red and 1 yellow, and roughly thinly sliced

- 1 teaspoon hot smoked paprika

- 1 teaspoon ground cumin

- 1 teaspoon coriander

- Fresh coriander leaves roughly chopped to serve

- 100g full-fat live Greek yogurt

- lime wedges, to serve

Instructions

Put the lettuce over and cut around the stalk end with a little knife to separate the leaves. At least eight leaves should be carefully peeled, removed, washed, and drained. Arrange the leaves on a serving dish or board. Cook the turkey, onion, and peppers in a large nonstick frying pan over medium heat for at least 5 to 10 minutes, or till the turkey is cooked and the veggies are softened and gently browned, tossing frequently. Stir in the spices and simmer for another 1–2 minutes. Season with a pinch of salt and a generous amount of freshly ground black pepper. Transfer the pan to the table or a hot dish and top with generous coriander. Fill the leaves with heated turkey, yogurt, and lime wedges for squeezing.

Nutritional facts

Calories: 195| Carbohydrates: 22 g| Protein: 19 g| Fat: 7 g| Sodium 236 mg |

33. Perfect Pulled Pork

Preparation time: 5 hours

Cooking time: 1 hour 30 minutes

Serving: 6

Ingredients

- 1kg pork shoulder joint, rind on

- For the marinade

- 45g tomato purée (around 3 tablespoons.)

- 30g chipotle paste (around 2 tablespoons.)

- juice 2 large oranges

- juice 2 limes

- 1 tsp. flaked sea salt

- 1 tsp. ground cumin

- 1 tsp. ground allspice

- 1 tsp. coarsely ground black pepper

Instructions

In a large non-metallic mixing basin, whisk the tomato purée, chipotle paste, orange and lime juice, salt, and spices to form the marinade. Please remove any remaining string from the pork and place it in the marinade. Turn the pork several times until it is well coated, then cover and marinate overnight in the refrigerator. Preheat the oven to 170 degrees Celsius. In a medium casserole, combine the pork and marinade, cover, and bake for 3 hours, or until the pork breaks apart when probed with a fork. After a couple of hours, check the pork and add a little more water if necessary to keep it moist. Shred the pork with forks on a board or hot dish, discarding the rind and fat. Serve with a spoonful of the spicy cooking liquid on top.

Nutritional facts

Calories: 159| Carbohydrates: 3 g| Protein: 18 g| Fat: 25 g| Sodium 262 mg |

34. Sausages with Onion Gravy and Cauliflower Mash

Preparation time: 5o minutes

Cooking time: 1 hour

Serving: 4

Ingredients

- 2 tsp. olive or rapeseed oil

- 12 good-quality, high-meat sausages (375-gram pack)

- 1 medium onion, peeled and thinly sliced

- 300ml hot broth (½ pork or ½ chicken broth cube)

- 2 tablespoon. reduced sugar tomato ketchup

- 2 teaspoons corn flour

For the cauliflower mash

- 1 medium cauliflower, trimmed, cut into small florets and stalk thinly sliced (700g prepared weight)

- 1 tablespoon olive oil

Instructions

Take a medium saucepan, half-full it with water, and bring it to a boil to prepare the cauliflower mash. Return the pot to a boil with the cauliflower. Cook for 15–20 minutes or until the vegetables are very soft. Return to the pan after draining. Add the olive oil, a pinch of sea salt, and powdered black pepper. Blend until smooth with a hand blending machine or in a food processor after cooling somewhat. You can also take a potato peeler to peel the potatoes well. Warm over low heat, stirring once in a while. Put the oil in a nonstick pan and gently cook the sausages for 5 minutes, flipping occasionally. Cook for 8 to 15 minutes, or until the sausages are fully cooked, and the onion is very soft and browned. Bring the stock and ketchup to a boil, then reduce to low heat. Mix the cornflour and one tablespoon of cold water in a small dish, then stir into the pan. Season with freshly ground black pepper and cook, constantly stirring, for 1–2 minutes, or until thickened and glossy. Season with salt and pepper to taste. Top the cauliflower mash with the sausages and gravy and serve on four hot plates.

Nutritional facts

Calories: 155| Carbohydrates: 40 g| Protein: 10 g| Fat: 21 g| Sodium 26 mg |

35. Cheat's One-Pot Cassoulet

Preparation time: 40 minutes

Cooking time: 1 hour

Serving: 4

Ingredients

- 1 tablespoon olive oil

- 6 spicy sausages (around 400g), such as Toulouse or spicy pork

- 1 large onion, peeled and thinly sliced

- 100 grams cubed smoked lardons, pancetta or bacon

- 400 grams can make haricot drained and rinsed

- 400 grams can of chopped tomatoes

- 1 teaspoon dried mixed herbs

- Generous handful of chopped fresh parsley to serve

Instructions

In a wide-based, nonstick skillet or flame-proof casserole, heat the oil, then add the sausages and cook, frequently rotating, for about 5 minutes, or until lightly browned on all sides. Remove from the pan and place on a cutting board. Cook for 3–5 minutes, frequently turning, until brown onion and pancetta. Return the sausages to the pan, cut them in half, and add the beans, tomatoes, and herbs. 150ml water was stirred in and brought to a slow simmer. Cook, stirring periodically, for 18–20 minutes, covered loosely. If the sauce is sticky too much, add a drop of water. Season to taste with sea salt and plenty of black pepper to serve, then toss in the parsley.

Nutritional facts

Calories: 276| Carbohydrates: 36 g| Protein: 11.5 g| Fat: 10 g| Sodium 339 mg |

36. Pan-Fried Pork with Apple and Leek

Preparation time: 50 minutes

Cooking time: 45 minutes

Serving: 2

Ingredients

- 2 pork loin steaks

- 1 tablespoon. olive

- 1 small apple

- 1 medium leek

- 200ml pork or chicken stock

- 1 tsp. Dijon

- 45g crème Fraiche

Instructions

Season each side of the pork with a pinch of sea salt and a generous amount of ground black pepper. Take a nonstick pan, warm the oil over medium heat, and fry the pork for 3 to 8 minutes, or until lightly browned and cooked through, depending on thickness. If you overcook the pork, it will become tough. Place on a platter that has been warmed. Cook for 2 minutes, or until the apple and leek are lightly browned and softened in the frying pan. Bring the broth and mustard to a boil, then reduce to low heat. Cook, constantly stirring, for 3 minutes, or until the leek is tender and the liquid has reduced by about two-thirds. Cook, constantly stirring, until the crème Fraiche has melted and is boiling. Before serving, place the pork in the pan and warm it.

Nutritional facts

Calories: 355| Carbohydrates: 32 g| Protein: 15 g| Fat: 8 g| Sodium 229 mg |

37. Peppered Pork Stir-Fry

Preparation time: 40 minutes

Cooking time: 45 minutes

Serving: 2

Ingredients

- 250 grams pork tenderloin sliced, cut in half lengthwise, then into 1cm slices

- 1 tablespoon coconut or rapeseed oil

- 320 to 350 grams pack mix vegetables

- 15 grams root ginger peeled and finely grated

For the spicy sauce

- 1 teaspoon cornflour

- 1 tablespoon soy sauce

- 1 teaspoon honey

- ¼ to ½ teaspoon chili flakes

Instructions

Season the pork with a little bit of salt and plenty of freshly ground black pepper. Take a large nonstick frying pan or wok, and heat the oil over medium-high heat. Stir in the pork for 3–4 minutes, tossing regularly, or until lightly browned and cooked through. Stir-fry the vegetables with the meat for 2–3 minutes. Cook for a few more seconds after adding the ginger. Combine the cornflour, soy sauce, honey, and chili in a separate bowl for the spicy sauce. Stir the veggies into the pan and toss everything together for 1–2 minutes or until cooked and shiny. If desired, top with a bit of additional soy sauce.

Nutritional facts

Calories: 276| Carbohydrates: 16 g| Protein: 12 g| Fat: 6 g| Sodium 39 mg |

38. Parma Pork

Preparation time: 1 hour

Cooking time: 1 hour

Serving: 3

Ingredients

- 1-kilogram butternut

- 400-gram pork tenderloin (fillet) trimmed of fat and sinew

- 3 slices Parma ham or prosciutto

Instructions

Preheat the oven to 200 °F and coat the baking tray with foil. Prick the whole, unpeeled squash with the tip of a knife 8–10 times on the baking tray. 1 hour in the oven. Wrap the pork in Parma ham or prosciutto in the meantime. Place the pork again in the oven, along with the squash, for another 20 to 30minutes, or till the pork is cooked completely and the squash is soft. (You should be able to easily pierce the squash with a knife.) Place the pork on a heating platter and cover with foil to rest.

Meanwhile, split the squash in half vertically, scoop out, and discard the seeds using a large spoon. Place the flesh in a basin after scooping it out of the skin. Season with salt and freshly ground black pepper, then mash thoroughly. Put the pork on a cutting wood board and slice it thickly, saving the resting juices. Serve the mash on hot plates with the pork on top. To serve, drizzle with the juices.

Nutritional facts

Calories: 308| Carbohydrates: 35 g| Protein: 25 g| Fat: 10 g| Sodium 39 mg |

39. Courgetti Spaghetti with Nuts, Spinach and Pancetta

Preparation time: 45 minutes

Cooking time: 30 minutes

Serving: 2

Ingredients

- 80g dried spaghetti

- 1 large courgette

- 50g cubed smoked lardons

- 1 tablespoon. olive oil

- 150g young spinach leaves

- 80g feta

Instructions

Bring a big pot half-filled with water to a boil. Bring to a boil again and simmer for 10 to 15 minutes, until either the spaghetti is cooked. Add the spiralized courgette and mix rapidly to combine, then drain through a colander and run under cold water for a few seconds. Meanwhile, in a nonstick saucepan with half the oil, toast the pine nuts and lardons for 2 to 3 minutes, frequently turning, until lightly browned. Return the pan to the heat after tipping it out onto a platter. Cook, frequently turning, for 1–2 minutes, or until the spinach is tender, with the remaining oil and spinach. Sprinkle with salt and pepper and simmer till two-thirds of the feta has melted, creating a creamy coating for the spinach. Return the spaghetti and courgette to the pot, add the spinach and feta sauce, and mix thoroughly for 1– 2 minutes over medium heat, using two forks. Divide the feta between two shallow bowls, top with the pancetta and pine nuts, and crumble the remaining feta on top.

Nutritional facts

Calories: 246| Carbohydrates: 46 g| Protein: 11 g| Fat: 19 g| Sodium 239 mg |

40. Lamb Chops with Minted Peas and Feta

Preparation time: 2 hours

Cooking time: 1 hour 45 minutes

Serving: 2

Ingredients

- 2 thick lamb loin chops around 175 grams or 4 lamb cutlets

- 1 teaspoon olive oil. For the crushed peas and feta

- 200g frozen peas

- 1 tablespoon olive oil

- 15-gram pine nuts toasted

- 1 red chili finely diced

- 10 grams fresh mint leaves finely chopped

- 50 grams feta

Instructions

Sauté the lamb on both sides with sea salt and powdered black pepper. Cook the chops for at least 3 to 7 minutes on each side, depending on thickness, or until done to taste, on a grill, barbeque, or frying pan over medium-high heat. In the end, switch to the fat side for 30 seconds. In the meantime, fill a pan halfway with water and bring it to a boil to create the minted peas. Cook for 3 minutes after adding the peas. Return the peas to the pan and lightly mash them. Add the olive oil, pine nuts, and chili, then top with the mint and feta crumbles. Toss lightly with a generous amount of ground black pepper. To serve, divide the lamb and smashed peas between two plates.

Nutritional facts

Calories: 286| Carbohydrates: 26 g| Protein: 17 g| Fat: 19 g| Sodium 289 mg |

41. Pork Meatballs

Preparation time: 10 minutes

Cooking time: 10 minutes

Servings: 4

Ingredients:

- 1 pound pork, ground

- 1/3 cup cilantro, chopped

- 1 cup red onion, chopped

- 4 garlic cloves, minced

- 1 tablespoon ginger, grated

- 1 Thai chili, chopped

- 2 tablespoons olive oil

Instructions:

In a bowl, combine the meat with cilantro, onion, garlic, ginger and chili, stir well and shape medium meatballs out of this mix. Heat a pan with the oil over medium-high heat, add the meatballs, cook them for 5 minutes on each side, divide them between plates and serve with a side salad.

Nutritional Facts:

Calories: 206| Carbohydrates: 6 g| Protein: 17 g| Fat: 4 g| Sodium 89 mg |

42. Pork with Peanuts

Preparation time: 10 minutes

Cooking time: 16 minutes

Servings: 4

Ingredients:

- 2 tablespoons lime juice

- 2 tablespoons coconut amino

- 1 and 1/2 tablespoons brown sugar

- 5 garlic cloves, minced

- 3 tablespoons olive oil

- Black pepper to the taste

- 1 yellow onion, cut into wedges

- and 1/2-pound pork tenderloin, cubed

- 3 tablespoons peanuts, chopped

- 2 scallions, chopped

Instructions:

Mix lime juice with amino and sugar in a bowl and stir well. Mix garlic with 1 and 1/2 teaspoon oil and some black pepper in another bowl and stir. Heat a frying pan or saucepan with the rest of the oil over medium-high heat, add meat, cook for 3 minutes and transfer to a bowl. Heat the same frying pan or saucepan over medium-high heat, add onion, stir and cook for 3 minutes. Add the garlic mix, return the pork, add the amino mix, toss, cook for 6 minutes, divide between plates, sprinkle scallions and peanuts, and serve.

Nutritional Facts:

Calories: 296| Carbohydrates: 20 g| Protein: 11 g| Fat: 8 g| Sodium 139 mg |

43. Pork and Veggies

Preparation time: 15 minutes

Cooking time: 1 hour

Servings: 6

Ingredients:

- 4 eggplants, cut into halves lengthwise
- 4 ounces olive oil
- 2 yellow onions, chopped
- 4 ounces pork meat, ground
- 2 green bell peppers, chopped
- 1-pound tomatoes, chopped
- 4 tomato slices
- 2 tablespoons low-sodium tomato paste
- 1/2 cup parsley, chopped
- 4 garlic cloves, minced
- 1/2 cup hot water
- Black pepper to the taste

Instructions:

Heat a frying pan or saucepan with the olive oil over medium-high heat, add eggplant halves, cook for 5 minutes and transfer to a plate. Heat the same frying pan or saucepan over medium-high heat, add onion, stir and cook for 3 minutes. Add bell peppers, pork, tomato paste, pepper, parsley and chopped tomatoes, stir and cook for 7 minutes. Arrange the eggplant halves in a baking tray, divide garlic in each, spoon meat filling and top with a tomato slice. Pour the water over them, cover the tray with foil, bake in the oven at 350 degrees for 40 minutes, divide between plates and serve.

Nutritional Facts:

Calories: 253| Carbohydrates: 12 g| Protein: 17 g| Fat: 8 g| Sodium 119 mg |

44. Pork and Sweet Potatoes

Preparation time: 10 minutes

Cooking time: 1 hour and 20 minutes

Servings: 8

Ingredients:

- 2 pounds sweet potatoes, chopped
- A drizzle of olive oil
- 1 yellow onion, chopped
- 2 pounds pork meat, ground
- 1 tablespoon chili powder
- Black pepper to the taste
- 1 teaspoon cumin, ground
- 1/2 teaspoon garlic powder
- 1/2 teaspoon oregano, chopped
- 1/2 teaspoon cinnamon powder
- 1 cup low-sodium veggie stock
- 1/2 cup cilantro, chopped

Instructions:

Heat a pan with the oil over medium-high heat, add sweet potatoes and onion, stir, cook for 15 minutes and transfer to a bowl. Heat the pan again over medium-high heat, add pork, stir and brown for 5 minutes. Add black pepper, cumin, garlic powder, oregano, chili powder, and cinnamon, stock, return potatoes and onion, stir and cook for 1 hour over medium heat. Add the cilantro, toss, divide into bowls and serve.

Nutritional Facts:

Calories: 296| Carbohydrates: 26 g| Protein: 11 g| Fat: 8 g| Sodium 209 mg |

45. Pork and Pumpkin Chili

Preparation time: 10 minutes

Cooking time: 1 hour and 30 minutes

Servings: 6

Ingredients:

- 1 green bell pepper, chopped
- 2 cups yellow onion, chopped
- 1 tablespoon olive oil
- 6 garlic cloves, minced
- 28 ounces canned tomatoes, no-salt-added and chopped
- and 1/2-pounds pork, ground
- 6 ounces low-sodium tomato paste
- 14 ounces pumpkin puree
- 1 cup low-sodium chicken stock
- 2 and 1/2 teaspoons oregano, dried

- 1 and 1/2 teaspoon cinnamon, ground
- 1 and 1/2 tablespoon chili powder
- Black pepper to the taste

Instructions

Heat a pot with the oil over medium-high heat, add bell peppers and onion, stir and cook for 7 minutes. Add garlic and the pork, toss and cook for 10 minutes. Add tomatoes, tomato paste, pumpkin puree, stock, oregano, cinnamon, chili powder and pepper, stir, cover, cook over medium heat for 1 hour and 10 minutes, divide into bowls and serve.

Nutritional Facts:

Calories: 276| Carbohydrates: 36 g| Protein: 11.5 g| Fat: 10 g| Sodium 339 mg |

46. Kale Steak Salad

Preparation time: 10 minutes

Cooking time: 12 minutes

Servings: 2

Ingredients:

- 2 peaches, chopped
- 3 handfuls kale, chopped
- 8 ounces pork steak, cut into strips
- 1 tablespoon avocado oil
- A drizzle of olive oil
- 1 tablespoon balsamic vinegar

Instructions:

Heat a pan with the avocado oil over medium-high heat, add steak strips, cook them for 6 minutes and transfer to a salad bowl. Add peaches, kale, olive oil and vinegar, toss and serve.

Nutritional Facts:

Calories: 244| Carbohydrates: 1 g| Protein: 21 g| Fat: 2 g| Sodium 56 mg |

47. Pork Roast

Preparation time: 10 minutes

Cooking time: 3 hours and 20 minutes

Servings: 6

Ingredients:

- 2- and 1/2-pounds pork roast
- Black pepper to the taste
- 1 teaspoon chili powder

- 1/2 teaspoon onion powder
- 1/4 teaspoon cumin, ground
- 1 teaspoon cocoa powder

Instructions:

In a roasting pan, combine the roast with black pepper, chili powder, onion powder, cumin and cocoa, rub, cover the pan, introduce it to the oven and bake at 325 degrees F for 3 hours and 20 minutes. Slice, divide between plates and serve with a side salad.

Nutritional Facts:

Calories: 155| Carbohydrates: 20 g| Protein: 10 g| Fat: 18 g| Sodium 276 mg |

48. Smoky Pork Chops

Preparation time: 10 minutes

Cooking time: 20 minutes

Servings: 4

Ingredients:

- 2 tablespoons olive oil
- 4 pork chops
- 1 tablespoon chili powder
- Black pepper to the taste
- 1 teaspoon sweet paprika
- 1 garlic clove, minced
- 1 cup coconut milk
- 1 teaspoon liquid smoke
- 1/4 cup cilantro, chopped
- Juice of 1 lemon

Instructions:

Mix pork chops with pepper, chili powder, paprika, and garlic in a bowl and rub well. Heat a pan with the oil over medium-high heat, add pork chops and cook for 5 minutes on each side. In a blender, mix coconut milk with liquid smoke, lemon juice and cilantro, blend well, pour over the chops, cook for 10 minutes more, divide everything between plates and serve.

Nutritional Facts:

Calories: 594.19| Carbohydrates: 60.42 g| Protein: 11.68 g| Fat: 34.08 g|

49. Pork with Dates Sauce

Preparation time: 10 minutes

Cooking time: 40 minutes

Servings: 6

Ingredients:

- and 1/2-pounds pork tenderloin
- 2 tablespoons water
- 1/3 cup dates, pitted
- 1/4 teaspoon onion powder
- 1/4 teaspoon smoked paprika
- 2 tablespoons mustard
- 1/4 cup coconut amino
- Black pepper to the taste

Instructions

In your food processor, mix dates with water, coconut amino, mustard, paprika, pepper and onion powder and blend well. Put pork tenderloin in a roasting pan, add the dates sauce, toss to coat very well, introduce everything in the oven at 400 degrees F, bake for 40 minutes, slice the meat, divide it and the sauce between plates and serve.

Nutritional Facts:

Calories: 332| Carbohydrates: 50 g| Protein: 7.4 g| Fat: 13.7 g| Sodium 226 mg |

50. Pork Chops and Apples

Preparation time: 10 minutes

Cooking time: 1 hour

Servings: 4

Ingredients:

- 1 and 1/2 cups chicken stock
- Black pepper to the taste
- 4 pork chops
- 1 yellow onion, chopped
- 1 tablespoon olive oil
- 2 garlic cloves, minced
- 3 apples, cored and sliced
- 1 tablespoon thyme, chopped

Instructions:

Heat a pan with the oil over medium-high heat, add pork chops, season with black pepper and cook for 5 minutes. Add onion, garlic, apples, thyme and stock, toss, introduce in the oven and bake at 350 degrees F for 50 minutes. Divide everything between plates and serve.

Nutritional Facts:

Calories: 332| Carbohydrates: 50 g| Protein: 7.4 g| Fat: 13.7 g| Sodium 226 mg |

51. Summer Shrimp

Preparation time: 10 minutes

Cooking time: 1 hour 5 minutes

Serving: 4

Ingredients

- 2 cloves garlic (smashed)
- 1 tablespoon olive oil
- 2 teaspoons fresh lime juice
- 1 teaspoon low-sodium Worcestershire sauce
- 1 teaspoon dried oregano
- 1/4 teaspoon freshly ground black pepper

Shrimp:

- 1 small red onion
- 16 serrano chilies
- 8 bamboo skewers (10 inches long, soaked in water for 30 minutes)
- 24 large fresh shrimp (about 1 pound, peeled and deveined)

Instructions

Blend or process all marinade ingredients until smooth in a blender or small food processor. Toss the shrimp with the marinade to thoroughly coat them in a mixing dish. Allow at least 10 minutes, but no more than 2 hours. Half the onion and then quarter each half. Using a skewer, thread 1 chili onto each skewer. Repeat with 1 shrimp and a piece of onion. Finish with a second chili on each skewer; heat a cast-iron grill pan or an electric or gas grill over high heat. Cook skewers, covered, for 5 minutes on each side, or until shrimp are cooked through and onions are browned and just soft. Serve with a side of salsa.

Nutritional facts

Calories: 360| Carbohydrates: 4 g| Protein: 28 g| Fat: 24 g| Sodium 166 mg |

52. Coffee-Ancho Chile Rubbed Flat Iron Steak

Preparation time: 10 minutes

Cooking time: 35 minutes

Serving: 4

Ingredients

- 4 4-ounce flat iron steaks Coffee-Ancho Chile Rub
- 1/2 cup chicken stock
- 1 1/2 teaspoons of water
- 1 teaspoon cornstarch

Instructions

Rub the spice rub all over the steaks and set aside 30 minutes before cooking. Cook to your desired level of doneness. Take the meat out, but keep it on the stovetop. Add the stock. Add the ingredients, including cornstarch and water, to a mixing bowl. Bring the broth to a boil, then whisk in the cornstarch slurry. Remove the stock from the heat as soon as it thickens, and dish it over the meat.

Nutritional facts

Calories: 128.6| Carbohydrates: 2.47 g| Protein: 12.96 g| Fat: 5.96 g| Sodium 221 mg |

53. Mushroom and Broccoli Risotto

Preparation time: 10 minutes

Cooking time: 15 minutes

Serving: 4

Ingredients

- 2 1/2 cups chicken stock
- 8 ounces button mushrooms (washed and sliced)
- 1/2 medium onion (diced)
- 1/4 pound broccoli florets (cut into bite-size pieces)
- 1 tablespoon olive oil
- 1 cup Arborio rice
- 2 cloves garlic (minced)
- 1/3 cup white wine
- 2 tablespoons Parmesan cheese (grated)
- Pepper to taste

Instructions

Bring chicken stock to a boil. Prepare the veggies and weigh the dry ingredients. Remove the stock from the heat after it has reached a boil and put it aside. Heat the olive oil in a medium-sized cooking pan and add the onion, mushrooms, and garlic. Cook until the onions are tender. Cook for a few minutes after adding the risotto and rice. Reduce the wine to half its original volume. 1 cup hot stock; continually mix rice while it absorbs the stock. Continue stirring as you add additional stock. Mix in the broccoli once all of the stock has been added. Add the ingredients, including Parmesan cheese and season to taste when the liquid has been absorbed, and the rice is tender.

Nutritional facts

Calories: 237| Carbohydrates: 7 g| Protein: 16 g| Fat: 14 g| Sodium 196 mg |

54. Sloppy Joe

Preparation time: 5 – 8 minutes

Cooking time: minutes

Servings: 3

Ingredients:

- ½ pound (225g) lean ground beef
- ½ cup chopped onions
- 3 whole-wheat hamburger buns, split
- ½ cup chopped green bell pepper
- 1 cup low-sodium tomato soup, undiluted

Instructions:

Cook beef in a nonstick pan over medium flame and onion and pepper until the beef is brown. Discard excess fat from the pan. Add tomato soup and mix well. Slow the flame and cook till the mixture is dry. Toast the buns if desired. Place the beef mixture on the bottom half of the buns.

Nutritional Facts:

Calories: 136| Carbohydrates: 22 g| Protein: 5 g| Fat: 6 g| Sodium 162 mg |

55. Sesame Chicken Veggie Wraps

Preparation time: 10 minutes

Cooking time: 5 – 10 minutes

Servings: 4

Ingredients:

For dressing:

- tablespoon orange juice
- ½ teaspoon sesame oil
- 1 tablespoon olive oil
- A pinch pepper
- ¼ teaspoon ground ginger
- A pinch salt

For wraps:

- 4 whole-wheat tortillas (8 inches/20cm each)
- ½ cup frozen shelled edamame
- 1 cup fresh baby spinach
- ½ cup chopped fresh sugar snap peas
- ¼ cup thinly sliced sweet red pepper
- ½ cup thinly sliced cucumber
- ¼ cup shredded carrots
- ½ cup cooked, chopped chicken breast

Instructions:

Follow the directions on the package and cook the edamame. Drain in a colander and rinse under cold running water.

To make the dressing:

Whisk together orange juice, sesame oil, olive oil, pepper, ginger, and salt in a bowl. Place drained edamame, chicken, spinach, sugar snap peas, red pepper, cucumber, and carrots in a bowl and toss well. Warm the tortillas. Spread the vegetable mixture on the tortillas. Fold like a burrito and serve.

Nutritional Facts

Calories: 221| Carbohydrates: 15 g| Protein: 5 g| Fat: 18 g| Sodium 26 mg |

56. Greek Chicken & Cucumber Pita Sandwiches with Yogurt Sauce

Preparation time: 15 minutes + marinating time

Cooking time: 8 minutes

Servings: 2

Ingredients:

- ½ teaspoon grated lemon zest
- 2 ½ teaspoons olive oil, divided
- 4 cloves garlic, minced, divided
- ½ pound (225g) chicken tenders
- ¼ teaspoon salt, divided
- 1 teaspoon chopped fresh dill
- 1 teaspoon chopped fresh mint
- 1 whole-wheat pita bread
- ¼ cup sliced red onion
- 1 tablespoon fresh lemon juice
- ½ tablespoon chopped fresh oregano or ½ teaspoon dried oregano
- Crushed red pepper to taste
- ½ English cucumber, halved, deseeded grated
- ¼ English cucumber, halved, sliced
- 6 tablespoons nonfat plain Greek yogurt
- ½ teaspoon ground pepper
- 2 lettuce leaves
- ½ cup chopped plum tomatoes

Instructions:

To make the marinade: Place lemon juice, lemon zest, oregano, crushed red pepper, 1 ½ teaspoon oil, and half the garlic in a bowl and stir. Place chicken and toss well. Cover and chill for 1 – 4 hours. Place grated cucumber in a fine wire mesh strainer to make cucumber sauce. Sprinkle 1/8 teaspoon salt over it. Let it remain this way for 15 minutes. Squeeze the cucumber for excess moisture. Place the squeezed cucumber in a bowl. Add

yogurt, dill, mint, 1 teaspoon oil, pepper, 1/8 teaspoon salt and remaining garlic and stir until well combined. Cover and chill until use. Set up your grill and preheat it to medium-high heat. Grease the grill grate with some oil and place chicken on the grill. Cook for 3 – 4 minutes. Flip sides and cook for another 3 – 4 minutes or until the internal temperature in the thickest part of the meat shows 165°F (75°C) on a meat thermometer. Spoon some cucumber sauce in half the pita and spread it evenly. Divide the chicken tenders among the pita halves and stuff the chicken tenders in the pita pockets along with lettuce, tomatoes, red onion, and cucumber slices.

Nutritional Facts

Calories: 311| Carbohydrates: 24g| Protein: 18.5g| Fat: 16g| Sodium 304 mg |

57. Lemon Tahini Couscous with Chicken & Vegetables

Preparation time: 10 minutes

Cooking time: 18 – 20 minutes

Servings: 2

Ingredients:

- ½ cup whole-wheat pearl couscous
- 1/8 cup water
- 1 tablespoon lemon juice
- ¼ teaspoon salt
- 1/8 teaspoon crushed red pepper
- 1 cup sliced mushrooms
- 2 cups coleslaw mix
- 6oz (170g) cooked, chopped chicken breast
- 2 tablespoons crumbled low-fat feta cheese
- Lemon wedges to serve (optional)
- 2 tablespoons tahini
- 1 teaspoon grated lemon zest
- 1 tablespoon olive oil, divided
- 1/8 teaspoon ground pepper
- 2 small cloves garlic, minced
- ¼ medium red bell pepper, chopped
- 2 cups baby spinach
- 1/8 cup toasted, sliced almonds
- ½ tablespoon chopped fresh parsley

Instructions:

Follow the directions on the package and cook the couscous. Once cooked, fluff the couscous using a fork. While the couscous is cooking, combine tahini, lemon juice, salt, crushed red pepper, water, ½ tablespoon oil, and pepper in a bowl. Pour ½ tablespoon oil into a nonstick skillet and heat over medium-high flame. When the oil is heated, add garlic and sauté for a few seconds until you get a nice aroma. Stir in mushrooms until mushrooms are slightly tender. Add coleslaw mix and spinach and stir well. Once spinach turns limp, add chicken, tahini sauce mixture, and couscous and toss well. Heat thoroughly. Divide into 2 plates. Garnish with almonds, parsley, feta cheese, lemon zest, and lemon wedges and serve.

Nutritional Facts:

Calories: 246| Carbohydrates: 40g| Protein: 6.2g| Fat: 9g| Sodium 399 mg |

58. Baked Chicken and Wild Rice

Preparation time: 10 minutes + soaking time

Cooking time: 60 minutes

Servings: 3

Ingredients:

- ½ pound (225g) boneless, skinless chicken breast halves, cut into 1-inch pieces (2,5cm)

- ¾ cup whole pearl onions

- 1 cup unsalted chicken broth

- 6 tablespoons uncooked wild rice

- ¾ cup chopped celery

- ½ teaspoon chopped fresh tarragon

- 6 tablespoons uncooked long-grain white rice

- ¾ cup dry white wine

Instructions:

Place chicken, onions, celery, ½ cup broth, and tarragon in a pan. Place the pan over medium flame and cook until the chicken is tender. Turn off the heat. Combine white rice, wild rice, ½ cup broth, and dry white wine in a baking dish. Set aside for 30 minutes to soak. Stir chicken and vegetable mixture into the baking dish of rice mixture. Cover the dish with foil and place it in an oven that has been preheated to 300°F (150°C) and bake until the rice is tender. It should take 45 – 50 minutes. If you see that there is no broth in the baking dish and the rice is not cooked, add more broth. Divide into 3 plates and serve.

Nutritional Facts:

Calories 214| Carbohydrates 19g| Protein 6.3g| Fat 14g| Sodium 91 mg |

59. Thai Chicken Pasta Skillet

Preparation time: 10 minutes

Cooking time: 20 minutes

Servings: 3

Ingredients:

- 3oz (85g) uncooked whole-wheat spaghetti

- ½ package (from a 10oz/280g package) of fresh sugar snap peas, trimmed, cut into strips on the diagonal

- 1 cup cooked shredded chicken

- 1 small cucumber, halved lengthwise, deseeded, cut into slices on the diagonal

- 1 teaspoon canola oil

- 1 cup julienne-cut carrot

- ½ cup Thai peanut sauce

- Fresh cilantro, chopped, to garnish (optional)

Instructions:

Follow the directions on the package and cook the spaghetti. Pour oil into a skillet and heat over medium-high flame. When the oil is heated, add carrot and sugar, snap peas and cook until the vegetables are crisp and tender. Stir in peanut sauce and chicken and mix well. Add spaghetti and toss well. Heat thoroughly. Divide into 3 plates. Scatter cucumber and cilantro on top and serve.

Nutritional Facts:

Calories 201| Carbohydrates 14 g| Protein 5 g| Fat 14 g| Sodium 222 mg |

60. Grilled Chicken with Pasta

Preparation time: 10 minutes

Cooking time: 25 minutes

Servings: 3

Ingredients:

- 1 boneless, skinless chicken breast (4oz/115g)

- 1 small white onion, chopped

- ½ cup canned or cooked white beans, unsalted

- 1/8 cup chopped fresh basil

- 1/8 cup grated parmesan cheese

- ½ tablespoon olive oil

- ½ cup sliced mushrooms

- 1 tablespoon chopped garlic

- 6oz (170g) uncooked Roselle pasta

- Pepper to taste

Instructions:

Follow the directions on the package and cook the pasta. You can grill the chicken on a grill or broil it in an oven. If you are using the grill, preheat the grill to high heat. Set the oven to broil mode and preheat the oven if you use the oven. Place rack 5–6 inches (12-15cm) below the heating element. Grease the grill grate or broiler pan with some oil.

Place chicken on the grill rack or in the broiler pan and grill the chicken for 5 minutes. Place chicken on your cutting board. When the chicken cools a little, cut it into strips. Place a nonstick pan on flame. Once the oil heats, stir in the onions and mushrooms. Once the mushrooms are tender, add white beans, basil, garlic, and chicken and stir. Add pasta and toss well. Sprinkle parmesan and pepper on top and serve.

Nutritional Facts:

Calories 262| Carbohydrates 41 g| Protein 7 g| Fat 8 g| Sodium 152 mg |

61. Chicken Chili

Preparation time: 15 minutes

Cooking time: 20 minutes

Servings: 10

Ingredients:

- 4 tablespoons extra-virgin olive oil
- 6 cloves garlic, minced
- 2 medium green bell peppers, chopped
- 2 large onions, chopped
- 4 cups cubed sweet potatoes
- 4 teaspoons ground cumin
- 4 tablespoons chili powder
- 2 teaspoon dried oregano
- 2 cans (15oz/425g each) of low-sodium cannellini beans, rinsed
- 2 cups frozen corn
- 1 ½ teaspoons salt
- 4 cups chicken stock
- 4 cups cooked, cubed chicken
- ½ teaspoon pepper or to taste

To serve:

- Sour cream
- Chopped cilantro
- Avocado, peeled, pitted, chopped

Instructions:

Whisk oil into a large soup pot and heat over the flame. When the oil is heated, add garlic and onion and cook for a couple of minutes. Stir in sweet potatoes and bell pepper and cook until vegetables are slightly cooked.

Add spices and oregano and stir for a few seconds until you get a nice aroma. Stir in beans and broth. Slow down the heat, cover the pot partially and cook for around 20 minutes when it begins to boil. Add corn and cook for a couple of minutes. Stir in chicken and heat thoroughly. Turn off the heat. Add salt and pepper and stir. Ladle into bowls. Serve with suggested toppings.

Nutritional Facts:

Calories 365| Carbohydrates 47 g| Protein 15 g| Fat 13 g| Sodium 551mg |

62. Chicken & Goat Cheese Skillet

Preparation time: 10 minutes

Cooking time: 10 minutes

Servings: 4

Ingredients:

- 1-pound (450g) boneless, skinless chicken breast, cut into 1-inch pieces (2,5cm)
- ¼ teaspoon pepper
- 2 cups 1-inch (2,5cm) cut fresh asparagus
- 6 plum tomatoes, chopped
- ¼ cup crumbled herbed fresh goat cheese +extra to serve
- ½ teaspoon salt
- 4 teaspoons olive oil
- 2 cloves garlic, minced
- 6 tablespoons low-fat milk
- Hot cooked rice or pasta to serve

Instructions:

Put a pan on flame, add oil, and let it heat. Sprinkle salt and pepper over the chicken and place in the pan. Cook until it is not pink anymore. Remove the chicken and place it in a bowl using a slotted spoon. Keep it warm. Place asparagus in the same pan and cook over medium-high flame for a minute. Stir in garlic and cook until you get a nice aroma. Add milk, tomatoes, and goat cheese and stir. Cover and cook for a few minutes until the cheese melts. Add chicken and stir. To serve: Place 1 ½ cups chicken mixture on each of the 4 serving plates. Place some hot cooked rice or pasta. Garnish with some more feta cheese, and serve.

Nutritional Facts:

Calories 524| Carbohydrates 51 g| Protein 13 g| Fat 31 g |Sodium 525 mg |

63. Chicken Chop Suey

Preparation time: 10 minutes

Cooking time: 20 minutes

Servings: 3

Ingredients:

- 2 teaspoons olive oil
- ¼ teaspoon dried tarragon
- ¼ teaspoon dried marjoram
- ¼ teaspoon dried basil
- ¼ teaspoon grated lemon zest
- 1 ½ tablespoon low-sodium teriyaki sauce
- ¼ cup pineapple tidbits
- 1 ½ tablespoon unsweetened pineapple juice
- 1 tablespoon cornstarch
- ½ pound (225g) boneless skinless chicken breasts, cut into 1-inch pieces (2,5cm)
- ¾ cup chopped carrots
- ½ can (from 8oz/225g can) sliced water chestnuts, drained
- ¼ cup chopped onion
- ½ medium tart apple, cored, chopped
- ½ cup cold water, divided
- 1 ½ cups hot cooked brown rice

Instructions:

Put a pan on flame, add oil, and let it heat. Pour oil into it and let it heat. Once the oil is heated, place the chicken in the skillet. Sprinkle lemon zest and the dry herbs and cook until the chicken is light brown. Add carrots, apple, water chestnut, onion, and pineapple and stir.   Add teriyaki sauce, pineapple juice, and half the water and stir. Lower the flame and cook until the chicken gets mushy or when it begins to boil. Whisk the remaining water and cornstarch in a bowl and pour into the skillet. Stir constantly until thick. Let it come back to a boil. To serve: Place ½ cup of rice on each plate. Spoon chicken chop Suey over the rice and serve.

Nutritional Facts:

Calories 221|Carbohydrates 0.9 g |Protein 11 g |Fat 17 g |Sodium 180 mg |

64. Cauliflower and Potato Curry

Preparation time: 10 minutes

Cook time: 15 minutes

Servings: 4

Ingredients

- 2 tablespoons of oil
- ½ onion, chopped
- 2-inch piece of ginger
- 3 garlic cloves
- 1 teaspoon of turmeric
- 1 teaspoon Of cumin
- 1 small cauliflower
- 1 medium potato
- 2 small tomatoes
- 1 small green chili
- ½ cup of water
- Juice of lemon
- ¼ cup of cilantro (leaves)
- 1 teaspoon of garam masala
- Rice or bread (for serving)

Instructions

Heat and cook in a saucepan or fry pan on medium heat. Cook, constantly stirring, until the onion is softened. Fry it until ginger and garlic are fragrant. Contribute the turmeric and cumin and mix well. Toss the cauliflower, potato, tomatoes, chili, and water in a bowl and whisk. Carry to a gentle simmer, then lower to low heat and cover. Cook for 25 minutes, stirring periodically, until the potatoes and cauliflower are cooked. Combine the lemon juice, cilantro, and garam masala in a mixing bowl. Serve with rice or toast as a side dish.

Nutritional Facts

Calories 387| Carbohydrates 42 g| Protein 17 g| Fat 15.7 g | Sodium 557 mg |

65. Wheat Bean Veggie Burgers

Preparation time: 10 minutes

Cook time: 15 minutes

Servings: 4

- Ingredients
- 1 cup canned white beans
- 1 cup cooked white rice
- 1 teaspoon of garlic powder
- 2 teaspoons of thyme
- ½ teaspoon of chipotle pepper
- ½ sweet onion
- ½ cup of corn
- ½ cup of red pepper
- Juice of 1 lemon

- 1/3 cup of flour
- 1 large egg
- Black pepper
- 2 teaspoons of oil (olive)

Instructions

Mash the beans using a potato masher in a large mixing dish, leaving a few whole beans if desired. Continuous stirring to integrate the rice, garlic powder, thyme, chipotle pepper, onion, corn, bell pepper, lemon, flour, and egg. Season with salt and pepper. Mold the material into four patties using your hands. Stir the olive oil in a large pan over medium heat. Cook the burgers for 5 minutes on one side until browned, then turn and cook for another 5 minutes on the other side.

Nutritional Facts

Calories: 594.19| Carbohydrates: 60.42 g| Protein: 11.68 g| Fat: 34.08 g| Sodium 216 mg |

66. Spinach Falafel Wrap

Preparation time: 10 minutes

Cook time: 15 minutes

Servings: 4

Ingredients

- 6 ounces spinach
- 1 Can chickpeas
- 2 teaspoons of ground cumin
- ¾ cup of flour
- 2 tablespoons of canola oil for frying
- ¼ cup 0f plain yogurt
- 2 garlic cloves
- Juice of 1 lemon
- Black pepper
- 4 tortillas
- 1 cucumber
- 2 slices onion
- Salad greens (for serving)

Instructions

To whither the spinach, please place it in a colander in the sink and pour boiling water over it. Allow cooling before pressing as much water as possible out of the spinach. Toss the spinach, chickpeas, cumin, and flour in a food processor. Pulse until everything is well combined. Spoon the mixture into tablespoon-size balls and flatten them into patties with your palms. One tablespoon oil, heated in a large pan over medium-high heat. Sauté for some minutes on each side, or until browned and crisp,

using half of the falafel patties. Carry on with the remaining falafel patties in the same manner. Combine the yogurt, garlic, lemon juice, and pepper in a small bowl. Place 3 falafel patties, a few cucumber spears, a few red onion rings, and a handful of salad leaves on each tortilla. 1 tablespoon yogurt sauce on top of each.

Nutritional Facts

Calories: 700.78| Carbohydrates: 34.91 g| Protein: 4.12 g| Fat: 4.79 g| Sodium 136 mg |

67. Chicken Baked

Preparation Time: 15 Minutes

Cooking Time: 35 Minutes

Servings: 2

Ingredients:

- 2 lbs. Chicken tenders
- 1 large zucchini
- 1 cup grape tomatoes
- 2 tablespoons olive oil
- 3 Dill sprigs

For the topping:

- 2 tablespoons feta cheese, crumbled
- 1 tablespoon olive oil
- 1 tablespoon fresh lemon juice
- 1 tablespoon fresh dill, chopped

Instructions:

Warm the oven to 200°C/400°F. Drizzle the olive oil on a baking tray, then place the chicken, zucchini, dill, and tomatoes on the tray—season with salt. Bake the chicken within 30 minutes. Meanwhile, in a small bowl, stir all the topping ingredients. Place the chicken on the serving tray, then top with veggies and discard dill sprigs. Sprinkle the topping mixture on top of the chicken and vegetables. Serve and enjoy.

Nutritional Facts:

Calories: 332| Carbohydrates: 50 g| Protein: 7.4 g|

Fat: 13.7 g| Sodium 226 mg |

68. Garlic Chicken with Pepper

Preparation Time: 15 Minutes

Cooking Time: 21 Minutes

Servings: 2

Ingredients:

- 2 chicken breasts, cut into strips
- 2 Bell peppers, cut into strips

- 5 garlic cloves, chopped
- 3 tablespoons water
- 2 tablespoons olive oil
- 1 tablespoon paprika
- 2 teaspoon black pepper
- ½ teaspoon salt

Instructions:

Warm the olive oil, add garlic and sauté for 2-3 minutes. Add peppers and cook for 3 minutes. Add chicken and spices and stir to coat. Add water and stir well. Bring to a boil. Cover and simmer for 10-15 minutes. Serve and enjoy.

Nutritional Facts:

Calories: 330| Carbohydrates: 35 g| Protein 11 g| Fat: 4 g| Sodium 188 mg |

69. Mustard Chicken

Preparation Time: 15 Minutes

Cooking Time: 20 Minutes

Servings: 2

Ingredients:

- 1 lb. Chicken tenders
- 2 tablespoons fresh tarragon, chopped
- ½ cup whole grain mustard
- ½ teaspoon paprika
- 1 garlic clove, minced
- 1/2 oz. Fresh lemon juice
- ½ teaspoon pepper
- ¼ teaspoon kosher salt

Instructions:

Warm the oven to 425°F. Except for chicken, put all ingredients in a large bowl and mix well. Put the chicken in a bowl, then stir until well-coated. Place the chicken on a baking dish and cover. Bake within 15-20 minutes. Serve and enjoy.

Nutritional Facts:

Calories: 289.6| Carbohydrates: 2.5 g| Protein: 13.16 g| Fat: 26.6 g| Sodium 276 mg |

70. Honey Chicken

Preparation Time: 10 Minutes

Cooking Time: 25 Minutes

Servings: 2

Ingredients:

- 1 teaspoon paprika
- 8 Saltine crackers, 2 inches square
- 2 chicken breasts, 4 ounces each
- 4 teaspoons honey

Instructions:

Set the oven to heat at 375°F. Grease a baking dish with cooking oil. Smash the crackers in a Ziploc bag and toss them with paprika in a bowl. Brush the chicken with honey and add it to the crackers. Mix well and transfer the chicken to the baking dish. Bake the chicken for 25 minutes until golden brown, and serve.

Nutritional Facts:

Calories: 529.8 | Carbohydrates: 68.28 g| Protein: 12.08 g| Fat: 24.96 g| Sodium 176 mg |

71. Chicken Leeks and Tarragon

Preparation Time: 10 Minutes

Cooking Time: 20 Minutes

Servings: 2

Ingredients:

- 1 teaspoon of oil
- 1 small onion
- 2 leeks
- 3 garlic cloves, minced
- 1-pound boneless, skinless chicken breast2 large tomatoes, chopped
- 1 Red pepper
- 2/3 cup of brown rice
- 1 teaspoon of tarragon
- 2 cups of chicken broth
- 1 cup frozen peas
- ¼ cup of parsley
- 1 Lemon

Instructions:

Preheat a nonstick pan with olive oil over medium heat. Toss in leeks, onions, chicken strips, and garlic. Sauté for 5 minutes. Stir in red pepper slices and tomatoes. Stir and cook for 5 minutes. Add tarragon, broth, and rice. Continue cooking, add peas and continue cooking until the liquid is thoroughly cooked. Garnish with parsley and lemon. Serve.

Nutritional Facts:

Calories: 188.1| Carbohydrates: 35 g| Protein: 8.5 g| Fat: 14.5 g| Sodium 209 mg |

72. Chicken and Pasta

Preparation Time: 10 Minutes

Cooking Time: 10 Minutes

Servings: 2

Ingredients:

- 1 cup uncooked whole-wheat rigatoni
- 2 chicken breasts, cut into cubes
- ¼ cup of salsa
- 1 ½ cup of canned unsalted tomato sauce
- 1/8 teaspoon garlic powder
- 1 teaspoon cumin
- ½ teaspoon chili powder
- ½ cup canned black beans, drained
- ½ cup of fresh corn
- ¼ cup Monterey Jack and Colby cheese, shredded

Instructions:

Fill a pot with water up to ¾ full and boil it. Add pasta to cook until it is al dente, then drain the pasta while rinsing under cold water. Preheat a skillet with cooking oil, then cook the chicken for 10 minutes until golden from both sides. Add tomato sauce, salsa, cumin, garlic powder, black beans, corn, and chili powder. Cook the mixture while stirring, then toss in the pasta. Serve with two tablespoons of cheese on top. Enjoy.

Nutritional Facts:

Calories: 519| Carbohydrates: 82 g| Protein: 23 g| Fat: 124 g| Sodium 136 mg |

73. Chicken Breasts

Preparation Time: 15 Minutes

Cooking Time: 30 Minutes

Servings: 2

Ingredients:

- 3 tablespoon seedless raisins
- ½ cup of chopped onion
- ½ cup of chopped celery
- ¼ teaspoon garlic, minced
- 1 Bay leaf
- 1 cup apple with peel, chopped
- 2 tablespoons chopped water chestnuts
- 4 large chicken breast halves, 5 ounces each
- 1 tablespoon olive oil
- 1 cup fat-free milk
- 1 teaspoon curry powder
- 2 tablespoons all-purpose (plain) flour
- 1 Lemon, cut into 4 wedges

Instructions:

Set the oven to heat at 425°F. Grease a baking dish with cooking oil. Soak raisins in warm water until they swell. Grease a heated skillet with cooking spray. Add celery, garlic, onions, and bay leaf. Sauté for 5 minutes. Discard the bay leaf, then toss in apples. Stir and cook for 2 minutes. Drain the soaked raisins and pat them dry to remove excess water. Add raisins and water chestnuts to the apple mixture. Pull apart the chicken's skin and stuff the apple raisin mixture between the skin and the chicken. Preheat olive oil in another skillet and sear the breasts for 5 minutes per side. Place the chicken breasts in a baking dish and cover them. Bake for 15 minutes until temperature reaches 165°F. Prepare the sauce by mixing milk, flour, and curry powder in a saucepan. Stir and cook until the mixture thickens, about 5 minutes. Pour this sauce over the baked chicken. Bake again the covered dish for 10 minutes. Serve.

Nutritional Facts

Calories: 131| Carbohydrates: 5 g| Protein: 22 g| Fat: 2 g| Sodium 236 mg |

74. Chicken Sliders

Preparation Time: 10 Minutes

Cooking Time: 10 Minutes

Servings: 2

Ingredients:

- 10 ounces ground chicken breast
- 1 tablespoon black pepper
- 1 tablespoon minced garlic
- 1 tablespoon balsamic vinegar
- ½ cup minced onion
- 1 Fresh chili pepper, minced
- 1 tablespoon fennel seed, crushed
- 4 Whole-wheat mini buns
- 4 Lettuce leaves
- 4 Tomato slices

Instructions:

Combine all the ingredients except the wheat buns, tomato, and lettuce. Mix well and refrigerate the mixture for 1 hour. Then, divide the mixture into four patties. Broil these patties in a greased baking tray until golden brown. Place the chicken patties in the wheat buns along with lettuce and tomato. Serve.

Nutritional Facts:

Calories: 360| Carbohydrates: 4 g| Protein: 28 g| Fat: 24 g| Sodium 166 mg |

75. Oaxacan Chicken

Preparation Time: 15 Minutes

Cooking Time: 28 Minutes

Servings: 2

Ingredients:

- 1 4-ounce chicken breast, skinned and halved
- ½ cup uncooked long-grain rice
- 1 teaspoon of extra-virgin olive oil
- ½ cup Low-sodium salsa
- ½ cup chicken stock, mixed with 2 tablespoons water
- ¾ cup baby carrots
- 2 tablespoons green olives, pitted and chopped
- 2 tablespoons dark raisins
- ½ teaspoon ground Cinnamon
- 2 tablespoons fresh cilantro

Instructions:

Warm oven to 350°F. Heat the olive oil in a baking pan that can go in the oven. Add the rice. Sauté the rice until it begins to pop, approximately 2 minutes. Add the salsa, baby carrots, green olives, dark raisins, halved chicken breast, chicken stock, and ground cinnamon. Bring the mix to a simmer, and stir once. Cover the mixture tightly, and bake in the oven until the chicken stock has been completely absorbed approximately 25 minutes. Sprinkle fresh cilantro or parsley, and mix. Serve immediately.

Nutritional Facts

Calories: 178| Carbohydrates: 9.2 g| Protein: 6 g| Fat: 19 g| Sodium 196 mg |

76. Crusted Whitefish

Preparation Time: 10 minutes

Cooking Time: 20 minutes

Servings: 2

Ingredients:

- ¼ cup of pistachios
- 1 tablespoon of parsley
- 1 tablespoon of cheese
- 1 tablespoon of bread crumbs
- 2 tablespoons of olive oil
- ¼ teaspoon of salt
- 10 ounces skinless whitefish

Instructions:

The oven was preheated to 350°F, and positioned the center rack in the oven. Applying foil, line a sheet pan. In a tiny food processor, pulse all ingredients except the fish until the nuts are finely crushed. Place the fish on the baking sheet. Spread the nut mixture evenly on the fish and softly smooth it down. Depending on the thickness of the fish, bake it for 20 to 30 minutes or until it flakes easily with a fork. Remember that baking a thicker fish cut will take a little longer. You know it's done when it's opaque and flakes apart easily.

Nutritional Facts:

Calories: 275| Carbohydrates: 4 g| Protein: 20 g| Fat: 20 g| Sodium 186 mg |

77. Sauced Shellfish in Wine

Preparation Time: 10 minutes

Cooking Time: 10 minutes

Servings: 2

Ingredients:

- 2-lbs fresh cuttlefish
- ½-cup olive oil
- 1-pc large onion, finely chopped
- 1-cup of Roble white wine
- ¼-cup lukewarm water
- 1-pc bay leaf
- ½-bunch parsley, chopped
- 4-pcs tomatoes, grated
- Salt and pepper to taste

Instructions:

Remove the cuttlefish's hard cartilage centerpiece (cuttlebone), the ink bag, and the guts. Clean the cuttlefish under running water. Drain any extra water before slicing it into thin pieces. In a medium-high-heat saucepan, heat the oil and sauté the onion for 3 minutes or until tender. Pour the white wine over the cuttlefish slices. Cook for 5 minutes, or until it reaches a simmer. After pouring it into the water, add all the ingredients, including tomatoes, bay leaves, parsley, tomatoes, salt, and pepper. Cook, occasionally stirring, until the cuttlefish pieces are cooked, and the sauce has thickened. Warm them up and serve them with rice. If you overcook the cuttlefish, the texture will become quite hard. Before using the cuttlefish in any dish, it's a good idea to grill it for 3 minutes over a fire.

Nutritional Facts:

Calories: 230 | Carbohydrates: 8 g | Protein: 12 g | Fat: 17 g | Sodium 210 mg |

78. Pistachio Fish

Preparation Time: 5 minutes

Cooking Time: 10 minutes

Servings: 2

Ingredients:

- 4 (5 ounces) boneless sole fillets
- ½ cup pistachios, finely chopped
- Juice of 1 lemon
- Teaspoon extra virgin olive oil

Instructions:

Preheat oven. Wrap parchment paper around the baking sheet and set it aside. Dry the fish with kitchen towels and season gently with salt and pepper. Pistachios should be added to a small bowl. Place the sol on the prepared sheet and cover each fillet with 2 teaspoons of the pistachio mixture. Lemon juice and olive oil are applied to the fish. Bake for 10 minutes, or until golden brown and the fish flakes easily with a fork.

Nutritional Facts:

Calories: 143.7 | Carbohydrates: 34.62 g | Protein: 3.44 g | Fat: 3.19 g | Sodium 236 mg |

79. Speedy Tilapia Onion and Avocado

Preparation time: 10 minutes

Cooking time: 5 minutes

Servings: 2

Ingredients:

- 1 tablespoon of olive oil
- 1 tablespoon of orange juice
- ¼ teaspoon of salt
- 4 tilapia fillets
- ¼ cup chopped red onion
- 1 avocado, pitted

Instructions:

Meld the oil, orange juice, and salt with a fork in a 9-inch glass pie plate. Place each fish on the pie plate, one at a time, and flip to coat on both sides. Arrange the fillets in a wagon-wheel pattern, with one end of each fillet in the middle of the dish, and the other briefly stretched over the dish's edge. 1 tablespoon onion on top of each fillet, then fold the end of the fillet that hangs over the edge in half over the onion. You should have four layered fillets with the flap against the dishes outside edge and the ends all in the middle when you're done. Enclose the dish with cling film, leaving a tiny gap at the side to allow steam to escape. Microwave for roughly 3 minutes on high. When gently pushed with a fork, the fish will split into flakes (chunks). Serve the fillets with avocado on top.

Nutritional Facts:

Calories: 53.85 | Carbohydrates: 2.42 g | Protein: 8.5 g | Fat: 0.9 g | Sodium 172 mg |

80. Steamed Mussels in Wine Sauce

Preparation time: 5 minutes

Cooking time: 10 minutes

Servings: 2

Ingredients:

- 2 pounds of small mussels
- 1 tablespoon of olive oil
- 1 cup thinly sliced onion
- 3 garlic cloves
- 1 cup of white wine
- 2 lemon slices
- ¼ teaspoon of black pepper
- ¼ teaspoon of salt
- Fresh lemon

Instructions:

Strain cold water well over mussels in a big funnel in the sink. All shells should be tightly closed; any slightly open or broken shells should be discarded. Remove the mussels from the colander and set them aside until ready to use. Heat the oil in a large skillet stirring occasionally. Cook, stirring periodically, for 4 minutes after adding the onion. Cook, frequently stirring, for 1 minute after adding the garlic. Bring the wine, lemon slices, pepper, and salt to a simmer in a saucepan. For 2 minutes in the oven, cover and add the mussels. Cook until the mussels open their shells, about 3 minutes. While they're cooking, gently shake the pan two or three times. All of the shells should be fully open at this point. Discard any mussels that are still unopened using a slotted spoon. Pour the broth over the mussels that have been opened in a shallow serving dish. If desired, garnish with more fresh lemon slices.

Nutritional Facts:

Calories: 178 | Carbohydrates: 1 g | Protein: 7.72 g | Fat: 13 g | Sodium 276 mg |

81. Orange and Garlic Shrimp

Preparation time: 20 minutes

Cooking time: 10 minutes

Servings: 2

Ingredients:

- 1 large orange
- 3 tablespoons of olive oil
- 1 tablespoon of Rosemary
- 1 tablespoon Of thyme
- 3 garlic cloves
- ¼ teaspoon of black pepper
- ¼ teaspoon of sea salt
- 1½ pounds of raw shrimp

Instructions:

Using a citrus grater, zest the whole orange. Combine the orange zest, 2 tablespoons oil, Rosemary, thyme, garlic, pepper, and salt in a large zip-top plastic bag. Add the shrimp, zip the bag, and gently massage the shrimp until all of the spices are evenly distributed, and the shrimp is thoroughly coated. Remove from the equation. Over medium heat, heat a grill, grill pan, or big skillet. The remaining 1 tablespoon of oil may be brushed on or swirled in. Cook for 4 to 6 minutes, or until the shrimp become pink and white, turning halfway through if cooking on the grill or tossing every minute if cooking in a pan. In a large serving dish, place the shrimp. Add the remaining shrimp to the dish and repeat with the remaining shrimp. Peel the orange and chop the flesh into bite-size pieces while the shrimp boil. Toss in with the cooked shrimp in a serving dish. Serve right now, or chill and serve later.

Nutritional Facts:

Calories: 286| Carbohydrates: 26 g| Protein: 13 g| Fat: 15 g| Sodium 186 mg |

82. Shrimp-Gnocchi Bake

Preparation time: 10 minutes

Cooking time: 20 minutes

Servings: 2

Ingredients:

- 1 cup tomato
- 2 tablespoons of olive oil
- 2 garlic cloves
- ½ teaspoon of black pepper
- ¼ teaspoon of red pepper
- 1 jar of roasted red peppers
- 1-pound of shrimp
- 1-pound of frozen gnocchi
- ½ cup of cheese
- 1/3 cup of basil leaves

Instructions:

Preheat the oven. Combine the tomatoes, oil, garlic, black pepper, and crushed red pepper in a baking dish. Roast for 10 minutes in the oven. Combine the roasted peppers and shrimp in a mixing bowl. Cook for a further 10 minutes or until the shrimp are pink and white. Cook the gnocchi on the stovetop according to the package instructions while the shrimp cooks. Drain and keep it heated in a colander. Take the dish out of the oven. Serve with cooked gnocchi, feta, and basil.

Nutritional Facts:

Calories: 237| Carbohydrates: 7 g| Protein: 16 g| Fat: 14 g| Sodium 196 mg |

83. Cod with Bake Vegetables

Preparation Time: 15 minutes

Cooking Time: 25 minutes

Serving: 2

Ingredients:

- 454 g thick cod fillet
- ¼ teaspoon of onion powder (optional)
- ¼ teaspoon of paprika
- 3 tablespoons olive oil
- 4 medium of scallions
- ½ cup of fresh chopped basil
- 3 tablespoons of minced garlic (optional)
- 2 teaspoons of salt
- 2 teaspoons black pepper
- ¼ teaspoon powder marjoram (optional)
- 6 dried tomato slices
- ½ cup of dry white wine
- ½ cup of cheese
- 1 can of oil-packed artichoke hearts, drained
- 1 lemon
- 1 cup olives
- 1 teaspoon of capers
- 4 small red potatoes

Instructions:

Set oven to 375°f. Season the fish with paprika and onion powder (if desired). Heat an ovenproof skillet over medium heat and sear the top side of the cod for about 1 minute until golden. Set aside. Heat the olive oil in the same skillet and overheat. Add the scallions, ¼ cup of basil, garlic (if desired), salt, pepper, marjoram (if desired), tomato slices, and white wine and stir. Boil then removes from heat. Evenly spread the sauce on the bottom of the skillet. Place the cod on top of the tomato basil sauce and scatter with feta cheese. Place the artichokes in the skillet and top with the lemon slices. Scatter with the olives, capers (if desired), and the remaining ¼ cup of basil. Pull out from the heat and transfer to the preheated oven. Bake for 15 to 20 minutes. Meanwhile, place the quartered potatoes on a baking sheet or wrapped in aluminum foil. Bake in the oven for 15 minutes. Cool for 5 minutes before serving.

Nutritional Facts:

Calories: 276| Carbohydrates: 41 g| Protein: 13.8 g| Fat: 11 g| Sodium 236 mg |

84. Cooker Salmon in Foil

Preparation Time: 5 minutes

Cooking Time: 2 hours

Serving: 2

Ingredients:

- 2 (6-ounce / 170-g) salmon fillets

- 1 tablespoon olive oil

- 2 cloves garlic, minced

- ½ tablespoon lime juice

- 1 teaspoon finely chopped fresh parsley

- ¼ teaspoon black pepper

Instructions

Spread a length of foil onto a work surface and place the salmon fillets in the middle. Blend olive oil, garlic, lime juice, parsley, and black pepper. Brush the mixture over the fillets. Fold the foil over and crimp the sides to make a packet. Place the packet into the slow cooker, cover it, and cook on High for 2 hours. Serve hot.

Nutritional Facts:

Calories: 276| Carbohydrates: 41 g| Protein: 13.8 g| Fat: 11 g| Sodium 236 mg |

85. Garlic Parmesan Salmon and Asparagus

Preparation Time: 10 minutes

Cooking Time: 15 minutes

Serving: 2

Ingredients:

- 2 salmon fillets

- ½ teaspoon of salt

- Black pepper to taste

- 1 pound of fresh asparagus.

- 3 tablespoons of almond butter

- 2 garlic cloves

- ¼ cup of grated Parmesan cheese

Instructions:

Preheat the oven. A wrapper should be used to line a baking pan. Season the salmon fillets on both sides. Place the salmon in the center of the parchment paper and surround it with asparagus. In a small saucepan over medium heat, melt the almond butter. Cook garlic that has been minced. Drizzle the garlic butter sauce over the fish and asparagus, then sprinkle with the Parmesan cheese. Preheat the oven to 350°F and bake for 12 minutes. To create a lovely sear on the asparagus, turn the oven to broil for approximately 3 minutes towards the end of cooking. Allow 5 minutes to cool before serving.

Nutritional Facts:

Calories: 218| Carbohydrates: 2.8 g| Protein: 17 g| Fat: 15 g| Sodium 201 mg |

86. Lemon Rosemary Branzino

Preparation Time: 15 minutes

Cooking Time: 30 minutes

Serving: 2

Ingredients:

- 4 tablespoons extra-virgin olive oil

- 2 Branzino fillets

- 1 garlic clove

- 1 bunch of scallions

- 12 small cherry tomatoes

- 1 large carrot

- ½ cup of white wine

- 2 tablespoons of paprika

- 2 teaspoons of salt

- ½ tablespoon of chili pepper

- 2 rosemary sprigs

- 1 small lemon

- ½ cup of sliced olives

Instructions:

Cooking spray preheated oven overheating for two min, or until hot. Sauté 1 tablespoon of olive oil in a small saucepan. Sear the Branzino fillets for 2 minutes, skin-side up. Cook the fillets on the other side. Remove from the equation. 2 tablespoons of olive oil swirled around the pan to coat it evenly. Sauté for 5 minutes with the garlic, onions, tomatoes, and carrot. Stir in the wine until all of the ingredients are fully mixed. Place the fish on top of the sauce with care. Preheat the oven to 450 degrees Fahrenheit (235 degrees Celsius). Season the fillets with paprika, salt, and chili pepper and brush with the remaining 1 tablespoon of olive oil. A rosemary sprig and lemon slices should be placed on each fillet. Arrange the olives on top of the fish and all over the pan. Roast the lemon slices for approximately 10 minutes or until they are caramelized. Serve immediately.

Nutritional Facts:

Calories: 150| Carbohydrates: 19 g| Protein: 6.8 g| Fat: 5 g| Sodium 226 mg |

87. Lemon Pesto Salmon

Preparation Time: 5 minutes

Cooking Time: 10 minutes

Serving: 2

Ingredients:

- 10 ounces salmon fillet

- 2 tablespoons of pesto sauce

- 1 fresh lemon

- Cooking spray

Instructions:

Preheat your grill to medium-high. Using cooking spray, coat the grill grates. Season the fish with salt and pepper. On top, spread the pesto sauce. Place the salmon fillet on a bed of fresh lemon slices approximately the same size as the salmon fillet on the hot grill. Any remaining lemon slices should be placed on top of the salmon. Cook the fish for 10 minutes on the grill.

Nutritional Facts:

Calories: 231| Carbohydrates: 43 g| Protein: 13 g| Fat: 4 g| Sodium 176 mg |

88. Chicken with Minty Couscous

Preparation Time: 15 Minutes

Cooking Time: 25 Minutes

Servings: 2

Ingredients:

- 2 small chicken breasts, sliced

- 1 Red chili pepper, finely chopped

- 1 garlic clove, crushed

- 1 Ginger root, 2 cm long peeled and grated

- 1 teaspoon ground cumin

- ½ teaspoon turmeric

- 2 tablespoons extra-virgin olive oil

- 1 pinch of sea salt

- ¾ cup couscous

- 1 bunch of mint leaves,

- 2 Lemons, grate the rind and juice them

Instructions:

Place the chicken breast slices and chopped chili pepper in a large bowl. Sprinkle with crushed garlic, ginger, cumin, turmeric, and a pinch of salt. Add the grated rind of both lemons and the juice of 1 lemon. Pour one tablespoon of olive oil over the chicken, and coat evenly. Cover the dish and freeze it within 1 hour. After 1 hour, coat a skillet with olive oil and fry the chicken. As the chicken is cooking, pour the couscous into a bowl, pour hot water over it, and let it absorb the water (approximately 5 minutes). Fluff the couscous. Add some chopped mint, the other tablespoon of olive oil, and juice from the second lemon. Top the couscous with the chicken. Garnish with chopped mint. Serve immediately.

Nutritional Facts:

Calories: 159| Carbohydrates: 35 g| Protein: 4 g| Fat: 1 g| Sodium 217 mg |

89. Chicken Pasta and Peas

Preparation Time: 15 minutes

Cooking Time: 20 minutes

Servings: 2

Ingredients:

- 1-pound chicken breasts

- 2 ½ cups penne pasta

- 1 cup snow peas, trimmed and halved

- 1 teaspoon olive oil

- 1 Standard jar of Tomato and Basil pasta sauce

- Fresh ground pepper

Instructions

In a medium frying pan, heat the olive oil. Flavor the chicken breasts with salt and pepper. Cook the chicken breasts until cooked through (approximately 5 – 7 minutes on each side). Cook the pasta, as stated in the instruction on the package. Cook the snow peas with the pasta. Scoop 1 cup of the pasta water. Drain the pasta and peas, and set them aside. Once the chicken is cooked, slice it diagonally. Return the chicken to the frying pan. Add the pasta sauce. Add some pasta water to the desired consistency. Heat, then divide into bowls. Serve immediately.

Nutritional Facts:

Calories: 202| Carbohydrates: 19 g| Protein: 9 g| Fat: 13 g| Sodium 26 mg |

90. Chicken Divan

Preparation Time: 15 Minutes

Cooking Time: 30 Minutes

Servings: 2

Ingredients:

- 1/2-pound cooked chicken, boneless, skinless, diced in bite-size pieces
- 1 cup broccoli, cooked, diced into bite-size pieces
- 1 cup extra sharp cheddar cheese, grated
- 1 can mushroom soup
- ½ cup of water
- 1 cup croutons

Instructions:

Warm the oven to 350°F. In a large pot, heat the soup and water. Add the chicken, broccoli, and cheese. Combine thoroughly. Pour into a greased baking dish. Place the croutons over the mixture. Bake within 30 minutes or until the casserole is bubbling and the croutons are golden brown.

Nutritional Facts:

Calories: 386| Carbohydrates: 12 g| Protein: 16 g| Fat: 30 g| Sodium 276 mg |

91. Honey Cajun Chicken

Preparation Time: 15 Minutes

Cooking Time: 20 Minutes

Servings: 2

Ingredients:

- 2 chicken breasts, skinless, boneless
- 1 tablespoon butter or margarine
- 1 pound of linguini
- 3 large mushrooms, sliced
- 1 large tomato, diced
- 2 tablespoons regular mustard
- 4 tablespoons honey
- 3 ounces low-fat table cream
- Parsley, roughly chopped

Instructions:

Wash and dry the chicken breasts—warm one tablespoon of butter or margarine in a large pan. Add the chicken breasts, and season with salt and pepper. Cook on each side for 6 – 10 minutes, until cooked thoroughly. Pull the chicken breasts from the pan. Set them aside. Cook the linguini as stated in the instructions on the package in a large pot. Save 1 cup of pasta water. Drain the linguine. Add the mushrooms and tomatoes to the pan from cooking the chicken. Heat until they are tender. Add

the honey, pasta, water, mustard, and cream. Combine thoroughly. Add the chicken and linguine to the pan. Stir until coated. Garnish with parsley. Serve immediately.

Nutritional Facts:

Calories: 289| Carbohydrates: 5 g| Protein: 14 g| Fat: 22 g| Sodium 223 mg |

92. Parsley Chicken Breast

Preparation Time: 15 Minutes

Cooking Time: 15 Minutes

Servings: 2

Ingredients:

- 2 chicken breasts, skinless, boneless
- 1/3 cup white wine
- 1/3 cup lemon juice
- 4 garlic cloves, minced
- 3 tablespoons bread crumbs
- 2 tablespoons flavorless oil (olive, canola, or sunflower)
- ¼ cup fresh parsley

Instructions:

Mix the wine, lemon juice, plus garlic in a measuring cup. Pound each chicken breast until they are ¼ inch thick. Coat the chicken with bread crumbs, and heat the oil in a large skillet. Fry the chicken within 6 minutes on each side until they turn brown. Stir in the wine mixture over the chicken. Simmer for 5 minutes. Pour any extra juices over the chicken. Garnish with parsley.

Nutritional Facts

Calories: 289| Carbohydrates: 5 g| Protein: 14 g| Fat: 22 g| Sodium 223 mg |

93. Shrimp Skewers with Mango Cucumber Salsa

Preparation time: 10 minutes + 30 minutes to marinate

Cooking Time: 15 minutes

Serving: 6

Ingredients

For Shrimp

- Juice of 2 limes
- 2 tablespoons honey
- 1 teaspoon canola oil
- 1-inch piece of ginger (minced)

- 1 pound large shrimp

For Salsa

- ¼ cup diced sweet onion
- 1 small red chili (finely diced)
- Juice of 1 lime
- 1 medium cucumber (seeded and diced)
- 1 mango (peeled and diced)

Instructions

Combine the lime juice, honey, and ginger in a medium mixing basin. Toss in the shrimp to coat them. To marinate, cover and chill for 30 minutes. Using skewers, thread the shrimp onto the skewers. Brush a grill with oil and heat over medium-high heat. Cook the skewers for 3 to 6 minutes on each side, or until the shrimp are opaque and done.

For salsa:

Toss the onion, chili, cucumber, mango, and lime juice in a small bowl. Toss in the shrimp to coat them.

Nutritional facts

Calories: 107| Carbohydrates: 5. g| Protein: 3.1 g| Fat: 8.5 g| Sodium 225 mg |

94. Shrimp and Bok Choy in Parchment

Preparation time: 10 minutes

Cooking Time: 15 minutes

Serving: 4

Ingredients

- 12 ounces shrimp (peeled and deveined)
- 3 garlic cloves (minced)
- 1 teaspoon toasted sesame oil
- 2 tablespoons rice vinegar
- 2 teaspoons honey
- 2 tablespoons freshly squeezed lime juice
- 1 pound choy (white and green parts thinly sliced)
- 2 scallions (thinly sliced)
- 2-inch piece of ginger (minced)
- 1 jalapeño pepper (thinly sliced)
- ¼ cup chopped cilantro

Instructions

Preheat the oven to 375 degrees Fahrenheit. Combine the shrimp, garlic, and ginger in a small bowl. Combine the sesame oil, honey, lime juice, and rice vinegar in a small bowl. Cut four huge circles out of parchment paper, each

about 12 inches in diameter. Place a big bunch of choy on each piece, then top with the shrimp, garlic-ginger mixture, scallions, and jalapeno slices. Drizzle one-quarter of the vinegar–lime juice mixture over each mound. To make a half-moon shape, fold the parchment paper in half. To make a seal, fold the edges together. Cook the packets for 15 minutes on a rimmed baking sheet. Before serving, remove the pan from the oven and set it aside for 5 minutes. Keep an eye out for leaking steam while opening the package. Serve with white rice and cilantro as a garnish.

Nutritional facts

Calories: 71| Carbohydrates: 0.4 g| Protein: 9 g| Fat: 4 g| Sodium 193 mg |

95. Shrimp Fried Rice

Preparation time: 10 minutes

Cooking Time: 15 minutes

Serving: 6

Ingredients

- 1 tablespoon extra-virgin olive oil
- ½ sweet onion (chopped)
- 1 cup sugar snap peas
- 2-inch piece of ginger (minced)
- 3 garlic cloves (minced)
- 1 pound shrimp (peeled and deveined)
- 3 cups cooked rice

Instructions

Warm the oil in a pot over medium-high heat. Cook, constantly stirring, for 3 to 5 minutes or until the onion softens. Stir in the ginger and garlic until they are fragrant.

Cook, often tossing, for approximately 5 minutes or until the shrimp is opaque and almost cooked through. Stir in the snap peas and rice until well combined and heated. Serve.

Nutritional facts

Calories: 211| Carbohydrates: 17 g| Protein: 9 g| Fat: 7 g| Sodium 266 mg |

96. Creamy Shrimp Fettuccine

Preparation time: 10 minutes

Cooking Time: 30 minutes

Serving: 4

Ingredients

- 8 ounces dried fettuccine
- 3 garlic cloves (minced)

- 2 tablespoons extra-virgin olive oil (divided)
- 10 ounces shrimp (peeled and deveined)
- 1 cup Homemade Rice Milk or unsweetened store-bought rice milk
- 1 teaspoon garlic powder
- 2 tablespoons all-purpose flour
- ¼ cup grated Parmesan cheese
- 2 tablespoons chopped parsley
- Lemon, cut into wedges (for serving)
- Freshly ground black pepper

Instructions

A big stockpot of salted water should be brought to a boil. Add the fettuccine and simmer, turning regularly, until the noodles are al dente. Drain. Add 1 tablespoon olive oil, and heat it in a large pan over medium heat. Cook, stirring periodically, for 3 to 5 minutes, or until the shrimp are pink and opaque. Remove the shrimp from the pan in the same skillet, and add the remaining tablespoon of oil. Constantly stir until the garlic is fragrant. Combine the flour and water and stir until the paste forms. Slowly drizzle in the rice milk, a little at a time, constantly whisking until the mixture is smooth. Add the garlic powder and mix well. Slow down the heat to low and cook until the sauce thickens. Add the Parmesan cheese and mix well. Season with salt and pepper. Toss in the noodles and toss well to coat. Add the shrimp and mix well. Serve with lemon wedges and parsley on the side.

Nutritional facts

Calories: 236| Carbohydrates: 27 g| Protein: 11 g| Fat: 11 g| Sodium 136 mg |

97. White Fish and Broccoli Curry

Preparation time: 10 minutes

Cooking Time: 10 minutes

Serving: 6

Ingredients

For Curry Paste:

- ½ sweet onion (chopped)
- 1 medium red chili (chopped)
- 1 teaspoon turmeric powder
- 1-inch piece of ginger (peeled and chopped)
- ½ teaspoon cumin seeds
- 1 lemongrass stalk (outer leaves removed, tender bottom portion chopped)
- ¼ cup roughly chopped fresh cilantro stems
- 2 tablespoons extra-virgin olive oil

For Curry:

- ¾ cup Homemade Rice Milk/unsweetened store-bought rice milk
- ½ cup cream cheese
- 3 cups broccoli florets
- 1 pound tilapia fillets
- Juice of 1 lime
- 1 teaspoon sugar

Instructions

For Curry Paste:

Combine the onion, chili, ginger, lemongrass, cilantro, turmeric, cumin seeds, and olive oil in a mortar and pestle or blender, and mix until smooth.

For Curry:

Heat the curry paste in a large pan over medium-high heat for 2 to 3 minutes, stirring periodically, until aromatic. Stir in the rice milk until it is completely mixed. Bring to a low boil, then reduce to low heat. Meanwhile, place the cream cheese. Stir in a few tablespoons of the heated rice-milk mixture until smooth. Add the tilapia and broccoli to the pan, then gently whisk in the cream cheese mixture to combine. Cook till the fish is perfectly cooked, the broccoli is tender, and the curry is bubbling. Combine the lime juice and sugar in a mixing bowl. Take the pan off the heat and serve over white rice.

Nutritional facts

Calories: 127| Carbohydrates: 11.6 g| Protein: 6 g| Fat: 6 g| Sodium 266 mg |

98. Oven-Fried Fish with Pineapple Salsa

Preparation time: 10 minutes

Cooking Time: 20 minutes

Serving: 4

Ingredients

For Salsa

- 1 cup diced pineapple
- ½ jalapeño pepper (seeded and diced)
- Juice of ½ lime
- ¼ cup diced red onion
- ¼ cup chopped fresh cilantro

For Fish

- 1 tablespoon butter
- 1 pound white fish fillets
- ½ teaspoon garlic powder
- ¼ cup yellow cornmeal

- ¼ cup all-purpose flour

- 1 egg (beaten)

- ½ teaspoon paprika

- 2 tablespoons Homemade Rice Milk/unsweetened store-bought rice milk

Instructions

Combine the pineapple, onion, jalapeno, lime juice, and cilantro in a small bowl. While you prepare the fish, toss the salad and put it aside.

For Fish:

Preheat the oven to 400 degrees Fahrenheit. Using butter, grease a small baking dish. Garlic powder and paprika are used to season the fish fillets. Combine the cornmeal and flour. Combine the egg and rice milk in a separate small bowl. Each fish should be dipped in the egg mixture and then rolled into the flour mixture. In the preheated pan, arrange the fish in a single layer. Bake for 20 minutes or until the fish is golden brown and easily flaked with a fork.

Nutritional facts

Calories: 305| Carbohydrates: 6.3 g| Protein: 19.6 g| Fat: 21.8 g| Sodium 270 mg |

99. Salmon and Kale in Parchment

Preparation time: 10 minutes

Cooking Time: 15 minutes

Serving: 4

Ingredients

- 2 cups thinly sliced kale leaves

- 2 small zucchini, sliced

- 1 pound salmon fillets

- 4 fresh thyme sprigs

- ½ teaspoon paprika

- 4 fresh rosemary sprigs

- 1 lemon (sliced)

- ¼ cup dry white wine

- Freshly ground black pepper as required

Instructions

Preheat the oven to 450 degrees Fahrenheit. Cut four pieces of parchment paper with approximately 12 inches each. 12 cup kale leaves, topped with many slices of zucchini, 12 cup kale leaves, 12 cup kale leaves, 12 cup kale leaves, 12 cup kale leaves, 12 cup kale leaves, 12 cup Season with salt and pepper. Season the salmon fillets with paprika, then garnish with a sprig of thyme, rosemary, and a slice of lemon. 1 tablespoon white wine, poured over each fillet to seal the seams, fold the parchment paper, and wrinkle the edges. 15 minutes in

the oven. Remove the fillets from the oven and set them aside to cool for 5 minutes before serving.

Nutritional facts

Calories: 285| Carbohydrates: 4 g| Protein: 25 g| Fat: 19 g| Sodium 206 mg |

100. Salmon Burgers

Preparation time: 10 minutes

Cooking Time: 10 minutes

Serving: 4

Ingredients

- 1 pound salmon

- 1 tablespoon of mustard

- Zest of 1 lemon

- 1 tablespoon of lemon juice

- 2 scallions

- ½ cup of coarse bread crumbs

- 1 tablespoon extra-virgin olive oil

- Buns or greens

- Black pepper as required

Instructions

Remove any pin bones from the fish and chop them into slices. Add half of the salmon to a food processor and pulse until pasty. Mix mustard, lemon zest, and lemon juice. Add salt and pepper. Fill a bowl halfway with the fish mixture. Add the scallions and 14 cups of bread crumbs and mix well. Make four patties out of the mixture. Spread the remaining bread crumbs on a dish and gently cover each burger. Heat the olive oil in a large pan over medium-high heat. Cook the burgers. Serve with a green salad, such as Mixed Green Leaf and Citrus Salad or Spinach Salad with Orange Vinaigrette, on a bun or over a bed of greens.

Nutritional facts

Calories: 261| Carbohydrates: 1 g| Protein: 14 g| Fat: 22 g| Sodium 256 mg |

101. Roasted Salmon with Herb Gremolata

Preparation time: 10 minutes

Cooking Time: 15 minutes

Serving: 4

Ingredients

- ½ cup loosely packed

- Juice of 1 lemon

- 2 garlic cloves

- 1 tablespoon of thyme
- 1 tablespoon of rosemary
- 1 pound salmon fillets
- Black pepper

Instructions

Preheat the oven to 200 degrees Celsius. In a separate bowl, incorporate the parsley, lemon zest, lemon juice, garlic, rosemary, and thyme. Stir the ingredients together to mix them. After pushing the fillets into the herb mixture to coat one side, place them herb-side up on a baking pan. Salt & pepper to taste. Cooking for eight minutes, or when a fork easily penetrates the salmon.

Nutritional facts

Calories: 107| Carbohydrates: 4 g| Protein: 6 g| Fat: 8 g| Sodium 136 mg |

102. Chicken Kebab Sandwich

Preparation time: 15 minutes

Cooking Time: 15 minutes

Serving: 4

Ingredients

- 12 ounces of chicken breast
- 2 tablespoons lemon juice
- 4 white flatbreads
- 1 tablespoon extra-virgin olive oil
- 4 garlic cloves, minced
- ¼ cup plain
- 1 cucumber (sliced)
- 1 cup lettuce (shredded)
- Black pepper

Instructions

Simply throw the chicken breasts with lemon juice, olive oil, and half of the garlic to coat in a serving pot. Salt & pepper to taste. At the same time, the remainder of the ingredients is prepared and set aside to marinate. In a small dish, combine the yogurt and the remaining garlic. Salt & pepper to taste and stir well. Take it out of the equation. In a large skillet over medium-high heat, combine the chicken and the marinade. Simmer for fifteen minutes until the chicken is evenly browned on the outside. And from the other side, simmer until the chicken is slightly browned and the liquid flow. Start taking the turn off the heat and leave it aside for 5 minutes to cool. In each flatbread, incorporate the chicken, cucumber, and lettuce. To serve, top with a tablespoon of yogurt sauce.

Nutritional facts

Calories: 160| Carbohydrates: 13 g| Protein: 6 g| Fat: 10

g| Sodium 220 mg |

103. Chicken with Cabbage

Preparation time: 10 minutes

Cooking Time: 10 minutes

Serving: 4

Ingredients

- 1 teaspoon canola oil
- ¼ cup water
- 10 ounces of chicken breast
- 3 cups of green cabbage
- 1 teaspoon of ginger
- ½ teaspoon of garlic powder
- 1 tablespoon of cornstarch
- Black pepper

Instructions

In a pan over medium heat, bring to a simmer on low flame. Cook, frequently stirring, until the chicken is caramelized and cooked completely. Before adding the cabbage to the pan, cook for another 2 to 3 minutes, until it is tender but still crisp and green. Merge the cornstarch, ginger, garlic, and water in a shallow dish. Heat the mixture in the pan for 1 minute or until the sauce has thickened somewhat. Salt & pepper to taste.

Nutritional facts

Calories: 242| Carbohydrates: 9 g| Protein: 9 g| Fat: 7 g| Sodium 276 mg |

104. Chicken Chow Mein

Preparation time: 10 minutes

Cooking Time: 15 minutes

Serving: 6

Ingredients

- 2 teaspoons of cornstarch
- 1 teaspoon of soy sauce

- 1 teaspoon of rice wine
- 1 teaspoon of sugar
- 1 tablespoon of water
- 1 teaspoon of sesame oil
- 2 teaspoons of canola oil
- 8 ounces of chicken thighs
- 2 cups of green cabbage
- 1 carrot
- 3 garlic of cloves
- 4 scallions
- 10 ounces of noodles
- 1 cup of mung bean sprouts

Instructions

In a bowl, add all the ingredients, including cornstarch, water, and soy sauce. Combine the rice wine, sugar, and sesame oil. Substitute. Over medium-high heat, heat the canola oil in a large skillet or wok. Continue cooking, often stirring, until the garlic is aromatic. Cook for 1 minute, regularly flipping, until the chicken is golden brown but not fully done. Cook for 1–2 minutes, or until the cabbage begins to wilt and the chicken is fully cooked, before adding the cabbage, carrot, and scallions. In a bowl, combine the pasta, chicken, and vegetables. Add the sauce and blend thoroughly. Incorporate the bean sprouts with a whisk. Serve immediately after turning off the heat.

Nutritional facts

Calories: 264| Carbohydrates: 39 g| Protein: 6 g| Fat: 9 g| Sodium 236 mg |

105. Chicken Satay with Peanut Sauce

Preparation time: 10 minutes + 2 hours to marinate

Cooking Time: 15 minutes

Serving: 6

Ingredients

- 1 pound of chicken breast
- ½ cup of plain unsweetened yogurt
- 2 garlic cloves
- 1-inch piece ginger
- 2 teaspoons of curry powder
- 1 teaspoon canola oil

For Sauce:

- ¾ cup of peanut butter
- 1 teaspoon of soy sauce

- 1 tablespoon of brown sugar
- ½ teaspoon of chili flakes
- ¼ cup of hot water
- Fresh cilantro leaves
- Lime wedges
- Juice of 2 limes

Instructions

Combine the yogurt, garlic, ginger, and curry powder in a bowl. Stir everything together to blend. Combine the chicken strips and marinate in a separate bowl. After covering, refrigerate for 2 hours. Thread the chicken pieces together using skewers.

In a grill pan over medium-high heat, heat the oil. Cook for 3 to 5 minutes on each side or until the chicken skewers are cooked.

To make the sauce in a food processor, combine the peanut butter, soy sauce, brown sugar, lemon juice, chili flakes, and hot water. Blend on high speed until absolutely smooth. Transfer to a mixing bowl and sprinkle with cilantro, if desired

Nutritional facts

Calories: 244| Carbohydrates: 32 g| Protein: 4 g| Fat: 7 g| Sodium 206 mg |

106. Chicken, Pasta, and Broccoli Bake

Preparation time: 10 minutes

Cooking Time: 30 minutes

Serving: 6

Ingredients

- 8 ounces egg noodles
- 3 cups of chicken breast
- 1 package of broccoli florets
- 2 tablespoons of butter
- ½ sweet onion
- ¼ cup of all-purpose flour
- 1½ cups Simple Chicken broth
- Black pepper
- ¾ cup of rice milk
- ¼ cup of cheese

Instructions

A small cup of yogurt, garlic, ginger, and curry powder. Stir everything together. Meanwhile, mix the chicken strips and marinate. Cover and refrigerate for 2 hours. Thread the chicken on skewers.

In a grill pan, with medium-high heat, the oil. 3–5

minutes on each side for the chicken skewers to cook thoroughly.

Then combine the mixture in a food processor with the soy sauce, lime juice, red chili flakes, and water. Blend until smooth. Add cilantro to a mixing dish. Lemon wedges to squeeze over skewers and Chicken Satay.

Nutritional facts

Calories: 190| Carbohydrates: 26 g| Protein: 4 g| Fat: 9 g| Sodium 223 mg |

107. Turkey Meatballs with Spaghetti in Garlic Sauce

Preparation time: 15 minutes

Cooking Time: 20 minutes

Serving: 4

Ingredients

- ¾ pound turkey
- ½ teaspoon of onion powder
- ½ cup of bread crumbs
- 1 large egg
- ½ teaspoon of garlic powder

For Pasta

- 8 ounces spaghetti noodles
- 2 cups chopped broccoli rabe
- 1 tablespoon of olive oil
- 5 garlic cloves
- ¼ cup of cheese
- Black pepper

Instructions

Preheat the oven to 375°F. Line a baking sheet with parchment. Mix the turkey, bread crumbs, egg, onion powder, and garlic powder. Mix well. Form the turkey mixture into 2-inch meatballs on a baking sheet. Bake for 20 minutes, rotating halfway until browned and cooked through.

Pasta: Boil water, add noodles, and cook until al dente. Drain, saving 1 cup of cooking liquid. The oil should be hot. Soak in hot water for 10 min. Add the broccoli rabe and 12 cups of boiling water. Cook for 5 minutes, covered until the broccoli rabe is fork-tender. Mix in the noodles. Add a few tablespoons of the remaining cooking water to the pan to moisten the noodles. After the Parmesan, sprinkle some salt and pepper. Serve meatballs over spaghetti.

Nutritional facts

Calories: 136| Carbohydrates: 22 g| Protein: 5 g| Fat: 6 g| Sodium 162 mg |

108. Marinated Pork Tenderloin

Preparation time: 15 minutes + 2 hours to marinate

Cooking Time: 20 minutes

Serving: 4

Ingredients

- 4 tablespoons of olive oil
- 3 garlic cloves
- 2 tablespoons of Dijon mustard
- 1 tablespoon of thyme leaves
- ½ teaspoon of black pepper
- 2 pounds pork
- Juice of 2 lemons

Instructions

2 tablespoons olive oil, garlic, mustard, and pepper; add the pork, cover, and refrigerate for 2 hours. Prepare and heat the oven to 400°F. 2 tablespoons. Olive oil in an oven-safe pan on medium-high heat. Remove tenderloin from marinade and sear on both sides in a pan. In the oven for 20 minutes, wrap it with foil until the juices run clear. After 10 minutes, slice it into 12-inch thick slices and serve.

Nutritional facts

Calories: 221| Carbohydrates: 15 g| Protein: 5 g| Fat: 18 g| Sodium 26 mg |

109. Meatloaf with Mushroom Gravy

Preparation time: 15 minutes

Cooking Time: 50 minutes

Serving: 8

Ingredients

- Nonstick cooking spray
- 1 tablespoon of olive oil
- 1 package of sliced cremini mushrooms
- 1 teaspoon of dried oregano
- 1 sweet onion
- 3 garlic cloves
- 1 large egg
- 1½ pounds of beef
- 1 slice of white bread for bread crumbs
- ¼ teaspoon of black pepper
- 1 tablespoon of flour
- 1 cup of beef broth

Instructions

Preheat the oven to 350°F. Coat a loaf pan with nonstick spray. 1 tablespoon olive oil heated in a big pan Oregano and mushroom 5 minutes, occasionally stirring 5 minutes, stirring periodically, until the mushrooms and onion are soft. Stop the heat. The mushroom mixture should be coarsely chopped and split into two equal portions. Keep the other half. Combine chopped mushrooms, beef, egg, bread crumbs, and pepper in a medium mixing bowl. Mix well. Assemble the meat mixture into a loaf in the bread pan. 45 minutes or until done. Add the remaining mushroom mixture to the 1 teaspoon olive oil and heat through. Mix in the flour evenly. Pour in the broth slowly, stirring to avoid clumps. Heat to a simmer, then reduce to a simmer for five min, or until the sauce thickens. Serve the gravy over the meatloaf.

Nutritional facts

Calories: 325| Carbohydrates: 50.1 g| Protein: 8.6 g| Fat: 14.2 g| Sodium 226 mg |

110. Flank Steak with Chimichurri Sauce

Preparation time: 15 minutes

Cooking Time: 15 minutes

Serving: 6

Ingredients

For Sauce:

- ¼ cup of parsley
- ¼ cup of cilantro
- ¼ cup of onion
- 2 garlic cloves
- 2 tablespoons of apple cider
- ¼ cup of olive oil
- ¼ teaspoon of black pepper
- ¼ teaspoon of chili flakes

For Steak

- 1½ pounds of steak
- 1 teaspoon of garlic powder
- ½ teaspoon of oregano
- Black pepper

Instructions

Mix parsley, cilantro, onion, garlic, olive oil, vinegar, pepper, and chili flakes in a big bowl. Use immediately or freeze it for up to three days.

Steak:

Preheat the broiler oven as close as getting an oven shelf to the broiler. Garlic powder, oregano, and pepper on both sides of the flank steak for 5 minutes per side on a baking sheet Cook for 3-5 minutes on the other side, or until done. Then tent it with aluminum foil. Allow 5 minutes rest. Serve with a cross-grain chimichurri sauce.

Nutritional facts

Calories: 224| Carbohydrates: 29 g| Protein: 5 g| Fat: 8 g| Sodium 226 mg |

111. Chili Rice with Beef

Preparation time: 15 minutes

Cooking Time: 15 minutes

Serving: 4

Ingredients

- 2 cups of rice
- 2 tablespoons of vegetable oil
- 1 pound of beef
- 1 cup onion
- 1 ½ teaspoon of chili powder
- ⅛ teaspoon of black pepper
- ½ teaspoon of sage

Instructions

Then add the meat and onion. Stir often until golden. In a big bowl, mix rice and seasonings. Mix all ingredients. Turn off the heat. Set aside for 10-14 minutes.

Nutritional facts

Calories: 127| Carbohydrates: 10 g| Protein: 7 g| Fat: 7 g| Sodium 192 mg |

112. Salisbury Steak

Preparation time: 15 minutes

Cooking Time: 22 minutes

Serving: 4

Ingredients

- 1 pound chopped beef
- 1 small onion
- ½ cup water
- ½ cup of green pepper
- 1 teaspoon of black pepper
- 1 egg
- 1 tablespoon of vegetable oil
- 1 tablespoon of corn starch

Instructions

Mix beef, onion, green pepper, black pepper, and egg.

Then form patties. Heat the oil and cook the patties on both sides. Add half the water and simmer for 15 minutes. Remove the patties. Mix in the remaining water and cornstarch. Cooking while stirring, thickens the gravy. Serve the steak hot with gravy.

Nutritional facts

Calories: 197 | Carbohydrates: 3 g | Protein: 5 g | Fat: 7 g | Sodium 182 mg |

113. Parsley Burger

Preparation time: 15 minutes

Cooking Time: 20 minutes

Serving: 4

Ingredients

- 1 pound lean ground beef
- 1 tablespoon of lemon juice
- ¼ teaspoon of black pepper
- ¼ teaspoon of thyme
- 1 tablespoon of parsley flakes
- ¼ teaspoon of oregano

Instructions

Ensure that all components are mixed. 4 little patties (34 g) "ado

A lightly greased broiler pan 3 minutes broiling" Remove from heat and rotate for 10-15 minutes.

Nutritional facts

Calories: 221 | Carbohydrates: 3 g | Protein: 8 g | Fat: 19 g | Sodium 213 mg |

114. Swedish Meatballs

Preparation time: 15 minutes

Cooking Time: 20 minutes

Serving: 25

Ingredients

Meatballs:

- 1 pound beef
- ¼ cup of onions
- 1 tablespoon of lemon juice
- 1 teaspoon of poultry seasoning
- 1 teaspoon of black pepper
- ¼ teaspoon of mustard
- ¾ teaspoon of onion powder
- 1 teaspoon of sugar

- 1 teaspoon of Tabasco sauce
- 1 teaspoon of Italian seasoning

Sauce:

- ¼ cup of vegetable oil
- 2 teaspoons of sugar
- 2 tablespoons flour
- 1 teaspoon of onion powder
- 2 teaspoons of vinegar
- 1 teaspoon of Tabasco sauce
- 2-3 cups of water

Instructions

Meatballs:

Preheat the oven to 425°F. In a big mixing basin, combine

all ingredients. Make meatballs using one tablespoon of the meat mixture.

Bake the meatballs for 20 minutes

Sauce prep. Discard the sauce and meatballs from the oven. Keep heated till serving.

Cook the flour and oil, stirring regularly, until golden brown. Turn off the heat. Mix onion powder, vinegar, sugar, Tabasco sauce, and water. Return the sauce to heat and stir until thickened.

Nutritional facts

Calories: 197 | Carbohydrates: 2 g | Protein: 12 g | Fat: 3 g | Sodium 270 mg |

115. Steak & Onion Sandwich

Preparation time: 15 minutes

Cooking Time: 10 minutes

Serving: 4

Ingredients

- 4 chopped steaks
- 1 tablespoon of lemon juice
- 1 tablespoon of vegetable oil
- 1 tablespoon of Italian seasoning
- 1 tablespoon of black pepper
- 1 medium onion
- 4 hoagie rolls

Instructions

Mix the meat with lemon juice, Italian seasoning, and black pepper.

Heat the oil in a frying pan. Brown, both sides of seasoned steaks until done. Bring the tray out and drain it.

Add the onion and simmer until tender, with sliced hoagie bread and onion rings on the side.

Nutritional facts

Calories: 233| Carbohydrates: 30 g| Protein: 9 g| Fat: 9 g| Sodium 267 mg |

116. Basic Meat Loaf

Preparation time: 15 minutes

Cooking Time: 45 minutes

Serving: 8

Ingredients

- 1 pound ground turkey
- 1 egg white
- ½ cup of chopped onions
- 1 tablespoon of lemon juice
- ½ teaspoon of onion powder
- ½ teaspoon of Italian seasoning
- ¼ teaspoon of black pepper
- ½ cup of plain bread crumbs
- ½ cup of diced green pepper
- ¼ cup of water

Instructions

Preheat the oven to 400°F. Pour lemon juice over the meat.

The rest of the ingredients are in a mixing bowl. Mix well with meat. Prepare the oven at 350°F and bake the loaf for 45 minutes.

Nutritional facts

Calories: 161| Carbohydrates: 30 g| Protein: 7 g| Fat: 1 g| Sodium 83 mg |

117. Barbecue Cups

Preparation time: 15 minutes

Cooking Time: 12 minutes

Serving: 10

Ingredients

- ¾ pounds ground turkey
- ½ cup of spicy barbecue sauce
- 2 teaspoons of onion flakes
- Dash of garlic powder
- 10-ounces package of low-fat refrigerator biscuits

Instructions

Brown the turkey. Afterward, incorporate the barbecue sauce and onion flakes. Mix well. Flatten each biscuit and push it into a muffin tin. Half-fill each biscuit cup with beef mixture. Prepare the oven to 400°F and bake for 10-12 minutes.

Nutritional facts

Calories: 304| Carbohydrates: 12 g| Protein: 9 g| Fat: 11 g| Sodium 266 mg |

118. Zesty Caribbean Chicken

Preparation time: 10 minutes

Cook time: 45 minutes

Servings: 4

Ingredients

- 3 pounds of skinless chicken thighs
- 1/4 cup of butter
- 1/4 cup of honey
- 1 tablespoon of mustard
- 2 teaspoons of curry powder
- 1 garlic clove
- 1 tablespoon Jamaican spice
- 1 lemon
- 1 cup of rice (brown)
- 1/2 cup of green peas

Instructions

Oven preheated to 350°F. Merge the butter, honey, mustard, garlic, and spices in a bowl and whisk through the chicken. Stir to combine the chicken in a baking dish with the marinade and bake for 35-40 minutes. On the other hand, bring a pot of water to a boil, add the rice, cover it, and cook for 20 minutes. In the last 5 minutes, pour the peas into the pan. Transfer the rice to the stove for 5 minutes after draining and covering it. When the chicken is cooked properly, serve it over a bed of rice and peas with a splash of lime juice on top.

Nutritional Facts

Calories: 180| Carbohydrates: 32 g| Protein: 4 g| Fat: 6 g| Sodium 190 mg |

119. Cajun Chicken and Shrimp Fiesta

Preparation time: 10 minutes

Cook time: 40 minutes

Servings: 4

Ingredients

- 3 pounds of skinless chicken breasts
- 1 onion

- 1 bell pepper
- 2 garlic cloves
- 10 king prawns
- 1 cup of brown rice
- 1 tablespoon olive oil
- 1 cup of chicken stock

For the Cajun spice blend:

- 1 teaspoon of cayenne pepper
- 1 teaspoon of paprika
- 1 teaspoon of oregano (dried)
- 1 teaspoon of thyme (dried)

Instructions

To prepare your Cajun spice mix, gather the spices and herbs in a pitcher. Burn the olive oil in a large frying or saucepan over med to low heat. Tan the chicken one for about 4-5 minutes on each side. Set to the side. Sautéed the onion in the pan until it was golden. Sauté for 5 minutes, until either the prawns are glossy, pour the garlic, prawns, Cajun spice, and red pepper into the saucepan. Fold the brown rice, chicken, and chicken broth into the pan. Continue cooking lasted for approximately 25 minutes, or when the rice is fluffy, and the chicken is perfectly cooked.

Nutritional Facts

Calories: 204| Carbohydrates: 12 g| Protein: 9 g| Fat: 11 g| Sodium 246 mg |

120. Ginger and Scallion Chicken Stir Fry

Preparation time: 5 minutes

Cook time: 30 minutes

Servings: 4

Ingredients

- 1 tablespoon of coconut oil
- 2 cups of rice noodles
- 3 pounds of chicken breasts
- 1 carrot chopped finely
- 1/4 cup of celery
- 1/2 cup of scallions
- 1/2 cup of mushrooms
- 1 tablespoon ginger
- 1 garlic clove, minced
- 1 lime

Instructions

Carry a skillet of water to a boil on direct heat, and immediately add the noodles. Sauté for around about 15 minutes. Secondly, in a wok on direct heat, bring the oil to a boil and add the chopped chicken breasts, stirring for at least 20 minutes anyway until well cooked, then set aside. Stir for 10 minutes with the carrots, celery, and chestnut mushrooms in the wok before adding the scallions, ginger, garlic, and cooked chicken back into the pan. Keep cooking for a few minutes until everything is boiling, then drain the noodles and add them to the pan. Before serving, put some lime juice over the top.

Nutritional Facts

Calories: 182| Carbohydrates: 32 g| Protein: 4 g| Fat: 6 g| Sodium 195 mg |

121. Harissa Spiced Chicken Tray-Bake

Preparation time: 15 minutes

Cook time: 30 minutes

Servings: 4

Ingredients

- 4 chicken breasts
- 1 spaghetti squash
- 2 onion

For harissa:

- 1 red pepper, diced
- 1 teaspoon red chili (dried)
- 1 garlic clove
- 1 teaspoon caraway seeds
- 1 teaspoon cumin
- 1 teaspoon cilantro
- 2 tablespoon olive oil

Instructions

In a mixing pitcher, incorporate the harissa spices and olive oil. Wrap and marinate the chicken breast and vegetables in the harissa mixture in the refrigerator for as long as needed. Preheat the oven while ready to cook. Put the breast chicken on a baking rack in the oven and bake for thirty minutes.

Nutritional Facts

Calories: 331| Carbohydrates: 42 g| Protein: 6 g| Fat: 11 g| Sodium 141 mg |

122. Chicken with Spiced Red Cabbage and Cranberry Sauce

Preparation time: 2 minutes

Cook time: 30 minutes

Servings: 2

Ingredients

- 1 tablespoon of olive oil
- 1/4 red onion, finely sliced
- 3-pound chicken breasts
- 1 red cabbage
- 1 tablespoon of nutmeg
- 1 tablespoon of apple vinegar
- 1 cup of cranberries
- 1 teaspoon of brown sugar

Instructions

Hold a pot to simmer water, after which add the remaining cabbage slices, nutmeg, and cinnamon to the water. Continue cooking for 15-twenty minutes on low flame. In a pot on moderate to high heat, bring the oil to a boil. Sauté the onions for some minutes or until tender. The chicken breasts should now be added and cooked for 10 minutes on each side. Combine the cranberries, water, apple vinegar, and brown sugar in a single small boiler.

Cover and cook, then decrease flame to low and cook for 10 minutes, or until cranberries are limp. Watch the water level and top it out as needed. Blend the cranberries until smooth in a food processor after they've softened. Season the cabbage with salt and pepper. Toss the chicken breast with cranberry sauce and serve over a bed of red cabbage.

Nutritional Facts

Calories: 197| Carbohydrates: 32 g| Protein: 6 g| Fat: 4 g| Sodium 66 mg |

123. Baked Eggs in Avocado

Preparation Time: 15 minutes

Cooking Time: 15 minutes

Servings: 2

Ingredients:

- 2 avocados
- Juice 2 limes
- Freshly ground black pepper
- 4 eggs
- 2 whole-wheat or corn tortillas, warmed (ø 8"/20cm)
- Optional for Servings: halved cherry tomatoes and chopped cilantro

Instructions:

Adjust the oven rack to the middle position and preheat the oven to 450°F. Scrape out the center of halved avocado using a spoonful of about 1 1/2 tablespoons. Press lime juice over the avocados and season with black pepper to taste, and then place it on a baking sheet. Crack an egg into the avocado. Bake within 10 to 15 minutes. Remove from oven and garnish with optional cilantro and cherry tomatoes and serve with warm tortillas.

Nutritional Facts:

Calories: 270| Carbohydrates: 19 g| Protein: 5 g| Fat: 10 g| Sodium 146 mg |

124. Beans and Rice

Preparation Time: 15 minutes

Cooking Time: 45 minutes

Servings: 2

Ingredients:

- 1/2 cup brown rice
- 1 cup of water
- 1 can bean
- 1 tablespoon of cumin
- Juice 1 lime
- 4 handfuls of spinach
- Optional toppings: avocado, chopped tomatoes, yogurt, onions

Instructions

Mix rice plus water in a pot and bring to a boil. Cover and reduce heat to a low simmer. Cook within 30 to 40 minutes or according to package instructions. Meanwhile, add the beans, 1/4 cup of water, cumin, and lime juice to a medium skillet. Simmer within 5 to 7 minutes. Remove it from the heat once the liquid is mostly gone, and add spinach. Cover and let spinach wilt slightly, 2 to 3 minutes. Mix in with the beans. Serve beans with rice. Add toppings if using.

Nutritional Facts:

Calories: 169| Carbohydrates: 34 g| Protein: 1 g| Fat: 4 g| Sodium 148 mg |

125. Butternut-Squash Macaroni and Cheese

Preparation Time: 15 minutes

Cooking Time: 20 minutes

Servings: 2

Ingredients:

- 1 cup of wheat ziti macaroni
- 2 cups of butternut squash
- 1 cup of milk
- Black pepper
- 1 teaspoon of mustard
- 1 tablespoon of olive oil

- 1/4 cup of shredded cheese

Instructions:

Cook the pasta al dente. Put the butternut squash plus 1/2 cup milk in a medium saucepan and place over medium-high heat. Season with black pepper. Bring it to a simmer. Lower the heat, then cook until fork-tender, 8 to 10 minutes. To a blender, add squash and Dijon mustard. Purée until smooth.

Meanwhile, place a frying pan or saucepan over medium heat and add olive oil. Add the squash purée and the remaining 1/2 cup of milk. Simmer within 5 minutes. Add the cheese and stir to combine. Add the pasta to the sauté pan and stir to combine.

Nutritional Facts:

Calories: 263| Carbohydrates: 33 g| Protein: 4 g| Fat: 11 g| Sodium 66 mg |

126. Pasta with Tomatoes and Peas

Preparation Time: 15 minutes

Cooking Time: 15 minutes

Servings: 2

Ingredients:

- 1/2 cup of pasta
- 8 cups of water
- 1 cup of peas
- 1 tablespoon of olive oil
- 1 cup of tomatoes
- 1/4 teaspoon of black pepper
- 1 teaspoon of basil
- 1/4 cup of cheese

Instructions:

Cook the pasta al dente. Add the water to the same pot you used to cook the pasta, and when it's boiling, add the peas. Cook within 5 minutes. Drain and set aside. Heat the oil skillet. Add the tomatoes, put a lid and let the tomatoes soften for about 5 minutes, stirring a few times. Season with black pepper and basil. Toss in the pasta, peas, and 1/4 cup of water, stir and remove from the heat.

Nutritional Facts:

Calories: 291| Carbohydrates: 12 g| Protein: 15 g| Fat: 13 g| Sodium 40 mg |

127. Healthy Vegetable Fried Rice

Preparation Time: 15 minutes

Cooking Time: 10 minutes

Servings: 4

Ingredients:

For the Sauce:

- 1/3 cup of garlic vinegar
- 1 and 1/2 tablespoons of molasses
- 1 teaspoon of onion powder

For the Fried Rice:

- 1 teaspoon of olive oil
- 2 lightly beaten whole eggs + 4 egg whites
- 1 cup of mixed vegetable
- 1 cup of edamame
- 2 cups of brown rice (cooked)

Instructions:

Prepare the sauce by combining the garlic vinegar, molasses, and onion powder in a glass jar. Shake well. Heat-up oil in a large wok or skillet over medium-high heat. Add eggs and egg whites, and let cook until the eggs set for about 1 minute. Break up eggs with a spatula or spoon into small pieces. Add frozen mixed vegetables and frozen edamame. Cook for 4 minutes, stirring frequently. Add the brown rice and sauce to the vegetable-and-egg mixture. Cook for 5 minutes or until heated through. Serve immediately.

Nutritional Facts:

Calories: 390| Carbohydrates: 56 g| Protein: 8 g| Fat: 17 g| Sodium 42 mg |

128. Portobello-Mushroom Cheeseburgers

Preparation Time: 15 minutes

Cooking Time: 10 minutes

Servings: 4

Ingredients:

- 4 Portobello mushrooms
- 1 tablespoon of olive oil
- 1/2 teaspoon of black pepper
- 1 tablespoon of vinegar
- 4 slices of cheese
- 4 wheat
- 1/2 avocado

Instructions:

Set the temperature to a medium-high skillet or grill pan. Remove the stems from the mushrooms. Brush with olive oil and pepper each cap. Cook for 4 minutes cap-side up in a skillet. Cook for 4 minutes on the flip. Flip with red wine vinegar. Cook for 2 minutes with the cheese. Loosen the cover to maximize melting. Toast the sandwich thins. Top your burgers with avocado slices.

Nutritional Facts

Calories: 247| Carbohydrates: 50 g| Protein: 8 g| Fat: 5 g| Sodium 140 mg |

129. Aromatic Chicken and Eggplant Curry

Preparation time: 10 minutes

Cook time: 35 minutes

Servings: 4

Ingredients

- 1 tablespoon of coconut oil
- 1 teaspoon of garam masala
- 1 teaspoon of cumin
- 1 teaspoon of turmeric
- 1/2 onion
- 1 clove garlic
- 1 eggplant
- 1/2 cup of chopped tomatoes
- 1 cup of water
- 3-pound chicken or turkey breasts
- 2 tablespoons of cilantro
- 2 cups of brown rice

Instructions

In a variable pan, bring to a boil and contribute the onions, constantly stirring for 3-4 minutes or until they begin to soften. Spices should be added one at a time and stirred for 4-5 minutes to release the flavors. Blend in the garlic at this point. Pour in the tomatoes and water, stirring constantly. Add the chicken and eggplant, cover, and cook for 25- 30 minutes or until the chicken is fully cooked. Leave the pot of water to a boil, add the rice, cover, and simmer for 20 minutes. Transfer the rice to the stove for 5 minutes after draining and covering it. Serve the chicken curry over the rice in separate pieces. To serve, garnish with fresh cilantro.

Nutritional Facts

Calories: 89| Carbohydrates: 4 g| Protein: 6 g| Fat: 6 g| Sodium 145 mg |

130. Marinated Olives

Preparation Time: 4 hours

Cooking Time: 0 minutes

Servings: 2

Ingredients:

- 2 cups of mixed green olives
- ¼ cup of vinegar
- ¼ cup of olive oil

- 4 garlic cloves
- Juice of 1 large orange
- 1 teaspoon of pepper flakes
- 2 bay leaves
- ½ teaspoon of cumin
- ½ teaspoon of allspice

Instructions:

Incorporate the olives, vinegar, oil, garlic, orange zest and juice, red pepper flakes, bay leaves, cumin, and allspice and mix well. Seal and chill for 4 hours or up to a week to allow the olives to marinate, tossing again before serving.

Nutritional Facts:

Calories: 468| Carbohydrates: 52 g| Protein: 17 g| Fat: 13 g| Sodium 156 mg |

131. Olive Tapenade with Anchovies

Preparation Time: 1hour and 10 minutes

Cooking Time: 0 minutes

Servings: 2

Ingredients

- 2 cups of Kalamata olives
- 2 anchovy fillets
- 2 teaspoons of minced capers
- 1 garlic clove
- 1 cooked egg yolk
- 1 teaspoon of mustard
- ¼ cup of olive oil
- Seedy Crackers

Instructions:

Rinse the olives in cold water. Place the drained olives, anchovies, capers, garlic, egg yolk, and Dijon in a food processor, blender, or large jar. Process until it forms a thick paste. While running, gradually stream in the olive oil. Hand over to a small bowl, cover, and refrigerate for at least 1 hour to develop the flavors. Serve with Seedy Crackers, atop a Versatile Sandwich Round, or with your favorite crunchy vegetables.

Nutritional Facts:

Calories: 232|Carbohydrates: 12g| Protein: 12.3g| Fat: 14g| Sodium 397 mg |

132. Italian Chicken

Preparation time: 10 minutes

Cook time: 20 minutes

Servings: 2

Ingredients

- 3 pounds of chicken breasts
- 1 tablespoon of olive oil
- 1 garlic clove
- 1 cup of chicken stock
- 1 teaspoon of thyme (dried)
- 1 teaspoon of rosemary (dried)
- 1 teaspoon basil (dried)
- 1/2 lemon
- 1 teaspoon of black pepper

Instructions

In some blending dishes, incorporate herbs. Place 1 chicken breast on a chopping board, sprinkle with 1/4 herb mix, and cover with plastic wrap; flatten the chicken breast with a meat pounder or rolling pin. Resume with the rest of the chicken breasts and herb mixture. Heat the oil over medium heat in a nonstick skillet and add the chicken breasts. Sauté for 8 minutes on each side or until completely done. Throw in the garlic for 2 minutes in the pan. Whisk the lemon juice, olive oil, and black pepper in a dressing bowl. Serve the chicken breasts with your favorite rice or couscous and vegetables with lemon dressing.

Nutritional Facts

Calories: 285| Carbohydrates: 16g| Protein: 16.1g| Fat: 12g| Sodium 316 mg |

133. Walnut and Basil Chicken Delight

Preparation time:

Cook time:

Servings:

Ingredients

- 3 pounds of skinless chicken
- 1 bunch of basil
- 1/2 cup of spinach
- 1 cup of walnuts
- 2 tablespoon olive oil
- 1/4 cup of brie
- 1/2 cup of arugula

Instructions

Oven preheated to 350°f. Split the chicken breasts and 'thin' them with a meat pounder.

Reserve a handful of nuts and arugula aside. In a mixture of pestle & mortar, combine the remaining

ingredients with a pinch of black pepper and mix until smooth. If the pesto has to be thinned, add a little water. Using the pesto, coat the chicken. Ready to oven to 350°F and bake the chicken for at least 30 minutes or until it is fully done. Place the remaining nuts on top of each chicken escalope and broil for 5 minutes to finish with a crispy coating. Serve on an arugula bed.

Nutritional Facts

Calories: 317| Carbohydrates: 50g| Protein: 12.8g| Fat: 9g| Sodium 473 mg |

134. Slow-Cooked Beef Brisket

Preparation time: 10 minutes

Cook time: 3.5 hours

Servings: 4

Ingredients

- 12-pound chuck roast
- 2 garlic cloves
- 1 tablespoon. thyme
- 1 tablespoon rosemary
- 1 tablespoon of mustard
- 1/4 cup of olive oil
- 1 teaspoon of black pepper
- 1 onion
- 1 cup of carrots
- 2 cups of chicken stock

Instructions

Set the oven to 300 °F. Strip the meat of any fatty deposits, and soak the veggies in lukewarm water. To make a thick paste, add all ingredients that include mustard, thyme, rosemary, and garlic, then add the oil and pepper. In an oven-safe baking dish, pour the mixture over the meat. Arrange the veggies around the meat at the bottom of the baking dish. Cover and round for about 3 hours or until vegetables are soft. Cook for another 30 minutes in the oven after uncovering the dish.

Nutritional Facts

Calories: 211| Carbohydrates: 24g| Protein: 18.5g| Fat: 16g| Sodium 304 mg

135. Homemade Avocado Sushi

Preparation Time: 20 minutes

Cook Time: 15 minutes

Serving: 4

Ingredients

- 1½ cups dry quinoa

- 3 cups water, plus additional for rolling
- ½ teaspoon of salt
- 6 nori sheets
- 3 avocados (halved)
- 1 small cucumber
- Coconut amino, for dipping (optional)

Instructions

In a fine-mesh strainer, rinse the quinoa. Combine the rinsed quinoa, water, and salt in a medium saucepan placed over high heat. Bring the water to a boil. Reduce the heat to a low setting. Cook for 15 minutes with the lid on. With a fork, fluff the quinoa.

Place 1 nori sheet on a chopping board. 12 cup quinoa, spread evenly over the sheet, leaving 2 to 3 inches uncovered at the top. Arrange 5 or 6 avocado slices in a row across the bottom of the nori sheet (facing you). Top with 5 or 6 cucumber matchsticks.

Roll up the nori sheet firmly, starting at the bottom. To seal the roll, dab the exposed top with water. Make 6 pieces out of the sushi roll. Replace the nori sheets, quinoa, and veggies with the remaining 5. Serve with coconut amino on the side (if using).

Nutritional facts

Calories: 557| Carbohydrates: 57g| Protein: 13 g| Fat: 33g| Sodium 309 mg

136. Red Lentil Stew

Preparation Time: 10 minutes

Cook Time: 35 minutes

Serving: 6

Ingredients

- 2 onions
- 4 celery stalks
- 6½ cups plus 2 tablespoons of water
- 3 cups red lentils
- 2 zucchini
- 1 teaspoon dried oregano
- 1 teaspoon of salt

Instructions

Sauté the onions and celery in 2 tablespoons of water in a large saucepan over medium heat for approximately 5 minutes, or until tender. Combine the lentils, zucchini, and the remaining 612 cups of water, oregano, and salt in a large mixing bowl. Bring the water to a boil. Reduce the heat to a low setting. Simmer for 30 minutes, covered, stirring periodically. Adjust the seasoning to taste if required.

Nutritional facts

Calories: 367| Carbohydrates: 64g| Protein: 26 g| Fat: 1g| Sodium 410 mg

137. Broccoli and Bean Casserole

Preparation Time: 10 minutes

Cook Time: 35 minutes

Serving: 4

Ingredients

- ¾ cup vegetable broth or water
- 2 broccoli heads
- 1 teaspoon salt
- 2 cups cooked pinto or navy beans, or 1 (14-ounce) can
- 1 to 2 tablespoons brown rice flour or arrowroot flour
- 1 cup walnuts

Instructions

Preheat the oven to 350 ° degrees Fahrenheit. Warm the broth in a large ovenproof saucepan over medium heat. Add the broccoli and season with salt. 6–8 minutes, or until the broccoli is brilliant green. Combine the pinto beans and brown rice flour in a mixing bowl. Cook for another 5 minutes, or until the liquid has slightly thickened. Over the top, scatter the walnuts. Preheat the oven to 350°F and bake the pot for 20 to 25 minutes. Toasted walnuts are recommended.

Nutritional facts

Calories: 410| Carbohydrates: 43g| Protein: 22 g| Fat: 20g| Sodium 635 mg

138. Brown Pasta with Cream Carrot Marinara

Preparation Time: 15 minutes

Cook Time: 20 minutes

Serving: 6

Ingredients

- 1¼ cups cashews, soaked in water for at least 4 hours
- 5 large carrots
- 1½ to 2 cups of water
- 1 tablespoon of basil
- 1 teaspoon of salt
- 1 (12-ounce) package of brown rice spaghetti
- 1 bunch kale (chopped into 1-inch pieces)

Instructions

The cashews should be drained and rinsed. Combine the carrots and 112 cups of water in a medium saucepan placed over high heat. Bring the water to a boil. Reduce the heat to low and cook for 5 to 8 minutes or until the vegetables are soft. Reserve the cooking water after draining the carrots. Combine the cashews, basil, and salt in a blender. Cook the carrots in the leftover cooking water. Blend till smooth, taking care not to burn yourself on the hot liquid. Thin the sauce with extra water if it's too thick.

Over high heat, bring a large saucepan of water to a boil. Cook the pasta according to the package instructions. Toss in the kale and let it wilt in the final minute of cooking time. Return the spaghetti to the saucepan after draining it. Toss with the marinara carrots. It's possible that you won't need all of the sauce. Leftover sauce keeps for 3 to 4 days in the refrigerator and freezes nicely.

Nutritional facts

Calories: 408| Carbohydrates: 65g| Protein: 10 g| Fat: 14g| Sodium 460 mg

139. Buckwheat Vegetable Polenta

Preparation Time: 15 minutes

Cook Time: 20 minutes

Serving: 6

Ingredients

- 3 cups buckwheat
- ¼ cup extra-virgin olive oil
- 6 garlic cloves
- 7 to 8 cups warm vegetable broth (homemade or purchased), divided
- 2 cups shredded zucchini
- 6 cups spinach
- 1 teaspoon salt

Instructions

Grind the buckwheat till fine in a spice grinder, high-powered blender, or food processor. Heat the olive oil in a large saucepan over medium-low heat. Sauté for 3 minutes with the garlic. Stir in the ground buckwheat to coat it with the garlic and oil. Add 1 cup vegetable broth, stirring. When all of the liquid has been absorbed, add another 1 cup of broth, zucchini, and spinach. 1 cup at a time, add the remaining 4 cups of liquid until the buckwheat is soft and has the consistency of thick polenta. You may not need all of the broth. Season with salt. Season to taste and adjust seasoning as needed.

Nutritional facts

Calories: 426| Carbohydrates: 65g| Protein: 18 g| Fat: 13g| Sodium 1307 mg

140. Quinoa Flatbread Pizza

Preparation Time: 10 minutes

Cook Time: 40 minutes

Serving: 6

Ingredients

- 1 Quinoa Flatbread
- 1 cup pearl onions
- 2 tablespoons extra-virgin olive oil
- 2 cups arugula
- 1 (14-ounce) can artichoke hearts in water
- 2 tablespoons pine nuts (optional)

Instructions

Follow the recipe's directions for making the flatbread. Remove the flatbread from the oven and raise the temperature to 375°F. Toss the pearl onions and olive oil in a small baking dish. Preheat the oven to 350°F and bake the dish for 10 minutes. Arrange the onions on top of the crust. Arugula, artichoke hearts, and pine nuts go on top (if used). Return the pizza to the oven and bake for another 12 minutes. Before slicing and serving, allow the pizza to cool somewhat.

Nutritional facts

Calories: 181| Carbohydrates: 13g| Protein: 4 g| Fat: 13g| Sodium 407 mg

141. Sardine Donburi

Preparation Time: 10 minutes

Cook Time: 50 minutes

Serving: 6

Ingredients

- 2 cups brown rice
- 4 cups water
- ½ teaspoon salt
- 3 (4-ounce) cans of sardines packed in water
- 3 scallions
- 1-inch piece ginger
- 4 tablespoons sesame oil or extra-virgin olive oil

Instructions

Combine the rice, water, and salt in a big saucepan. Over high heat, bring to a boil. Reduce the heat to a low setting. Cook for 45 to 50 minutes or until vegetables is soft. Sardines should be coarsely mashed in a medium basin. Add the sardines, scallions, and ginger to the saucepan after the rice is done. Combine everything well. Pour the rice into four bowls. 1 teaspoon to 1 tablespoon sesame oil drizzled over each bowl.

Nutritional facts

Calories: 604| Carbohydrates: 74g| Protein: 25g| Fat: 24g| Sodium 499 mg

142. Fish Tacos with Pineapple Salsa

Preparation Time: 15 minutes

Cook Time: 12 minutes

Serving: 6

Ingredients

FOR THE SALSA

- 1½ cups fresh or canned, pineapple chunks, cut into small dice

- 1 small red onion, minced

- Juice of 1 lime

- Zest of 1 lime

FOR THE TACOS

- 1 head of romaine lettuce

- 3 tablespoons coconut oil

- 14 ounces white fish, skinless and firm, such as cod or halibut

- Juice of 1 lime

- Zest of 1 lime

- ½ teaspoon salt

Instructions

HOW TO MAKE SALSA

Combine the pineapple and onion in a medium mixing basin. Mix in the lime juice and zest. Set aside after thoroughly stirring.

HOW TO MAKE TACOS

Separate the lettuce leaves into 6 to 12 big and adequate for holding the filling leaves. The leaves should be washed and dried. Heat the coconut oil in a large pan over medium-low heat. Brush the lime juice and zest over the fish. Season with salt and pepper. In the pan, place the fish. 8 minutes of cooking. Break up the fish into tiny pieces by flipping it over. Cook for another 3 to 4 minutes. The flesh should be translucent and readily flake with a fork. Fill the lettuce leaves with cooked fish (double the leaves for added strength) and top with salsa.

Nutritional facts

Calories: 198| Carbohydrates: 12g| Protein: 19g| Fat: 9g| Sodium 245 mg

Chapter 5: Soups and Salads

1. Eggplant Vegetable Soup

Preparation time: 10 minutes

Cooking time: 40 minutes

Serving: 12

Ingredients

- 1 pound 93 percent lean ground turkey
- 1/2 cup onion (chopped)
- 1 clove of garlic (minced)
- 1/2 cup celery (chopped)
- 1/2 cup carrots (chopped)
- 1 can (28 ounces) low-sodium or no-salt-added crushed tomatoes with liquid
- 1 medium eggplant (peeled and cubed)
- 28 ounces of low-sodium or no-salt-added beef broth
- 1/2 teaspoon salt
- 1 1/2 teaspoon ground nutmeg
- 2 teaspoons dried parsley
- 1/2 cup dry macaroni
- 3/4 cup grated Parmesan cheese for garnish
- Pepper to taste

Instructions

Brown the turkey in a pot. Combine the onions, celery, carrots, tomatoes, and broth in a large mixing bowl. Stir everything together thoroughly. Simmer for 30 minutes after adding the eggplant and seasonings. Cook for another 10 minutes or until the macaroni is done. Toss in the parsley. Serve with a sprinkling of cheese on top.

Nutritional facts

Calories 145|Carbohydrates 12 g| Proteins 13 g| Fats 5.6 g | Sodium 252 mg |

2. Turkey Vegetable Soup

Preparation time: 10 minutes

Cooking time: 14 minutes

Serving: 12

Ingredients

- 1/4 cup unsalted butter
- 1 1/2 teaspoon low-sodium curry powder
- 2 tablespoons flour
- 2 medium onions (chopped)
- 1 cup potatoes (chopped)
- 1/2 cup celery (chopped)
- 1/2 cup carrots (chopped)
- 2 tablespoons fresh parsley (chopped)
- 1/2 teaspoon fresh sage (chopped)
- 3 cups low-sodium chicken broth
- 2 pounds cooked 93 percent lean ground turkey
- 1 1/2 cups milk
- 10 ounces frozen chopped spinach
- Pepper to taste

Instructions

In a medium-high-heat saucepan, melt the butter. Add the onions and cook until they are transparent, about 10 minutes. Cook for 2 to 3 minutes after adding the flour and curry powder. Toss the potatoes, carrots, celery, parsley, and sage liquid. Bring the water to a boil. Reduce to a low heat setting, cover, and cook for 10 minutes. Combine the turkey, milk, and spinach in a mixing bowl. Simmer, covered, until well heated. Season with salt and pepper to taste.

Nutritional facts

Calories 245| Carbohydrates 8 g| Proteins 24 g| Fats 13.8 g | Sodium 125 mg |

3. Ginger Pork Soup

Preparation time: 10 minutes

Cooking time: 20 minutes

Serving: 8

Ingredients

- 1 tablespoon olive oil
- 2 cups shiitake mushrooms (sliced)
- 12 ounces lean boneless pork (cut into thin pieces)
- 2 cloves garlic (minced)

- 32 ounces of low-sodium chicken broth
- 2 teaspoons fresh ginger
- 2 tablespoons dry sherry
- 2 tablespoons low-sodium soy sauce
- 1/2 teaspoon crushed red pepper
- 2 cups Chinese cabbage (thinly sliced)
- 1 scallion (thinly sliced)

Instructions

Warm the oil in a pot over medium heat. Cook for 2-3 minutes, or until the pork is slightly pink in the middle. Take the pork out of the pan and put it aside. Cook until the garlic and mushrooms are soft in the pot. Bring to a boil with the broth, soy sauce, ginger, sherry, and red pepper. Combine the pork, green onion and Chinese cabbage in a mixing bowl. Heat till heated all the way through.

Nutritional facts

Calories 140| Carbohydrates 8 g| Proteins 13 g| Fats 6.0 g| Sodium 194 mg |

4. Creamy Carrot Thyme Soup

Preparation time: 10 minutes

Cooking time: 1 hour 5 minutes

Serving: 12

Ingredients

- 3 pounds of baby carrots or carrot chunks (peeled)
- 1/2 teaspoon ground ginger
- 8 cups low-sodium vegetable or chicken broth
- 1/3 cup honey
- 1/3 cup heavy cream
- 2 sprigs of fresh thyme
- Pepper to taste

Instructions

In a saucepan, combine the carrots, stock, and thyme. Bring to a boil, lower to low heat and continue to cook for 15 minutes. 45 minutes to an hour is a good length of time. Remove the soup from the heat and mix it in two batches. Completely puree the soup. Combine the honey and cream in a mixing bowl. As desired, season with pepper. Serve when still hot.

Nutritional facts

Calories 100| Carbohydrates 17 g| Proteins 3 g| Fat 2.6 g| Sodium 433 mg |

5. Beef Chili

Preparation time: 10 minutes

Cooking time: 2 hours

Serving: 8

Ingredients

- 1/2 cup onion (chopped)
- 1 large (11 to 12 inches) stalk of celery
- 1 tablespoon canola oil
- 2 tablespoons chili powder
- 1/2 cup green bell pepper
- 1 1/2 pounds of beef
- 16 ounces tomatoes
- 1 1/2 cup water

Instructions

Chop the onion, celery, and bell pepper into small pieces. On medium heat, heat a big skillet. Toss in the onion, celery, and bell pepper with the oil. Cook until the vegetables are soft but not brown. Cook until the ground beef is brown, dividing it into tiny pieces. Puree the tomatoes and add them to the meat mixture in a blender. Combine the chili powder and water in a mixing bowl. Reduce heat to low after completely mixing. Cook for many hours at a low temperature.

Nutritional facts

Calories 175| Carbohydrates 5 g| Proteins 16 g| Fats 10.5 g| Sodium 83 mg |

6. Strawberry Spinach Salad

Preparation time: 10 minutes

Cooking time: 0 minutes

Serving: 6

Ingredients

- 3 cups fresh spinach or a 6-ounce package of pre-washed spinach
- 1 tablespoon red wine vinegar
- 1 cup fresh strawberries (finely sliced)
- 1 tablespoon fresh lemon juice
- 1/8 teaspoon dry mustard
- 2 tablespoons honey
- 3 tablespoons olive oil

Instructions

The spinach leaves should be washed and dried. Place in a dish and tear into bite-size pieces. Strawberries, cut, and go on top of the spinach. Combine the vinegar, lemon juice, honey, dry mustard, and oil in a separate bowl. Dress the spinach and strawberries with the dressing. Toss thoroughly and serve right away.

Nutritional facts

Calories 95 | Carbohydrates 9 g | Proteins 1 g | Fats 6.9 g | Sodium 13 mg |

7. Roasted Corn & Edamame Salad

Preparation time: 45 minutes

Cooking time: 15 minutes

Serving: 6

Ingredients

- 2 ears fresh corn, unhusked / 1 1/4 cups cooked corn kernels
- 1/4 cup red onion (chopped)
- 1/4 cup red bell pepper (diced small)
- 1 tablespoon light mayonnaise
- 1 tablespoon fresh lemon juice
- 1 tablespoon fresh cilantro (finely chopped)
- 1 1/2 teaspoon ginger (finely chopped or grated)
- 1/2 cup edamame (shelled)
- 1/8 teaspoon salt
- 1/8 teaspoon black pepper

Instructions

Soak fresh corn for 30 minutes in cold water. Preheat the grill to high. Grill for 10 to 15 minutes in the husk, flipping once. Allow cooling before removing the husks. Cut the corn off the cob and place it in a basin. Combine the remaining ingredients in a mixing bowl. Refrigerate until ready to serve, covered in plastic wrap.

Nutritional facts

Calories 65 | Carbohydrates 10 g | Proteins 3 g | Fats 2.0 g | Sodium 71 mg |

8. Summertime Salad

Preparation time: 20 minutes

Cooking time: 0 minutes

Serving: 6

Ingredients

Salad:

- 6 cups spring lettuce mix (loosely packed)
- 1 avocado, peeled (pitted and diced)
- 1/2 cup walnuts (toasted and chopped)
- 1/2 cup goat cheese (crumbled)

- 1/4 cup red onion (thinly sliced)
- 2 cups seedless grapes (halved)

Creamy Poppy Seed dressing:

- 3 tablespoons apple cider vinegar
- 1/4 cup sugar
- 1/8 teaspoon dry mustard
- 1 tablespoon freshly squeezed orange juice
- 1/8 teaspoon salt
- 3 tablespoons light mayonnaise
- 3 tablespoons vegetable oil
- 1 tablespoon onion (finely chopped)
- 1/2 teaspoon poppy seeds

Instructions

Combine the vinegar, sugar, onion, dry mustard, salt, mayonnaise, and orange juice in a food processor. Blend everything well. While the machine is still running, drizzle the vegetable oil in a steady stream and process until well integrated. Add the poppy seeds and pulse just until combined. Refrigerate until ready to use in an airtight container. Toss the salad ingredients together in a bowl. Drizzle vinaigrette over salad and toss to mix.

Nutritional facts

Calories 305 | Carbohydrates 24 g | Proteins 6 g | Fats 22.1 g | Sodium 185 mg |

9. Zucchini-Ribbon Salad

Preparation time: 10 minutes

Cooking time: 0 minutes

Serving: 6

Ingredients

- 2 medium zucchinis
- 1 tablespoon sesame oil
- 2 medium yellow squash
- 3 tablespoons low-sodium soy sauce
- 1/8 teaspoon red pepper flakes
- 2 tablespoons rice wine vinegar
- 1/4 teaspoon sugar
- 1/2 teaspoon sesame seeds

Instructions

Peel the zucchini and squash into long ribbons. Whisk together the remaining ingredients in a large mixing basin. Toss in the zucchini and squash to combine thoroughly. Season with freshly ground pepper to taste.

Nutritional facts

Calories 50| Carbohydrates 5 g| Proteins 2 g| Fats 2.8 g| Sodium 272 mg |

10. Mandarin Salad

Preparation time: 5 minutes

Cooking time: 0 minutes

Serving: 4

Ingredients

Salad:

- 1/2 cup dried cherries
- 4 cups leaf lettuce/spinach
- 1 cup mandarin oranges (packed in water or juice)
- 1/4 cup toasted almonds
- 3 to 5 strips of low-sodium bacon or turkey bacon (cooked and crumbled)
- 2 medium apples (sliced)

Dressing:

- 2 tablespoons sugar substitute (Splenda, or can use sugar)
- 2 tablespoons of water
- 2 tablespoons apple cider vinegar
- 2 tablespoons olive oil
- Pepper to taste
- 1/4 teaspoon salt

Instructions

Toss the salad ingredients together. In a separate dish, combine the dressing ingredients in the order stated. Just before serving, toss the salad with the dressing.

Nutritional facts

Calories 295| Carbohydrates 37 g| Proteins 7 g| Fats 14.8 g| Sodium 245 mg |

11. Chipotle Chicken Salad

Preparation time: 5 minutes

Cooking time: 0 minutes

Serving: 4

Ingredients

- 2 cups cooked chicken (shredded)
- 1 cup celery (chopped)
- 2 tablespoons chipotle peppers in adobo sauce

- 1/4 cup red onions (diced)
- 1/4 teaspoon sea salt
- 1/2 cup light or homemade mayonnaise
- 1/8 teaspoon black pepper

Instructions

In a large mixing basin, combine all of the ingredients. Mix thoroughly.

Nutritional facts

Calories 195| Carbohydrates 5 g| Proteins 21| Fats 9.8 g| Sodium 442 mg |

12. Spinach, Apple and Walnut Salad

Preparation time: 5 minutes

Cooking time: 0 minutes

Serving: 4

Ingredients

- 2 large apples (Golden Delicious or another favorite, cored, diced large)
- 8 cups (2 5-ounce packages) of baby spinach leaves
- ¼ cup fresh lemon juice
- 3 tablespoons extra-virgin olive oil
- 1 tablespoon apple cider vinegar
- Ground black pepper as per taste
- 2 tablespoons honey
- 2/3 cup crumbled goat cheese
- 1/2 cup chopped walnuts (toasted)

Instructions

2 tablespoons of lemon juice tossed with apples. Remove long stems and damaged leaves from the spinach and place it in a large mixing basin. To taste, combine the remaining juice, olive oil, vinegar, honey, and powdered pepper in a mixing bowl. Toss spinach with apples and dressing in a large mixing bowl. Divide the mixture into four bowls. Cheese and walnuts go on top.

Nutritional facts

Calories 380| Carbohydrates 29 g| Proteins 9 g| Fats 27.1 g| Sodium 170 mg |

13. Mexican Vegetable Salad

Preparation time: 5 minutes

Cooking time: 0 minutes

Serving: 6

Ingredients

- 2 medium tomatoes (seeded and chopped)
- 1 cucumber (cut into bite-size chunks)
- 1 jalapeño (seeded and finely chopped)
- 1/2 medium red onion (chopped)
- 1 medium red bell pepper (cut into chunks)
- 2 large (11 to 12 inches) stalks of celery (chopped)
- 2 teaspoons Tabasco
- 2 limes (juiced)
- 2 tablespoons fresh cilantro
- 2 tablespoons olive oil
- Salt and pepper to taste

Instructions

In a mixing bowl, combine the veggies. Serve with chopped cilantro on top. The salad should be dressed with spicy sauce, lime juice, and olive oil. Salt & pepper to taste. Chill before serving.

Nutritional facts

Calories 70| Carbohydrates 7 g| Proteins 1 g| Fats 4.8 g| Sodium 88 mg |

14. Fall Harvest Orzo Salad

Preparation time: 5 minutes

Cooking time: 0 minutes

Serving: 8

Ingredients

- 4 cups cooked orzo
- 1 cup dried cranberries
- 1/4 cup fresh lemon juice
- 2 cups apple
- 1/4 cup olive oil
- 1/2 teaspoon black pepper
- 2 tablespoons fresh basil
- 1/4 cup blanched almonds
- 1/2 cup cheese

Instructions

Prepare the orzo according to the package directions. Combine all ingredients in a medium mixing bowl, except the blue cheese and almonds, and gently combine until thoroughly combined. Serve by transferring the mixture to a serving dish and topping it with crumbled blue cheese and almonds.

Nutritional facts

Calories 305| Carbohydrates 40 g| Proteins 7 g| Fats 13.5 g| Sodium 121 mg |

15. Bow-Tie Pasta Salad

Preparation time: 5 minutes

Cooking time: 0 minutes

Serving: 8

Ingredients

- 2 cups cooked bow-tie pasta
- 1/4 cup chopped celery
- 1/2 teaspoon sugar
- 2 tablespoons shredded carrot
- 2 tablespoons minced onion
- 1/8 teaspoon pepper
- 2 tablespoons chopped green pepper
- 2/3 cup mayonnaise
- 1 tablespoon lemon juice

Instructions

Combine the spaghetti, green pepper, celery, onion and carrot in a mixing bowl. Blend pepper, sugar, mayonnaise, and lemon juice in a separate small bowl until it becomes smooth. Pour it over the pasta and veggies and toss to coat. Chill.

Nutritional facts

Calories 189| Carbohydrates 12g| Proteins 2g| Fats 15g| Sodium 111 mg |

16. Chili Con Carne

Preparation time: 15 minutes

Cooking time: 0 minutes

Serving: 5

Ingredients

- 1 lb. lean ground beef
- 1 cup chopped onion
- 2 tablespoons chili powder
- 1/2 cup chopped green pepper
- 6 oz. no-salt tomato paste
- 1 teaspoon garlic powder
- 1/2 teaspoon paprika
- 1-quart water
- 1/2 teaspoon ground cumin

Instructions

Brown the ground beef in a large saucepan. Fat should be drained. Add the green pepper and onion. Cook until the onion is completely translucent. Simmer for 1 1/2 hours with the other ingredients. Measure the chili and add enough water to create 5 cups before serving. Bring to a boil.

Nutritional facts

Calories 254| Carbohydrates 11g| Proteins 21g| Fats 14g| Sodium 118 mg |

17. Cottage Cheese Salad

Preparation time: 5 minutes

Cooking time: 0 minutes

Serving: 11

Ingredients

- 2 lb. creamed cottage cheese
- 1 6-oz can juice packed crushed pineapple (drained)
- 1 8-oz carton of whipped cream
- 1 3-oz package Jell-O-lime or raspberry

Instructions

Cottage cheese should be mixed with dry Jell-O. Drain the pineapple and add it to the mix. Whip up the cream and fold it in. Refrigerate.

Nutritional facts

Calories 191| Carbohydrates 5g| Proteins 17g| Fats 11g| Sodium 348 mg |

18. Cranberry Frozen Salad

Preparation time: 10 minutes

Cooking time: 0 minutes

Serving: 9

Ingredients

- 1 8-oz package of cream cheese
- 1/2 pint whipping cream (whipped)
- 1 16-oz can of cranberry sauce
- 1/2 teaspoon vanilla extract

Instructions

Cream the cream cheese with an electric mixer until frothy. Combine the vanilla, whipped cream, and cranberry sauce in a mixing bowl. Fill a 9 x 9-inch baking pan halfway with the batter. Freeze. Serve frozen, cut into squares.

Nutritional facts

Calories 255| Carbohydrates 21g| Proteins 2.5g| Fats 19g| Sodium 99 mg |

19. Spiced Lamb Meatballs with Roasted Vegetables

Preparation time: 10 minutes

Cooking time: 40 minutes

Serving: 5

Ingredients

For Vegetables:

- 1 medium head cauliflower (cut into florets)
- 2 cups carrots, cut into medallions
- 1 teaspoon ground cumin
- 2 tablespoons avocado or olive oil
- ½ teaspoon paprika
- ½ teaspoon ground cinnamon
- ¼ teaspoon freshly ground black pepper
- 1¼ cup frozen corn

For Meatballs

- 1 pound ground lamb
- ¼ cup whole-wheat bread crumbs
- 1 teaspoon garlic powder/1 garlic clove (minced)
- ½ teaspoon ground coriander
- 1 large egg (lightly beaten)
- ½ teaspoon ground cumin
- ½ teaspoon ground cinnamon
- ½ teaspoon freshly ground black pepper
- ½ teaspoon paprika
- ½ teaspoon ground cayenne pepper (optional)

For Sauce

- ¼ cup tahini
- 2 tablespoons finely chopped fresh mint/1 tablespoon dried mint
- Freshly squeezed lemon juice
- 3 to 4 tablespoons of warm water

Instructions

Preheat the oven to 400 degrees Fahrenheit. Spread the carrots and cauliflower in a single layer on a baking tray lined with parchment paper. Drizzle with oil and toss to cover with cumin, cinnamon, paprika, and black pepper. Roast for 20–25 minutes or until golden brown.

To make Meatballs:

Meanwhile, add the lamb, bread crumbs, egg, garlic powder, coriander, cumin, paprika, cinnamon, black pepper, and cayenne (if using) in a large mixing bowl and stir until well blended. Overworking the flesh will result in toughness. Make 1-inch balls out of the dough. After 20 to 25 minutes of cooking, turn the veggies and add the meatballs to the pan. Put the meatballs in the middle of the veggies and return the pan to the oven. Bake for 15 minutes or until well done.

To make Mint Tahini Sauce:

Meanwhile, whisk the tahini, water, mint, and lemon juice to taste in a small bowl. Toss the corn with the vegetable and meatball combination after heating it according to package directions. When the dish is done, divide it into four equal parts and top with the sauce.

Refrigerate the leftovers for up to 5 days and freeze them for 3 months in an airtight container. The sauce can be kept in the refrigerator; however, freezing it is not recommended. Make the sauce when you're ready to reheat frozen meals.

Nutritional facts

Calories: 436| Carbohydrates: 26 g| Protein: 18 g| Fat: 19 g| Sodium 226 mg

20. Baked Apple Pork Chops with Wild Rice and Green Beans

Preparation time: 10 minutes

Cooking time: 1 hour

Serving: 4

Ingredients

- ½ cup water
- Avocado or olive oil cooking spray
- 2 tablespoons avocado or olive oil
- 2 tablespoons brown sugar or honey
- 2 tablespoons apple cider vinegar
- 9 ounces center loin pork chops
- 2 medium apples (cored and sliced)
- 1 pound of green beans (trimmed)
- ½ teaspoon freshly ground black pepper
- 1 cup cooked wild rice
- ½ teaspoon salt

Instructions

Preheat the oven to 325 degrees Fahrenheit. Spray an oven-safe pan with cooking spray and line it with foil. Heat the oil in a skillet or pan over medium-high heat. Brown the pork chops for 2 to 3 minutes on each side. Remove the pan from heat and set it in the oven pan with the cut apples on top. Spray the green beans gently with cooking spray and arrange them in a single layer in the pan. Deglaze the skillet with the water, scraping up the browned bits from the bottom with a spatula. Over the pork chops and green beans, pour the sauce. Brown sugar, vinegar, salt, and pepper are sprinkled over the pork chops. Bake for 30 minutes with the pan covered with foil. Cook for a further 15 to 20 minutes after uncovering.

Meanwhile, microwave the wild rice until it is hot. Serve the pork with green beans, apples, and rice on the side. Refrigerate the leftovers for up to 5 days and freeze them for 3 months in an airtight container.

Nutritional facts

Calories: 304| Carbohydrates: 35 g| Protein: 10 g| Fat: 21 g| Sodium 116 mg

21. Lamb Chops with Redcurrant and Mint Sauce

Preparation time: 10 minutes

Cooking time: 40 minutes

Serving: 4

Ingredients

- 4 Lean lamb chops
- 4 tablespoon Redcurrant jelly
- 1 tablespoon Lemon juice
- 4 tablespoon Water
- 1 tablespoon Mint sauce

Instructions

Combine the redcurrant jelly, mint sauce, lemon juice, and water in an ovenproof dish.

Trim the chops and set them on the sauce-coated plate, rotating to coat each chop well.

Bake uncovered for 35-40 minutes at 180°C (Gas Mark 4) in a preheated oven until the lamb is cooked. Before serving, the sauce may need to be thinned with cornflour and a little water.

Nutritional facts

Calories: 352| Carbohydrates: 55 g| Protein: 41 g| Fat: 15 g| Sodium 166 mg

22. Lamb and Ginger Stir Fry

Preparation time: 10 minutes

Cooking time: 8 minutes

Serving: 2

Ingredients

- 225g Minced lamb
- 1 teaspoon Ginger root (chopped or grated)

- 1 tablespoon Cooked peas
- A little sunflower oil
- Pepper to taste

Instructions

Fry, the lamb for 3-4 minutes in the sunflower oil or until lightly browned. Add the ginger and continue to cook for another 2-3 minutes, stirring constantly. Season with pepper, and add the peas.

Nutritional facts

Calories: 177| Carbohydrates: 18 g| Protein: 13 g| Fat: 12 g| Sodium 126 mg

23. Spicy Chicken

Preparation time: 10 minutes

Cooking time: 18 minutes

Serving: 4

Ingredients

- 450g Chicken (cut into 2.5cm cubes)
- 1 medium onion (finely chopped)
- ½ teaspoon Ginger powder
- 300ml homemade chicken stock or water
- 2 tablespoons Cooking oil
- 2 tablespoon Mango chutney
- 1 teaspoon soft dark brown sugar
- 150ml Cream

Seasoning:

- 55g Plain flour
- 1 tablespoon hot curry powder
- 1 teaspoon Paprika
- 1 teaspoon Cayenne pepper
- 1 tablespoon Turmeric
- 1 teaspoon ground coriander
- 1 teaspoon Chili powder
- 1 teaspoon ground cumin

Instructions

Mix all of the seasoning ingredients and coat the chicken in it. In a big heavy-bottomed frying pan, heat the oil. Fry the chicken until it is completely sealed. Cook for 1-2 minutes after adding the onion and ginger. Combine the stock of water, chutney, and sugar in a mixing bowl. Bring to a boil, then reduce heat and cook for 15 minutes. Stir in the cream and heat until the sauce is warmed through. Be careful not to boil the sauce.

Nutritional facts

Calories: 394| Carbohydrates: 40 g| Protein: 10 g| Fat: 22 g| Sodium 236 mg

24. Chicken and Sweetcorn Stir fry

Preparation time: 10 minutes

Cooking time: 20 minutes

Serving: 2

Ingredients

- 200g Chicken breast (cut into strips)
- 2 small Shallots (chopped)
- 1 small can of sweetcorn (drained)
- 2 tablespoon half fat crème fraiche (heaped)
- 30g Frozen peas
- Black pepper to taste
- Oil for frying

Instructions

In a little oil, fry the shallots and chicken for around 15 minutes, stirring periodically until done. Add peas and sweetcorn and cook for another 5 minutes. Stir in the crème Fraiche and season with black pepper.

Nutritional facts

Calories: 390| Carbohydrates: 40 g| Protein: 19 g| Fat: 23 g| Sodium 136 mg

25. Spicy Barbeque Chicken

Preparation time: 10 minutes

Cooking time: 15 minutes

Serving: 4

Ingredients

- 4 chicken breasts (skinned)
- 25g Plain flour
- 2 tablespoons Sunflower oil
- 1 tablespoon Red wine vinegar
- 4 tablespoons Lemon juice
- 1 Garlic clove (skinned and crushed)
- 2 tablespoon Low-fat natural yogurt
- 1 teaspoon Ginger root (grated)
- 1 teaspoon Paprika
- 1 teaspoon crushed peppercorns

Instructions

Mix 2 tablespoons of lemon juice, yogurt, flour, vinegar, oil, garlic, paprika, and peppercorns.

Make 1cm-wide parallel incisions in the chicken and sprinkle with lemon juice. Cover the chicken with the yogurt better in a mixing dish. Chill for many hours, rotating now and then. Cook the chicken for about 10-13 minutes on each side on the grill or barbecue or until the juices flow clear.

Nutritional facts

Calories: 278| Carbohydrates: 42 g| Protein: 16 g| Fat: 21 g| Sodium 206 mg

26. Sweet and Sour Pork

Preparation time: 10 minutes

Cooking time: 12 minutes

Serving: 4

Ingredients

- 225g Lean pork (cut into 2.5cm cubes)
- 1 teaspoon Olive oil
- 1 teaspoon ground ginger
- Black pepper to taste
- Vegetable oil for frying

Batter

- 175g Plain flour
- 300ml Water
- ½ teaspoon Oil
- 1 small Egg

Sweet and sour sauce

- 2 tablespoons White sugar
- 6 tablespoon Vinegar
- 200ml Water
- 2 teaspoon Cornflour (heaped)
- 2 tablespoon Pineapple juice (can be drained from a tin)
- Black pepper to taste
- A few drops of red food coloring

Instructions

Make a well with a spoon in the center of the flour in a basin. Gradually beat in the water while adding the egg. Set aside for 20 minutes after adding the oil. In a saucepan, combine the sugar, pepper, vinegar, water, and pineapple juice and bring to a boil for 2 minutes. Maintain a high temperature.

Combine the pork cubes, olive oil, pepper, and ground ginger in a mixing dish. Mix thoroughly. Remove any extra flour from the pork after coating it in 2 tablespoons. In a mixing bowl, combine the meat and the batter. In a deep pot, heat the oil until it is hot but not smoking. Cook the battered pork for 8-9 minutes or until golden brown in the oil. Drain it on absorbent paper. Serve in a hot serving dish with the sauce on top.

Nutritional facts

Calories: 676| Carbohydrates: 22 g| Protein: 18 g| Fat: 24 g| Sodium 336 mg

27. Fried Pork with Noodles

Preparation time: 10 minutes

Cooking time: 15 minutes

Serving: 2

Ingredients

- 225g Lean pork fillet (chicken may also be used)
- 2 medium Carrots (pre-boiled and drained)
- ½ teaspoon Thai seven-spice powder
- 1 medium Courgette (pre-boiled and drained)
- 1 small Red pepper (pre-boiled and drained)
- Oil for frying

Instructions

Cut the pork into thin strips and cook them in a wok or frying pan with a tiny oil. Carrot, courgette, and pepper should be cut into strips and added to the pork. Stir in the Thai seven-spice powder and simmer, often stirring, until the meat is well cooked.

Nutritional facts

Calories: 280| Carbohydrates: 40 g| Protein: 39 g| Fat: 11 g| Sodium 136 mg

28. Texas Hash

Preparation time: 10 minutes

Cooking time: 45 minutes

Serving: 4

Ingredients

- 450g Minced beef
- 2 tablespoon Rice
- 1 large onion (chopped)
- 1 tin of Tomatoes
- 1 teaspoon Sugar
- 1 Green pepper (deseeded and thinly sliced)
- 1 tablespoon Worcestershire sauce
- Pepper to taste
- Oil for frying

Instructions

In a little amount of oil, fry the onion until golden. Stir in the mince until it is fully broken up. Toss in the pepper and whisk to combine. Add the Worcestershire sauce and rice to the tin of tomatoes (fruit and liquid) in the pan. Stir well and boil for a few minutes until part of the tomato juice has evaporated. Cook for about 45 minutes in a moderate oven at 180°C (Gas Mark 4) in a greased ovenproof dish.

Nutritional facts

Calories: 324| Carbohydrates: 30 g| Protein: 27 g| Fat: 17 g| Sodium 136 mg

29. Shepherd's Pie

Preparation time: 10 minutes

Cooking time: 40 minutes

Serving: 4

Ingredients

- 450g Minced lamb (or beef)
- 1 large onion (chopped)
- 1 tablespoon Oil
- 2 medium Carrots (chopped)
- 1 tablespoon Flour
- 1 Stock cube
- 300ml Boiling water
- 675g Potatoes
- 25g Grated cheese
- Knob of margarine
- Dash of milk
- Black pepper to taste

Instructions

In a large pot, heat the oil, then add the onion and sauté until golden. Brown the mince in a little amount of oil. Boil carrots, drain and add to the mince and onions in a separate pan. Combine 300ml boiling water with the stock cube, add to the meat and season with black pepper. Boil the potatoes until they become tender, then drain and mash with a splash of milk, a knob of margarine, and a pinch of black pepper. Place the mince in an ovenproof dish, top with mashed potatoes, and then cheese. Cook for 30-40 minutes at 190°C (Gas Mark 5) until the potato is golden brown.

Nutritional facts

Calories: 478| Carbohydrates: 35 g| Protein: 34 g| Fat: 22 g| Sodium 136 mg

30. Spicy Beef

Preparation time: 10 minutes

Cooking time: 10 minutes

Serving: 4

Ingredients

- 560g Sirloin/rump steak
- 4 small Tomatoes (peeled, de-seeded and sliced)
- 1-2 Garlic cloves (crushed)
- 4 Celery sticks
- 2 tablespoons clear honey
- 2-3 teaspoons Mild chili powder
- 2 tablespoon Paprika
- 1 Beef stock cube
- 4 Spring onions (thinly sliced)
- 300ml Water
- 2 tablespoons Red wine vinegar
- 2 tablespoons Sunflower oil
- 1 tablespoon Worcestershire sauce

Instructions

The steak should be cut into 1cm pieces. Mix in the paprika and chili powder until the steak is uniformly coated. Allow for an hour of marinating time. Celery should be cut into 5cm lengths and then 5mm thick strips. Add the stock cube to the water and the Worcestershire sauce, honey, and red wine vinegar to make the stock. Before adding the steak, heat the oil and sauté the celery and garlic for a minute. Fry for another 3-4 minutes on high heat. Cook until the meat is fully covered and sizzling hot before adding the sauce. Heat the tomatoes until they are hot. Serve right away.

Nutritional facts

Calories: 414| Carbohydrates: 38 g| Protein: 46 g| Fat:

21 g| Sodium 96 mg

31. Saffron and Coriander Rice

Preparation time: 10 minutes

Cooking time: 10 minutes

Serving: 2

Ingredients

- 100g Basmati rice
- 5 Cloves
- 2 tablespoons fresh coriander (chopped)
- 5 Whole cardamom pods (optional)
- Pinch of saffron threads

Instructions

Combine the rice, cloves, and cardamom in a pan of boiling water. Cook according to the package directions. Remove the spices and drain the rice. Toss the rice back into the pan.

Stir in the saffron threads, cover them, and set aside 5-10 minutes. Serve immediately after adding the chopped coriander.

Nutritional facts

Calories: 184| Carbohydrates: 7 g| Protein: 4 g| Fat: 1 g| Sodium 116 mg

32. Tomato Pasta

Preparation time: 10 minutes

Cooking time: 15 minutes

Serving: 2

Ingredients

- 1 tablespoon Olive oil
- 1 small onion (chopped)
- Pinch Sugar
- 1 Garlic clove (chopped)
- A 400g Tin of chopped tomatoes (drained)

- Pinch Mixed herbs
- Pinch Black pepper
- 200g Dried pasta

Instructions

In a pot, brown the onion and garlic. Combine the tomato tin, black pepper, herbs, and sugar in a mixing bowl. Cook for 10 to 15 minutes. Meanwhile, cook the pasta until it is well-boiled. Drain and combine with the tomato sauce for a delicious meal.

Nutritional facts

Calories: 452| Carbohydrates: 17 g| Protein: 14 g| Fat: 21 g| Sodium 336 mg

33. Salmon Pasta with Butter

Preparation time: 10 minutes

Cooking time: 15 minutes

Serving: 4

Ingredients

- 350g Salmon fillets
- 600ml Water
- 400g Dried pasta
- 15g Butter or margarine
- 2 tablespoons Plain flour
- 2 tablespoons fresh tarragon (chopped)
- 1 Bay leaf
- Black pepper to taste

Instructions

Poach the salmon fillets for 15 minutes or until cooked in the water with the bay leaf. Remove the fish from the water and save the cooking liquid (450ml). In a big pot of boiling water, cook the pasta. Flake the fish while the pasta is boiling, discarding the skin and any bones. In a small saucepan, melt the butter or margarine, add the flour and whisk for 1 minute. Remove the pot from the heat and slowly stir in the fish stock. Return the sauce to heat and whisk until it thickens. Stir in the tarragon after seasoning the sauce with black pepper. Drain the pasta and set it aside. Mix the pasta with the salmon and sauce and toss gently.

Nutritional facts

Calories: 394| Carbohydrates: 30 g| Protein: 27 g| Fat: 15 g| Sodium 126 mg

34. Tuna and Potato Bake

Preparation time: 10 minutes

Cooking time: 40 minutes

Serving: 2

Ingredients

- 450g Boiled potatoes
- 1 medium Onion
- A 550g Tin of tuna (drained)
- ½ Lemon juice
- 2 pinches Nutmeg
- Black pepper to taste
- 4 Eggs (beaten)
- Butter/margarine as required

Instructions

Cook the onion for 10 minutes at a low temperature. Combine the onion and potato in a mixing bowl. Combine the pepper, lemon juice, nutmeg, and beaten eggs in a mixing bowl.

Toss the tuna with the potato mixture and flake it up. Brush the top of the mixture with melted butter or margarine and place it in an ovenproof dish that has been properly buttered. Preheat the oven to about 200°C (Gas Mark 6) and bake for 30 minutes until the top is well browned.

Nutritional facts

Calories: 521| Carbohydrates: 70 g| Protein: 76 g| Fat: 6 g| Sodium 146 mg

35. Lemon Sole with Ginger and Lime

Preparation time: 10 minutes

Cooking time: 15 minutes

Serving: 2

Ingredients

- 2 medium plaice fillets
- 1 teaspoon Ginger
- 2 tablespoons Sunflower oil
- ½ Lime
- Lime slices to garnish
- 2 metal skewers

Instructions

Each sole fillet should be cut in half along the middle. Each strip should be cut in half lengthwise. Roll the sole strips neatly on each skewer, and thread four rolls. Brush the remaining ingredients over the fish. Refrigerate for 10 minutes or up to 3 hours, covered. Grill over medium heat until done, flipping once and sprinkling with any residual marinade. Serve with lime slices as a garnish.

Nutritional facts

Calories: 245| Carbohydrates: 35 g| Protein: 31 g| Fat: 21 g| Sodium 176 mg

36. Root Vegetable Loaf

Preparation time: 20 minutes

Cooking time: 55 minutes

Serving: 6 to 8

Ingredients

- 1 onion
- 2 tablespoons of water
- 2 cups of grated carrots
- 1½ cups of sweet potatoes
- 1½ cups of gluten-free rolled oats
- ¾ cup of butternut squash purée
- 1 teaspoon of salt

Instructions

Preheat the oven to 350 degrees Fahrenheit. Using parchment paper, line a loaf pan. Sauté the onion in the water in a large saucepan over medium heat for approximately 5 minutes or until tender. Add the sweet potatoes and carrots. 2 minutes after cooking, Take the saucepan off the heat. Combine the oats, butternut squash purée, and salt in a mixing bowl. Mix thoroughly. Press the mixture evenly into the loaf pan that has been prepared. Bake for 50 to 55 minutes, uncovered, and in a preheated oven until the bread is firm and brown. Allow 10 minutes to cool before slicing.

Nutritional facts

Calories: 169| Carbohydrates: 34 g| Protein: 5 g| Fat: 2 g| Sodium 442 mg

37. Baked Falafel

Preparation time: 15 minutes

Cooking time: 30 minutes

Serving: 6 to 8

Ingredients

- 3 cups cooked chickpeas
- ⅓ Cup of tahini
- 1 tablespoon ground cumin
- 4 garlic cloves
- ½ teaspoon of salt
- 1 small bunch of basil
- Water (for thinning)

Instructions

Preheat the oven to 350 degrees Fahrenheit. Using parchment paper, line a baking sheet. Combine the chickpeas, cumin, tahini, garlic, and salt in a food processor. Blend until almost completely smooth. Toss in the basil. Pulse until fully combined. If required, add 1 or 2 tablespoons of water to assist the ingredients in forming a ball, but don't overdo it. Wet and pasty mixtures should be avoided. 2 tablespoons of dough, rolled into a ball, should go on the baking sheet. Press the ball into a 1-inch thick patty with the bottom of a glass or your palm. Repeat with the remaining chickpea mixture; 24 patties should result. Preheat the oven to 350°F and bake the patties for 30 minutes. The falafels will be mushy right out of the oven, but they will firm up as they cool.

Nutritional facts

Calories: 242| Carbohydrates: 24 g| Protein: 12 g| Fat: 12 g| Sodium 225 mg

38. Bean Burgers

Preparation time: 15 minutes

Cooking time: 35 minutes

Serving: 4 to 6

Ingredients

- 1 tablespoon of ginger

- 1 cup gluten-free rolled oats

- 3 cups cooked navy beans (1½ cups dried)

- 2 cups yam/sweet potato purée (about 2 yams/sweet potatoes, steamed and mashed)

- ½ cup sunflower seed butter or tahini

- ½ teaspoon of salt

Instructions

Pulse the oats a few times in a food processor until a rough meal forms. Combine the beans, yam purée, sunflower seed butter, ginger, and salt in a large mixing bowl. Blend until well combined. You may smooth it out entirely or leave it somewhat lumpy. Refrigerate for thirty minutes to firm up the mixture.

Preheat the oven to 350 degrees Fahrenheit. Use parchment paper or Silpat to line a baking sheet. Scoop the mixture onto the prepared sheet using a 13-cup or 12-cup measuring. (The scoop size is determined by the size of the burgers you desire.)

Gently pat the ingredients down to make 1-inch thick patties. This recipe makes around 12 patties. Preheat the oven to 350°F and bake the sheet for 35 minutes. Halfway through the cooking period, flip the burgers.

Nutritional facts

Calories: 581| Carbohydrates: 81 g| Protein: 27 g| Fat: 19 g| Sodium 355 mg

39. Black Bean Chili

Preparation time: 10 minutes

Cooking time: 60 minutes

Serving: 6

Ingredients

- 2 onions

- 2 tablespoons water

- 4 cups cooked black beans

- 1 (28-ounce) can of crushed tomatoes

- 4 teaspoons of chili powder

- 1½ teaspoons salt

Instructions

Sauté the onions in the water in a large saucepan over medium heat for approximately 5 minutes or until tender. Combine the black beans, tomatoes, chili powder, and salt in a bowl. Bring the water to a boil. Reduce heat to a low setting. Cook, stirring periodically, for 1 hour. Adjust the seasoning to taste if required.

Nutritional facts

Calories: 294| Carbohydrates: 55 g| Protein: 18 g| Fat: 1 g| Sodium 858 mg

40. Vegetable Spring Roll Wraps

Preparation time: 20 minutes

Cooking time: 0 minutes

Serving: 6

Ingredients

- 10 rice paper wrappers

- 2 cups of baby spinach

- 1 cup grated carrot

- 1 cucumber (cut into thin, 4-inch-long strips)

- 1 avocado (cut into thin strips)

Instructions

Place the veggies in front of you on a chopping board on a level surface. Fill a large, shallow basin halfway with heated water—hot enough to fry the wrappers but not too hot to touch.1 wrapper should be soaked in water before placing it on the cutting board. 14 cups spinach, 2 tablespoons shredded carrot, a few cucumber slices, and 1 or 2 avocado slices go into the wrapper's center. Fold the sides over the center, then burrito-style roll the wrapper from the bottom (the side closest to you). Continue with the rest of the wrappers and veggies. Serve right away.

Nutritional facts

Calories: 246| Carbohydrates: 36 g| Protein: 4 g| Fat: 10 g| Sodium 145 mg

41. Tahini-Kale Noodles

Preparation time: 5 minutes

Cooking time: 10 minutes

Serving: 4

Ingredient

- ½ cup tahini

- 8 ounces brown rice spaghetti or buckwheat noodles

- 4 cups of kale

- ¾ cup hot water

- ¼ teaspoon of salt

- ½ cup of chopped parsley

Instructions

Follow the package directions for cooking the noodles. Toss in the greens in the final 30 seconds of cooking time. Drain the noodles and greens in a colander. Place in a large mixing basin. Combine the tahini, boiling water, and salt in a medium mixing bowl. Add extra water if you want a thinner sauce. Toss the noodles with parsley and sauce. Toss to coat evenly. Adjust the seasoning to taste if required. Serve warm or chilled.

Nutritional facts

Calories: 404| Carbohydrates: 54g| Protein: 15 g| Fat: 18 g| Sodium 223 mg

Chapter 6: Appetizers, Snack and Sides

1. Mango Salsa Wontons

Preparation time: 5 minutes

Cooking time: 15 minutes

Serving: 24

Ingredients

- Vegetable oil cooking spray
- 1 tablespoon olive oil
- 1 large ripe mango
- 1 small cucumber
- 1/2 medium red onion
- 2 to 3 tablespoons fresh lime juice
- 2 to 3 tablespoons chopped
- fresh cilantro
- 24 wonton sheets
- Pinch of cayenne pepper

Instructions

Preheat the oven to 350 degrees Fahrenheit. Coat mini-muffin pans with cooking spray and use wonton sheets to line the molds. Preheat the oven to 350°F and bake for 9 to 12 minutes, or until golden brown. Allow the wonton cups to cool. Toss in the other ingredients and a pinch of black pepper to taste. Serve each wonton filled with salsa.

Nutritional facts

Calories: 40 | Carbohydrates: 7 g | Proteins: 1 g | Fats: 0.7 g | Sodium 6 mg |

2. Artichoke Dip

Preparation time: 5 minutes

Cooking time: 40 minutes

Serving: 10

Ingredients

- 1 cup artichoke
- 1/4 cup cream
- 1 large garlic clove
- 2 tablespoons cream cheese
- 2 teaspoons hot sauce
- 1 tablespoon Parmesan cheese
- 1/4 cup mayonnaise

Instructions

Preheat the oven to 375 degrees Fahrenheit. Cover artichoke hearts with water in a saucepan and bring them to a boil. Reduce the heat to medium and continue to cook for another 6 minutes. To cool, drain with cold water. Chop the artichoke hearts into small pieces. Combine mayonnaise, sour cream, cream cheese, spicy sauce, and garlic in a medium mixing bowl. Fill a baking dish halfway with the mixture. Parmesan cheese should be sprinkled on top. Preheat the oven to 350°F and bake for 30 minutes, or until the top is bubbly.

Nutritional facts

Calories: 40 | Carbohydrates: 4 g | Proteins: 1 g | Fats: 2.4 g | Sodium 113 mg |

3. Fresh Tzatziki

Preparation time: 20 minutes

Cooking time: 0 minutes

Serving: 10

Ingredients

- 1 large cucumber
- 1 tablespoon lemon juice
- 1 cup plain nonfat yogurt
- 1 teaspoon dried dill weed
- 4 large cloves of garlic
- Pinch of salt

Instructions

In a mixing dish, combine all of the ingredients. Allow for a 20-minute rest period. Serve with cucumbers, broccoli, and carrots as a side dish. Use it as a salad dressing or a spread on a sandwich. The leftovers will last 3 to 4 days in the refrigerator.

Nutritional facts

Calories: 20 | Carbohydrates: 3 g | Proteins: 2 g | Fats: 0.1 g | Sodium 35 mg |

4. Chicken Lettuce Wraps

Preparation time: 10 minutes

Cooking time: 10 minutes

Serving: 6

Ingredients

- Vegetable oil cooking spray
- 2 large stalks of celery
- 4 medium carrots
- 1 can of water chestnuts
- 1 large red bell pepper

- 3 medium scallions
- 2 tablespoons fresh ginger
- 4 cloves garlic
- 1 pound ground chicken
- 2 tablespoons rice vinegar
- 1/4 teaspoon black pepper
- 1/3 cup Chinese plum sauce
- 2 tablespoon soy sauce
- 1 teaspoon hot pepper sauce
- 1/4 cup cilantro
- 1 head lettuce

Instructions

Preheat a large skillet over medium-high heat, liberally sprayed with cooking spray. Carrots, celery, bell pepper, water, scallions, ginger, chestnuts, and garlic should all be added. Cook, stirring periodically, for approximately 5 minutes or until the veggies soften slightly. To avoid burning, add a tablespoon of water as needed. If necessary, reapply the cooking spray and add the ground chicken to the skillet. Cook until the chicken is no longer pink, breaking it up with a wooden spoon as it cooks into a fine crumble. Season with salt and pepper. Combine the plum sauce, vinegar, soy sauce, and chili paste in a mixing bowl. Toss to coat. Reduce the heat and cook until the mixture is thoroughly heated. Stir in the cilantro after removing the pan from the heat. Allow 5 minutes for the mixture to cool somewhat. Clean the lettuce and separate the leaves into 12 pieces. Trim the stem ends of the lettuce leaves if they are rough while collecting them. Half a cup of the chicken mixture should be placed in each lettuce cup. If desired, top with more cilantro.

Nutritional facts

Calories: 155 | Carbohydrates: 18 g | Proteins: 11 g | Fats: 5.0 g | Sodium 364 mg |

5. Sweet and Spicy Meatballs

Preparation time: 10 minutes

Cooking time: 25 minutes

Serving: 18

Ingredients

- Vegetable oil cooking spray
- 1/4 cup onion
- 1 pound of ground beef
- 1 large egg white
- 1/3 cup fine dry breadcrumbs
- 1/4 cup fresh parsley

- 1/8 teaspoon nutmeg
- 1/4 cup creamer
- 1/2 cup cranberries
- 1/2 cup grape jelly
- 2 teaspoons dry mustard
- 1/8 teaspoon cayenne pepper
- 1 teaspoon fresh lemon juice

Instructions

Preheat the oven to 375 degrees Fahrenheit. Spray a small pot with cooking spray and set it on the stovetop on medium-high heat. Add the onion and cook until it is soft. In a mixing dish, combine the onion and the other 6 ingredients. Make 36 1-inch meatballs out of the mixture. Cooking sprays a jelly roll pan or a small baking dish. On a baking sheet, place the meatballs and bake for 18 minutes.

Meanwhile, make the sauce by mixing the cranberries and the sugar. In a small saucepan, combine the remaining ingredients. Cook over medium heat until well heated. Pour the sauce over the meatballs into a serving dish. Toothpicks are used to serve.

Nutritional facts

Calories: 80 | Carbohydrates: 8 g | Proteins: 5 g | Fats: 2.9 g | Sodium 34 mg |

6. Hot Crab Dip

Preparation time: 10 minutes

Cooking time: 25 minutes

Serving: 10

Ingredients

- 1 package cheese
- 1 tablespoon onion
- 2 teaspoons Worcestershire sauce
- 1/8 teaspoon black pepper
- 2 tablespoons creamer
- 1 cab crab meat
- 1 teaspoon lemon juice
- Cayenne pepper to taste

Instructions

Preheat the oven to 375 degrees Fahrenheit. In a mixing dish, soften the cream cheese. Combine the onion, lemon juice, Worcestershire sauce, black pepper, and cayenne pepper in a large mixing bowl. Mix thoroughly. Add the non-dairy creamer and mix well. Stir in the crab meat until everything is well combined. Fill an oven-safe dish halfway with the mixture. Bake for 15 minutes, or until hot and bubbling, uncovered.

Nutritional facts

Calories 65 | Carbohydrates 3 g | Protein 5 g | Fat 3.7 g | Sodium 179 mg |

7. Mexican Layer Dip

Preparation time: 10 minutes

Cooking time: 0 minutes

Serving: 15

Ingredients

- 1 tablespoon lemon juice
- A 15-ounce of can beans
- 1/2 cup cream
- 3 avocados
- 1/2 cup plum tomato
- 1/2 cup of cheese
- 1 tablespoon mayonnaise
- 2 tablespoons fresh cilantro
- 3 tablespoons taco seasoning
- 1/2 cup diced onion
- 2 bell peppers
- 2 to 3 cups of lettuce

Instructions

Evenly put the ingredients in a baking pan. Refried black beans are the first layer. 2nd layer: mayonnaise, lemon juice, and mashed potatoes with ripe avocados. Layer 3: Combine sour cream, cilantro, and reduced-sodium taco seasoning. Peppers (bell) (layer 4) (layer 5), shredded cheese, shredded lettuce (layer 6), 7th layer: diced plum tomato and onion.

Nutritional facts

Calories: 110 | Carbohydrates: 11 g | Proteins: 4 g | Fats: 6.7 g |

8. Hummus

Preparation time: 15 minutes

Cooking time: 1 hour 40 minutes

Serving: 8

Ingredients

- 2/3 cup dry garbanzo beans
- 2 cloves Garlic
- 2 tablespoons onion
- 2 tablespoons fresh parsley
- 2 to 3 tablespoons tahini sauce

- Juice from 1 lemon
- Pinch of salt

Instructions

Beans:

Place beans in a large mixing basin and cover with cold water by several inches. Because they will double in size while soaking, make sure you choose a big enough basin. Any floating beans should be removed and discarded. Allow it to soak overnight by covering the bowl with a clean cloth. Before cooking, drain and rinse. Fill a big saucepan halfway with water and add the beans (about 1 quart of water for each cup of soaked beans). Bring to a boil, then lower to low heat. Cook for 60 to 90 minutes or until vegetables is soft. As you cook, keep an eye on the water level; you may need to add extra. Allow draining in a colander and cool. Fill an airtight container or a sealable bag halfway with cooked and drained beans (keep liquid out). They will last 3 to 4 days in the refrigerator.

Hummus:

Make a thick paste out of cooked garbanzo beans. Combine the remaining ingredients in a mixing bowl. Add a little extra lemon juice if the consistency is too thick.

Nutritional facts

Calories: 95 | Carbohydrates: 12 g | Proteins: 4 g | Fats: 3.9 g | Sodium 28 mg |

9. Chili Lime Shrimp

Preparation time: 5 minutes

Cooking time: 7 minutes

Serving: 4

Ingredients

- Vegetable oil cooking spray
- ¼ cup low-sodium or no-salt-added tomato paste
- 1 clove garlic
- 1-pound fresh medium shrimp
- 1 teaspoon chili powder
- 1 lime

Instructions

Combine tomato paste, garlic, and chili powder in a small bowl. Cook for 1 minute on high in a wok or big pan sprayed with cooking spray. Cook for 5 minutes or until shrimp become pink, turning often. Toss in the tomato paste mixture to evenly coat the shrimp.

Nutritional facts

Calories: 95 | Carbohydrates: 2 g | Proteins: 20 g | Fats: 0.8 g | Sodium 105 mg |

10. Easy Bruschetta

Preparation time: 5 minutes

Cooking time: 10 minutes

Serving: 8

Ingredients

- 1/2 cup tomatoes
- 1/2 cup red bell pepper
- 1 tablespoon minced garlic
- 2 tablespoons cheese
- 2 tablespoons Parmesan cheese
- 1 1/2 teaspoons basil leaves
- 1 baguette
- 1 1/2 teaspoons oregano leaves
- 1 can tomatoes

Instructions

Combine and mix all ingredients in a saucepan, except the baguette slices. Bring to a boil, seasoning with pepper to taste. Reduce heat to low and cook for 10 minutes.

Nutritional facts

Calories: 170 | Carbohydrates: 31 g | Proteins: 8 g | Fats: 1.9 g | Sodium 368 mg |

11. Warm Potato and Kale Mix

Preparation time: 10 minutes

Cooking time: 18 minutes

Serving: 2

Ingredients

- 2 large potatoes
- 1 cup fresh kale leaves
- 1/2 cup onion
- 1 clove garlic
- 1 small tomato
- 1/2 teaspoon dried thyme
- 1/2 cup beans
- 1 tablespoon olive oil
- Pepper to taste

Instructions

Potatoes should be diced and steamed until just tender (about 10 minutes). Remove from the equation. Kale should be washed and stems removed before being cut into 1/2-inch pieces. Heat the oil in a nonstick skillet over medium heat. Sauté the onion, garlic, and thyme until the onion is tender (about 3 minutes). Add the kale and tomato and cook for another 1 to 2 minutes, or until the kale has wilted. Stir in the potatoes and beans until everything is well combined and heated. Season with salt and pepper to taste, and serve right away.

Nutritional facts

Calories 350 | Carbohydrates 65 g | Proteins 10 g | Fats 7.4 g | Sodium 162 mg |

12. Spicy Sweet Potato Fries

Preparation time: 10 minutes

Cooking time: 30 minutes

Serving: 6

Ingredients

- 6 medium sweet potatoes
- 2 teaspoons sugar
- Vegetable cooking spray
- 1/4 teaspoon ground red pepper
- 1/8 teaspoon black pepper
- 1/2 teaspoon salt

Instructions

Preheat the oven to 500 degrees Fahrenheit. Potatoes should be peeled and chopped lengthwise. Transfer to a large mixing bowl and spray with cooking spray. Toss the potatoes with the sugar, salt, and pepper, stirring well to coat. Arrange potatoes in a single layer on a baking sheet, and cut sides down. Bake for 10 minutes, then flip the wedges. Bake for another 10 minutes, or until the potatoes are soft and in color.

Nutritional facts

Calories: 115 | Carbohydrates: 25 g | Proteins: 2 g | Fats: 0.8 g | Sodium 238 mg |

13. Mashed Tomato Potatoes

Preparation time: 10 minutes

Cooking time: 25 minutes

Serving: 8

Ingredients

- 2 pounds potatoes
- 5 medium tomatoes
- 1/4 cup butter
- 2 garlic cloves
- 1/2 cup cheese
- 1/2 cup milk

- 1/4 cup parsley
- 3 medium scallions
- 1/2 teaspoon kosher salt

Instructions

Fill a big saucepan halfway with water and add the potatoes and garlic. Bring to a boil, then reduce to low heat and cook for 25 minutes, or until a fork easily pierces a potato. Drain the garlic and potatoes. Use a potato masher or a fork to mash until smooth. Combine the milk, parsley, butter, Parmesan, scallions, and salt in a mixing bowl. Fold in the tomatoes gently.

Nutritional facts

Calories 190| Carbohydrates 25 g| Proteins 6 g| Fats 8.1 g| Sodium 262 mg |

14. Grilled Sweet Potatoes and Scallions

Preparation time: 10 minutes

Cooking time: 15 minutes

Serving: 4

Ingredients

- 4 potatoes
- 2 tablespoons Dijon mustard
- 8 medium scallions
- 2 teaspoons honey
- 3/4 cup olive oil
- 1/2 cup apple cider vinegar
- 1/4 cup balsamic vinegar
- Freshly ground pepper per taste
- 1/4 cup parsley

Instructions

Preheat the grill to medium-high. Brush the potatoes and onions with oil before placing them on the grill. 3 to 4 minutes on each side on the grill, or until potatoes are just tender. Scallions should be grilled until tender and marked. Remove the scallions from the grill and slice them thinly. Combine 1/2 cup olive oil, mustard, tablespoons of vinegar, and honey in a large mixing basin. To taste, season with pepper. Toss in the potatoes, scallions, and parsley until well coated. Serve immediately on a plate.

Nutritional facts

Calories: 570| Carbohydrates: 46 g| Proteins: 5 g| Fats: 41.3 g| Sodium 257 mg |

15. Roasted Brussels sprouts

Preparation time: 10 minutes

Cooking time: 45 minutes

Serving: 6

Ingredients

- 1 pound Brussels sprout
- 2 tablespoons olive oil
- 1 tablespoon garlic
- 1 teaspoon fresh lemon juice
- black pepper per taste
- Salt per taste
- 1/4 cup cheese

Instructions

Preheat the oven to 350 degrees Fahrenheit. In a frying pan or a roasting pan, place Brussels sprouts. Add the garlic and mix well. Lemon juice should be drizzled over Brussels sprouts. Toss the sprouts in the oil until they are fully covered. Season with a sufficient amount of salt (at least 1/2 teaspoon) and a few grinds of black pepper. Cook for 20 minutes on the top shelf of the oven, then toss to coat Brussels sprouts with the oil in the pan. Cook for a further ten minutes. Cook for another 5 minutes after adding the Parmesan (if using). Warm the dish before serving.

Nutritional facts

Calories 85| Carbohydrates 6 g| Proteins 4 g| Fats 6.1 g| Sodium 128 mg |

16. Grilled Asparagus with Mozzarella

Preparation time: 5 minutes

Cooking time: 10 minutes

Serving: 4

Ingredients

Asparagus:

- 20 asparagus stalks
- 1/4 pound mozzarella

Dressing:

- 4 tablespoons fresh lemon juice
- 1/4 cup olive oil
- 1 teaspoon dried oregano
- 1 small shallot
- 1 tablespoon fresh parsley
- Freshly ground pepper to taste

Instructions

Preheat the grill to high. Combine all of the dressing ingredients in a small dish and set aside. Season asparagus with pepper to taste after brushing with an olive oil mixture. 3–4 minutes on the grill, or until just tender. Distribute the asparagus among four dishes and top with a piece of mozzarella right away.

Nutritional facts

Calories 230| Carbohydrates 7 g| Proteins 10 g| Fats 19.5 g| Sodium 200 mg |

17. Grilled Vegetables

Preparation time: 5 minutes

Cooking time: 25 minutes

Serving: 4

Ingredients

- 1 medium onion (cut into large chunks)
- 1 medium zucchini (cut into thick slices)
- 2 tablespoons olive oil
- 1 medium yellow squash (cut into thick slices)
- 1 small sweet potato (cut into small cubes)
- 1 clove of garlic (minced)
- Pinch of salt
- Pepper to taste

Instructions

In a large mixing basin, combine all of the veggies. Combine the oil, garlic, salt, and pepper; pour over the veggies. Stir to coat all of the veggies. Arrange veggies in a grill basket or on a flat baking sheet. Cook on a medium-high grill for 10 to 20 minutes, or until the veggies are cooked and beginning to brown. Serve right away.

Nutritional facts

Calories: 80| Carbohydrates: 11 g| Proteins: 2 g| Fats: 3.9 g| Sodium 45 mg |

18. Noodles Romano

Preparation time: 5 minutes

Cooking time: 10 minutes

Serving: 6

Ingredients

- 1/2 cup unsalted butter (divided)
- 2 tablespoons dried parsley
- 1 garlic clove
- 1 teaspoon dried basil
- 6 ounces light or reduced-fat cream cheese
- 8 ounces whole-wheat spaghetti
- 3/4 cup Parmesan cheese

- 1/8 teaspoon pepper

Instructions

Combine 1/4 cup butter, parsley flakes, and basil in a small mixing bowl. Cream together the cream cheese and pepper with the butter mixture. 2/3 cup boiling water, stirred in. Blend the ingredients well. Warm over a pan of boiling water. Cook noodles until just soft in unsalted water; drain. Cook for 1 to 2 minutes in 1/4 cup butter, then pour over noodles and mix gently and rapidly to coat thoroughly. Toss with 1/2 cup Parmesan cheese once more. Noodles should be piled high on a heated serving plate. Warm the cream cheese sauce and pour it over the noodles. The remaining 1/4 cup Parmesan cheese should be sprinkled on top. Add more parsley as a garnish.

Nutritional facts

Calories: 380| Carbohydrates: 32 g| Proteins: 13 g| Fats: 23.9 g| Sodium 332 mg |

19. Quinoa with Black Beans and Avocado

Preparation time: 5 minutes

Cooking time: 12 minutes

Serving: 6

Ingredients

- 1 3/4 cups water
- 1 tablespoon olive oil
- 1 avocado (chopped into chunks)
- 1 cup dry quinoa (rinsed)
- 1 can (16 ounces) of low-sodium black beans, drained and rinsed (rinse twice to reduce sodium)
- 1 small garlic clove (minced)
- 3/4 cup cherry tomatoes (quartered)
- 1/2 medium red onion (diced)
- 1 medium red bell pepper (chopped into chunks)
- 1/4 cup fresh cilantro (chopped)

Dressing:

- 1 lime (juiced)
- 1/2 teaspoon cumin
- 1/2 tablespoon olive oil

Instructions

In a medium saucepan over medium heat, warm the olive oil. Toast-washed quinoa for 2 to 3 minutes or until it begins to smell nutty. Add the water, stir once, cover, and cook for 20 minutes. Prepare the dressing by blending the lime juice, oil, and cumin while heating the quinoa. Whisk vigorously. Season with salt and pepper to taste. Remove the quinoa from the pan and fluff it with a fork when done. Toss in the black beans to warm them up. Allow 5 minutes for the quinoa to cool before mixing the additional ingredients, including the dressing. If required, adjust the seasoning.

Nutritional facts

Calories: 260| Carbohydrates: 37 g| Proteins: 9 g| Fats: 9.1 g| Sodium 8 mg |

20. Roasted Vegetables

Preparation time: 10 minutes

Cooking time: 52 minutes

Serving: 8

Ingredients

- 1 small butternut squash (cubed)
- 2 small Yukon Gold potatoes (cubed)
- 2 medium red bell peppers (seeded and diced)
- 1 small sweet potato (peeled and cubed)
- 1 medium red onion (quartered)
- 1 tablespoon fresh thyme (chopped)
- 3 tablespoons olive oil
- 2 tablespoons fresh rosemary (chopped)
- 1 1/2 tablespoons balsamic vinegar
- Salt to taste
- Freshly ground black pepper

Instructions

Preheat the oven to 475 degrees Fahrenheit. Combine the squash, sweet potato, red bell peppers, and Yukon Gold potatoes in a large mixing basin. Red onion quarters should be cut into pieces and added to the mixture. Combine the thyme, rosemary, vinegar, olive oil, salt, and pepper in a small bowl. Toss the veggies in the oil mixture until they are well-covered. In a big pan, spread evenly. Roast for 30–40 minutes, tossing every 10 minutes, or until veggies are cooked and browned in the oven.

Nutritional facts

Calories: 95| Carbohydrates: 16 g| Proteins: 2 g| Fats: 3.6 g| Sodium 46 mg |

21. Couscous and Feta-Stuffed Peppers

Preparation time: 10 minutes

Cooking time: 40 minutes

Serving: 4

Ingredients

- Vegetable oil cooking spray
- 1 1/4 cups low-sodium chicken or vegetable broth
- 4 large bell peppers (mixed colors)
- 1/2 teaspoon dried oregano
- 1 1/4 tablespoon olive oil
- 1/2 cup onion (chopped)
- 2/3 cup couscous
- 6 ounces zucchini (quartered lengthwise, then sliced across thinly)
- 6 ounces yellow squash (quartered lengthwise, then sliced across thinly)
- 1/2 teaspoon fennel seeds
- 1 cup cherry tomatoes (cut in half)
- 15 ounces canned low-sodium garbanzo beans (drained and rinsed)
- 4 ounces low-fat or reduced-fat crumbled feta cheese

Instructions

Preheat the oven to 350 degrees Fahrenheit. Using cooking spray, coat a small baking dish. In a saucepan, bring the broth to a boil, add the couscous, cover, and remove from the heat. Meanwhile, bring a big pot of water to a boil. Cut the bell peppers' stems and tops off, then scoop out the seeds and membranes. Boil peppers, trim for 5 minutes, then drain upside down. In a nonstick skillet, heat the oil. Combine the onion, zucchini, yellow squash, fennel seeds, and oregano in a large mixing bowl. Cook for 5 minutes or until softened, stirring often. Take the pan off the heat and add the tomatoes and garbanzo beans. Scrape the couscous into the pan with a fork and stir with the veggies. Add the crumbled feta cheese and mix well. Fill the peppers with couscous and stand them upright in the roasting dish. 15 minutes in the oven. Serve right away.

Nutritional facts

Calories: 400| Carbohydrates: 57 g| Proteins: 19 g| Fats: 12.1 g| Sodium 385 mg |

22. Chili Wheat Treats

Preparation time: 10 minutes

Cooking time: 15 minutes

Serving: 8

Ingredients

- 1/2 cup margarine
- 1/2 teaspoon garlic powder
- Dash cayenne pepper
- 1/2 teaspoon ground cumin
- 4 cups spoon-size shredded wheat

- 1 tablespoon chili powder

Instructions

Preheat the oven to 300 degrees Fahrenheit. In a 10 x 15-inch baking pan, melt margarine. Add the spices and mix well. Toss in the cereal to coat it evenly. Preheat the oven to 350°F and bake for 15 minutes, or until crisp. Keep in an airtight container.

Nutritional facts

Calories 184 | Carbohydrates 16g | Protein 3 g | Fat 12g | Sodium 107 mg |

23. Holiday Eggnog

Preparation time: 5 minutes

Cooking time: 10 minutes

Serving: 6

Ingredients

- 1 1/2 teaspoons vanilla
- 1 1/2 cups liquid non-dairy coffee creamer
- 1/2 cup frozen eggs / 1/2 cup liquid low-cholesterol egg substitute
- 2 tablespoons sugar
- Nutmeg

Instructions

In a blender or an electric mixer, thoroughly combine the first four ingredients. Allow cooling completely. Finish with a nutmeg sprinkling.

Nutritional facts

Calories 134 | Carbohydrates 13g | Protein 3g | Fat 8g | Sodium 88 mg |

24. Onion Bagel Chips

Preparation time: 10 minutes

Cooking time: 20 minutes

Serving: 4

Ingredients

- 2 3-1/2-oz plain bagels
- 2 tablespoons margarine (melted)
- 1/2 teaspoon onion powder

Instructions

Using an electric knife, cut each bagel in half vertically. Place one bagel half on a flat surface, cut side down, and cut vertically into 8 slices. Proceed with the remaining bagel halves in the same manner. On a baking sheet, arrange the slices. Brush bagels with a mixture of margarine and onion powder. Preheat the oven to 325°F and bake for 20 minutes, or until golden and crisp.

Remove from pan and set aside to cool fully. Keep the container sealed. This recipe makes 32 chips.

Nutritional facts

Calories: 128 | Carbohydrates: 16g | Protein: 3g | Fat: 6g | Sodium 208 mg |

25. Oriental Egg Rolls

Preparation time: 10 minutes

Cooking time: 40 minutes

Serving: 14

Ingredients

- 1 lb. diced cooked chicken
- 1/2 lb. bean sprouts
- 2 tablespoons vegetable oil
- 1/2 lb. shredded cabbage
- 1 clove of garlic (minced)
- 1 medium (1 cup) chopped onion
- 1 tablespoon low sodium soy sauce
- 1 package (20) egg roll wrappers
- Oil for frying

Instructions

Combine all ingredients except the wrappers and frying oil in a mixing dish. Allow 30 minutes for marinating. Divide the filling among the wrappers and fold according to the directions on the wrapper packaging. Preheat the oil to 350 degrees Fahrenheit. Fry egg rolls (1 inch or more) in heated oil until golden brown. Using paper towels, absorb any excess liquid.

Nutritional facts

Calories 168 | Carbohydrates 15g | Protein 9g | Fat 8g | Sodium 152 mg |

26. Parmesan Cheese Spread

Preparation time: 40 minutes

Cooking time: 0 minutes

Serving: 7

Ingredients

- 1 3-oz package of cream cheese
- 4 tablespoons margarine (softened)
- 2 tablespoons grated
- 1 tablespoon dry white wine
- 1 tablespoon minced parsley
- 1/4 teaspoon garlic powder

- Parmesan cheese
- Dash of thyme
- Dash of marjoram

Instructions

Combine all ingredients in a large mixing bowl and stir until thoroughly combined. Refrigerate for at least 4 hours. Serve with Melba toast and unsalted crackers, or use it as a celery stuffing.

Nutritional facts

Calories 109| Carbohydrates 1g| Protein 2g| Fat 11g| Sodium 115 mg |

27. Polynesian Turkey Kabobs

Preparation time: 10 minutes

Cooking time: 20 minutes

Serving: 15

Ingredients

- 1 lb. ground raw turkey
- 1/3 cup unsalted crackers (crushed, 5 crackers)
- 1 egg or 1/4 cup liquid egg substitute
- 1/4 cup chopped onion
- 1 teaspoon ground ginger
- 1 clove of garlic (crushed)
- 1 20-oz can pineapple chunks in juice (drained, reserving 1/3 cup juice)
- 1 large red pepper (cut into 22 pieces)
- 1 large green pepper (cut into 23 pieces)
- 1/3 cup reserved pineapple juice
- 2 tablespoons margarine (melted)
- 2 tablespoons orange marmalade
- 1 1/2 teaspoons ground ginger

Instructions

Combine the first six ingredients in a medium mixing basin. Make 30 meatballs out of the mixture. Arrange pineapple chunks and pepper slices on 15 8-inch wooden skewers. Place the pan under the broiler. Combine pineapple juice, margarine, marmalade, and ginger in a small mixing dish. Brush the kabobs with a brush. Broil for 20 minutes at 4 inches from the heat source, flipping once and basting with sauce.

Nutritional facts

Calories 122| Carbohydrates 20g| Protein 2g| Fat 4g| Sodium 49 mg |

28. Snack Mix

Preparation time: 5 minutes

Cooking time: 10 minutes

Serving: 6

Ingredients

- 1 cup rice cereal squares
- 1/3 cup margarine (melted)
- 3 cups unsalted popped popcorn
- 1 cup corn cereal squares
- 1 cup unsalted tiny pretzel twists
- 1/2 teaspoon garlic powder
- 1/2 teaspoon onion powder
- 1 tablespoon Parmesan cheese

Instructions

In a large mixing dish, combine cereals, pretzels, and popcorn. Melt the margarine and add the garlic and onion powders. Toss the cereal mixture in the sauce to coat it. Parmesan cheese should be added at this point. Preheat the oven to 350°F and bake for 7–10 minutes. Cool. Keep in a tightly sealed container.

Nutritional facts

Calories 180| Carbohydrates 19g| Protein 2.5g| Fat 11g| Sodium 386 mg |

29. Spiced Pineapple Appetizer

Preparation time: 5 minutes

Cooking time: 8 minutes

Serving: 10

Ingredients

- 1/4 cup white wine vinegar
- 2 tablespoons lime juice
- 1/4 teaspoon crushed red pepper
- 3 tablespoons sugar
- 1/8 teaspoon garlic powder
- 1/2 teaspoon Dijon mustard
- 1 20-oz can of pineapple chunks in juice (drained)

Instructions

Combine the vinegar, sugar, lime juice, Dijon mustard, pepper, and garlic powder in a saucepan. Bring the water to a boil. Reduce heat to low and cook uncovered for 3 minutes. Combine the vinegar mixture and the pineapple; stir well. Serve with toothpicks while still heated.

Nutritional facts

Calories 47| Carbohydrates 12g| Protein 0g| Fat 0g| Sodium 4 mg |

30. Zippy Dip

Preparation time: 5 minutes

Cooking time: 0 minutes

Serving: 12

Ingredients

- 1/2 cup margarine (softened)
- 1 teaspoon horseradish
- 3 tablespoons green onion (chopped)
- 1 1/2 teaspoons lemon juice
- 1 package (8 oz.) cream cheese (softened)
- 1 1/2 teaspoons hot dry mustard
- 2 tablespoons mayonnaise
- 1 teaspoon paprika
- 1/2 teaspoon tarragon
- 1/2 teaspoon garlic powder
- 1 tablespoon vinegar
- Dash of cayenne pepper

Instructions

Combine all ingredients in a blender and blend until smooth. Serve with fresh veggies or unsalted crackers.

Nutritional facts

Calories 155| Carbohydrates 2g| Protein 2g| Fat 16g| Sodium 133 mg |

31. Asparagus Bruschetta with Garlic and Basil

Preparation time: 5 minutes

Cooking time: 10 minutes

Serving: 2

Ingredients

- 1 tablespoon Olive oil
- 1 Ciabatta loaf or any other uncut small white loaf
- 4 Fresh asparagus spears (boiled until tender)
- ½ Garlic clove (crushed and finely chopped)
- 1 tablespoon basil (finely chopped)

Instructions

Cut four 2cm thick slices of bread from the loaf and set them on a baking pan under a medium grill, lightly brown one side. Cut the asparagus spears lengthwise and then into two or three shorter strips. Combine the olive oil, garlic, and basil in a bowl and distribute over the bread's untoasted side. Return to the grill until the edges are browned, then top with asparagus and a light brushing of olive oil. While the dish is still hot, serve it right away.

Nutritional facts

Calories 230| Carbohydrates 13g| Protein 8g| Fat 8g| Sodium 16 mg |

32. Roasted Onion Garlic Dip

Preparation time: 15 minutes + 1 hour for chilling

Cooking time: 1 hour

Serving: 6

Ingredients

- 1 large sweet onion (peeled and cut into eighths)
- 8 garlic cloves
- 2 teaspoons olive oil
- ½ cup light sour cream
- 1 tablespoon fresh lemon juice
- 1 tablespoon chopped fresh parsley
- 1 teaspoon chopped fresh thyme
- Freshly ground black pepper

Instructions

Set the oven to 425 degrees Fahrenheit. Toss the onion and garlic with the olive oil in a small bowl. Place the onion and garlic on aluminum foil and gently wrap them in a package. Place the foil package on a small baking sheet and bake it for 15 minutes. Roast for 50 minutes to an hour or until the veggies are aromatic and golden. Allow 15 minutes for the packet to cool after removing it from the oven. Combine the sour cream, lemon juice, parsley, thyme, and black pepper in a medium mixing bowl. Carefully open the foil wrapper and place the veggies on a chopping board. Chop the veggies and toss them in with the sour cream. To blend, stir everything together. Before serving, cover the dip and chill it in the refrigerator for 1 hour.

Nutritional facts

Calories 44| Carbohydrates 5g| Protein 1g| Fat 3g| Sodium 10 mg |

33. Baba Ghanoush

Preparation time: 20 minutes

Cooking time: 30 minutes

Serving: 6

Ingredients

- 1 medium eggplant (halved and scored with a

crosshatch pattern on the cut sides)

- 1 teaspoon ground cumin
- 1 tablespoon olive oil (plus extra for brushing)
- 1 tablespoon lemon juice
- 1 large sweet onion (peeled and diced)
- 2 garlic cloves (halved)
- 1 teaspoon ground coriander
- Freshly ground black pepper

Instructions

Preheat the oven to 400 degrees Fahrenheit. Preheat the oven to 350°F. Line two baking pans with parchment paper. Brush one baking sheet with olive oil and arrange the eggplant pieces cut-side down. Combine the onion, garlic, 1 tablespoon olive oil, cumin, and coriander in a small bowl. On the second baking sheet, spread the seasoned onions. Roast the onions for approximately 20 minutes and the eggplant for 30 minutes, or until softened and browned on both baking pans. Scrape the eggplant flesh into a basin after removing the veggies from the oven. Toss the onions and garlic with the eggplant on a chopping board and roughly chop. Add the lemon juice and pepper to taste. Warm or cooled is fine.

Nutritional facts

Calories: 45| Carbohydrates: 6g| Protein: 1g| Fat: 2g| Sodium 3 mg |

34. Cheese Herb Dip

Preparation time: 20 minutes

Cooking time: 0 minutes

Serving: 8

Ingredients

- 1 cup cream cheese
- 1 teaspoon minced garlic
- ½ scallion (green part only, finely chopped)
- 1 tablespoon chopped fresh parsley
- 1 tablespoon chopped fresh basil
- ½ cup unsweetened rice milk
- 1 tablespoon freshly squeezed lemon juice
- ½ teaspoon chopped fresh thyme
- ¼ teaspoon freshly ground black pepper

Instructions

Combine the cream cheese, milk, scallion, parsley, basil, lemon juice, garlic, thyme, and pepper in a medium mixing bowl. Refrigerate the dip for up to one week in an airtight container.

Nutritional facts

Calories 108| Carbohydrates 3g| Protein 2g| Fat 10g| Sodium 112 mg |

35. Spicy Kale Chips

Preparation time: 20 minutes

Cooking time: 25 minutes

Serving: 6

Ingredients

- 2 cups kale
- 2 teaspoons olive oil
- ¼ teaspoon chili powder
- Pinch cayenne pepper

Instructions

Preheat the oven to 300 degrees Fahrenheit. Set aside 2 baking sheets lined with parchment paper. Remove the kale stems before tearing the leaves into 2-inch pieces. Wash and dry the kale well. Drizzle olive oil over the kale in a large mixing basin. Toss the kale with the oil with your hands, ensuring each leaf is well coated. Toss the kale with chili powder and cayenne pepper to blend completely. On each baking sheet, spread the seasoned kale in a single layer. Make sure the leaves aren't overlapping. Bake the kale for 20 to 25 minutes, flipping the pans once or until crisp and dry. Remove the pans from the oven and let the chips cool for 5 minutes on the trays. Serve right away.

Nutritional facts

Calories 24| Carbohydrates 2g| Protein 1g|Fat 2g| Sodium 13 mg |

36. Cinnamon Tortillas Chips

Preparation time: 15 minutes

Cooking time: 10 minutes

Serving: 6

Ingredients

- 2 teaspoons granulated sugar
- ½ teaspoon ground cinnamon
- 3 (6-inch) flour tortillas
- Cooking spray (for coating the tortillas)
- Pinch ground nutmeg

Instructions

Preheat the oven to 350 degrees Fahrenheit. Using parchment paper, line a baking sheet. Combine the sugar, cinnamon, and nutmeg in a small bowl. Spray both sides of the tortillas with cooking spray and place them in a clean work area. Using a pastry brush, evenly coat both sides of each tortilla with cinnamon sugar. Place the tortillas on the baking sheet, and cut them into 16 wedges each. Bake the tortilla wedges for approximately 10 minutes, rotating once or until crisp. Cool the chips completely before storing them in an airtight jar at room temperature for up to a week.

Nutritional facts

Calories 51| Carbohydrates 9g| Protein 1g| Fat 1g| Sodium 103 mg |

37. Sweet and Spicy Kettle Corn

Preparation time: 1 minute

Cooking time: 5 minutes

Serving: 8

Ingredients

- 1 cup popcorn kernels
- 3 tablespoons olive oil
- ½ cup brown sugar
- Pinch cayenne pepper

Instructions

Add the olive oil and a few popcorn kernels to a big saucepan covering medium heat. Lightly shake the saucepan until the popcorn kernels pop. Toss in the remaining kernels as well as the sugar in the saucepan. Shake the pot regularly while popping the kernels until they are all popped. Remove the popcorn from the kettle and place it in a large mixing dish. Serve the popcorn with a dash of cayenne pepper.

Nutritional facts

Calories 186| Carbohydrates 30g| Protein 3g| Fat 6g| Sodium 5 mg |

38. Blueberries and Cream Ice Pops

Preparation time: 10 minutes + 3 hours to freeze

Cooking time: 0 minutes

Serving: 6

Ingredients

- 3 cups fresh blueberries
- 1 teaspoon freshly squeezed lemon juice
- ¼ cup unsweetened rice milk
- ¼ cup granulated sugar
- ½ teaspoon pure vanilla extract
- ¼ cup light sour cream
- ¼ teaspoon ground cinnamon

Instructions

Puree the blueberries, lemon juice, rice milk, sour cream, sugar, vanilla, and cinnamon in a blender until smooth. Fill ice pop molds halfway with the mixture and freeze for 3 to 4 hours, or until extremely solid.

Nutritional facts

Calories 78| Carbohydrates 18g| Protein 1g| Fat 1g| Sodium 12 mg |

39. Candied Ginger Ice Milk

Preparation time: 20 minutes + 1 hour to freeze

Cooking time: 15 minutes

Serving: 4

Ingredients

- 4 cups vanilla rice milk
- ½ cup granulated sugar
- ¼ teaspoon ground nutmeg
- 1 (4-inch) piece of fresh ginger (peeled and sliced thin)
- ¼ cup finely chopped candied ginger

Instructions

Combine the milk, sugar, and fresh ginger in a large saucepan over medium heat. Heat the milk mixture for approximately 5 minutes or until it is nearly boiling, stirring regularly. Reduce to low heat and cook for 15 minutes. Remove the milk from the heat and stir in the nutmeg powder. To infuse the taste, let the mixture rest for 1 hour. Strain the milk mixture through a fine strainer into a medium basin to remove the ginger. Place the mixture in the refrigerator to cool fully before adding the candied ginger. In an ice cream machine, freeze the ginger ice according to the manufacturer's instructions. Freeze the completed dessert in an airtight container for up to 3 months.

Nutritional facts

Calories 108| Carbohydrates 24g| Protein 0g| Fat 1g| Sodium 47 mg |

40. Meringue Cookies

Preparation time: 30 minutes

Cooking time: 30 minutes

Serving: 24

Ingredients

- 4 egg whites (at room temperature)
- 1 cup granulated sugar
- 1 teaspoon pure vanilla extract
- 1 teaspoon almond extract

Instructions

Preheat the oven to 300 degrees Fahrenheit. Set aside 2 baking sheets lined with parchment paper. Beat the egg whites until firm peaks form in a large stainless steel mixing basin. 1 tablespoon granulated sugar at a time, beating thoroughly after each addition to integrate until all of the sugar is used, and the meringue is thick and shiny. Combine the vanilla and almond extracts in a mixing bowl. Drop the meringue batter onto the baking pans with a tablespoon, spreading the cookies equally. Bake for approximately 30 minutes or until the cookies are crisp. Take the cookies out of the oven and place them on wire racks to cool. Keep the cookies at room temperature for up to a week in an airtight container.

Nutritional facts

Calories 36| Carbohydrates 8g| Protein 1g| Fat 0g| Sodium 9 mg |

41. Corn Bread

Preparation time: 10 minutes

Cooking time: 20 minutes

Serving: 10

Ingredients

- Cooking spray (for greasing the baking dish)
- ¾ cup all-purpose flour
- 1 tablespoon baking soda
- 1¼ cup yellow cornmeal
- ½ cup granulated sugar
- 2 eggs
- 1 cup unsweetened (unfortified rice milk)
- 2 tablespoons olive oil

Instructions

Preheat the oven to 425 degrees Fahrenheit. Set aside an 8-by-8-inch baking dish that has been lightly sprayed with cooking spray. Combine the cornmeal, flour, baking soda replacement, and sugar in a medium mixing basin. Whisk together the eggs, rice milk, and olive oil in a small bowl until well combined. Combine the wet and dry ingredients in a mixing bowl and whisk until completely blended. Fill the baking dish halfway with batter and bake for 20 minutes or golden. Warm the dish before serving.

Nutritional facts

Calories 198| Carbohydrates 34g| Protein 4g| Fat 5g| Sodium 25 mg |

42. Roasted Red Pepper and Chicken Crostini

Preparation time: 10 minutes

Cooking time: 5 minutes

Serving: 4

Ingredients

- 2 tablespoons olive oil
- 4 slices of French bread
- ½ teaspoon minced garlic
- 1 roasted red bell pepper (chopped)
- 4 ounces cooked chicken breast (shredded)
- ½ cup chopped fresh basil

Instructions

Preheat the oven to 400 degrees Fahrenheit. Use aluminum foil to line a baking pan. Combine the olive oil and garlic in a small bowl. Brush the olive oil mixture on both sides of each slice of bread. Place the bread on the baking pan and toast for approximately 5 minutes, rotating once, or until golden and crisp on both sides. Combine the red pepper, chicken, and basil in a medium mixing basin. Serve the red pepper mixture on top of each toasted bread piece.

Nutritional facts

Calories: 184| Carbohydrates: 19g| Protein: 9g| Fat: 8g| Sodium 175 mg |

43. Cucumber Wrapped Vegetable Rolls

Preparation time: 30 minutes

Cooking time: 0 minutes

Serving: 8

Ingredients

- ½ cup finely shredded red cabbage
- ½ cup grated carrot
- ¼ cup chopped cilantro
- ¼ cup julienned scallion (both green and white parts)
- ¼ cup julienned red bell pepper
- 1 tablespoon olive oil
- ¼ teaspoon ground cumin
- ¼ teaspoon freshly ground black pepper
- 1 English cucumber (sliced into 8 very thin strips with a vegetable peeler)

Instructions

Toss the cabbage, carrot, red pepper, scallion, cilantro, olive oil, cumin, and black pepper in a medium mixing bowl until thoroughly combined. Distribute the vegetable filling evenly among the cucumber strips, putting the filling at one end of each strip. Roll up the cucumber strips and fasten with a wooden pick around the filling. Carry on with each cucumber strip in the same manner.

Nutritional facts

Calories 26| Carbohydrates 3g| Protein 0g| Fat 2g| Sodium 7 mg |

44. Antojitos

Preparation time: 20 minutes

Cooking time: 0 minutes

Serving: 8

Ingredients

- 6 ounces plain cream cheese (at room temperature)
- ½ jalapeño pepper (finely chopped)
- ½ teaspoon ground cumin
- ½ scallion, green part only (chopped)
- ¼ cup finely chopped red bell pepper
- ½ teaspoon ground coriander
- ½ teaspoon chili powder
- 3 (8-inch) flour tortillas

Instructions

Combine the cream cheese, jalapeno pepper, scallion, red bell pepper, cumin, coriander, and chili powder in a medium mixing bowl. Distribute the cream cheese mixture equally among the three tortillas, spreading it thinly and leaving a 14-inch border all the way around. Wrap each tortilla securely in plastic wrap like a jelly roll. Refrigerate for approximately 1 hour or until the rolls are firm. To serve, cut the tortilla rolls into 1-inch pieces and place them on a dish.

Nutritional facts

Calories 110| Carbohydrates 7g| Protein 2g| Fat 8g| Sodium 215 mg |

45. Chicken Vegetable Kebabs

Preparation time: 15 minutes + 1 hour to marinate

Cooking time: 12 minutes

Serving: 4

Ingredients

- 2 tablespoons olive oil
- ½ teaspoon minced garlic
- ½ teaspoon chopped fresh thyme
- 2 tablespoons freshly squeezed lemon juice
- 4 ounces boneless (skinless chicken breast, cut into 8 pieces)
- 1 small summer squash (cut into 8 pieces)
- ½ medium onion (cut into 8 pieces)

Instructions

Combine the olive oil, lemon juice, garlic, and thyme in a medium mixing bowl. Toss the chicken into the dish and toss it around to coat it. Cover the bowl with plastic wrap and refrigerate the chicken for 1 hour to marinate. Thread the squash, onion, and chicken pieces onto four big skewers, equally distributing the veggies and meat. Preheat the grill to medium and cook the skewers for 10 to 12 minutes, rotating at least twice or until the chicken is cooked through.

Nutritional facts

Calories 106| Carbohydrates 3g| Protein 7g| Fat 8g| Sodium 14 mg |

46. Five Spice Chicken Lettuce Wraps

Preparation time: 30 minutes

Cooking time: 0 minutes

Serving: 8

Ingredients

- 6 ounces of chicken breast
- 1 scallion
- ½ red apple
- ¼ English cucumber
- Juice of 1 lime
- Zest of 1 lime
- ½ cup bean sprouts
- 2 tablespoons Cilantro
- ½ teaspoon spice powder
- 8 Boston lettuce leaves

Instructions

Combine the chicken, sprouts, cucumber, cilantro, and other ingredients and five-spice powder in a large mixing bowl. Evenly distribute the chicken mixture among the 8 lettuce leaves. Serve the lettuce wrapped around the chicken mixture.

Nutritional facts

Calories 51| Carbohydrates 2g| Protein 7g| Fat 2g| Sodium 16 mg |

47. Side Ginger Cauliflower Rice

Preparation time: 10 minutes

Cooking time: 10 minutes

Serving: 4

Ingredients

- 5 cups cauliflower florets

- 3 tablespoons coconut oil
- 4 ginger slices (grated)
- 1 tablespoon coconut vinegar
- 3 garlic cloves (minced)
- 1 tablespoon chives (minced)
- A pinch of sea salt
- Black pepper to taste

Instructions

Pulse the cauliflower florets in a food processor until they are finely chopped. Heat the oil in a skillet over medium-high heat, add the ginger and cook for 3 minutes, stirring occasionally. Cook for 7 minutes after adding the cauliflower rice and garlic. Stir in the salt, black pepper, vinegar, and chives, simmer for a few seconds longer, then divide among plates and serve. Enjoy!

Nutritional facts

Calories: 125| Carbohydrates: 7.9 g| Protein: 2.7 g| Fat: 10.4g| Sodium 75 mg |

48. Basil Zucchini Spaghetti

Preparation time: 1 hour + 10 minutes

Cooking time: 10 minutes

Serving: 4

Ingredients

- ¼ cup basil (chopped)
- 1/3 cup coconut oil (melted)
- 4 zucchinis (cut with a spiralizer)
- A pinch of sea salt
- ½ cup walnuts (chopped)
- 2 garlic cloves (minced)
- Black pepper to taste

Instructions

Mix zucchini spaghetti with salt and pepper in a mixing basin, tossing to coat, set aside for 1 hour, drain thoroughly, and place in a bowl. Heat the oil in a pan over medium-high heat, then add the zucchini spaghetti and garlic, constantly stirring for 5 minutes. Stir in the basil, walnuts, and black pepper, and simmer for another 3 minutes. Serve as a side dish by dividing the mixture across plates. Enjoy!

Nutritional facts

Calories 287| Carbohydrates 8.7g| Protein 6.3 g| Fat 27.8g| Sodium 75 mg |

49. Braised Sweet Cabbage

Preparation time: 10 minutes

Cooking time: 10 minutes

Serving: 4

Ingredients

- 2 tablespoons water
- 1 small cabbage head (shredded)
- 6 ounces shallots (cooked and chopped)
- A pinch of black pepper
- A pinch of sweet paprika
- 1 tablespoon dill (chopped)
- A drizzle of olive oil

Instructions

Heat the oil in a pan over medium heat, then add the cabbage and water, mix, and cook for 5 minutes. Toss in the remaining ingredients, simmer for another 5 minutes, then divide amongst plates and serve as a side dish!

Nutritional facts

Calories 91| Carbohydrates 20.8g| Protein 4.1g| Fat 0.5g| Sodium 75 mg |

50. Cauliflower and Leeks

Preparation time: 10 minutes

Cooking time: 20 minutes

Serving: 4

Ingredients

- 1 and ½ cups leeks (chopped)
- 1 and ½ cups cauliflower florets
- 1 + ½ cups artichoke hearts
- 2 tablespoons coconut oil (melted)
- 2 garlic cloves (minced)
- Black pepper to taste

Instructions

Heat the oil in a skillet over medium-high heat, then add the garlic, leeks, cauliflower florets, and artichoke hearts and simmer for 20 minutes, stirring occasionally. Stir in the black pepper, divide across plates, and serve.

Nutritional facts

Calories: 192| Carbohydrates: 35.1g| Protein: 5.1g| Fat: 6.9g| Sodium 76 mg |

51. Eggplant and Mushroom Sauté

Preparation time: 10 minutes

Cooking time: 30 minutes

Serving: 4

Ingredients

- 2 pounds of oyster mushrooms (chopped)
- 6 ounces shallots (peeled, chopped)
- 3 celery stalks (chopped)
- 1 yellow onion (chopped)
- 2 eggplants (cubed)
- 1 tablespoon parsley (chopped)
- Black pepper to taste
- 1 tablespoon savory (dried)
- 3 tablespoons coconut oil (melted)
- A pinch of sea salt

Instructions

Over medium-high heat, heat the oil in a pan, then add the onion, stir, and cook for 4 minutes. Stir in the shallots and simmer for another 4 minutes. Cook for 15 minutes after adding the eggplant pieces, mushrooms, celery, savory, and black pepper to taste. Stir in the parsley, simmer for a few minutes longer, then divide across plates and serve.

Nutritional facts

Calories 101.3| Carbohydrates 156.5 g| Proteins 69.1 g| Fat 10.9 g| Sodium 105 mg |

52. Mint Zucchini

Preparation time: 10 minutes

Cooking time: 7 minutes

Serving: 4

Ingredients

- 2 tablespoons mint
- ½ tablespoon dill (chopped)
- 2 zucchinis (halved lengthwise and then sliced into half-moons)
- 1 tablespoon coconut oil (melted)
- A pinch of cayenne pepper

Instructions

Heat the oil in a skillet over medium-high heat, add the zucchinis and cook for 6 minutes, stirring occasionally. Stir in the cayenne, dill, and mint, heat for another minute, then divide amongst plates and serve.

Nutritional facts

Calories 46| Carbohydrates 3.5g| Protein 1.3g| Fat 3.6g| Sodium 75 mg |

53. Celery and Kale Mix

Preparation time: 10 minutes

Cooking time: 20 minutes

Serving: 4

Ingredients

- 2 celery stalks (chopped)
- 1 tablespoon coconut oil (melted)
- 1 small red bell pepper (chopped)
- 3 tablespoons water
- 5 cups kale (torn)

Instructions

Over medium-high heat, heat the oil in a skillet, add the celery, stir, and cook for 10 minutes. Cook for another 10 minutes after adding the kale, water, and bell pepper. Serve by dividing the mixture across plates.

Nutritional facts

Calories 81| Carbohydrates 11.3 g| Protein 2.9 g| Fat 3.5 g| Sodium 75 mg |

54. Kale, Mushrooms, and Red Chard Mix

Preparation time: 10 minutes

Cooking time: 17 minutes

Serving: 4

Ingredients

- ½ pound brown mushrooms (sliced)
- 5 cups kale (roughly chopped)
- 3 cups red chard (chopped)
- 1 and ½ tablespoons coconut oil
- 2 tablespoons water
- Black pepper to taste

Instructions

Heat the oil in a skillet over medium-high heat, add the mushrooms, stir, and cook for 5 minutes. Cook for 10 minutes after adding red chard, kale, and water. Toss in a pinch of black pepper, stir and simmer for another 2 minutes. Serve by dividing the mixture across plates.

Nutritional facts

Calories 97| Carbohydrates 13.3g| Protein 5.4g| Fat 3.4g| Sodium 79 mg |

55. Bok Choy and Beets

Preparation time: 10 minutes

Cooking time: 30 minutes

Serving: 4

Ingredients

- 1 tablespoon coconut oil
- 4 cups bok choy (chopped)
- 2 tablespoons water
- 3 beets (cut into quarters and thinly sliced)
- A pinch of cayenne pepper

Instructions

Fill a large saucepan halfway with water, add the beets, and bring to a boil over medium heat. Cover and simmer for 20 minutes, then drain. Heat the oil in a pan over medium-high heat, add the bok choy and water, toss to combine, and simmer for 10 minutes. Stir in the beets and cayenne pepper, simmer for another 2 minutes, then divide among plates and serve as a side dish!

Nutritional facts

Calories 71| Carbohydrates 9g| Protein 2.3g| Fat 3.7g| Sodium 75 mg |

56. Spicy Sweet Potatoes

Preparation time: 10 minutes

Cooking time: 40 minutes

Serving: 4

Ingredients

- 4 sweet potatoes (peeled and thinly sliced)
- 2 teaspoons nutmeg (ground)
- 2 tablespoon coconut oil (melted)
- Cayenne pepper to taste

Instructions

Toss sweet potato slices in a basin with nutmeg, cayenne, and oil to coat thoroughly. Place them on a parchment-lined baking sheet and bake for 25 minutes at 350 degrees F. Bake for another 15 minutes after flipping the potatoes, then divide amongst plates and serve as a side dish.

Nutritional facts

Calories 242| Carbohydrates 42.4 g| Protein 2.4 g| Fat 7.5g| Sodium 75 mg |

57. Broccoli and Almonds Mix

Preparation time: 10 minutes

Cooking time: 11 minutes

Serving: 4

Ingredients

- 1 tablespoon olive oil
- 1 pound broccoli florets
- 1 garlic clove (minced)
- 1/3 cup almonds (chopped)
- Black pepper to taste

Instructions

Heat the oil in a pan over medium-high heat, add the almonds, toss to combine, and cook for 5 minutes before transferring to a bowl. Return the pan to medium-high heat, add the broccoli and garlic, stir, cover, and cook for 6 minutes. Stir in the almonds and season with black pepper to taste, then divide among plates and serve.

Nutritional facts

Calories 116| Carbohydrates 9.5g| Protein 4.9g| Fat 7.8g| Sodium 75 mg |

58. Squash and Cranberries

Preparation time: 10 minutes

Cooking time: 30 minutes

Serving: 2

Ingredients

- 1 butternut squash (peeled and cubed)
- 2 garlic cloves (minced)
- 1 small yellow onion (chopped)
- 1 tablespoon coconut oil
- 12 ounces coconut milk
- 1 teaspoon curry powder
- 1 teaspoon cinnamon powder
- ½ cup cranberries

Instructions

Spread squash pieces on a parchment-lined baking sheet, bake for 15 minutes at 425 degrees F, and set aside. Heat the oil in a pan over medium-high heat, then add the garlic and onion, constantly stirring for 5 minutes. Cook for 3 minutes after adding the roasted squash. Stir in the coconut milk, cranberries, cinnamon, and curry powder, and simmer for 5 minutes. Serve as a side dish by dividing the mixture across plates.

Nutritional facts

Calories 518| Carbohydrates 24.9 g| Proteins 5.3 g| Fat 47.6 g| Sodium 70 mg |

59. Creamy Chard

Preparation time: 10 minutes

Cooking time: 10 minutes

Serving: 2

Ingredients

- Juice of ½ lemon
- 12 ounces coconut milk
- 1 bunch chard
- A pinch of sea salt
- 1 tablespoon coconut oil
- Black pepper to taste

Instructions

Over medium-high heat, heat the oil in a skillet, add the chard, stir, and cook for 5 minutes. Stir in the lemon juice, a bit of salt, black pepper, and coconut milk, then cook for another 5 minutes. Serve as a side dish by dividing the mixture across plates.

Nutritional facts

Calories 453| Carbohydrates 10.1g| Protein 4.2g| Fat 47.4g| Sodium 85 mg |

60. Dill Carrots

Preparation time: 10 minutes

Cooking time: 30 minutes

Serving: 4

Ingredients

- 1 pound of baby carrots
- 1 tablespoon coconut oil (melted)
- 2 tablespoons dill (chopped)
- 1 tablespoon coconut sugar
- A pinch of black pepper

Instructions

In a large saucepan, combine the carrots and enough water to cover them. Bring to a boil over medium-high heat, then cover and cook for 30 minutes. Drain the carrots, place them in a mixing dish, and whisk the melted oil, black pepper, dill, and coconut sugar until well combined. Divide among plates and serve.

Nutritional facts

Calories 85| Carbohydrates 13.4 g| Proteins 1 g| Fat 3.6 g| Sodium 65 mg |

61. Mixes of snack

Preparation time: 10 minutes

Cooking time: 1 hour 15 minutes

Serving: 4

Ingredients

- 6 cup margarine
- 2 tablespoon Worcestershire sauce

- ½ teaspoon onion powder
- 1 cup pretzels
- ¾ cup garlic powder
- 3 cups crispy
- 3 cups cheerios
- 3 cups corn flakes
- 1 cup kix
- 1 cup of broken bagel chips into 1-inch pieces
- 1 ½ tablespoon spice salt

Instructions

Preheat the oven to 250 degrees Fahrenheit (120c) in a pan, and melt the margarine. Season with salt and pepper. Mix in the other ingredients gradually until the coating is homogeneous. Cook for 1 hour, stirring 15 minutes in between. Allow cooling on paper towels. Store in an airtight container.

Nutritional facts

Calories 200| Carbohydrates 27 g| Protein 3 g| Fat 9 g| Sodium 4 mg |

62. Cranberry dip with fresh fruit

Preparation time: 10 minutes

Cooking time: 0 minutes

Serving: 8

Ingredients

- 8-ounce sour cream
- 1/2 cup whole berry cranberry sauce
- 4 cups fresh pineapple (peeled, cubed)
- 4 medium apples (peeled, cored, and cubed)
- 1/4 teaspoon nutmeg
- 4 medium pears (peeled, cored, and cubed)
- 1/4 teaspoon ground ginger
- 1 teaspoon lemon juice

Instructions

Combine the cranberry sauce, sour cream, ginger, and nutmeg in a food processor. Transfer the mixture to a bowl after blending until smooth. Combine the pineapple, pears, apples, and lemon juice in a salad dish. Using small skewers, thread the fruits. Serve with the sauce on the side.

Nutritional facts

Calories 70| Carbohydrates 13 g| Protein 0 g| Fat 2 g| Sodium 8 mg |

63. Cucumbers with sour cream

Preparation time: 10 minutes

Cooking time: 0 minutes

Serving: 4

Ingredients

- 2 medium cucumbers (peeled and sliced thinly)
- 1 tablespoon canola oil
- 1/2 cup reduced-fat sour cream
- 1/2 medium sweet onion (sliced)
- 1/4 cup white wine vinegar
- 1/8 teaspoon black pepper

Instructions

Combine the cucumber, onion, and other ingredients in a medium-sized mixing bowl. Refrigerate for 2 hours after thoroughly mixing. Toss one more before serving.

Nutritional facts

Calories 64| Carbohydrates 4 g| Protein 1 g| Fat 5 g| Sodium 72 mg |

64. Sweet, savory Meatballs

Preparation time: 10 minutes

Cooking time: 20 minutes

Serving: 12

Ingredients

- 1-pound ground turkey
- 1/4 cup bread crumbs
- 6-ounce grape jelly
- 2 tablespoon onion (finely chopped)
- 1 teaspoon garlic powder
- 1 large egg
- 1/2 teaspoon black pepper
- 1/4 cup canola oil
- 1/4 cup chili sauce

Instructions

In a large mixing bowl, combine all ingredients except the chili sauce and jelly. Make little balls out of the mixture after thoroughly mixing it. It will yield around 48 meatballs. On a burner, spread them out on a buttered pan. Cook until golden brown on both sides over medium heat. Combine the chili sauce and jelly in a microwave-safe bowl and heat for 2 minutes. Toss the meatballs in the pan with the chili sauce mixture. Preheat the oven to 350°F and place the meatballs in the pan for 20 minutes. Serve hot and fresh.

Nutritional facts

Calories 127| Carbohydrates 14 g| Protein 9 g| Fat 4 g| Sodium 129 mg |

65. Spicy Corn Bread

Preparation time: 10 minutes

Cooking time: 30 minutes

Serving: 8

Ingredients

- 1 cup all-purpose white flour
- 1 egg
- 1 cup plain cornmeal
- 1 tablespoon sugar
- 1 teaspoon chili powder
- 1 cup rice milk (unenriched)
- 1 egg white
- 2 tablespoon canola oil
- 1/4 teaspoon black pepper
- 2 teaspoon baking powder
- 1/2 cup scallions (finely chopped)
- 1/4 cup carrots (finely grated)
- 1 garlic clove (minced)

Instructions

Preheat the oven to 400 degrees Fahrenheit. Combine the flour, baking powder, sugar, cornmeal, pepper, and chili powder in a mixing bowl. Combine the oil, milk, egg white, and egg in a mixing bowl. Stir in the carrots, garlic, and scallions after thoroughly mixing until smooth. Stir everything well, then pour the batter into an 8-inch baking pan sprayed with cooking spray. Preheat the oven to 350°F and bake for 30 minutes or golden brown. Slice and serve immediately.

Nutritional facts

Calories: 188| Carbohydrates: 31 g| Protein: 5 g| Fat: 5 g| Sodium 155 mg |

66. Sweet and spicy tortilla chips

Preparation time: 10 minutes

Cooking time: 8 minutes

Serving: 6

Ingredients

- 1/4 cup butter
- 6 flour tortillas (6" size)

- 1 teaspoon brown sugar
- 1/2 teaspoon garlic powder
- 1/2 teaspoon ground cumin
- 1/4 teaspoon ground cayenne pepper
- · 1/2 teaspoon ground chili powder

Instructions

Preheat the oven to 425 degrees Fahrenheit. Using cooking spray, grease a baking pan. Combine all spices, brown sugar, and melted butter in a small mixing dish. Combine all of the ingredients in a mixing bowl and set aside. Brush the tortillas with the sugar mixture after slicing them into 8 wedges. Bake for 8 minutes after spreading them out on the baking sheet. Serve immediately.

Nutritional facts

Calories 115| Carbohydrates 11 g| Protein 2 g| Fat 7 g| | Sodium 156 mg |

67. Addictive pretzels

Preparation time: 10 minutes

Cooking time: 1 hour

Serving: 6

Ingredients

- 32-ounce bag of unsalted pretzels
- 3 teaspoon garlic powder
- 1 cup canola oil
- 2 tablespoon seasoning mix
- 3 teaspoon dried dill weed

Instructions

Preheat the oven to 175 degrees Fahrenheit. Break the pretzels into pieces and place them on a baking pan. Combine garlic powder and dill; set aside half of the mixture. Combine the remaining half with the spice mix and 34 cups of canola oil in a mixing bowl. Brush a generous amount of this oil over the pretzels. Bake for 1 hour, rotate the pieces and bake for another 15 minutes. Allow to cool before sprinkling with the remaining dill mixture and drizzling with additional oil. Serve hot and fresh.

Nutritional facts

Calories 184| Carbohydrates 22 g| Protein 2 g| Fat 8 g| Sodium 60 mg |

68. Shrimp Spread with Crackers

Preparation time: 10 minutes

Cooking time: 0 minutes

Serving: 6

Ingredients

- 1/4 cup light cream cheese
- 1 tablespoon parsley
- 2 1/2-ounce cooked (shelled shrimp, minced)
- 1 tablespoon no-salt-added ketchup
- 1 teaspoon Worcestershire sauce
- 1/2 teaspoon herb seasoning blend
- 1/4 teaspoon hot sauce
- 24 matzo cracker miniatures

Instructions

First, combine the minced shrimp and cream cheese in a mixing dish. Combine Worcestershire sauce, spicy sauce, herb spice, and ketchup in a large mixing bowl. Combine all ingredients in a large mixing bowl and top with chopped parsley. With the crackers, serve the spread.

Nutritional facts

Calories 57| Carbohydrates 7 g| Protein 3 g| Fat: 1g| Sodium 69 mg |

69. Buffalo chicken dip

Preparation time: 10 minutes

Cooking time: 3 hours

Serving: 4

Ingredients

- 4-ounce cream cheese
- 1 cup reduced-fat sour cream
- 1/2 cup bottled roasted red peppers
- 4 teaspoon hot pepper sauce
- 2 cups cooked (shredded chicken)

Instructions

Pour half a cup of drained red peppers into a food processor until smooth. Thoroughly combine cream cheese, sour cream, and pureed peppers in a mixing dish. Transfer the mixture to a slow cooker after adding the shredded chicken and spicy sauce. Cook on low heat for 3 hours. Serve with celery, carrots, cauliflower, and

cucumber while still warm.

Nutritional facts

Calories 73| Carbohydrates 2 g| Protein 5 g| Fat 5 g | Sodium 66 mg |

70. Chicken pepper bacon wraps

Preparation time: 10 minutes

Cooking time: 15 minutes

Serving: 4

Ingredients

- 1 medium onion (chopped)

- 12 strips of bacon (halved)

- 2 pounds boneless (skinless chicken breast)

- 12 fresh jalapenos peppers

Instructions

Spray a grill rack with cooking spray and preheat the grill on low. Remove the seeds from the peppers after slicing them in half lengthwise. Cut the chicken into tiny pieces and distribute them among the peppers. Place the chopped onion on top of the chicken in the peppers now. The bacon strips should be wrapped around the filled peppers. Cook for 15 minutes on the grill with these covered peppers. Serve hot and fresh.

Nutritional facts

Calories 71| Carbohydrates 1 g| Protein 10 g| Fat 3 g| Sodium 96 mg |

71. Garlic Oyster Crackers

Preparation time: 10 minutes

Cooking time: 45 minutes

Serving: 4

Ingredients

- 1/2 cup butter-flavored popcorn oil

- 1 tablespoon garlic powder

- 7 cups oyster crackers

- 2 teaspoon dried dill weed

Instructions

Preheat the oven to 250 degrees Fahrenheit. In a large mixing bowl, combine garlic powder and oil. Toss in the crackers and toss well to coat evenly. Mix the crackers with the dill weed and toss well again. Bake the crackers for 45 minutes after spreading them out on the baking sheet. Every 15 minutes, toss them. Serve immediately.

Nutritional facts

Calories 118| Protein 2 g| Carbohydrates 12 g| Fat 7 g| Sodium 166 mg |

72. Lime Cilantro Rice

Preparation time: 5 minutes

Cooking time: 20 minutes

Serving: 2

Ingredients

- 0.75 cup White rice

- 1.5 cups water

- 0.25 teaspoon Bay leaf (ground)

- 1 tablespoon Lime juice

- 1.5 tablespoons Olive oil

- 0.25 teaspoon Lime Zest

- 0.25 cup cilantro (chopped)

Instructions

In a medium-sized saucepan, combine the white rice and water and bring to a boil over medium heat. Simmer and cover the saucepan with a lid until all the water has been absorbed, around eighteen to twenty minutes. After the ground bay leaf, olive oil, lime juice, lemon juice, lime zest, and cilantro have been cooked, stir in the ground bay leaf, olive oil, lime juice, lemon juice, lime zest, and cilantro. This should be done using a fork rather than a spoon since this will fluff the rice rather than compress it. Serve when still hot.

Nutritional facts

Calories 363| Carbohydrates 60g| Protein 5g| Fat 10 g| Sodium 5 mg |

73. Spicy Mushroom Stir Fry

Preparation time: 10 minutes

Cooking time: 12 minutes

Serving: 4

Ingredients

- 1 cup low-sodium vegetable broth

- 2 tablespoons cornstarch

- 1 red bell pepper (chopped)

- 1 teaspoon low-sodium soy sauce

- 1/8 teaspoon cayenne pepper

- 2 tablespoon olive oil

- 1/2 teaspoon ground ginger

- 2 (8-oz.) packages of sliced button mushrooms

- 1 jalapeño pepper (minced)

Instructions

Combine the broth, ginger, soy sauce, cornstarch, and cayenne pepper in a small bowl. After that, put it away. After that, heat the olive oil in a wok (or a heavy skillet) over high heat. After that, toss in the mushrooms and peppers. Stir-frying the veggies for 3–5 minutes, or until they are tender-crisp. Stir the broth mixture into the wok and cook for an additional 3–5 minutes, or until the veggies are cooked, and the sauce has thickened. Serve.

Nutritional facts

Calories 300| Carbohydrates 49 g| Protein 8 g| Fat 16 g| Sodium 56 mg |

74. Eggs Creamy Melt

Preparation time: 6 minutes

Cooking time: 4 minutes

Serving: 2

Ingredients

- 2 beaten eggs
- 1 tablespoon olive oil
- Italian seasoning as required
- 1 cup shredded tofu

Instructions

Combine beaten eggs and Italian spices in a small bowl. Toss the tofu on top. In a pan, heat the olive oil. Add the egg mixture to the pan. Cook for a total of 4 minutes on each side. Serve.

Nutritional facts

Calories 214| Carbohydrates 1.4 g| Protein 15.57 g| Fat 16.9 g| Sodium 78 mg |

75. Cauliflower Mash

Preparation time: 5 minutes

Cooking time: 10 minutes

Serving: 4

Ingredients

- 2 cups of "leached" potatoes
- 2 tablespoons of softened butter
- 3/4 cup of tepid low-fat milk
- 2 cups of cauliflower florets
- 1 teaspoon of ground black pepper

Instructions

Potatoes should be quartered. Break apart the cauliflower. In a big saucepan of boiling water, add the vegetables. Cook for approximately 10 minutes or until the vegetables are soft. Drain after removing the pan from the heat. Add the milk, butter, and pepper to taste. Cream the vegetables using an immersion blender. Serve immediately.

Nutritional facts

Calories 310 | Protein 10 g| Carbohydrates 37 g| Fat 11 g| Sodium 49 mg |

76. Jalapeno Crisp

Preparation time: 10 minutes

Cooking time: 1 hour 15 minutes

Serving: 20

Ingredients

- 1/2 cup sesame seeds
- 1/2 cup hulled hemp seeds
- 3 tablespoons Psyllium husk
- 1/2 cup flax seeds
- 1 teaspoon salt
- 1 teaspoon baking powder
- 1/2 cup sunflower seeds
- 2 cups of water

Instructions

Preheat the oven to 350 degrees Fahrenheit. Combine seeds, baking powder, salt, and Psyllium husk in a blender. Blend until you have a sand-like texture, then add the water and blend till you get a batter. Allow the batter to rest for 10 minutes or until it forms a thick dough-like substance. Whip the dough and place it on a parchment-lined cookie sheet. Spread it out evenly, ensuring a thickness of 1/4 inch all the way around. In your oven, bake for 75 minutes. Remove the spices and chop them into 20 pieces. Allow 30 minutes for cooling before serving.

Nutritional facts

Calories 700 |Carbohydrates 30 g| Protein 33.76 g| Fat 73 g| Sodium 60 mg |

77. Celeriac Tortilla

Preparation time: 10 minutes

Cooking time: 1 hour 15 minutes

Serving: 20

Ingredients

- 2 oz. celery root (peeled)
- 1 egg beaten
- 1 potato (peeled)
- 1 tablespoon almond flour
- 1 teaspoon olive oil
- 1/2 teaspoon salt

Instructions

Bake for 15 minutes at 355F with the potato and celery root in the tray. Vegetables cooked in the oven should be tender. After that, place them in a food processor. Blend until completely smooth. Combine the salt, almond flour, and egg in a mixing bowl. Knead the moist dough with your hands. Make the balls by cutting the dough into four parts. Roll the dough balls into tortilla shapes using the rolling pin. In a skillet, heat the olive oil. Place the first celeriac tortilla on top of the pan and cook for 1.5 minutes on each side. Repeat with the rest of the tortilla balls. Before serving, wrap the baked tortillas in the cloth.

Nutritional facts

Calories 163.81| Carbohydrates 22.04 g| Protein 6.02 g| Fat 6.16 g| Sodium 75 mg |

78. Caraway Mushroom Caps (Low Caloric)

Preparation time: 8 minutes

Cooking time: 25 minutes

Serving: 4

Ingredients

- 1 teaspoon caraway seeds

- 3 oz. Portobello mushroom caps

- 2 teaspoons butter (softened)

- 1/4 teaspoon salt

Instructions

If necessary, trim and wash the mushroom tops. Preheat the oven to 360 degrees Fahrenheit. Combine butter, salt, and caraway seeds in a food processor. Fill the mushroom caps halfway with the butter mixture and place them on the baking dish. Preheat the oven to 355°F and bake Portobello caps for 10 minutes.

Nutritional facts

Calories 45.75| Carbohydrates 1.95 g| Protein 1.57 g| Fat 4 g| Sodium 293 mg |

79. Stuffed Sweet Potato

Preparation time: 10 minutes

Cooking time: 20 minutes

Serving: 4

Ingredients

- 2 sweet potatoes

- 2 teaspoons butter

- 1/4 cup Cheddar cheese (shredded)

- 1 tablespoon fresh parsley (chopped)

- 1/2 teaspoon salt

Instructions

Make a lengthwise incision in each sweet potato and bake for 10 minutes at 360 degrees Fahrenheit. After that, take 1/2 of each sweet potato flesh and scoop it out. Salt, parsley, butter, and grated cheese are mixed into the veggies. Return the sweet potatoes to the oven and bake for an additional 10 minutes at 355F.

Nutritional facts

Calories 480.85| Carbohydrates 91.9 g| Protein 10.45 g| Fat 8.64 g| Sodium 924 mg |

80. Baked Olives

Preparation time: 5 minutes

Cooking time: 11 minutes

Serving: 3

Ingredients

- 1 1/2 cup olives

- 1/4 teaspoon dried thyme

- 1 tablespoon olive oil

- 1/3 teaspoon minced garlic

- 1/2 teaspoon salt

- 1 teaspoon dried oregano

Instructions

The baking paper should be used to line the baking pan. Arrange the olives in a single layer in the tray. Then add olive oil, dried oregano, dried thyme, chopped garlic, and salt to taste. Preheat the oven to 420°F and bake olives for 11 minutes.

Nutritional facts

Calories 182.07| Carbohydrates 7.08 g| Protein 0.93 g| Fat 17.94 g| Sodium 230 mg |

81. Lemon Cucumbers with Dill

Preparation time: 5 minutes

Cooking time: 30 minutes

Serving: 3

Ingredients

- 3 cucumbers

- 1 tablespoon olive oil

- 3 tablespoons lemon juice

- 3/4 teaspoon lemon zest

- 3 teaspoons dill (chopped)

- 3/4 teaspoon chili flakes

Instructions

Cucumbers should be peeled and chopped coarsely. In a large glass jar, place the cucumbers. Combine the lemon zest, lemon juice, dill, olive oil, and chili flakes in a mixing bowl. Close the lid and give it a good shake. Cucumbers should be marinated for 30 minutes.

Nutritional facts

Calories 115.93| Carbohydrates 13.05 g| Protein 2.14 g| Fat 7.64 g| Sodium 3 mg |

82. Honey Apple Bites

Preparation time: 10 minutes

Cooking time: 15 minutes

Serving: 2

Ingredients

- 1 tablespoon honey
- 1/2 teaspoon ground cardamom
- 2 apples

Instructions

Slice the apples into halves and detach the seeds. Then cut the apples into 4 bites more. Place the apple bits in the tray and sprinkle them with ground cardamom and honey. Bake apples for 15 minutes at 355F.

Nutritional facts

Calories 120.47 | Carbohydrates 32.22 g| Protein 0.58 g| Fat 0.27 g| Sodium 2 mg |

83. Sesame Seeds Escarole

Preparation time: 10 minutes

Cooking time: 25 minutes

Serving: 4

Ingredients

- 1 head escarole
- 1 tablespoon sesame oil
- 1 teaspoon balsamic vinegar
- 3/4 teaspoon ground black pepper
- 1 teaspoon sesame seeds
- 1/4 cup of water

Instructions

Roughly chop the escarole. Fill the skillet halfway with water and come to a boil. Add the escarole, chopped. Over high heat, sauté it for 2 minutes. Then, toss the sesame seeds, sesame oil, balsamic vinegar, and freshly ground black pepper. Mix thoroughly and continue to sauté the escarole for another minute or until it begins to boil again.

Nutritional facts

Calories 118 g| Carbohydrates 9.5 g| Protein 3.6 g| Fat 8.1 g| Sodium 3 mg |

84. Yogurt Eggplants

Preparation time: 10 minutes

Cooking time: 18 minutes

Serving: 4

Ingredients

- 1 cup Plain yogurt

- 1 teaspoon salt
- 1 tablespoon butter
- 1 teaspoon ground black pepper
- 2 eggplants (chopped)
- 1 tablespoon fresh dill (chopped)

Instructions

In a skillet, melt the butter. In a large mixing bowl, toss the eggplants with the heated butter. Season them with a pinch of salt and freshly ground black pepper. Over medium-high heat, roast the veggies for 5 minutes. They should be stirred now and again. Add fresh dill and Plain Yogurt after that. Mix everything up well. Close the lid and cook the eggplants for 10 minutes over medium-high heat.

Nutritional facts

Calories 214.14| Carbohydrates 27.04 g| Protein 7.86 g| Fat 10.19 g| Sodium 45 mg |

85. Tuna Dip

Preparation time: 10 minutes

Cooking time: 0 minutes

Serving: 20

Ingredients

- 2 (10 oz.) canned tuna chunks (drained)
- 1 1/2 cups Cheddar cheese
- 2 (8 oz.) packages of cream cheese (softened)
- 1 cup Ranch dressing
- 3/4 cup pepper sauce
- 1 bunch celery
- 1 (8 oz.) box of chicken-flavored crackers

Instructions

In a salad bowl, combine all of the tuna dip ingredients. Combine all of the ingredients in a large mixing bowl and toss thoroughly. Refrigerate for 1 hour. Serve.

Nutritional facts

Calories 256| Carbohydrates 1.4 g| Protein 30.2 g| Fat 14.6 g| Sodium 220 mg |

86. Apple Brie Pizza

Preparation time: 10 minutes

Cooking time: 15 minutes

Serving: 12

Ingredients

Pizza crust:

- ½ cup hot water
- 1 ¼ cup all-purpose flour
- 1 teaspoon instant yeast
- 4 teaspoon canola oil
- 2 teaspoons cornmeal

Toppings:

- 7 oz. Brie cheese with rind (softened)
- 1 teaspoon apple juice
- 2 tablespoon light sour cream
- ¼ tsp dill weed
- 1-2 red apples (with peel, cut into paper-thin wedges)
- 2 teaspoon Parmesan cheese (grated)

Instructions

Fill a food processor halfway with flour and yeast. Pour hot water and frying oil into the food chute with the cover on and the machine running. For approximately 50 seconds, process until the ball forms. Remove the dough from the pan and cover it in plastic wrap. Allow for a 10-minute rest period. Alternatively, you may mix the dough by hand if you don't have a food processor. Preheat the oven to 450 degrees Fahrenheit.

Separate the dough into two equal parts. 1 teaspoon cornmeal on the work surface 1 part of dough should be rolled out to a 10" diameter on cornmeal. Rep with the remaining dough part. Place on a baking sheet that has been buttered. With a fork, poke holes all over the dough. Bake each crust for approximately 10 minutes on the bottom rack. These may be baked one at a time. Before adding toppings to the pizza crusts, allow them to cool.

Toppings:

On a big platter, mash Brie cheese, sour cream, dill weed, and apple juice with a fork. Rather than mashing until smooth, mix roughly. Apply to both crusts.

Place a single layer of apple slices on top of each crust. Parmesan cheese should be sprinkled on top. Bake for approximately 5 minutes in the center of a 450°F oven, or until the crust is crisp and the top is starting to become golden. To make 24 wedges, cut each pizza into 12 wedges.

Nutritional facts

Calories 131| Carbohydrates 13 g| Protein 5 g| Fat 6 g| Sodium 135 mg |

87. Nuts and Bolts

Preparation time: 10 minutes

Cooking time: 1 hour

Serving: 20

Ingredients

- 4 cups real
- ½ teaspoon garlic powder
- 4 cups Cheerios cereal
- 2 cups white bread (cut into cubes)
- ¼ cup unsalted margarine (melted)
- ½ cup canola oil
- 1 teaspoon onion powder
- ¼ teaspoon pepper

Instructions

Combine bread cubes and cereals in a large mixing basin. Margarine should be poured over the cereal mixture. Toss the cereal mixture with the oil and seasonings. Stir everything together well. The mixture should be spread out on two cookie sheets. Preheat the oven to 250°F and bake for 1 hour. Allow cooling before storing in an airtight container.

Nutritional facts

Calories 143| Carbohydrates 16 g| Protein 2.3 g| Fat 3 g| Sodium 119 mg |

88. Snack Dip

Preparation time: 10 minutes

Cooking time: 0 minutes

Serving: 4

Ingredients

- 4 oz. (120 g) light cream cheese (softened)
- 1 tablespoon green onion (chopped)
- 1 tablespoon mayonnaise
- ¼ teaspoon garlic powder
- 1 ½ teaspoon white vinegar
- ¾ teaspoon lemon juice
- ¾ teaspoon mustard powder
- ½ teaspoon horseradish (prepared)
- ½ teaspoon paprika
- ¼ teaspoon cayenne pepper

Instructions

In a small mixing dish, combine all of the ingredients. Mix thoroughly. Refrigerate until ready to use.

Nutritional facts

Calories 88| Carbohydrates 3 g| Protein 2.5 g| Fat 3 g| Sodium 105 mg |

89. Devilled Eggs

Preparation time: 10 minutes

Cooking time: 10 minutes

Serving: 6

Ingredients

- 6 hard-boiled eggs (cooled and peeled)

- 1 teaspoon Dijon mustard

- 1/8 teaspoon pepper

- ½ cup mayonnaise

- 1/8 teaspoon paprika

Instructions

Invert the eggs and cut them in half lengthwise. Scoop out the yolks and set them in a small basin. With a fork, mash the yolks. Combine the mayonnaise, mustard, and pepper in a mixing bowl. Mix thoroughly. Divide the yolk mixture equally among the egg white halves. Paprika should be sprinkled on top.

To boil eggs:

Put raw eggs in a kettle of cold water to hard-boil them. Bring the water to a boil, remove the saucepan from the heat and set it aside. Cook for 10 minutes with the lid on the pot. Cool the eggs in cold water after draining the boiling water. When the shells are cold enough to handle, break them and peel them.

Nutritional facts

Calories 147| Carbohydrate 0.7 g| Protein 6 g| Fat 7 g| Sodium 92 mg |

90. Candied Carrots and Apple

Preparation time: 10 minutes

Cooking time: 10 minutes

Serving: 8

Ingredients

- 3 cups sliced carrots

- ½ teaspoon ground nutmeg

- ½ cup packed brown sugar

- ¼ teaspoon pepper

- 3 medium Granny Smith apples (cored, peeled, and sliced)

- 2 tablespoons unsalted margarine

Instructions

Carrots should be cooked for 15-20 minutes in water until tender. Drain. Combine brown sugar and spices in a mixing bowl. Using cooking spray, coat a baking dish. Alternate layers of apples and carrots, topping each layer with brown sugar and spices. Dot with margarine bits. Cover and bake for 30-40 minutes at 350 degrees F or until apples are tender. Remove the lid and bake for

another 10 minutes. Carrots should be soaked in water for 4 hours before cooking if you're on a low potassium diet.

Nutritional facts

Calories 128| Carbohydrates 1 g| Protein 128 g| Fat 130 g| Sodium 60 mg |

91. Mac & Cheese

Preparation time: 10 minutes

Cooking time: 10 minutes

Serving: 4

Ingredients

- 2 cups elbow, shell, or bowtie pasta

- 5 oz. cream cheese spread

- 4 oz. can dice green chilies (rinsed and drained)

- Pepper to taste

Instructions

Cook pasta according to package directions in boiling water without salt or butter. Drain. Combine the cream cheese spread and the chilies in a mixing bowl. Stir in the cream cheese spread until it has completely melted into the spaghetti. Serve immediately. Season with salt and pepper to taste. Add cooked and drained ground beef for more protein.

Nutritional facts

Calories 220| Carbohydrates 24 g| Protein 7 g| Fat 9 g| Sodium 205 mg |

92. Ground Beef and Black Beans Appetizer

Preparation time: 10 minutes

Cooking time: 0 minutes

Serving: 18

Ingredients

- 1 can of no-salt-added petite tomatoes

- 1 can low sodium black beans (washed and rinsed)

- 1 pound of extra-lean ground beef (cooked and drained)

- 1 container (8-oz) of fat-free sour cream

- 2 cups frozen corn (thawed)

- 1 package salt-free taco seasoning

Instructions

Combine all ingredients in a mixing bowl. If preferred, top with fat-free cheddar cheese. Serve with tortilla chips that haven't been seasoned.

Nutritional facts

Calories: 115| Carbohydrates: 45 g| Protein: 11 g| Fat: 13 g | Sodium 150 mg |

93. Cinnamon Apple Chips

Preparation time: 5 minutes

Cooking time: 2 or 3 hours

Serving: 4

Ingredients

- 4 apples
- 1 teaspoon ground cinnamon

Instructions

Preheat the oven to 200 degrees Fahrenheit. Using parchment paper, line a baking sheet. Apples should be cored and sliced into 18-inch pieces. Toss the apple slices with the cinnamon in a medium basin. Arrange the apples in a single layer on the prepared baking sheet. Cook for 2–3 hours or until the apples are completely dry. They'll be squishy when they're hot, but after they've cooled entirely, they'll be crisp. For up to four days, store in an airtight container.

Nutritional facts

Calories 96| Carbohydrates 26g| Protein 1g| Fat 0g| Sodium 2 mg |

94. Savory Collard Chips

Preparation time: 5 minutes

Cooking time: 20 minutes

Serving: 4

Ingredients

- 1 bunch of collard greens
- 1 teaspoon extra-virgin olive oil
- Juice of ½ lemon
- ½ teaspoon garlic powder
- ¼ teaspoon freshly ground black pepper

Instructions

Preheat your oven to 350 degrees Fahrenheit. Using parchment paper, line a baking sheet. Collards should be cut into 2-by-2-inch squares and dried with paper towels. Toss the greens with olive oil, lemon juice, garlic powder, and pepper in a large mixing bowl. Mix thoroughly with your hands, kneading the dressing into the greens until they are equally covered. Place the collards in a single layer on the baking sheet and bake for 8 minutes. Cook for a further 8 minutes or until the pieces are crisp. Remove it from the oven, cool it, and store it in an airtight container for up to three days in a cool spot.

Nutritional facts

Calories 24| Carbohydrates 3g| Protein 1g| Fat 1g| Sodium 8 mg |

95. Roasted Red Pepper Hummus

Preparation time: 10 minutes

Cooking time: 10 minutes

Serving: 8

Ingredients

- 1 red bell pepper
- 2 garlic cloves
- 1 (15-ounce) can of chickpeas (drained and rinsed)
- Juice of 1 lemon
- 2 tablespoons tahini
- 2 tablespoons extra-virgin olive oil

Instructions

Raise an oven rack to the top of the oven. Increase the temperature of the broiler to high. Cut the pepper into three or four big pieces after removing the core. Place them skin-side up on a baking pan. Broil the peppers until the skins are browned, about 5 to 10 minutes. Remove the peppers from the oven and place them in a small dish. Wrap them in plastic wrap and steam for 10 to 15 minutes or until they're cool enough to handle. Remove the charred peel from the peppers and puree the peppers. Combine the chickpeas, lemon juice, tahini, garlic, and olive oil in a large mixing bowl. Process until smooth, adding up to 1 tablespoon of water if necessary to get the required consistency.

Nutritional facts

Calories 103| Carbohydrates 10g| Protein 3g| Fat 6g| Sodium 72 mg |

96. Thai Style Eggplant Dip

Preparation time: 10 minutes

Cooking time: 30 minutes

Serving: 4

Ingredients

- 1 pound Thai eggplant (or Japanese or Chinese eggplant)
- 2 tablespoons rice vinegar
- 1 teaspoon low-sodium soy sauce
- 1 jalapeño pepper
- 2 teaspoons sugar
- 2 garlic cloves

- ¼ cup chopped basil
- Cut vegetables or crackers (for serving)

Instructions

Preheat the oven to 425 degrees Fahrenheit. Using a skewer or knife, pierce the eggplant in various places. Cook until soft, approximately 30 minutes, on a rimmed baking sheet. Allow cooling before cutting in half and scooping the eggplant flesh into a blender. Combine the rice vinegar, sugar, soy sauce, jalapeno, garlic, and basil in a blender. Blend until completely smooth. Serve with crackers or chopped veggies.

Nutritional facts

Calories: 40| Carbohydrates: 10g| Protein: 2g| Fat: 0g| Sodium 47 mg |

97. Collard Salad Rolls with Peanut Dipping Sause

Preparation time: 20 minutes

Cooking time: 0 minutes

Serving: 4

Ingredients

For The Dipping Sauce

- ¼ cup peanut butter
- 2 tablespoons honey
- Juice of 1 lime
- ¼ teaspoon red chili flakes

For The Salad Rolls

- 4 ounces extra-firm tofu
- 1 bunch of collard greens
- 1 cup thinly sliced purple cabbage
- 2 carrots (cut into matchsticks)
- 1 cup bean sprouts
- ½ cup cilantro leaves and stems

Instructions

For Sauce:

Mix the peanut butter, honey, lime juice, and chili flakes in a blender and mix until smooth. Add 1 to 2 tablespoons of water to get the appropriate consistency.

For rolls:

Press the excess liquid from the tofu using paper towels. Cut the matchsticks into 12-inch thick matchsticks. Remove and discard any tough stems from the collard greens. Arrange all of the ingredients in a convenient location. In your hand, place a couple of pieces of tofu and a little bit of cabbage, bean sprouts, and carrots. Roll into a cylinder with a couple of cilantro

sprigs on top. While creating the remainder of the rolls, place each seam-side down on a serving tray. Serve with dipping sauce on the side.

Nutritional facts

Calories: 174| Carbohydrates: 20g| Protein: 8g| Fat: 9g| Sodium 42 mg |

98. Roasted Broccoli

Preparation time: 5 minutes

Cooking time: 20 minutes

Serving: 6

Ingredients

- 2 small heads of broccoli (cut into florets)
- 1 tablespoon extra-virgin olive oil
- 3 garlic cloves (minced)

Instructions

Heat the oven to 425 degrees Fahrenheit. Toss the broccoli with olive oil and garlic in a medium mixing bowl. Arrange them on baking paper in a single layer. Cook the broccoli for 10 minutes, then turn it and roast for another 10 minutes. Serve.

Nutritional facts

Calories 38| Carbohydrates 4g| Protein 1g|Fat 2g| Sodium 15 mg |

99. Mint Carrots Roasted

Preparation time: 5 minutes

Cooking time: 20 minutes

Serving: 6

Ingredients

- 1 pound of carrots (trimmed)
- 1 tablespoon extra-virgin olive oil
- ¼ cup thinly sliced mint
- Freshly ground black pepper

Instructions

Preheat the oven to 425 degrees Fahrenheit. Arrange the carrots on a rimmed baking sheet in a single layer. Drizzle the olive oil over the carrots on the baking sheet and toss to coat. Season with salt and pepper. Roast for 20 minutes or until the vegetables are soft and browned, tossing twice throughout the cooking process. Serve with a garnish of mint.

Nutritional facts

Calories 51| Carbohydrates 7g| Protein 1g| Fat 2g| Sodium 52 mg |

100. Root Vegetables Roasted

Preparation time: 5 minutes

Cooking time: 20 minutes

Serving: 6

Ingredients

- 1 cup chopped turnips
- 1 cup chopped rutabaga
- 1 teaspoon fresh chopped rosemary
- 1 cup chopped parsnips
- 1 tablespoon extra-virgin olive oil
- Freshly ground black pepper

Instructions

Preheat the oven to 400 degrees Fahrenheit. Stir the turnips, rutabaga, and parsnips with olive oil and rosemary in a large mixing basin. Season with pepper and arrange in a single layer on a baking sheet. Cook, stirring once, for 20 to 25 minutes, or until the veggies are soft and browned.

Nutritional facts

Calories 52 | Carbohydrates 7g | Protein 1g | Fat 2g | Sodium 22 mg |

101. Vegetable Couscous

Preparation time: 10 minutes

Cooking time: 15 minutes

Serving: 6

Ingredients

- 1 cup couscous
- 1 tablespoon extra-virgin olive oil
- ½ sweet onion (diced)
- ½ teaspoon garlic powder
- 1 carrot (diced)
- 1 celery stalk (diced)
- ½ cup diced red or yellow bell pepper
- 1 small zucchini (diced)
- 1½ cups Simple Chicken Broth or low-sodium store-bought chicken stock
- Freshly ground black pepper

Instructions

Heat the olive oil in a large pan over medium heat. Cook, occasionally stirring, until the onion, carrot, celery, and bell pepper begin to soften, approximately 5 to 7 minutes. Combine the zucchini, couscous, broth, and garlic powder in a large mixing bowl. Bring to a boil, stirring to combine. Cover and turn off the heat. Allow for 5 to 8 minutes of resting time. Serve by fluffing with a fork and seasoning with pepper.

Nutritional facts

Calories 154 | Carbohydrates 27g | Protein 5g | Fat 3g | Sodium 36 mg |

102. Garlic Cauliflower Rice

Preparation time: 5 minutes

Cooking time: 10 minutes

Serving: 8

Ingredients

- 1 medium head cauliflower
- 4 garlic cloves, minced
- 1 tablespoon extra-virgin olive oil
- Freshly ground black pepper

Instructions

Remove the end (core) of the cauliflower with a sharp knife and cut the cauliflower into pieces. Process the pieces in a food blender until they are the size of rice, being careful not to over-process them to the point where they become mushy. Heat the olive oil in a large pan over medium heat. Stir in the garlic until it is aromatic. Stir in the cauliflower until it is evenly coated. Lower the heat and add 1 tablespoon of water to the pan. Steam the cauliflower for 7 to 10 minutes or until it is soft. Serve with a pinch of black pepper.

Nutritional facts

Calories 37 | Fat 0 g | Protein 2 g | Carbohydrates 4 g | Sodium 22 mg |

103. Healthy Tahini Buns

Preparation Time: 10 Minutes

Cooking Time: 15-20 Minutes

Servings: 2

Ingredients

- 1 egg
- 4 tablespoons of Tahini paste
- ½ teaspoon of baking powder
- 1 teaspoon of fresh lime juice
- 1 pinch of salt for taste

Instructions

Preheat the oven to 350 degrees Fahrenheit. Place a parchment-lined baking sheet to one side. Blend all ingredients in a blender and process until a homogeneous batter is obtained.

Form the buns by scooping the mixture onto a baking pan. Baking time is between 17 and 20 minutes. Take it out and let it cool down before serving.

Nutritional facts

Calories: 172 | Carbohydrates: 7 g | Protein: 6 g | Fat: 14 g | Sodium: 112 mg

104. Chickpeas and Pepper Hummus

Preparation Time: 10 Minutes

Cooking Time: 0 Minutes

Servings: 2

Ingredients

- 14 ounces canned chickpeas, no-salt-added, drained and rinsed
- 1 tablespoon sesame paste
- 2 Roasted red peppers, chopped
- Juice of ½ lemon
- 4 Walnuts, chopped

Instructions

Combine the chickpeas, sesame paste, red peppers, lemon juice, and walnuts in a blender and pulse until smooth. Divide into bowls and serve as a snack.

Nutritional facts:

Calories: 231| Fat: 12 g | Carbohydrates: 15 g | Protein: 14 g | Sodium: 120 mg

105. Lemony Chickpeas Dip

Preparation Time: 10 Minutes

Cooking Time: 0 Minutes

Servings: 2

Ingredients

- 14 ounces canned chickpeas, drained, no-salt-added, rinsed
- Zest of 1 lemon, grated
- Juice of 1 lemon
- 1 tablespoon olive oil
- 4 tablespoons pine nuts
- ½ cup coriander, chopped

Instructions

Combine the chickpeas, lemon zest, lemon juice, coriander, and oil in a blender and pulse until smooth. Divide into small bowls, garnish with pine nuts, and serve

as a party dip.

Nutritional facts:

Calories: 200 | Fat: 12 g | Carbohydrates: 9 g | Protein: 7 g | Sodium: 846 mg

106. Chili Nuts

Preparation Time: 10 Minutes

Cooking Time: 10 Minutes

Servings: 2

Ingredients

- ½ teaspoon chili flakes
- 1 Egg white
- ½ teaspoon curry powder
- ½ teaspoon b powder
- 4 tablespoons coconut sugar
- A pinch of cayenne pepper
- 14 ounces mixed nuts

Instructions

Whisk the egg white, chili flakes, curry powder, ginger powder, coconut sugar, and cayenne in a mixing bowl. Toss in the nuts lay them out on a baking sheet lined with parchment paper, and bake for 10 minutes at 400°F. Serve the nuts as a snack by dividing them into dishes.

Nutritional Facts

Calories: 234 | Fat: 12 g | Carbohydrates: 14 g | Protein: 7 g | Sodium: 107 mg

107. Artichoke Spread

Preparation Time: 10 Minutes

Cooking Time: 15 Minutes

Servings: 2

Ingredients:

- 10 ounces spinach, chopped
- 12 ounces canned artichoke hearts, no-salt-added, drained and chopped
- 1 cup coconut cream
- 1 cup low-fat cheddar, shredded
- A pinch of black pepper

Instructions:

Combine the spinach, artichokes, cream, cheese, and black pepper in a mixing bowl, stir well, transfer to a baking dish, and bake at 400 degrees F for 15 minutes. Serve in individual bowls.

Nutritional facts:

Calories: 200 | Fat: 4 g | Carbohydrates: 14 g | Protein: 8 g | Sodium: 396 mg

108. Avocado Salsa

Preparation Time: 10 Minutes

Cooking Time: 0 Minutes

Servings: 2

Ingredients:

- 1 small yellow onion, minced
- 1 Jalapeno, minced
- ¼ cup cilantro, chopped
- A pinch of black pepper
- 2 Avocados, peeled, pitted, and cubed
- 2 tablespoons lime juice

Instructions:

Toss the onion with the jalapeño, cilantro, black pepper, avocado, and lime juice in a mixing bowl, and then serve.

Nutritional facts:

Calories: 198 | Fat: 2 g | Carbohydrates: 14 g | Protein: 7 g | Sodium: 34 mg

109. Onion Spread

Preparation Time: 10 Minutes

Cooking Time: 35 Minutes

Servings: 2

Ingredients:

- 2 tablespoons olive oil
- 2 Yellow onions, sliced
- A pinch of black pepper
- 8 ounces low-fat cream cheese
- 1 cup coconut cream
- 2 tablespoons chives, chopped

Instructions:

Heat oil over low heat, add onions and pepper, and simmer for 35 minutes, stirring occasionally. Mix onions, coconut cream, cream cheese, and chives in a bowl for a party spread.

Nutritional facts:

Calories: 212 | Fat: 3 g | Carbohydrates: 14 g | Protein: 8 g | Sodium: 82 mg

110. Lime Grilled Pineapple

Preparation Time: 10 Minutes

Cooking Time: 10 Minutes

Servings: 2

Ingredients

- 1 tablespoon lime juice
- 2 tablespoons honey
- 1 tablespoon olive oil
- 1 teaspoon cinnamon, ground
- 1 Pineapple, peeled and cut into medium pieces
- ¼ teaspoon cloves, ground
- 1 tablespoon dark rum
- 1 tablespoon lime zest, grated

Instructions

Mix lime juice, honey, oil, cinnamon, and cloves. Brush pineapple with marinade and skewer, and cook over medium-high heat. 5 minutes on each side, basting with marinade. Brush with rum, sprinkle with lime zest and serve warm or chilled.

Nutritional facts:

Calories: 50 | Fat: 1 g | Carbohydrates: 10 g | Protein: 0.5 g | Sodium: 94 mg

111. Sherry Hummus

Preparation Time: 10 Minutes

Cooking Time: 1 Hour

Servings: 2

Ingredients

- 2/3 cup chickpeas, soaked overnight and drained
- 4 garlic cloves
- 3 cups water
- 1 Bay leaf
- 1 tablespoon olive oil
- A pinch of salt
- 2 tablespoons sherry vinegar
- ¾ cup green onions, chopped
- 1 teaspoon cumin, ground
- 3 tablespoons cilantro, chopped

Instructions

Add chickpeas to water and salt, and stir. Stir in garlic and bay leaf, then simmer for 1 hour. Reserve 1/2 cup bay leaf liquid. Blend the chickpeas, saved liquid, green onions, vinegar, oil, garlic, cilantro, and cumin. Serve.

Nutritional facts

Calories: 113 | Fat: 1 g | Carbohydrates: 10 g | Protein: 3 g | Sodium: 62 mg

112. Fruit Potpourri

Preparation Time: 10 Minutes

Cooking Time: 0 Minutes

Servings: 2

Ingredients

- 1 teaspoon lime zest
- 1 teaspoon lime juice
- 6 ounces yogurt
- 1 Banana
- 4 Strawberries
- 1 Kiwi
- 4 Red grapes
- 4 Pineapple pieces

Instructions

Alternate banana, strawberry, kiwi, grape, pineapple, and grape slices on skewers. Refrigerate lemon yogurt with lime zest and juice until serving with fruit kebabs.

Nutritional facts:

Calories: 145 | Fat: 2 g | Carbohydrates: 34 mg | Protein: 4 g | Sodium: 120 mg

113. Pearl Asparagus

Preparation Time: 4 Weeks

Cooking Time: 0 Minutes

Servings: 2

Ingredients

- 3 cups asparagus spears, trimmed and cut in halves
- ¼ cup pearl onions
- ¼ cup apple cider vinegar
- 1 Dill spring
- ¼ cup white wine vinegar
- 2 cloves
- 1 cup water
- 3 garlic cloves, sliced
- ¼ teaspoon red pepper flakes

- 8 Black peppercorns
- 6 Coriander seeds

Instructions

Asparagus, onions, dill, cloves, pepper flakes, garlic, coriander, and peppercorns. Stir together apple cider vinegar, wine vinegar, and water. Put the lids on and seal the jars. Four weeks before serving, keep the jars in the fridge.

Nutritional facts

Calories: 30 | Fat: 0 g | Carbohydrates: 4 g | Protein: 2 g | Sodium: 103 mg

114. Shrimps Ceviche

Preparation Time: 3 Hours and 10 minutes

Cooking Time: 6 Minutes

Servings: 2

Ingredients

- ¼ pound shrimps, peeled, deveined, and chopped
- Zest and juice of 2 limes
- Zest and juice of 2 lemons
- 2 teaspoons cumin, ground
- 3 tablespoons olive oil
- 1 cup tomato, chopped
- ½ cup red onion, chopped
- 2 tablespoons garlic, minced
- 1 Serrano chili pepper, chopped
- 1 cup black beans, canned and drained
- 1 cup cucumber, chopped
- ¼ cup cilantro, chopped

Instructions

Toss shrimp with lime and lemon juice, cover, and refrigerate for 3 hours. Heat oil over medium-high heat, add shrimp and citrus liquids and fry for 2 minutes on each side. Toss lime and lemon zest, cumin, tomato, onion, chili pepper, garlic, cucumber, black beans, and cilantro with tortilla chips.

Nutritional facts

Calories: 100 | Fat: 3 g | Carbohydrates: 10 g | Protein: 5 g | Sodium: 124 mg

115. Hot Marinated Shrimps

Preparation Time: 1 Hour and 10 minutes

Cooking Time: 2 Minutes

Servings: 2

Ingredients

- 2 tablespoons capers
- ½ cup lime juice
- 1 Red onion, chopped
- ½ teaspoon chili powder
- 1 tablespoon mustard
- ½ cup rice vinegar
- 1 cup water
- 1 Bay leaf
- 3 cloves
- 1-pound shrimps, peeled and deveined

Instructions

Whisk capers, mustard, onion, lime juice, and chili in a baking dish. Heat the water over medium heat. Add cloves, bay leaf, and vinegar; boil. Removing the shrimps from the pan and placing them in the baking dish Cover and refrigerate for 1 hour. Serve in bowls.

Nutritional facts:

Calories: 50 | Fat: 0 g | Carbohydrates: 3 g | Protein: 12 g | Sodium: 76 mg

116. Garlicky White Bean Dip

Preparation Time: 10 Minutes

Cooking Time: 0 Minutes

Servings: 2

Ingredients

- 10 ounces canned white beans, drained
- 2 tablespoons olive oil
- 2 garlic cloves, roasted in the oven at 350°F for 40 minutes
- 2 tablespoons lemon juice

Instructions

Blend everything in the food processor. Serve with red bell pepper strips.

Nutritional facts

Calories: 89 | Fat: 4 g | Carbohydrates: 7 g | Protein: 2 g | Sodium: 45 mg

117. Spinach and Mint Dip

Preparation Time: 20 Minutes

Cooking Time: 0 Minutes

Servings: 2

Ingredients

- 1 bunch of spinach leaves, roughly chopped
- 1 Scallion, sliced
- 2 tablespoons mint leaves, chopped
- ¾ cup low-fat sour cream
- Black pepper to the taste

Instructions

Cook spinach in boiling water for 20 seconds, drain, rinse, and chop. Add sour cream, scallion, pepper to taste, and mint, mix well, and serve with pita chips.

Nutritional facts

Calories: 140 | Fat: 3 g | Carbohydrates: 6 g | Protein: 5 g | Sodium: 92 mg

118. Cilantro Spread

Preparation Time: 5 Minutes

Cooking Time: 0 Minutes

Servings: 2

Ingredients

- 2 Bunches of cilantro leaves
- ½ cup ginger, grated
- 3 tablespoons balsamic vinegar
- ½ cup avocado oil
- 2 tablespoons coconut amino

Instructions

Blend everything in a blender, then serve.

Nutritional facts:

Calories: 178 | Fat: 4 g | Carbohydrates: 14 g | Protein: 6 g | Sodium: 49 mg

119. Cheesy Broccoli Dip

Preparation Time: 6 Minutes

Cooking Time: 0 Minutes

Servings: 2

Ingredients:

- 7 ounces broccoli florets
- 1 cup low-fat cottage cheese
- A pinch of cayenne pepper

Instructions:

Blend everything, then serve as a party dip.

Nutritional facts:

Calories: 215 | Fat: 4 g | Carbohydrates: 15 g | Protein: 7 g | Sodium: 110 mg

120. Peach and Bacon Appetizer

Preparation Time: 2 Minutes

Cooking Time: 0 Minutes

Servings: 2

Ingredients:

- 1 Peach, cut into 8 wedges
- 8 Bacon slices

Instructions:

Wrap one peach wedge with bacon and serve on a plate. Serve as an appetizer with the remaining ingredients.

Nutritional facts:

Calories: 180 | Fat: 2 g | Carbohydrates: 11 g | Protein: 9 g | Sodium 56 mg

121. Garlic Sesame Dip

Preparation Time: 2 Minutes

Cooking Time: 0 Minutes

Servings: 2

Ingredients:

- 1 cup sesame seed paste
- 1 cup veggie stock
- ½ cup lemon juice
- ½ teaspoon cumin, ground
- 3 garlic cloves, chopped

Instructions:

Blend sesame paste, stock, cumin, lemon juice, and garlic until smooth. Serve in bowls.

Nutritional facts:

Calories: 170 | Fat: 12 g | Carbs: 12 g | Protein: 6 g | Sodium: 78 mg

122. Garlic Cottage Cheese Crispy

Preparation Time: 5 Minutes

Cooking Time: 2 minutes

Servings: 2

Ingredients:

- 1 cup cottage cheese
- ½ teaspoon Garlic powder
- A pinch of pepper

- A pinch of onion powder

Instructions:

Mix cheese and seasonings. Cook half a teaspoon of cheese mix in a skillet over medium heat for one minute. Repeat until done.

Nutritional facts:

Calories: 70 | Fat: 6 g | Carbohydrates: 1 g | Protein: 6 g | Sodium: 195 mg

123. Lemon Fat Bombs

Preparation Time: 10 Minutes

Cooking Time: 0 Minutes

Servings: 2

Ingredients:

- 1 Whole lemon
- 4 ounces cream cheese
- 2 ounces butter
- 2 teaspoons natural sweetener

Instructions:

Zest your lemon. Squeeze juice and zest into a basin. Combine butter, cream cheese, zest, salt, sugar, and juice in a bowl. With a hand mixer, blend until smooth. Freeze the mix for 2 hours.

Nutritional facts:

Calories: 404 | Carbohydrates: 4 g | Protein: 4 g | Fat: 43 g | Sodium: 19 mg

Chapter 7: Sauces and Kitchen Staples Recipes

1. Homemade Salt-Free Mexican Spice Mix

Preparation time: 5 minutes

Cooking time: 0 minutes

Serving: 8

Ingredients

- 2 tablespoons chili powder
- 4 1/2 teaspoons cumin
- 5 teaspoons paprika
- 2 1/2 teaspoons garlic powder
- 3 teaspoons onion powder

Instructions

Combine all of the ingredients and store them in an airtight jar. Add a few teaspoons to chicken, lean ground beef, or any meal to give it a Mexican flavor.

Nutritional facts

Calories 20| Carbohydrates 4 g| Protein 1 g| Fat 0.7 g| Sodium 37 mg

2. Homemade Mayonnaise

Preparation time: 10 minutes

Cooking time: 0 minutes

Serving: 24

Ingredients

- 1 large pasteurized egg (at room temperature)
- 1 1/4 cup olive oil (divided)
- 1/4 teaspoon salt (or less, to taste)
- 2 to 3 teaspoons fresh lemon juice (or white wine vinegar or a mix of the two)
- 1/2 teaspoon dry mustard
- A pinch or two of sugar (optional)

Instructions

In a blender, food processor, or mixer, combine the egg, 1/4 cup oil, dry mustard, salt, and sugar (if preferred). Make a thorough mix. While the mixer is running, trickle in the remaining oil a few drops at a time, allowing the oil to absorb the mixture before adding it more fully. After all of the oil has been added and the mixture has emulsified (it will seem to thicken and lighten), whisk in the lemon juice/vinegar with a spoon. Serve after chilling for 1 to 2 hours. Mayonnaise will stay in the refrigerator for approximately a week.

Nutritional facts

Calories 105| Carbohydrates 0 g| Protein 0 g| Fat 11.5 g| Sodium 27 mg

3. Coffee-Ancho Chile Rub

Preparation time: 10 minutes

Cooking time: 0 minutes

Serving: 14

Ingredients

- 1/4 cup espresso coffee beans, finely ground
- 1/3 cup packed brown sugar
- 2 teaspoons salt
- 1 tablespoon paprika
- 1 tablespoon garlic (granulated)
- 1 teaspoon black pepper
- 1 teaspoon dried oregano
- 1 teaspoon dry mustard
- 1 tablespoon ancho chili powder

Instructions

Coffee beans should be ground to fine powder. Place in a small mixing basin after removing from the grinder. Combine the remaining ingredients in a mixing dish and stir thoroughly. It may be kept in an airtight container or a baggie. To be served with lamb or beef.

Nutritional facts

Calories 30| Carbohydrates 7 g| Protein 0 g| Fat 0 g| Sodium 340 mg

4. Simple Kebob Marinade

Preparation time: 5 minutes

Cooking time: 0 minutes

Serving: 8

Ingredients

- 1/4 cup low-sodium soy sauce
- 2 tablespoons honey or agave
- 2 tablespoons fresh lemon juice
- 1 clove of crushed garlic
- 3/4 cup olive oil

Instructions

Combine all ingredients in a mixing bowl, finishing with the oil. Overnight marinate chicken, pig, or lean beef and vegetables (onions, mushrooms, bell peppers, tomatoes, squash, cauliflower, and more). Broil or grill. For every pound of meat, use 8 teaspoons of marinade. This recipe makes 2 pounds of meat.

Nutritional facts

Calories 200| Carbohydrates 5 g| Protein 1 g| Fat 20.3 g| Sodium 266 mg

5. Roasted Garlic

Preparation time: 15 minutes

Cooking time: 60 minutes

Serving: 36

Ingredients

- 3 heads of garlic
- Water

Instructions

Preheat the oven to 350 degrees Fahrenheit. Remove the skin from the garlic heads, but leave the cloves alone. Remove the tops of each head. Fill a shallow baking dish with enough water to cover the bottom of the heads (approximately 1/4 inch). Cover with foil or a lid. Bake for 60 minutes or until the cloves are tender.

Nutritional facts

Calories 5| Carbohydrates 1 g| Protein 0 g| Fat 0 g| Sodium 1 mg

6. Basic Chicken Stock

Preparation time: 15 minutes

Cooking time: 1 hour 30 minutes

Serving: 10

Ingredients

- 1 pound of chicken bones (washed, roasted)
- 3 tablespoons olive oil (divided)
- 2 bay leaves
- 1 yellow onion, peeled (coarsely chopped)
- 2 carrots, peeled (coarsely chopped)
- 2 stalks of celery (washed, coarsely chopped)
- 1 tablespoon black peppercorns
- 2 ½ quarts of water
- 2 cloves garlic (peeled)

Instructions

Preheat the oven to 400 degrees Fahrenheit. Wash the chicken bones and coat them in 2 tablespoons of olive oil in a mixing dish. Bake the bones for 30 minutes or golden brown on a sheet tray or in a suitable roasting pan. Heat 1 tablespoon olive oil in a gallon-size stockpot high on the stovetop. Sauté the onion, carrots, celery, garlic, bay leaves, and peppercorns for 10 minutes in the stockpot.

Cover with water and add the bones. Bring to a boil, then lower to low heat. After 45 minutes of simmering, pour the stock into a heat-resistant container.

Nutritional facts

Calories 65| Carbohydrates 3 g| Protein 4 g| Fat 4 g| Sodium 32 mg

7. Taco Seasoning

Preparation time: 5 minutes

Cooking time: 0 minutes

Serving: 4 tablespoons

Ingredients

- 1 tablespoon ground cumin
- 2 teaspoons paprika
- ½ teaspoon ground cinnamon
- 2 teaspoons garlic powder
- 1 teaspoon dried oregano
- 2 teaspoons freshly ground black pepper
- 1 teaspoon red pepper flakes
- ½ teaspoon onion powder

Instructions

In a sealable container, combine the cumin, paprika, garlic powder, black pepper, oregano, red pepper flakes, cinnamon, and onion powder and stir well. This seasoning may be kept at room temperature for up to a year in an airtight container. Before storage, be sure you label and date everything.

Nutritional facts

Calories 20| Carbohydrates 4 g| Protein 0 g| Fat 1 g| Sodium 5 mg

8. Curry Garlic Seasoning

Preparation time: 5 minutes

Cooking time: 0 minutes

Serving: 10 tablespoons

Ingredients

- 4 tablespoons dried onion flakes
- 1½ tablespoons curry powder
- 3 tablespoons garlic powder
- ½ tablespoon freshly ground black pepper
- ⅛ teaspoon ground cayenne pepper

Instructions

Mix the onion flakes, garlic powder, curry powder,

black pepper, and cayenne in a sealable container and stir thoroughly. This seasoning may be kept for up to a year at room temperature. Before storage, be sure you label and date everything.

Nutritional facts

Calories 21| Carbohydrates 5 g| Protein 0.08 g| Fat 0 g| Sodium 3 mg

9. Italian Seasoning Blend

Preparation time: 5 minutes

Cooking time: 0 minutes

Serving: 8 tablespoons

Ingredients

- 2 tablespoons basil
- 2 tablespoons oregano
- 1 tablespoon thyme
- 2 tablespoons parsley
- 1 tablespoon rosemary
- 1 tablespoon red pepper flakes
- 2 teaspoons garlic powder

Instructions

Combine the basil, oregano, parsley, rosemary, thyme, red pepper flakes (if using), and garlic powder in a sealable container and stir well. This seasoning may be kept for up to a year at room temperature. Before storage, be sure you label and date everything.

Nutritional facts

Calories 9| Carbohydrates 2 g| Protein 0.5 g| Fat 0 g| Sodium 3 mg

10. Barbecue Rub Seasoning Blend

Preparation time: 5 minutes

Cooking time: 0 minutes

Serving: 4 tablespoons

Ingredients

- 1 tablespoon brown sugar
- 1 teaspoon smoked paprika
- 1 teaspoon onion powder
- 1 teaspoon chili powder
- 1 teaspoon garlic powder
- 1 teaspoon ground cumin
- ¼ teaspoon dry mustard
- ⅛ teaspoon allspice

- ⅛ teaspoon red pepper flakes (optional)

Instructions

Combine the brown sugar, paprika, chili powder, garlic powder, onion powder, cumin, mustard, allspice, and red pepper flakes (if using) in an airtight container and stir well. This seasoning may be kept for up to a year at room temperature. Before storage, be sure you label and date everything.

Nutritional facts

Calories 16| Carbohydrates 4 g| Protein 0.4 g| Fat 0 g| Sodium 18 mg

11. Roasted Tomatillo Salsa

Preparation time: 5 minutes

Cooking time: 15 minutes

Serving: 2 cups

Ingredients

- 16 tomatillos (halved)
- 1 bunch of fresh cilantro
- 3 jalapeños (stemmed)
- 10 garlic cloves (peeled)
- 2 tablespoons avocado oil (plus more for drizzling)
- ¼ cup freshly squeezed lime juice
- ¼ cup water

Instructions

Preheat the broiler to high and place parchment paper on a baking pan. On a baking sheet, spread the tomatillos, jalapenos, and garlic. Drizzle the oil over the top and gently toss it to coat. Broil the tomatillos for 10 to 15 minutes or until browned. Puree the ingredients in a food processor or blender with cilantro, lime juice, water, and avocado oil until smooth. Keep leftovers refrigerated for up to 7 days in an airtight container. Before storing, let cool fully, label, and date.

Nutritional facts

Calories 22| Carbohydrates 4 g| Protein 0.7 g| Fat 1 g| Sodium 1 mg

12. Low-Sodium Dijon Mustard

Preparation time: 5 minutes

Cooking time: 0 minutes

Serving: 12 teaspoons

Ingredients

- 1 cup dry white wine
- ½ cup white vinegar

- ½ tablespoon sugar

- 1 bay leaf

- 2 garlic cloves (minced)

- 1 teaspoon allspice

- ¼ cup chopped onion

- ½ teaspoon dried tarragon

- ¼ teaspoon ground cayenne pepper

- ¼ cup cold water

- ½ cup dry mustard

Instructions

Combine the wine, vinegar, onion, sugar, garlic, allspice, bay leaf, tarragon, and cayenne in a medium saucepan. Boil, the mixture for approximately 20 minutes or until it is reduced by half. Meanwhile, put the water and mustard in a large mixing basin and set aside for 10 minutes. Strain the vinegar mixture and add it to the mustard mixture in a separate bowl. Return the mixture to the saucepan and simmer for another 10 minutes over medium-low heat, stirring often. This mustard can keep for up to 3 months in the refrigerator. Before storing, let cool fully, label, and date.

Nutritional facts

Calories 39| Carbohydrates 3 g| Protein 1.2 g| Fat 0 g| Sodium 6 mg

13. Mango Teriyaki Sauce

Preparation time: 5 minutes

Cooking time: 30 minutes

Serving: ¼ cups

Ingredients

- 3 Medjool dates (pitted)

- 2 cups water

- ½ cup chopped mango

- 1 tablespoon low-sodium soy sauce

- 1 teaspoon rice wine vinegar

- ¼ teaspoon ground ginger

- 1 tablespoon sesame oil

- ¼ teaspoon garlic powder

Instructions

Soak the dates with water in a small dish and set aside for 15 minutes. Drain the dates and save 1 cup of the liquid. Puree the dates and reserved water, mango, soy sauce, sesame oil, vinegar, ginger, and garlic powder until smooth in a blender or food processor. Fill a pot halfway with water and bring to a boil over medium heat. Remove off the flame after it has reached a boil and reduce to low

heat, stirring periodically. In 10 to 15 minutes, the sauce should thicken. Keep leftovers refrigerated for up to 7 days in an airtight container.

Nutritional facts

Calories 20| Carbohydrates 4 g| Protein 0.2 g| Fat 1 g| Sodium4 mg

14. Peanut Apple Sauce

Preparation time: 5 minutes

Cooking time: 0 minutes

Serving: 8 tablespoons

Ingredients

- ¼ cup creamy unsalted peanut butter

- 2 tablespoons unsweetened applesauce

- 3 to 4 tablespoons of warm water

- 1 tablespoon rice vinegar

- ¼ teaspoon ground ginger

Instructions

Combine the peanut butter, warm water, applesauce, vinegar, and ginger in a small bowl or jar until thoroughly blended. Keep the container sealed. Keep leftovers in an airtight jar in the refrigerator for 7 days.

Nutritional facts

Calories 50| Carbohydrates 2 g| Protein 0 g| Fat 4 g| Sodium 2 mg

15. Enchilada Sauce

Preparation time: 5 minutes

Cooking time: 20 minutes

Serving: 3 cups

Ingredients

- 2 tablespoons all-purpose flour

- 8 ounces of no-salt-added tomato sauce

- 2 tablespoons no-salt-added tomato paste

- 2 tablespoons olive or avocado oil

- 1 teaspoon ground cumin

- 1 teaspoon garlic powder

- ½ teaspoon dried oregano

- 1 tablespoon chili powder

- ¼ teaspoon ground cinnamon

- 2 cups of no-salt-added vegetable broth

Instructions

Heat the flour in a medium saucepan over medium-high heat for a minute to warm it up. Add the tomato sauce, tomato paste, oil, chili powder, cumin, garlic powder, oregano, and cinnamon, and stir. In 12-cup increments, add the broth to the mixture, stirring frequently. Reduce the heat to low and cook for 10 to 15 minutes, or until the sauce has thickened. Keep leftovers refrigerated for up to 7 days in an airtight container.

Nutritional facts

Calories 80| Carbohydrates 8 g| Protein 2.2 g| Fat 5 g| Sodium 66 mg

16. Unsweetened Almond Milk

Preparation time: 10 minutes + 12 hours to soak

Cooking time: 0 minutes

Serving: 3 cups

Ingredients

- 1 cup raw almonds

- 3 cups filtered water + more for soaking

Instructions

Place the almonds and enough water to cover them in a quart jar. Set aside for 6 to 8 hours or overnight in the refrigerator to soak. Transfer the almonds to a blender after draining them. Blend on high until the almonds are finely crushed, and the liquid is white, then add the filtered water. Place a sieve over a big bowl and cover it with a cheesecloth. Pour the almond mixture into the cheesecloth in stages, pressing the fabric to remove all of the liquid. Remove the almond pulp and toss it out. If desired, add any flavorings. Refrigerate for up to three days in an airtight container.

Nutritional facts

Calories 40| Carbohydrates 2 g| Protein 1 g| Fat 0 g| Sodium 6 mg

17. Beetroot Sauce

Preparation time: 10 minutes

Cooking time: 0 minutes

Serving: 4

Ingredients

- 1 cup of canned beetroot (no added sugar or salt)

- 1 teaspoon dry mustard

- A pinch of black pepper to taste

- 1 juiced lemon

Instructions

In a blender, purée all of the ingredients until smooth. Serve right away or keep in the fridge for up to two days

in an airtight container. It's delicious with turnip chips or eggplant fries cooked from scratch.

Nutritional facts

Calories 25| Carbohydrates 4 g| Protein 0 g| Fat 0 g| Sodium 4 mg

18. Hot Sauce

Preparation time: 5 minutes

Cooking time: 20 minutes

Serving: 5

Ingredients

- 1/4 cup onion (chopped)

- 2 tablespoon canola oil

- 1 tablespoon all-purpose white flour

- 1/2 cup tarragon vinegar

- 1 cup water

- 2 teaspoon dry mustard

- 1 teaspoon chili powder

Instructions

To produce a paste, combine the oil and flour, add the rest of the ingredients and transfer to a pan. Cook the mixture over low heat for 15-20 minutes or until it thickens. Before cooking, brush the sauce over the meats, fish, or vegetables.

Nutritional facts

Calories 67| Carbohydrates 2 g| Protein 0 g| Fat 6 g| Sodium 6 mg

19. Homemade Pork Gravy

Preparation time: 5 minutes

Cooking time: 25 minutes

Serving: 5

Ingredients

- 6 oz. lean ground pork (minced)

- 1 teaspoon ground sage

- 1 teaspoon paprika

- 1 teaspoon ground basil

- 1 teaspoon black pepper

- 1 tablespoon cornstarch

- 1 teaspoon fennel seeds

- 2 cups water

Instructions

Toss the minced pork with herbs and spices. Cook the pork mixture in a saucepan over medium to high heat for

15 minutes or until cooked through. Add the water and cornstarch to the saucepan and cook for another 10 minutes on low heat. Blend until a liquid consistency is achieved in a food processor, then sieve to remove any lumps. Once cold, store it in an airtight container as a meat gravy.

Nutritional facts

Calories 112| Carbohydrates 3 g| Protein 9 g| Fat 7 g| Sodium 12 mg

20. White Cheese Sauce

Preparation time: 5 minutes

Cooking time: 20 minutes

Serving: 5

Ingredients

- 1/4 cup all-purpose white flour
- 4 oz. cream cheese
- 1/2 cup brie
- 3/4 cup 1% low-fat milk or rice milk (unenriched)
- 1 tablespoon butter
- 1/4 teaspoon white pepper
- 1 teaspoon black pepper

Instructions

Preheat the pot over medium-high heat. Place the butter on the side of the pan closest to the handle. Tilt the pan towards you and melt the butter; be careful not to let it cover the whole pan. Add the flour to the other side of the pan and gently incorporate it into the butter, mixing until smooth. Stir in the milk for 10 minutes or until all lumps are gone. Stir in the cheese (optional) for another 5 minutes. Remove from the heat and serve right away.

Nutritional facts

Calories 156| Carbohydrates 9 g| Protein 4 g| Fat 12 g| Sodium 10 mg

21. Spicy Mango Chutney

Preparation time: 5 minutes

Cooking time: 15 minutes

Serving: 4

Ingredients

- 1 cup mango (finely diced)
- 1 tablespoon canola oil
- 1/2 cup onion (chopped)
- 2 teaspoon fresh ginger root (minced)
- 1 teaspoon chili powder

- 1 teaspoon cumin

Instructions

In a skillet, heat the oil over medium to high heat. Cook for 5 minutes or until the onion is tender. Stir in the ginger for 2 minutes. Add the other ingredients, cover, and reduce heat to low. Cook for 10 to 15 minutes. Remove from the heat and set aside to cool. Refrigerate for 2-3 days in an airtight jar.

Nutritional facts

Calories 76| Carbohydrates 3 g| Protein 9 g| Fat 7 g| Sodium 34 mg

22. Honey and Mustard Dressing

Preparation time: 5 minutes

Cooking time: 0 minutes

Serving: 2

Ingredients

- 1 tablespoon French mustard
- 1 tablespoon extra-virgin olive oil
- 1 tablespoon honey

Instructions

In a mixing basin, whisk together all ingredients until well blended. Refrigerate for up to one week after covering.

Nutritional facts

Calories 90| Carbohydrates 9 g| Protein 0 g| Fat 7 g| Sodium 2 mg

23. Cajun Spice Rub

Preparation time: 5 minutes

Cooking time: 0 minutes

Serving: 2

Ingredients

- 1 garlic clove (minced)
- 2 teaspoon black pepper
- 2 teaspoon cayenne pepper
- 2 teaspoon chili powder
- 2 teaspoon dried thyme
- 2 teaspoon dried oregano

Instructions

Combine all ingredients in an airtight container and keep them in a dry location. Use as a pre-cooking rub for meats and fish.

Nutritional facts

Calories 25| Carbohydrates 5 g| Protein 1 g| Fat 1 g| Sodium 17 mg

24. Sweet Chili and Lime

Preparation time: 5 minutes

Cooking time: 7 minutes

Serving: 4

Ingredients

- 2 garlic cloves
- 1 red jalapeno chili pepper
- 2 tablespoons white vinegar
- 2 tablespoons brown sugar
- 1/2 cup water
- 1 lime

Instructions

The lime, cornstarch, and 2 tablespoons of water should be set aside. In a blender or food processor, combine the remaining ingredients until smooth. Place the mixture in a pan over medium-high heat for 5 minutes or until it thickens. To loosen the mixture a bit further, add the cornstarch, 1 lime juice, and 2 tablespoons of water for another 2 minutes. Remove from the heat and set aside to cool. Refrigerate for 2-3 days in an airtight jar.

Nutritional facts

Calories 59| Carbohydrates 15 g| Protein 0 g| Fat 0 g| Sodium 3 mg

25. Mixed herb Marinade

Preparation time: 10 minutes

Cooking time: 35 minutes

Serving: 5

Ingredients

- 1 teaspoon black pepper
- 1 garlic clove (minced)
- 1 celery stalk (minced)
- 2 teaspoon mustard seeds (crushed)
- 1 teaspoon dried basil
- 1 teaspoon dried thyme
- 1 teaspoon dried oregano

Instructions

In a food processor, combine all ingredients and process until a fine powder is created. Keep in a sealed jar in a cool, dry location. When ready to use, combine 1 tablespoon olive oil with the spices and baste meats, seafood, and vegetables, or use it as a dry rub for broiling.

Nutritional facts

Calories 25| Carbohydrates 1 g| Protein 0 g| Fat 0 g| Sodium 3 mg

26. Wild Garlic Pesto

Preparation time: 5 minutes

Cooking time: 0 minutes

Serving: 5

Ingredients

- 1/2 cup fresh basil
- 1/2 cup fresh spinach/arugula
- 1/4 cup extra virgin olive oil
- 1/4 cup of wild garlic leaves (or 2 garlic cloves as an alternative)
- 1 lemon (juiced)
- 1 teaspoon black pepper

Instructions

In a food processor or blender, combine all ingredients until desired texture is achieved: chunky for a rustic feel or smooth for a dressing. Refrigerate for 3-4 days in an airtight container. Serve with spaghetti, roasted veggies, or raw vegetables as a dip.

Nutritional facts

Calories 59| Carbohydrates 0 g| Protein 0 g| Fat 0 g| Sodium 4 mg

27. Mexican salsa

Preparation time: 10 minutes

Cooking time: 35 minutes

Serving: 2

Ingredients

- 1/4 red onion (finely diced)
- 1 lime (juiced)
- 1 teaspoon white vinegar
- 1 teaspoon black pepper
- 1/4 cup mango/pineapple (diced)
- 1 tablespoon fresh cilantro (chopped)
- 1/2 lemon (juiced)

Instructions

Vegetables should be soaked in warm water. Toss all of the ingredients together in a bowl to coat. Serve immediately or store in an airtight jar in the fridge for 2-3 days. Serve with fish, meats, tacos, and salads.

Calories 41| Carbohydrates 12 g| Protein 0 g| Fat 0 g| Sodium 7 mg

28. Fajita Rub

Preparation time: 5 minutes

Cooking time: 0 minutes

Serving: 1

Ingredients

- 1½ teaspoons chili powder
- 1 teaspoon garlic powder
- 1 teaspoon dried oregano
- 1 teaspoon roasted cumin seed
- ½ teaspoon ground coriander
- ¼ teaspoon red pepper flakes

Instructions

Pulse the chili powder, garlic powder, cumin seed, oregano, coriander, and red pepper flakes in a blender until the spices are finely mixed and thoroughly incorporated. Fill a small jar with the spice mixture and close it. Store for up to 6 months in a cool, dry location.

Nutritional facts

Calories 1| Carbohydrates 0 g| Protein 0 g| Fat 0 g| Sodium 7 mg

29. Dried Herb Rub

Preparation time: 5 minutes

Cooking time: 0 minutes

Serving: 1

Ingredients

- 1 tablespoon dried thyme
- 2 teaspoons onion powder
- 1 tablespoon dried oregano
- 1 tablespoon dried parsley
- 1 teaspoon paprika
- 2 teaspoons dried basil
- 2 teaspoons ground coriander
- 1 teaspoon ground cumin
- 1 teaspoon garlic powder
- ½ teaspoon cayenne pepper

Instructions

In a blender, mix the thyme, oregano, parsley, basil,

coriander, onion powder, cumin, garlic powder, paprika, and cayenne pepper and pulse until thoroughly incorporated. Place the rub in a small, lidded jar. Store for up to 6 months in a cool, dry location.

Nutritional facts

Calories 3| Carbohydrates 1 g| Protein 0 g| Fat 0 g| Sodium 1 mg

30. Mediterranean Seasoning

Preparation time: 5 minutes

Cooking time: 0 minutes

Serving: 1

Ingredients

- 2 tablespoons oregano
- 2 teaspoons rosemary
- 2 teaspoons basil
- 1 teaspoon dried marjoram
- 1 tablespoon dried thyme
- 1 teaspoon dried parsley flakes

Instructions

Combine the oregano, thyme, rosemary, basil, marjoram, and parsley in a small basin and stir well. Fill a small container with the spice mixture and close it. Store for up to 6 months in a cool, dry location.

Nutritional facts

Calories 1| Carbohydrates 0 g| Protein 0 g| Fat 0 g| Sodium 0 mg

31. Hot Curry Powder

Preparation time: 5 minutes

Cooking time: 0 minutes

Serving: 1

Ingredients

- ¼ cup ground cumin
- ¼ cup ground coriander
- 3 tablespoons turmeric
- 1 teaspoon ground cinnamon
- 2 tablespoons sweet paprika
- 1 tablespoon fennel powder
- ½ teaspoon green chili powder
- 2 teaspoons ground cardamom
- 2 tablespoons ground mustard
- ½ teaspoon ground cloves

Instructions

In a blender, pulse the cumin, coriander, turmeric, paprika, mustard, fennel powder, green chili powder, cardamom, cinnamon, and cloves until finely crushed and thoroughly blended. Put the curry powder in a small, lidded jar. Store for up to 6 months in a cool, dry location.

Nutritional facts

Calories 19| Carbohydrates 3 g| Protein 1 g| Fat 1 g| Sodium 5 mg

32. Apple Pie Spice

Preparation time: 5 minutes

Cooking time: 0 minutes

Serving: 1

Ingredients

- ¼ cup ground cinnamon
- 2 teaspoons ground nutmeg
- 2 teaspoons ground ginger
- 1 teaspoon allspice
- ½ teaspoon ground cloves

Instructions

Combine the cinnamon, nutmeg, ginger, allspice, and cloves in a small bowl and stir until thoroughly blended. Fill a small jar with the spice mixture and close it. Store for up to 6 months in a cool, dry location.

Nutritional facts

Calories 6| Carbohydrates 1 g| Protein 0 g| Fat 0 g| Sodium 5 mg

33. Ras-el Hanout

Preparation time: 5 minutes

Cooking time: 0 minutes

Serving: 1

Ingredients

- 2 teaspoons ground nutmeg
- 2 teaspoons ground coriander
- 2 teaspoons ground cumin
- 2 teaspoons turmeric
- 2 teaspoons cinnamon
- 1 teaspoon cardamom
- 1 teaspoon sweet paprika
- 1 teaspoon cayenne pepper
- 1 teaspoon ground mace

- 1 teaspoon freshly ground black pepper
- ½ teaspoon ground allspice
- ½ teaspoon ground cloves

Instructions

Mix the nutmeg, coriander, cumin, turmeric, cinnamon, cardamom, paprika, mace, black pepper, cayenne pepper, allspice, and cloves in a small bowl until thoroughly blended. Fill a small container with the spice mixture and close it. Store for up to 6 months in a cool, dry location.

Nutritional facts

Calories 5| Carbohydrates 1 g| Protein 0 g| Fat 0 g| Sodium 1 mg

34. Poultry Seasoning

Preparation time: 5 minutes

Cooking time: 0 minutes

Serving: 1

Ingredients

- 2 tablespoons ground thyme
- 2 tablespoons ground marjoram
- 1 tablespoon ground sage
- 1 tablespoon ground celery seed
- 1 teaspoon ground rosemary
- 1 teaspoon freshly ground black pepper

Instructions

Mix the thyme, marjoram, sage, celery seed, rosemary, and pepper in a small bowl until everything is thoroughly blended. Fill a small container with the spice mixture and close it. Store for up to 6 months in a cool, dry location.

Nutritional facts

Calories 3| Carbohydrates 0 g| Protein 0 g| Fat 0 g| Sodium 1 mg

35. Berbere Spice Mix

Preparation time: 5 minutes

Cooking time: 5 minutes

Serving: 1

Ingredients

- 1 tablespoon coriander seeds
- 1 teaspoon cumin seeds
- 4 whole cloves
- 1 teaspoon fenugreek seeds
- ¼ teaspoon black peppercorns

- ¼ teaspoon whole allspice berries
- 4 dried chills (stemmed and seeded)
- 2 tablespoons ground cardamom
- 1 tablespoon sweet paprika
- 1 teaspoon ground ginger
- ¼ cup dried onion flakes
- ½ teaspoon ground nutmeg
- ½ teaspoon ground cinnamon

Instructions

Combine the coriander, cumin, fenugreek, peppercorns, allspice, and cloves in a small pan. Lightly roast the spices for approximately 4 minutes, or until aromatic, moving the pan continually. Remove the pan from the heat and set it aside for 10 minutes to allow the spices to cool. Combine the toasted spices, chills, and onion in a blender and process until the mixture is finely ground. In a small bowl, blend the cardamom, paprika, ginger, nutmeg, and cinnamon with the ground spice combination until fully incorporated. For up to 6 months, store the spice combination in a compact jar with a cover.

Nutritional facts

Calories 8| Carbohydrates 2 g| Protein 0 g| Fat 0 g| Sodium 14 mg

36. Creole Seasoning Mix

Preparation time: 5 minutes

Cooking time: 0 minutes

Serving: 1

Ingredients

- 1 tablespoon sweet paprika
- 1 tablespoon garlic powder
- 2 teaspoons dried oregano
- 2 teaspoons onion powder
- 1 teaspoon cayenne pepper
- 1 teaspoon ground thyme
- 1 teaspoon freshly ground black pepper

Instructions

In a small mixing bowl, combine the paprika, garlic powder, onion powder, oregano, cayenne pepper, thyme, and black pepper until thoroughly blended. Fill a small container with the spice mixture and close it. Store for up to 6 months in a cool, dry location.

Nutritional facts

Calories 7| Carbohydrates 2 g| Protein 0 g| Fat 0 g| Sodium 1 mg

37. Adobo Seasoning Mix

Preparation time: 5 minutes

Cooking time: 0 minutes

Serving: 1

Ingredients

- 4 tablespoons garlic powder
- 4 tablespoons onion powder
- 4 tablespoons ground cumin
- 3 tablespoons dried oregano
- 3 tablespoons freshly ground black pepper
- 2 tablespoons sweet paprika
- 2 tablespoons ground chili powder
- 1 tablespoon ground turmeric
- 1 tablespoon ground coriander

Instructions

Combine the garlic powder, onion powder, cumin, oregano, black pepper, paprika, chili powder, turmeric, and coriander in a small mixing bowl and stir well. Area the seasoning combination in a small jar with a cover and keep for up to 6 months in a cold, dry place.

Nutritional facts

Calories 8| Carbohydrates 2 g| Protein 0 g| Fat 0 g| Sodium 12 mg

38. Herbs de Provence

Preparation time: 5 minutes

Cooking time: 0 minutes

Serving: 1

Ingredients

- ½ cup dried thyme
- 3 tablespoons dried marjoram
- 3 tablespoons dried savory
- 2 tablespoons dried rosemary
- 2 teaspoons dried lavender flowers
- 1 teaspoon ground fennel

Instructions

Add the thyme, marjoram, savory, rosemary, lavender, and fennel in a blender. Pulse a few times to incorporate. Fill a small jar with the herb mixture and close it. Store for up to 6 months in a cool, dry location.

Nutritional facts

Calories 3| Carbohydrates 1 g| Protein 0 g| Fat 0 g| Sodium 0 mg

39. Lamb and Pork Seasoning

Preparation time: 5 minutes

Cooking time: 0 minutes

Serving: 1

Ingredients

- ¼ cup celery seed
- 2 tablespoons dried oregano
- 2 tablespoons onion powder
- 1 tablespoon dried thyme
- 1½ teaspoons garlic powder
- 1 teaspoon crushed bay leaf
- 1 teaspoon freshly ground black pepper
- 1 teaspoon ground allspice

Instructions

In a blender, mix the celery seed, oregano, onion powder, thyme, garlic powder, bay leaf, pepper, and allspice by pulsing a few times. Fill a small jar with the herb mixture and close it. Store for up to 6 months in a cool, dry location.

Nutritional facts

Calories 8| Carbohydrates 1 g| Protein 0 g| Fat 0 g| Sodium 2 mg

40. Asian seasoning

Preparation time: 5 minutes

Cooking time: 0 minutes

Serving: 1

Ingredients

- 2 tablespoons sesame seeds
- 2 tablespoons onion powder
- 2 tablespoons crushed star anise pods
- 2 tablespoons ground ginger
- 1 teaspoon ground allspice
- ½ teaspoon cardamom
- ½ teaspoon ground cloves

Instructions

In a small mixing bowl, combine the sesame seeds, onion powder, star anise, ginger, allspice, cardamom, and cloves. Fill a small jar with the spice mixture and close it. Store for up to 6 months in a cool, dry location.

Nutritional facts

Calories 10| Carbohydrates 1 g| Protein 0 g| Fat 0 g| Sodium 1 mg

41. Onion Seasoning Blend

Preparation time: 5 minutes

Cooking time: 0 minutes

Serving: 1

Ingredients

- 2 tablespoons onion powder
- 1 tablespoon dry mustard
- 1 teaspoon dried thyme
- 2 teaspoons sweet paprika
- 2 teaspoons garlic powder
- ½ teaspoon celery seeds
- ½ teaspoon freshly ground black pepper

Instructions

Combine the onion powder, mustard, paprika, garlic powder, thyme, celery seeds, and pepper in a small mixing bowl. Fill a small jar with the spice mixture and close it. Store for up to 6 months in a cool, dry location.

Nutritional facts

Calories 5| Carbohydrates 1 g| Protein 1 g| Fat 0 g| Sodium 3 mg

42. Coffee Dry Rub

Preparation time: 5 minutes

Cooking time: 0 minutes

Serving: 1

Ingredients

- 1 tablespoon ground coffee
- 2 teaspoons chili powder
- 2 teaspoons ground cumin
- 2 teaspoons sweet paprika
- 1 teaspoon brown sugar
- ¼ teaspoon freshly ground black pepper

Instructions

Mix the coffee, cumin, paprika, chili powder, brown sugar, and pepper in a small bowl until thoroughly blended. Place the rub in a small, lidded jar. Store for up to 6 months in a cool, dry location.

Nutritional facts

Calories 5| Carbohydrates 1 g| Protein 0 g| Fat 0 g| Sodium 18 mg

43. Balsamic Vinaigrette

Preparation time: 5 minutes

Cooking time: 0 minutes

Serving: 3 cups

Ingredients

- 1½ cups extra virgin olive oil
- 1 cup of good-quality balsamic vinegar
- 2 tablespoons chopped fresh parsley
- 2 tablespoons minced onion
- 1 teaspoon minced garlic
- 4 teaspoons chopped fresh basil
- Freshly ground black pepper

Instructions

Whisk together the olive oil and balsamic vinegar in a large mixing basin for 1 minute or until the ingredients emulsify. Combine the parsley, onion, garlic, and basil in a mixing bowl. Season with salt and pepper. Store the vinaigrette in a glass jar with a cover for 2 weeks at room temperature. Before usage, give it a good shake.

Nutritional facts

Calories 129| Carbohydrates 2 g| Protein 0 g| Fat 14 g| Sodium 3 mg

44. Balsamic Reduction

Preparation time: 5 minutes

Cooking time: 30 minutes

Serving: 1/2 cups

Ingredients

- 2 cups of good-quality balsamic vinegar
- 1 tablespoon granulated sugar

Instructions

Whisk the balsamic vinegar and sugar in a small saucepan over medium-high heat. Toss the vinegar mixture into a pot and bring it to a boil. Reduce the heat to low and cook for approximately 20 minutes, stirring regularly, or until the vinegar has reduced. Allow the vinegar reduction to cool fully after removing it from the heat. Fill a jar with the cooled reduction and keep it at room temperature for 2 weeks.

Nutritional facts

Calories 62| Carbohydrates 12 g| Protein 0 g| Fat 0 g| Sodium 15 mg

45. Herb Pesto

Preparation time: 10 minutes

Cooking time: 0 minutes

Serving: 1 1/2 cups

Ingredients

- 1 cup packed fresh basil leaves
- ½ cup packed fresh oregano leaves
- ¼ cup olive oil
- ½ cup packed fresh parsley leaves
- 2 garlic cloves
- 2 tablespoons freshly squeezed lemon juice

Instructions

Pulse the basil, oregano, parsley, and garlic for approximately 3 minutes, or until very finely chopped in a food processor. Drizzle the olive oil into the pesto, scraping down the edges at least once until thick paste forms. Pulse in the lemon juice until fully combined. Refrigerate the pesto for up to 1 week in an airtight jar.

Nutritional facts

Calories 22| Carbohydrates 0 g| Protein 0 g| Fat 2 g| Sodium 1 mg

46. Alfredo Sauce

Preparation time: 10 minutes

Cooking time: 10 minutes

Serving: 8

Ingredients

- 2 tablespoons unsalted butter
- 1 teaspoon minced garlic
- 1½ tablespoons all-purpose flour
- 1 cup plain unsweetened rice milk
- ¾ cup plain cream cheese
- 2 tablespoons Parmesan cheese
- ¼ teaspoon ground nutmeg
- Freshly ground black pepper (for seasoning)

Instructions

Melt the butter in a medium saucepan over medium heat. To make a paste, mix the flour and garlic, then whisk for 2 minutes to cook the flour. Whisk in the rice milk for another 4 minutes or until the sauce is thick and nearly boiling. For approximately 1 minute, whisk in the cream cheese, Parmesan cheese, and nutmeg until the sauce is smooth. Season with pepper after removing the sauce from the heat. Serve right immediately over spaghetti.

Calories 38| Carbohydrates 6 g| Protein 3 g| Fat 7 g| Sodium 141 mg

47. Apple Cranberry Chutney

Preparation time: 10 minutes

Cooking time: 30 minutes

Serving: 1 cup

Ingredients

- 1 large apple (peeled, cored, and sliced thin)
- ½ cup granulated sugar
- ½ red onion (finely chopped)
- ¼ cup apple juice
- ½ cup fresh cranberries
- Freshly ground black pepper (for seasoning)
- ¼ cup apple cider vinegar

Instructions

Combine the apple, sugar, cranberries, onion, apple juice, and vinegar in a medium saucepan. Bring the mixture to a boil, then lower to low heat and simmer for 25 to 30 minutes, stirring often, or until the cranberries are very soft. Season with salt and pepper. Remove the chutney from the heat and refrigerate for at least 3 hours, or until thoroughly chilled. Refrigerate the chutney for up to 1 week in an airtight jar.

Nutritional facts

Calories 36| Carbohydrates 9 g| Protein 0 g| Fat 0 g| Sodium 1 mg

48. Cooked Four Pepper Salsa

Preparation time: 15 minutes

Cooking time: 1 hour 15 minutes

Serving: 4 cups

Ingredients

- 1 pound red bell peppers (boiled and chopped)
- 2 small sweet banana peppers (chopped)
- 1 small sweet onion (chopped)
- 2 teaspoons minced garlic
- 1 jalapeño pepper (finely chopped)
- 1 green bell pepper (chopped)
- ½ cup apple cider vinegar
- 1 tablespoon granulated sugar
- 3 tablespoons chopped fresh cilantro

Instructions

Combine the red bell peppers, banana peppers, onion, jalapeno pepper, green bell pepper, apple cider vinegar, garlic, and sugar in a large skillet. Bring the mixture to a boil, constantly stirring. Reduce the heat to low and constantly stir for approximately 1 hour. Stir in the cilantro and cook for 15 minutes, stirring regularly. Allow 15 to 20 minutes for the salsa to cool once removed from the heat. Transfer the salsa to a jar and keep it refrigerated for up to a week or until ready to use. Serve chilled with tortilla chips cooked in the oven.

Nutritional facts

Calories 40| Carbohydrates 8 g| Protein 1 g| Fat 0 g| Sodium 4 mg

49. Cinnamon Apple Sauce

Preparation time: 10 minutes

Cooking time: 30 minutes

Serving: 3 cups

Ingredients

- 8 apples (peeled, cored, and sliced thin)
- ½ cup water
- ¼ teaspoon ground nutmeg
- 1 teaspoon ground cinnamon
- Pinch ground allspice

Instructions

In a medium saucepan over medium heat, combine the apples, water, cinnamon, nutmeg, and allspice. Heat the apple mixture for 25 to 30 minutes, stirring often, or until the apples soften. Remove the skillet from the heat and mash the apples with a potato masher until the desired texture is achieved. Allow the applesauce to cool before use. Keep refrigerated for up to one week.

Nutritional facts

Calories 106| Carbohydrates 28 g| Protein 1 g| Fat 0 g| Sodium 0 mg

50. Low Sodium Basil Oil

Preparation time: 15 minutes

Cooking time: 4 minutes

Serving: 3

Ingredients

- 2 cups olive oil
- 2 ½ cup fresh basil leaves patted dry

Instructions

In a food processor or blender, pulse the olive oil and basil leaves until the leaves are finely minced. Place everything in a medium saucepan over medium heat.

Heat the oil, stirring periodically, until it begins to boil around the edges, approximately 4 minutes. Remove it from the oven and set it aside to cool for approximately 2 hours. Pour the oil into a container through a fine-mesh sieve or a doubled piece of cheesecloth. Refrigerate the basil oil in an airtight glass bottle for two months. Remove the oil from the refrigerator and allow it to come to room temperature before using it for dressings, or scoop out cold spoons for cooking.

Nutritional facts

Calories 600| Carbohydrates 0 g| Protein 0 g| Fat 5 g| Sodium 3 mg

51. Basil Pesto

Preparation time: 15 minutes

Cooking time: 0 minutes

Serving: 1 ½ cup

Ingredients

- 2 cups gently packed fresh basil leaves
- 2 garlic cloves
- 1/4 cup olive oil
- 2 tablespoons pine nuts
- 2 tablespoons freshly squeezed lemon juice

Instructions

Within 3 minutes, pulse the basil, garlic, and pine nuts in a food processor or blender. Pour the olive oil into the butter and pulse until it becomes a thick paste. Pulse in the lemon juice until fully combined. Refrigerate the pesto for up to 2 weeks in an airtight glass jar.

Nutritional facts

Calories 310| Carbohydrates 0 g| Protein 0 g| Fat 33 g| Sodium 2 mg

52. Sweet Barbeque Sauce

Preparation time: 15 minutes

Cooking time: 11 minutes

Serving: 2 cups

Ingredients

- 1 teaspoon olive oil
- 1 tablespoon Dijon mustard
- 1/2 sweet onion (chopped)
- 1 teaspoon minced garlic
- 1/4 cup apple cider vinegar
- 1/4 cup honey
- 2 tablespoons low-sodium tomato paste

- 1 teaspoon hot sauce
- 1 teaspoon cornstarch

Instructions

In a medium saucepan over medium heat, warm the olive oil. Sauté the onion and garlic for 3 minutes or until softened. 3/4 cup water, honey, vinegar, tomato paste, mustard, and spicy sauce are combined in a mixing bowl. The cooking time is 6 minutes. 1/4 cup of water and the cornstarch should be combined in a small cup. Whisk the cornstarch into the sauce and simmer, constantly stirring, for approximately 2 minutes or until the sauce thickens. Cool. Place the sauce in a tightly sealed glass jar and refrigerate for up to 1 week.

Nutritional facts

Calories 190| Carbohydrates 3 g| Protein 0 g| Fat 33 g| Sodium 4 mg

53. Low Sodium Mayonnaise

Preparation time: 15 minutes

Cooking time: 0 minutes

Serving: 3

Ingredients

- 2 egg yolks
- 1 teaspoon Dijon mustard
- 2 tablespoons white vinegar
- 2 tablespoons freshly squeezed lemon juice
- 1 teaspoon honey
- 2 cups olive oil

Instructions

Combine the egg yolks, mustard, honey, vinegar, and lemon juice in a large mixing bowl. In a narrow stream, drizzle in the olive oil. It may be kept in the refrigerator for 2 weeks in a glass jar.

Nutritional facts

Calories 83| Carbohydrates 0 g| Protein 0 g| Fat 0 g| Sodium 12 mg

54. Citrus and Mustard Marinade

Preparation time: 15 minutes

Cooking time: 0 minutes

Serving: ¾ cup

Ingredients

- 1/4 cup lemon juice
- 1/4 cup orange juice
- 1/4 cup Dijon mustard

- 2 tablespoons honey
- 2 teaspoons chopped fresh thyme

Instructions

Whisk the lemon juice, orange juice, mustard, honey, and thyme in a medium mixing bowl until thoroughly combined. Refrigerate the marinade for up to 3 days in an airtight glass jar. Before usage, give it a good shake.

Nutritional facts

Calories 135.6| Carbohydrates 24.28 g| Protein 1 g| Fat 4 g| Sodium 5 mg

55. Creamy Vinaigrette

Preparation time: 15 minutes

Cooking time: 25 minutes

Serving: 4

Ingredients

- 2 tablespoon cider vinegar
- 2 tablespoon olive oil
- 2 tablespoons lime or lemon juice
- 1 teaspoon ground cumin
- 1 garlic clove (minced)
- 1 tsp. Dijon mustard
- 1/2 cup sour cream
- 1/4 teaspoon black pepper

Instructions

Combine all of the ingredients in a mixing bowl and combine well. Fill a carafe with mixed greens for each serving. Chill.

Nutritional facts

Calories 238.96| Carbohydrates 5 g| Protein 20 g| Fat 24.1 g| Sodium 44 mg

56. Mint Labneh

Preparation time: 10 minutes

Cooking time: 0 minutes

Serving: 6

Ingredients

- 32 ounces Plain Yogurt
- 1/2 teaspoon salt
- 1/4 cup olive oil
- 1/4 cup finely chopped fresh mint

Instructions

Combine the yogurt and salt in a mixing bowl. Place several layers of cheesecloth in a colander. Fill the lined colander halfway with the yogurt mixture. Place the colander over a sink or a bowl and set aside for 2 hours or until most of the liquid has been drained. In a small mixing bowl, blend the labneh, olive oil, and mint until thoroughly incorporated. For 1 to 2 weeks, keep the labneh refrigerated in an airtight container.

Nutritional facts

Calories 530.88| Carbohydrates 21.62 g| Protein 15.86 g| Fat 43.27 g| Sodium 22 mg

57. Fiery Honey Vinaigrette

Preparation time: 15 minutes

Cooking time: 0 minutes

Serving: ¾ cup

Ingredients

- 1/3 cup freshly squeezed lime juice
- 1/4 cup honey
- 1/4 cup olive oil
- 1 teaspoon chopped fresh basil leaves
- 1/2 teaspoon red pepper flakes

Instructions

In a medium mixing bowl, whisk the lime juice, honey, olive oil, basil, and red pepper flakes until thoroughly combined. Keep the dressing in a glass jar in the refrigerator for up to a week.

Nutritional facts

Calories 125| Carbohydrates 13 g| Protein 0 g| Fat 9 g| Sodium 22 mg

58. Buttermilk Herb Dressing

Preparation time: 15 minutes

Cooking time: 0 minutes

Serving: 1 ½ cup

Ingredients

- 1/2 cup skim milk
- 1/2 cup Low-Sodium lite Mayonnaise
- 2 tablespoons apple cider vinegar
- 1/2 scallion (green part only, chopped)
- 1 teaspoon chopped fresh thyme
- 1/2 teaspoon minced garlic
- 1 tablespoon chopped fresh dill
- Freshly ground black pepper

Instructions

Whisk the milk, mayonnaise, and vinegar until smooth in a medium mixing basin. Combine the scallion, dill, thyme, and garlic in a separate bowl. Season with salt and pepper. Store.

Nutritional facts

Calories 150| Carbohydrates 2 g| Protein 0 g| Fat 13 g| Sodium 5 mg

59. Poppy Seed Dressing

Preparation time: 15 minutes

Cooking time: 0 minutes

Serving: 2 cups

Ingredients

- 1/2 cup apple cider
- 1/3 cup honey
- 1 cup olive oil
- 1/4 cup lemon juice
- 1 tablespoon Dijon mustard
- 1/2 onion
- 2 tablespoons poppy seeds

Instructions

Combine the vinegar, honey, lemon juice, and mustard in a small bowl. Combine the oil, onion, and poppy seeds in a mixing bowl. Refrigerate the dressing for up to 2 weeks in an airtight glass jar.

Nutritional facts

Calories 151| Carbohydrates 7 g| Protein 0 g| Fat 14 g| Sodium 6 mg

60. Phosphorus-Free Baking Powder

Preparation time: 15 minutes

Cooking time: 0 minutes

Serving: ½ cup

Ingredients

- 6 tablespoons cream of tartar
- 2 tablespoons baking soda

Instructions

In a separate bowl, combine the cream of tartar and baking soda. Place in an airtight container and keep refrigerated for up to one month.

Nutritional facts

Calories 6| Carbohydrates 1 g| Protein 0 g| Fat 0 g|

Sodium 316 mg

61. Cilantro Lime Vinaigrette

Preparation time: 15 minutes

Cooking time: 0 minutes

Serving: ½ cup

Ingredients

- ½ cup packed cilantro leaves and stems
- ¼ cup extra-virgin olive oil
- 2 tablespoons freshly squeezed lime juice
- 2 tablespoons rice vinegar
- 2 garlic cloves, minced
- ¼ teaspoon freshly ground black pepper
- Zest of 1 lime

Instructions

Purée the cilantro, olive oil, lime juice and zest, rice vinegar, garlic, and pepper in a food processor or blender. Use right away or keep refrigerated for up to two days in an airtight container.

Nutritional facts

Calories 50| Carbohydrates 1 g| Protein 0 g| Fat 5 g| Sodium 1 mg

62. Creamy Herbed Dressing

Preparation time: 10 minutes

Cooking time: 0 minutes

Serving: 1 cup

Ingredients

- ¼ cup cream cheese (at room temperature)
- ¾ cup Homemade Rice Milk or unsweetened store-bought rice milk
- 1 garlic clove (minced)
- 1 tablespoon chopped fresh chives
- 1 tablespoon chopped fresh parsley
- Freshly ground black pepper

Instructions

Mix the cream cheese and rice milk in a small bowl. Mix garlic, chives, parsley, and pepper until completely combined. Use right away or keep in the refrigerator for up to three days in an airtight container.

Nutritional facts

Calories 57| Carbohydrates 7 g| Protein 2 g| Fat 3 g| Sodium 37 mg

63. Quick Herb and Oil Marinade

Preparation time: 10 minutes

Cooking time: 15 minutes

Serving: ¼ cup

Ingredients

- ¼ cup extra-virgin olive oil
- 1 tablespoon red or white wine vinegar
- 1 fresh rosemary sprig (leaves only, chopped)
- 2 fresh thyme sprigs (leaves only, chopped)
- 3 garlic cloves
- Freshly ground black pepper

Instructions

Combine the olive oil, vinegar, rosemary, thyme, garlic, and pepper in a small bowl and whisk to combine. Refrigerate for up to three days in an airtight container.

Nutritional facts

Calories 42| Carbohydrates 1 g| Protein 0 g| Fat 5 g| Sodium 0 mg

64. Cranberry Ketchup

Preparation time: 5 minutes

Cooking time: 20 minutes

Serving: 1 ½ cup

Ingredients

- 1 (12-ounce) package of fresh or frozen cranberries
- ½ cup chopped sweet onion
- 2 cups water
- ½ cup apple cider vinegar
- ¼ teaspoon ground cinnamon
- ¼ teaspoon ground allspice
- ½ cup sugar
- ¼ teaspoon ground mustard seeds
- Freshly ground black pepper

Instructions

Combine the cranberries, onion, and water in a small saucepan. Bring to a boil, lower to low heat, and cook, covered for approximately 10 minutes, or until the cranberries are softened. Remove the pan from the heat and puree the cranberries with an immersion blender. If you don't have an immersion blender, you may puree the mixture in a regular blender and return it to the saucepan. Stir in the vinegar, sugar, cinnamon, allspice, mustard seeds, and pepper, then cook, uncovered, for 5 to 10 minutes or until thickened.

Nutritional facts

Calories 25| Carbohydrates 6 g| Protein 0 g| Fat 0 g| Sodium 1

65. Apple Chutney

Preparation time: 5 minutes

Cooking time: 15 minutes

Serving: 6

Ingredients

- 2 medium apples (chopped)
- 1/2 teaspoon Cinnamon powder
- 2 teaspoon Refined Oil
- 2 tablespoon sugar
- 2 Bay leaf
- ½ teaspoon Ginger Paste

Instructions

Cook the apple chunks in a little water until mushy and pulpy. Set aside. Heat the oil and add the bay leaf and ginger paste to a wok. Add the apple pulp and cook it for a few minutes. Add the sugar to the apple (it can be replaced with sugar-free). Mix the sugar well and heat until it reaches chutney consistency. Mix in the cinnamon well. Take the chutney off the heat. Serve with rice, hot or cold.

Nutritional facts

Calories 65| Carbohydrates 27 g| Protein 0 g| Fat 2 g| Sodium 14 mg

Chapter 8: Drinks and Smoothies

1. Butternut Squash Smoothie

Preparation time: 5 minutes

Cooking time: 0 minutes

Serves: 2

Ingredients

- 2 cups butternut squash purée, frozen in ice cube trays
- 1 cup coconut milk
- ¼ cup tahini
- ¼ cup maple syrup
- 1 teaspoon cinnamon

Instructions

Place the butternut squash cubes in a blender after removing them from the ice cube trays. Combine the coconut milk, tahini, maple syrup, and cinnamon in a mixing bowl. Blend until completely smooth. To get the required consistency, thin with water or additional coconut milk if the consistency is too thick. Serve immediately in two glasses.

Nutritional facts

Calories: 660 | Fat: 48g | Carbohydrates: 59g | Protein: 10g | Sodium: 260mg

2. Tropical Green Smoothie

Preparation time: 5 minutes

Cooking time: 0 minutes

Serves: 2

Ingredients

- 2½ cups spinach
- 1½ cups water
- 1 cup frozen pineapple
- 1 cup frozen mango
- ¼ cup hemp seeds
- 1 teaspoon grated ginger

Instructions

Combine the spinach, water, pineapple, mango, hemp seeds, and ginger in a blender. Blend until completely smooth. Pour the mixture into two glasses and serve.

Nutritional facts

Calories: 196 | Fat: 7g | Carbohydrates: 29g | Protein: 7g | Sodium: 30mg

3. Eat your Greens Smoothie

Preparation time: 5 minutes

Cooking time: 0 minutes

Serves: 1

Ingredients

- ¾ to 1 cup of water
- 1 cup spinach leaves
- 2 kale leaves
- 2 romaine lettuce leaves
- ½ avocado
- 1 pear

Instructions

Combine the water, spinach, avocado, kale, romaine lettuce, and pear in a blender. Serve after blending until smooth.

Nutritional facts

Calories: 180 | Fat: 10g | Carbohydrates: 23g | Protein: 4g | Sodium: 45mg

4. Very Berry Smoothie

Preparation time: 5 minutes

Cooking time: 0 minutes

Serves: 1

Ingredients

- ¾ to 1 cup of water
- ½ cup frozen raspberries
- ½ cup frozen strawberries
- ¼ cup frozen blackberries
- 2 tablespoons of nut butter or seed butter, such as almond butter, sunflower seed butter, tahini, etc.

Instructions

Combine the water, strawberries, raspberries, blackberries, and nut butter in a blender. Serve after blending until smooth.

Nutritional facts

Calories: 186 | Fat: 9g | Carbohydrates: 24g | Protein: 4g | Sodium: 1mg

5. Strawberry Sunshine Smoothie

Preparation time: 5 minutes

Cooking time: 0 minutes

Serves: 2

Ingredients

- 2½ cups frozen strawberries
- 2 cups spinach
- 1¼ cups coconut milk
- ½ teaspoon ground cinnamon
- ⅛ to ¼ teaspoon ground turmeric

Instructions

Combine the strawberries, coconut milk, cinnamon, spinach, and turmeric in a blender. Blend until completely smooth. Pour the mixture into two glasses and serve.

Nutritional facts

Calories: 417 | Fat: 36g | Carbohydrates: 26g | Protein: 4g | Sodium: 46mg

6. Inflammation-Soothing Smoothie

Preparation time: 5 minutes

Cooking time: 0 minutes

Serves: 2

Ingredients

- 1 pear
- ½ fennel bulb
- 1 thin slice of ginger
- 1 cup spinach
- ½ cucumber
- ½ cup water
- ice (optional)

Instructions

Combine the pear, fennel, ginger, cucumber, spinach, water, and ice in a blender (if using). Blend until completely smooth.

Nutritional facts

Calories: 147 | Fat: 1g | Carbohydrates: 37g | Protein: 4g | Sodium: 89mg

7. Eat-your-Vegetables Smoothie

Preparation time: 10 minutes

Cooking time: 0 minutes

Serves: 1

Ingredients

- 1 carrot
- 1 small beet
- 1 celery stalk

- ½ cup raspberries
- 1 cup coconut water
- 1 teaspoon balsamic vinegar
- ice (optional)

Instructions

Blend the carrots, beets, celery, coconut water, raspberries, balsamic vinegar, and ice in a blender (if using). Blend until completely smooth.

Nutritional facts

Calories: 140 | Fat: 1g | Carbohydrates: 24g | Protein: 3g | Sodium: 293mg

8. Cherry Smoothie

Preparation time: 10 minutes

Cooking time: 0 minutes

Serves: 1

Ingredients

- 1 cup frozen no-added-sugar pitted cherries
- ¼ cup raspberries
- ¾ cup coconut water
- 1 tablespoon raw honey or maple syrup
- 1 teaspoon chia seeds
- 1 teaspoon hemp seeds
- Drop vanilla extract
- ice (optional)

Instructions

Blend the cherries, raspberries, coconut water, honey, chia seeds, hemp seeds, vanilla, and ice in a blender until smooth (if using). Blend until completely smooth.

Nutritional facts

Calories: 266 | Fat: 2g | Carbohydrates: 52g | Protein: 3g | Sodium: 122mg

9. Green Apple Smoothie

Preparation time: 10 minutes

Cooking time: 0 minutes

Serves: 1

Ingredients

- ½ cup coconut water
- 1 green apple
- 1 cup spinach
- ¼ lemon

- ½ cucumber
- 2 teaspoons raw honey or maple syrup
- ice (optional)

Instructions

Combine the coconut water, apple, spinach, lemon, cucumber, honey, and ice in a blender (if using). Blend until completely smooth.

Nutritional facts

Calories: 176 | Fat: 1g | Carbohydrates: 41g | Protein: 2g | Sodium: 110mg

10. One-for-All Smoothie

Preparation time: 10 minutes

Cooking time: 0 minutes

Serves: 1

Ingredients

- 1 cup spinach
- ½ cup blueberries
- ½ banana
- 1 cup coconut milk
- ½ teaspoon vanilla extract

Instructions

Combine the spinach, blueberries, banana, coconut milk, and vanilla in a blender. Blend until completely smooth.

Nutritional facts

Calories: 152 | Fat: 5g | Carbohydrates: 27g | Protein: 2g | Sodium: 90mg

11. Mango-Thyme Smoothie

Preparation time: 10 minutes

Cooking time: 0 minutes

Serves: 1

Ingredients

- 1 cup fresh or frozen mango chunks
- ½ cup fresh seedless green grapes
- ¼ fennel bulb
- ½ cup unsweetened almond milk
- ½ teaspoon fresh thyme leaves
- Pinch sea salt
- Pinch freshly ground black pepper
- Ice (optional)

Instructions

Blend the mango, grapes, fennel, almond milk, sea salt, thyme leaves, pepper, and ice in a mixer until smooth (if using). Blend until completely smooth.

Nutritional facts

Calories: 274 | Fat: 4g | Carbohydrates: 65g | Protein: 3g | Sodium: 125mg

12. Protein Powerhouse Smoothie

Preparation time: 10 minutes

Cooking time: 0 minutes

Serves: 1

Ingredients

- 1 cup packed kale leaves
- ¼ avocado
- 1 cup fresh grapes
- ¼ cup cashews (optional)
- 1 tablespoon hemp seed
- 1 or 2 mint leaves
- 1 cup coconut milk
- Ice (optional)

Instructions

Blend the kale, avocado, cashews (if used), grapes, hemp seed, mint leaves, coconut milk, and ice in a blender until smooth (if using). Blend until completely smooth.

Nutritional facts

Calories: 500 | Fat: 32g | Carbohydrates: 47g | Protein: 13g | Sodium: 199mg

13. Peachy Mint Punch

Preparation time: 15 minutes

Cooking time: 0 minutes

Serves: 4

Ingredients

- 1 (10-ounce) bag frozen no-added-sugar peach slices
- 3 tablespoons lemon juice
- 3 tablespoons raw honey or maple syrup
- 1 tablespoon of lemon zest
- 2 cups coconut water
- 2 cups sparkling water
- 4 fresh mint sprigs

- Ice

Instructions

Combine the peaches, lemon juice, honey, and lemon zest in a food processor. Process until completely smooth. Combine the peach purée and coconut water in a big pitcher. In the refrigerator, cool the mixture. Fill four large (16-ounce) glasses with ice when ready to serve. 1 sprig of mint in each glass. Fill each glass with approximately a third of a cup of peach mixture and fill with sparkling water.

Nutritional facts

Calories: 81 | Fat: 0g | Carbohydrates: 18g | Protein: 0g | Sodium: 85mg

14. Coconut-Ginger Smoothie

Preparation time: 10 minutes

Cooking time: 0 minutes

Serves: 1

Ingredients

- ½ cup coconut milk
- ½ cup coconut water
- ¼ avocado
- ¼ cup unsweetened coconut shreds or flakes
- 1 teaspoon raw honey or maple syrup
- 1 thin slice of fresh ginger
- Pinch of ground cardamom (optional)
- Ice (optional)

Instructions

Blend the coconut milk, coconut water, coconut, honey, avocado, ginger, cardamom (if used), and ice in a blender until smooth (if using). Blend until completely smooth.

Nutritional facts

Calories: 238| Fat: 18g | Carbohydrates: 16g | Protein: 5g | Sodium: 373mg

15. Green Smoothie

Preparation time: 5 minutes

Cooking time: 0 minutes

Serves: 2

Ingredients

- 3 cups baby spinach
- ¼ cup cilantro leaves
- 2 pears
- 3 cups unsweetened apple juice

- 1 tablespoon grated ginger
- 1 cup crushed ice

Instructions

Combine the spinach, cilantro, apple juice, pears, ginger, and ice in a blender. Blend until completely smooth.

Nutritional facts

Calories: 308 | Fat: 1g | Carbohydrates: 77g | Protein: 2g | Sodium: 50mg

16. Blueberry, Chocolate, and Turmeric Smoothie

Preparation time: 5 minutes

Cooking time: 0 minutes

Serves: 2

Ingredients

- 2 cups unsweetened almond milk
- 1 cup blueberries
- 2 tablespoons cocoa powder
- 1 to 2 packets of stevia
- 1 (1-inch) piece of turmeric
- 1 cup crushed ice

Instructions

Blend the almond milk, blueberries, cocoa powder, stevia, turmeric, and ice in a blender. Blend until completely smooth.

Nutritional facts

Calories: 97 | Fat: 5g | Carbohydrates: 16g | Protein: 3g | Sodium: 182mg

17. Kale and Banana Smoothie

Preparation time: 5 minutes

Cooking time: 0 minutes

Serves: 2

Ingredients

- 2 cups unsweetened almond milk
- 2 cups kale, stemmed, leaves chopped
- 2 bananas
- 1 to 2 packets of stevia, or to taste
- 1 teaspoon ground cinnamon
- 1 cup crushed ice

Instructions

Combine the almond milk, kale, stevia, bananas, cinnamon, and ice in a blender. Blend until completely smooth.

Nutritional facts

Calories: 181 | Fat: 4g | Carbohydrates: 37g | Protein: 4g | Sodium: 210mg

18. Green Tea and Pear Smoothie

Preparation time: 5 minutes

Cooking time: 0 minutes

Serves: 2

Ingredients

- 2 cups strongly brewed green tea
- 2 pears
- 2 tablespoons honey
- 1 (1-inch) piece of ginger
- 1 cup unsweetened almond milk
- 1 cup crushed ice

Instructions

Combine the green tea, pears, almond milk, honey, ginger, and ice in a blender. Blend until completely smooth.

Nutritional facts

Calories: 208 | Fat: 2g | Carbohydrates: 51g | Protein: 1g | Sodium: 94mg

19. Yogurt, Berry, and Walnut parfait

Preparation time: 10 minutes

Cooking time: 0 minutes

Serves: 2

Ingredients

- 2 cups plain yogurt, or plain unsweetened coconut yogurt or almond yogurt
- 2 tablespoons honey
- 1 cup fresh blueberries
- 1 cup fresh raspberries
- ½ cup walnut pieces

Instructions

Whisk the yogurt and honey together in a medium mixing basin. Spoon it into 2 serving dishes, spoon 12 cups blueberries, 12 cups raspberries, and 14 cups walnut bits on each.

Nutritional facts

Calories: 505 | Fat: 22g | carbohydrates: 56g |

Protein: 23g | Sodium: 174mg

20. Ginger-Berry Smoothie

Preparation time: 10 minutes

Cooking time: 0 minutes

Serves: 2

Ingredients

- 2 cups fresh blackberries
- 2 cups unsweetened almond milk
- 1 to 2 packets of stevia, or to taste
- 1 (1-inch) piece of ginger
- 2 cups crushed ice

Instructions

Combine the blackberries, almond milk, ginger, stevia, and ice in a blender. Blend until completely smooth.

Just chop off a piece and peel away the outer skin with a vegetable peeler to peel fresh ginger.

Nutritional facts

Calories: 95 | Fat: 3g | Carbohydrates: 16g | Protein: 3g | Sodium: 152mg

21. Turmeric and Green Tea Mango Smoothie

Preparation time: 5 minutes

Cooking time: 0 minutes

Serves: 2

Ingredients

- 2 cups cubed mango
- 2 teaspoons turmeric powder
- 2 tablespoons green tea powder
- 2 cups almond milk
- 2 tablespoons honey
- 1 cup crushed ice

Instructions

Combine the mango, turmeric, matcha, honey, almond milk, and ice in a blender. Blend until completely smooth.

Nutritional facts

Calories: 285 | Fat: 3g | Carbohydrates: 68g | Protein: 4g | Sodium: 94mg

22. Green Tea and Ginger Shake

Preparation time: 5 minutes

Cooking time: 0 minutes

Serves: 2

Ingredients

- 2 tablespoons grated ginger
- 2 tablespoons honey
- 2 tablespoons matcha (green tea) powder
- 2 scoops of low-fat vanilla ice cream
- 2 cups skim milk

Instructions

Combine the ginger, honey, matcha, ice cream, and milk in a blender. Blend until completely smooth.

To make this dairy-free, use any nondairy milk and nondairy ice creams, such as almond milk and almond milk ice cream. Frozen yogurt.

Nutritional facts

Calories: 340 |fat: 7g | Carbohydrates: 56g | Protein: 11g | Sodium: 186mg

23. Super Green Smoothie

Preparation time: 10 minutes

Cooking time: 0 minutes

Serves: 1

Ingredients

- 1 cup packed spinach
- ½ cucumber, peeled
- ½ pear
- ¼ avocado
- 1 teaspoon raw honey or maple syrup
- 1 cup unsweetened almond milk
- 2 mint leaves
- pinch salt
- ½ lemon
- Ice (optional)

Instructions

Blend the spinach, cucumber, avocado, pear, honey, almond milk, mint leaves, salt, 1 or 2 squeezes of lemon juice, and ice in a blender until smooth (if using). Blend until completely smooth.

Nutritional facts

Calories: 248 | Fat 14 g | Carbohydrates 33 g | Protein

5 g | Sodium 373 mg

24. Berry Shake

Preparation time: 5 minutes

Cook time: 0 minutes

Serving: 1

Ingredients

- Greek yogurt (25g)
- Semi-skimmed milk, 75 mL
- 40g frozen mixed berries, strawberries, blueberries, etc.
- 1/2 medium peeled and coarsely chopped bananas (about 50g)
- 1 tablespoon porridge oats
- 5 g almond flour
- 2 tablespoons water (cool)

Instructions

In a food grinder, add all ingredients and mix until smooth. If required, add additional water to get a smooth texture.

Nutritional Facts

Calories 190| Carbohydrates 22 g| Protein 3 g| Fat 2 g| Sodium 21 mg |

25. Strawberry and Chocolate Shake

Preparation time: 10 minutes

Cook time: 0 minutes

Serving: 1

Ingredients

- semi-skimmed milk (100 mL)
- 25 g live Greek yogurt (full fat)
- 100g strawberries (fresh or frozen)
- giant porridge oats (15g)
- 1 date with a soft pit
- a teaspoon of cocoa powder
- 2 tablespoon water (cool)

Instructions

In a food grinder, add all ingredients and mix until smooth. If required, add additional water to get a smooth texture.

Nutritional Facts

Calories 119| Carbohydrates 16 g| Protein 4 g| Fat 1 g| Sodium 10 mg |

26. Banana Nutty Shake

Preparation time: 5 minutes

Cook time: 0 minutes

Serving: 1

Ingredients

- 20g live Greek yogurt (full fat)
- semi-skimmed milk (100 mL)
- 1/2 medium bananas, peeled and coarsely chopped (about 50g peeled weight)
- 15g nut butter without sugar made from cashews or almonds
- 2 tablespoons water (cool)

Instruction

In a food grinder, add all ingredients and mix until smooth. If required, add additional water to get a smooth texture.

Nutritional Facts

Calories 214| Carbohydrates 22 g| Protein 1 g| Fat 4 g| Sodium 39 mg |

27. Minted Cucumber and Avocado Shake

Preparation time: 15 minutes

Cook time: 0 minutes

Serving: 1

Ingredients

- 1/2 medium avocados, chopped, skinned, and cut into quarters (about 75 grams)
- 200 g thickly sliced cucumber
- 25 g leaves of young spinach
- 15g full-fat live Greek yogurt
- Fresh mint leaves (12grams)
- 100 ml ice water

Instructions

In a food grinder, add all ingredients and mix until smooth. If required, add additional water to get a smooth texture.

Nutritional Facts

Calories 180| Carbohydrates 26 g| Protein 2 g| Fat 2.2 g| Sodium 11 mg |

28. Cashew, Carrot and Orange Shake

Preparation time: 20 minutes

Cook time: 0 minutes

Serving: 1

Ingredients

- 1/2 medium-size orange, skinned and cut into rough pieces
- 1/2 medium carrots (about 170g), trimmed and thinly sliced
- 15 g cashew nut butter or hazelnut butter with no added sugar
- 125 milliliters of cold water

Instructions

In a food grinder, add all ingredients and mix until smooth. If required, add additional water to get a smooth texture.

Nutritional Facts

Calories 215| Carbohydrates 20 g| Protein 5 g| Fat 1.8 g| Sodium 24 mg |

29. Ginger Shake

Preparation time: 20 minutes

Cook time: 0 minutes

Serving: 1

Ingredients

- 1 quartered green apple
- 1/2 medium courgette, chopped and finely chopped (about 65g)
- 8g peeled and finely chopped fresh root ginger
- 1/2 tsp turmeric powder
- 10 grams of mixed seeds (sunflower, pumpkin and flax)
- 2 teaspoons extra-virgin olive oil
- 100 mL ice water

Instructions

In a food mixing grinder, add all ingredients and mix until smooth. If required, add additional water to get a smooth texture.

Nutritional Facts

Calories 218| Carbohydrates 36 g| Protein 4 g| Fat 2 g| Sodium 8 mg |

30. Gazpacho Shake

Preparation time: 15 minutes

Cook time: 0 minutes

Serving: 1

Ingredients

- cucumber, 100g, coarsely chopped
- 2 to 3 healthy vine tomatoes, cut into quarters (about 125g)
- 1/2 red pepper, without seed and chopped
- 1/2 red pepper, without seed and chopped
- 25 g Greek yogurt (full fat)
- 10 g almond flour
- 1 tablespoon pureed tomatoes
- 1 teaspoon extra-virgin olive oil
- 2 tablespoons water (cool)
- to taste with salt and black pepper

Instructions

In a food mixing grinder, add all ingredients and mix until smooth. If required, add additional water to get a smooth texture.

Nutritional Facts

Calories 210| Carbohydrates 20.2 g| Protein 12.8 g| Fat 4.3 g| Sodium 12 mg |

31. Chai Smoothie

Preparation time: 40 minutes

Cooking time: 0 minutes

Serving: 1

Ingredients

- ½ cup boiling water
- 4 chai tea bags
- ¼ cup sugar
- 2 cups ice
- ½ cup 1% milk

Instructions

Combine boiling water, sugar, and chai tea bags in a small bowl. Cover and set aside for 5 minutes to steep. Discard tea bags, then refrigerate tea for 30 minutes or thoroughly chill. Place tea, ice, and milk in a blender and process until smooth. Serve immediately.

Nutritional facts

Calories 210| Carbohydrates 26 g| Protein 3 g| Fat 3 g| Sodium 166 mg |

32. Apple Chai Smoothie

Preparation time: 5 minutes+ 30 minutes to Steep

Cook time: 5 minutes

Servings: 2

Ingredients

- 1 cup rice milk, unsweetened
- 1 teabag
- 1 peeled, shelled, and shredded apple
- 2 quarts of ice

Instructions

Cook the rice milk in a moderate saucepan or pot over low heat for at least 5 minutes or until bubbling. Start taking the milk off the heat and infusing the teabag in it. Allow 30 minutes for the milk to settle in the refrigerator with the tea bag, remove the teabag and squeeze delicately to release all flavors. Pour the milk, apple, and ice into a blending machine and mix until smooth. *Put the smoothie into two glasses and serve.

Nutritional Facts

Calories 88| Carbohydrates 19 g| Protein 1 g| Fat 4 g| Sodium 55 mg |

33. Blueberry-Pineapple Smoothie

Preparation time: 15 minutes

Cook time: o minutes

Servings: 2

Ingredients

- 1 cup of blueberries, frozen
- 1/2 cup of Pineapple Clumps
- 1/2 cup of cucumber
- 1/2 apple
- 1/2 cup of water

Instructions

Take the blueberries, pineapple, cucumber, apple, and water and whirl till they are vicious and silky in a processor. Spoon the smoothie into two glasses and serve.

Nutritional Facts

Calories 87| Carbohydrates 22 g| Protein 1 g| Fat 1 g| Sodium 60 mg |

34. Watermelon- Raspberry Smoothie

Preparation time: 10 minutes

Cook time: 0 minutes

Servings: 2

Ingredients

- 1/2 cup of red cabbage, simmered, refrigerated, and diced
- 1 cup of watermelon, shredded
- 1/2 cup of raspberries, juicy

- 1 pound of ice

Instructions

In a processor, pulse the cabbage for 2 minutes, or till it is finely minced. Grind for nearly 1 minute until either the watermelon or raspberries are completely mashed. Grind in the ice again until the smoothie is extremely dense and perfect. Mixture and mix into two glasses and serve.

Nutritional Facts

Calories 47| Carbohydrates 11 g| Protein 1 g| Fat 0 g| Sodium 55 mg |

35. Cinnamon Hazelnut Latte

Preparation time: 10 minutes

Cook time: 0 minutes

Servings: 5

Ingredients

- 1 cup of almond milk, unsweetened
- 4 cups of freshly brewed coffee
- Torani Sugar-Free Classic Hazelnut Syrup (ten tablespoons)
- Cinnamon sticks (5)

Instructions

Take the almond milk and whisk until creamy in a big pitcher. Stir in the coffee until everything is well blended. To each cup, add 2 tablespoons of hazelnut syrup. Pour the coffee mixture equally into each of the five cups. Enjoy a cinnamon stick or a splash of ground cinnamon in each cup. Refrigerate remaining for up to three days in an airtight container.

Nutritional Facts

Calories 20| Carbohydrates 3 g| Protein 1.2 g| Fat 1 g| Sodium 130 mg |

36. Acai Berry Smoothie

Preparation time: 10 minutes

Cook time: 0 minutes

Serving: 5

Ingredients

- 1 (14-ounce) chilled acai packet, unsweetened
- 1 cup of frozen berries (various berries, strawberries, blueberries, or raspberries)
- 1/2 cup of plain yogurt
- 1/4 to 1/2 cup plain rice milk (relying on desired thickness)
- 1/4 medium pear or apple

- 1 tablespoon of berries (black)
- 1 tablespoon of raspberry compote
- 1 tablespoon of almonds, sliced
- 1 tablespoon of shredded unsweetened coconut

Instructions

Fill a blender halfway with the unsweetened cold acai packet. Break the product into little pieces if it's a large, pureed brick. Combine the frozen berries, yogurt, 1/4 cup rice milk, and apple in a blender. Blend until completely smooth. It should have a thick consistency. If necessary, add additional liquid to get the required consistency. Using a spatula, divide the combined mixture equally between the bowls. 1/2 tablespoon each of blackberries, raspberries, almonds, and coconut on top of each bowl.

Nutritional Facts

Calories 281| Carbohydrates 36 g| Protein 14.1 g| Fat 4 g| Sodium 56 mg |

37. Strawberry Juice

Preparation time: 10 minutes

Cooking time: 0 minutes

Serving: 2

Ingredients:

- 2 C. fresh strawberries, hulled
- 1 tsp. fresh lime juice
- 2 C. chilled filtered water

Instructions:

In a mixing blender, add all ingredients and pulse well. Through a strainer, strain the juice and transfer it into 2 glasses. Serve immediately.

Nutritional Facts:

Calories 46| Carbohydrates 11.1 g| Protein 1 g| Fat 0.4 g| Sodium 1 mg |

38. Kiwi Juice

Preparation time: 10 minutes

Cooking time: 0 minutes

Serving: 2

Ingredients:

- 4 medium kiwis, peeled and chopped
- 4 C. chilled filtered water

Instructions:

In a mixing blender, place kiwi and water and pulse well. Through a strainer, strain the juice and transfer it into 2 glasses and serve immediately.

Nutritional Facts:

Calories 93| Carbohydrates 22.3 g| Protein 1.7 g| Fat 0.8 g| Sodium 5 mg |

39. Grapefruit Juice

Preparation time: 10 minutes

Cooking time: 0 minutes

Serving: 2

Ingredients:

- 4 large grapefruits, peeled and sectioned

Instructions:

In a mixing juicer, add grapefruit and extract the juice according to the manufacturer's directions. Transfer into 2 glasses and serve immediately.

Nutritional Facts

Calories 212| Carbohydrates 53.7 g| Protein 4.2 g| Fat 0.7 g| Sodium 4 mg |

40. Orange Juice

Preparation time: 10 minutes

Cooking time: 0 minutes

Serving: 2

Ingredients:

- 6 medium oranges, peeled and sectioned
- Pinch of ground black pepper

Instructions:

In a mixing juicer, add orange pieces and extract the juice according to the manufacturer's directions. Transfer into 2 glasses and stir in black pepper. Serve immediately.

Nutritional Facts:

Calories 82| Carbohydrates 0.3 g| Protein 1.6 g| Fat 0.3 g| Sodium 5 mg |

41. Apple Juice

Preparation time: 10 minutes

Cooking time: 0 minutes

Serving: 2

Ingredients:

- 6 large apples, cored and sliced
- 1 tablespoon fresh lime juice

Instructions:

Add apple slices and extract the juice according to the manufacturer's directions in a juicer. Stir in lemon juice and transfer into 2 glasses. Serve immediately.

Nutritional Facts

Calories 349| Carbohydrates 92 g| Protein 10.6 g| Fat 1.2 g| Sodium 7.44 mg |

42. Apple & Pomegranate Juice

Preparation time: 10 minutes

Cooking time: 0 minutes

Serving: 2

Ingredients:

- 1 and ½ cup of fresh pomegranate seeds
- 2 teaspoons of fresh lemon juice
- 2 large apples
- Pinch of black pepper

Instructions:

Add all ingredients and extract the juice according to the manufacturer's directions in a juicer. Transfer into 2 glasses and serve immediately.

Nutritional Facts:

Calories 264| Carbohydrates 16 g| Protein 1.8 g| Fat 11.6 g| Sodium 5 mg |

43. Apple, Grapefruit & Carrot Juice

Preparation time: 10 minutes

Cooking time: 0 minutes

Serving: 2

Ingredients:

- 2 large apples
- 3 medium carrots
- 2 medium grapefruits
- 1 teaspoon of lemon juice

Instructions:

Add all ingredients and extract the juice according to the manufacturer's directions in a juicer. Transfer into 2 glasses and serve immediately.

Nutritional Facts:

Calories 195| Carbohydrates 50.2 g| Protein 2.2 g| Fat 0.6 g| Sodium 10 mg |

44. Apple & Celery Juice

Preparation time: 10 minutes

Cooking time: 0 minutes

Serving: 2

Ingredients:

- 4 large green apples, cored and sliced
- 4 medium celery stalks, chopped

Instructions:

Add celery and apple slices and celery in a juicer and extract the juice according to the manufacturer's directions. Transfer into 2 glasses and serve immediately.

Nutritional Facts:

Calories 237| Carbohydrates 62.1 g| Protein 1.4 g| Fat 0.9 g| Sodium 12 mg |

45. Apple, Carrot & Beet Juice

Preparation time: 10 minutes

Cooking time: 0 minutes

Serving: 2

Ingredients

- 3 large carrots, peeled and chopped
- 1 large apple, cored and sliced
- 1 large green apple, cored and sliced
- 2 medium red beets, trimmed, peeled and chopped

Instructions:

Add all ingredients and extract the juice according to the manufacturer's directions in a juicer. Transfer into 2 glasses and serve immediately.

Nutritional Facts:

Calories 204| Carbohydrates 51.4 g| Protein 3.2 g| Fat 0.6 g| Sodium 19 mg |

46. Apple & Spinach Juice

Preparation time: 10 minutes

Cooking time: 0 minutes

Serving: 2

Ingredients:

- 2 large green apples
- ¼ cup of parsley leaves
- 1 lemon
- 4 cups of spinach leaves
- 1 tablespoon of ginger
- 1 cup of filtered water

Instructions:

In a blender, add all ingredients and pulse well. Through a strainer, strain the juice and transfer it into 2 glasses. Serve immediately.

Nutritional Facts:

Calories 144| Carbohydrates 36 g| Protein 3 g| Fat 0.9 g| Sodium 6 mg |

47. Red Fruit & Veggies Juice

Preparation time: 10 minutes

Cooking time: 0 minutes

Serving: 2

Ingredients:

- 2 medium red beets
- 2 and ½ cups of fresh strawberries
- 1 large red bell pepper
- 1 large tomato
- ¼ cup of mint leaves

Instructions:

Add all ingredients and extract the juice according to the manufacturer's directions in a juicer. Transfer into 2 glasses and serve immediately.

Nutritional Facts:

Calories 131| Carbohydrates 30.5 g| Protein 4.1 g| Fat 1 g| Sodium 16 mg |

48. Green Fruit & Veggie Juice

Preparation time: 10 minutes

Cooking time: 0 minutes

Serving: 2

Ingredients:

- 2 apples
- 2 cups of spinach leaves
- 1 lemon
- 2 small pears
- 6 medium celery

Instructions:

Add all ingredients and extract the juice according to the manufacturer's directions in a juicer. Transfer into 2 glasses and serve immediately.

Nutritional Facts:

Calories 246| Carbohydrates 65.9 g| Protein 2.6 g| Fat 0.9 g| Sodium 100 mg |

49. Mixed Veggie Juice

Preparation time: 10 minutes

Cooking time: 0 minutes

Serving: 2

Ingredients:

- 3 cups of spinach
- 2 large seedless cucumbers
- Pinch of black pepper
- 2 medium fresh tomatoes
- 3 large celery stalks
- 3 tablespoons of basil leaves

Instructions:

Add all ingredients and extract the juice according to the manufacturer's directions in a juicer. Transfer into 2 glasses and serve immediately.

Nutritional Facts:

Calories 83| Carbohydrates 18.2 g| Protein 4.7 g| Fat 0.8 g| Sodium 90 mg |

50. Oat & Orange Smoothie

Preparation time: 10 minutes

Cooking time: 0 minutes

Serving: 4

Ingredients:

- 2/3 cup of oats
- 2 large bananas
- 1 cup of ice cubes
- 2 large oranges
- 2 and ½ cups of almond milk

Instructions:

In a high-speed blender, add rolled oats and pulse until finely chopped. Add all remaining ingredients and pulse until smooth. Transfer into 4 serving glasses and serve immediately.

Nutritional Facts

Calories 175| Carbohydrates 36.6 g| Protein 3 g| Fat 3 g| Sodium 20 mg |

51. Banana Smoothie

Preparation time: 10 minutes

Cooking time: 0 minutes

Serving: 2

Ingredients:

- 2 medium bananas
- ¼ teaspoon of ground cinnamon
- 1 and ½ cup of almond milk
- ½ teaspoon of vanilla extract

Instructions

In a mixing blender, add all ingredients and pulse until smooth. Transfer into 2 serving glasses and serve immediately.

Nutritional Facts:

Calories 139| Carbohydrates 29 g| Protein 2.1 g| Fat 3 g| Sodium 80 mg |

52. Mango Smoothie

Preparation time: 10 minutes

Cooking time: 0 minutes

Serving: 2

Ingredients:

- 2 medium mangoes
- ½ teaspoon of organic vanilla extract
- 1 medium banana
- 2 tablespoons almonds
- 1 and ½ cups of chilled milk

Instructions:

In a high-speed mixing blender, add all ingredients and pulse until smooth. Transfer into 2 serving glasses and serve immediately.

Nutritional Facts:

Calories 359| Carbohydrates 74.2 g| Protein 10.7 g| Fat 4.4 g| Sodium 78 mg |

53. Strawberry Smoothie

Preparation time: 10 minutes

Cooking time: 0 minutes

Serving: 2

Ingredients:

- 1 cup of strawberries
- 1 and ½ cup of milk
- 1 large banana
- 2 tablespoons of almonds

Instructions:

In a high-speed mixing blender, add all ingredients and pulse until smooth. Transfer into 2 serving glasses and serve immediately.

Nutritional Facts:

Calories 177| Carbohydrates 29 g| Protein 8.4 g| Fat 3.4 g| Sodium 45 mg |

54. Mixed Berries Smoothie

Preparation time: 10 minutes

Cooking time: 0 minutes

Serving: 2

Ingredients:

- 1 cup of strawberries
- ¼ cup of blackberries
- ½ cup of ice cubes
- ¼ cup of fresh raspberries
- 1 cup of fresh orange juice

Instructions:

In a high-speed mixing blender, add all ingredients and pulse until smooth. Transfer into 2 serving glasses and serve immediately.

Nutritional Facts:

Calories 95| Carbohydrates 22 g| Protein 1.8 g| Fat 0.7 g| Sodium 151 mg |

55. Apple & Pear Smoothie

Preparation time: 10 minutes

Cooking time: 0 minutes

Serving: 2

Ingredients:

- 2 green apples
- 2 cups of fresh mustard greens
- ¼ cup of ice cubes
- 2 pears
- ¼ teaspoon of cinnamon
- 1 and ½ cups of filtered water

Instructions:

In a high-speed mixing blender, add all ingredients and pulse until smooth. Transfer into 2 serving glasses and serve immediately.

Nutritional Facts:

Calories 252| Carbohydrates 65.5 g| Protein 2.9 g| Fat 0.8 g| Sodium 3 mg |

56. Apple & Kale Smoothie

Preparation time: 10 minutes

Cooking time: 0 minutes

Serving: 2

Ingredients:

- 2 cups of fresh kale

- 1 frozen banana
- 1 tablespoon of chia seeds
- 1 green apple
- 1 Medjool date
- 2 cups of chilled filtered water

Instructions:

In a high-speed mixing blender, add all ingredients and pulse until smooth. Transfer into 2 serving glasses and serve immediately.

Nutritional Facts:

Calories 198| Carbohydrates 1.6 g| Protein 4.2 g| Fat 1.6 g| Sodium 8 mg |

57. Kiwi & Cucumber Smoothie

Preparation time: 10 minutes

Cooking time: 0 minutes

Serving: 2

Ingredients:

- 2 kiwis
- 2 tablespoons of cilantro leaves
- 2 drops of liquid stevia
- 1 medium cucumber
- ½ teaspoon of ginger
- 2 cups of filtered water

Instructions:

In a high-speed mixing blender, add all ingredients and pulse until smooth. Transfer into 2 serving glasses and serve immediately.

Nutritional Facts:

Calories 71| Carbohydrates 17 g| Protein 1.9 g| Fat 0.6 g| Sodium 10 mg |

58. Grapes & Kale Smoothie

Preparation time: 10 minutes

Cooking time: 0 minute

Serving: 2

Ingredients:

- 2 cups of kale
- 4 drops of liquid stevia
- 1 and ½ cups of filtered water
- 1 cup of green grapes
- 1 tablespoon of fresh lime juice
- ¼ cup of ice cubes

Instructions:

In a high-speed mixing blender, add all ingredients and pulse until smooth. Transfer into 2 serving glasses and serve immediately.

Nutritional Facts:

Calories 65| Carbohydrates 15 g| Protein 2.3 g| Fat 0.2 g| Sodium 45 mg |

59. Pumpkin Smoothie

Preparation time: 10 minutes

Cooking time: 0 minutes

Serving: 2

Ingredients:

- 1 cup of pumpkin puree
- 1 teaspoon flaxseeds
- 1 and ½ cup of almond milk
- 1 medium banana
- ¼ teaspoon of cinnamon
- ¼ Cup of ice cubes

Instructions:

In a high-speed mixing blender, add all ingredients and pulse until smooth. Transfer into 2 serving glasses and serve immediately.

Nutritional Facts:

Calories 264| Carbohydrates 16 g| Protein 10.6 g| Fat 11.6 g| Sodium 23 mg |

60. Cucumber & Greens Smoothie

Preparation time: 10 minutes

Cooking time: 0 minutes

Serving: 2

Ingredients:

- 1 small cucumber
- ½ cup of lettuce
- ¼ cup of mint leaves
- 1 teaspoon of lemon juice
- ¼ cup of ice cubes
- 2 cups of mixed greens
- ¼ cup of parsley leaves
- 3 drops of liquid stevia
- 1 and ½ cup of filtered water

Instructions:

In a high-speed mixing blender, add all ingredients and pulse until smooth. Transfer into 2 serving glasses

and serve immediately.

Nutritional Facts:

Calories 50| Carbohydrates 11.3 g| Protein 2.5 g| Fat 0.5 g| Sodium 255 mg |

61. Chocolate Avocado Smoothie

Preparation time: 10 minutes

Cooking time: 8 minutes

Serving: 2

Ingredients:

- 1 medium avocado
- ½ teaspoon of vanilla extract
- ¼ cup of ice cubes
- 1 small banana
- 3 tablespoons of cocoa powder
- 1 and ¾ cups of chilled milk

Instructions:

In a high-speed mixing blender, add all ingredients and pulse until smooth. Transfer into 2 serving glasses and serve immediately.

Nutritional Facts:

Calories 358| Carbohydrates 36.5 g| Protein 11 g| Fat 21.3 g| Sodium 211 mg |

62. Homemade Rice Milk

Preparation time: 5 minutes+7 to 8 hours to soak

Cook time: 0 minutes

Servings: 4

Ingredients

- 1 cup of white rice
- 4 cups of water
- ½ teaspoon of vanilla extract

Instructions

Toast the rice in a medium-dry pan over medium heat until gently browned, approximately 5 minutes. Pour the water over the rice into a jar or dish. Cover and soak overnight in the refrigerator. Blend the rice, water, and vanilla extract (if using) in a blender until smooth. Pour the milk through a fine-mesh strainer set over a glass jar or basin. Serve right away, or cover and refrigerate for up to three days. Before usage, please give it a good shake.

Nutritional Facts

Calories 122| Carbohydrates 24 g| Protein 0 g| Fat 0 g| Sodium 155 mg |

63. Cinnamon Horchata

Preparation time: 5 minutes+ 3 hours to soak

Cook time: 0 minutes

Servings: 4

Ingredients:

- 1 cup of white rice
- 4 cups water
- 1 cinnamon stick, dices into pieces
- 1 cup Homemade Rice Milk.
- 1 teaspoon of vanilla extract
- 1 teaspoon of cinnamon
- ½ cup of sugar

Instructions:

Add the ingredients that including the rice, water, and cinnamon stick bits, to a blender. For approximately 1 minute, blend until the rice starts to break apart. Allow it to settle for at least 3 hours or overnight at room temperature. Pour the liquid into a wire fine-mesh sieve set over a pitcher. Remove the rice and throw it away. Place the milk, vanilla, ground cinnamon, and sugar in a stand mixer. To blend, whisk everything together. Serve with ice cubes.

Nutritional Facts

Calories 123| Carbohydrates 26 g| Protein 1 g| Fat 0 g| Sodium 122 mg |

64. Berry Mint Water

Preparation time: 5 minutes + 1 hour to cool

Cook time: 0 minutes

Servings: 6

Ingredients

- 8 cups of water
- ½ cup of strawberries
- ½ cup of blackberries
- 3 mint leaves

Instructions

Whisk the water, strawberries, blackberries, and mint in a big mixer before consuming, covering, and cooling for 1 hour. Please put it in the fridge for up to two days before serving.

Nutritional Facts

Calories 7| Carbohydrates 2 g| Protein 0 g| Fat 0 g| Sodium 3 mg |

65. Fennel Digestive Cooler

Preparation time: 5 minutes

Cooking time: 15 minutes

Servings: 2

Ingredients

- 2 cups Homemade Rice Milk
- ¼ cup fennel seeds, ground
- ¼ teaspoon ground cloves
- 1 tablespoon honey

Instructions

Put all the ingredients, including milk, fennel seeds, cloves, and honey, in a food processor. Permit 30 minutes to settle after processing until creamy. Sieve through a cheesecloth-lined wire mesh strainer or a coffee filter and put it over a glass or jar. Serve.

Nutritional Facts

Calories 163| Carbohydrates 30 g| Protein 3 g| Fat 2 g| Sodium 7 mg |

66. Mint Lassi

Preparation 5 minutes

Cook time: 0 minutes

Servings: 5

Ingredients

- 1 teaspoon cumin seeds
- ½ cup mint leaves
- 1 cup plain, unsweetened yogurt
- ½ cup water

Instructions

Sauté the cumin seeds in a dry pan over medium heat for 1 to 2 minutes, until fragrant.

Place the seeds in a blender with the mint, yogurt, and water and mix until smooth.

Nutritional Facts

Calories 114| Carbohydrates 5 g| Protein 0 g| Fat 3 g| Sodium 82 mg |

67. Vanilla Chai Smoothie

Preparation time: 5 minutes

Cook time: 5 minutes

Servings: 4

Ingredients

- 1 cup of Rice Milk

- 2 black tea bags

- 1 teaspoon of vanilla extract

- 1 cup of ice

- 1 teaspoon of honey

- 2 tablespoons of chia seeds

- ½ teaspoon of ground cinnamon

- ½ teaspoon of ground ginger

- ¼ teaspoon of ground cardamom

- ¼ teaspoon of ground cloves

Instructions

Put the rice milk in a saucepan when it is nearly scorching. Teabags should be steeped for 5 minutes before being discarded. Add all the ingredients, including rice milk, vanilla, ice, honey, chia seeds, cinnamon, ginger, cardamom, and cloves, in a blender and mix until smooth. Serve after processing until smooth.

Nutritional Facts

Calories 143| Carbohydrates 19 g| Protein 3 g| Fat 1 g| Sodium 120 mg |

68. Watermelon Kiwi Smoothie

Preparation time: 5 minutes

Cook time: 0 minutes

Servings: 2

Ingredients

- 2 cups watermelon cut into pieces

- 1 kiwifruit, mashed

- 1 cup of ice

Instructions

And all the ingredients, including watermelon, kiwi, and ice, are in a blender. Blend until completely smooth.

Nutritional Facts

Calories 67| Carbohydrates 17 g| Protein 1 g| Fat 0 g| Sodium 56 mg |

69. Strawberry Cheesecake Smoothie

Preparation time: 5 minutes

Cook time: 0 minutes

Servings: 4

Ingredients

- 1 cup of rice milk

- 1 cup of strawberries, mashed

- 2 tablespoons of cream cheese

- ½ teaspoon of honey

- 1 teaspoon of vanilla extract

- 5 ice cubes

Instructions

Add all the ingredients, including rice milk, strawberries, cream cheese, honey, vanilla, and ice cubes, to a blender and mix until smooth. Serve after processing until smooth.

Nutritional Facts

Calories 114| Carbohydrates 13 g| Protein 1 g| Fat 3 g| Sodium 90 mg |

70. Cucumber Spinach Green Smoothie

Preparation time: 5 minutes

Cook time: 0 minutes

Servings: 2

Ingredients

- ½ cucumber, mashed and roughly chopped

- ½ green apple, roughly chopped

- 1 cup of rice milk

- 2 cups of spinach

- 3 ice cubes

Instructions

Add all the ingredients, including rice milk, strawberries, cream cheese, honey, vanilla, and ice cubes, to a blender and mix until smooth. Serve after processing until smooth.

Nutritional Facts

Calories 75| Carbohydrates 13 g| Protein 1 g| Fat 2 g| Sodium 75 mg |

71. Hot Cocoa

Preparation time: 5 minutes

Cook time: 5 minutes

Servings: 1

Ingredients

- 1 tablespoon cocoa powder

- 2 teaspoons of Splenda

- 3 tablespoons of dessert topping

- 1 cup of normal water

- 2 tablespoons of cool water

Instructions

Heat a pot over medium heat until it is steaming.

Combine the cocoa powder and sugar in a cup, add the cold water and stir thoroughly. Then, gradually whisk in hot water until the cocoa mixture melts, and serve with whipped topping over the top. Serve immediately.

Nutritional Facts

Calories 120| Carbohydrates 23 g| Protein 1 g| Fat 3 g| Sodium 76 mg |

72. Almond Milk

Preparation time: 3 minutes

Cook time: 2 minutes

Servings: 2

Ingredients

- 1 cup of almonds soaked in warm water for 10 min
- 1 teaspoon of vanilla extract
- 3 cups of water

Instructions

Put the soaked almonds, lay them in a blender, add the water, and process for 2 minutes, or until the nuts are finely minced. Strain the milk into a dish via cheesecloth, remove the almond meal, and whisk the vanilla extract. Cover the milk and chill it until ready to serve. Whisk it thoroughly, pour the milk equally into the glasses, and serve when ready.

Nutritional Facts

Calories 30| Carbohydrates 1 g| Protein 1 g| Fat 2.5 g| Sodium 30 mg |

73. Lemon Cucumber- Flavored Water

Preparation time: 5 minutes

Cook time: 3 hours

Servings: 10

Ingredients

- 1 lemon, sliced
- ¼ cup of mint leaves, finely chopped
- 1 medium-size cucumber, sliced
- ¼ cup of basil leaves, trimmed
- 10 cups of freshwater

Instructions

In a large pitcher, combine the papaya and mint. Fill the container with water. Stir well and chill the pitcher overnight to let the flavors permeate. Allow cooling before serving.

Nutritional Facts

Calories 10| Carbohydrates 2.2 g| Protein 0.12 g| Fat 0 g| Sodium 3 mg |

74. Blackberry Sage Cocktail

Preparation time: 5 minutes

Cook time: 10 minutes

Servings: 6

Ingredients

- 1 cup of water
- 1 cup of sugar
- 8 fresh sage leaves+ a little bit more for garnish
- 1-pint of blackberries
- Juice of 1/2 a lemon
- seltzer water

Instructions

In a saucepan, add all the ingredients that including water and sugar. Cook for 7 to 10 minutes or until the sugar has dissolved. Remove the pan from the heat. Add the sage leaves, cover them, and set them aside for approximately 2 hours. Incorporate fresh blackberry juice, lemon juice, and simple sage syrup in a cocktail shaker. Add all the ingredients to a closed container and chill until well cold. Serve in ice-filled cocktail glasses with a sprig of fresh sage and a splash of seltzer water.

Nutritional Facts

Calories 6| Carbohydrates 15 g| Protein 3 g| Fat 1 g| Sodium 12 mg |

75. Apple Cinnamon Drink

Preparation time: 10 minutes

Cook time: 10 minutes

Servings: 4

Ingredients

- 13 apples
- 1 liter of cold water
- 4 tablespoons of cinnamon
- 2 tablespoons of sugar

Instructions

13 fresh apples, scraped, minced, and simmered. Soak once they're half-cooked and simmer for the next 2 minutes. Sprinkle a healthy portion of cinnamon in 4 teaspoons, and you can use as much as you like and 2 tablespoons of sugar. Heat and cook for a further few minutes. Rinse and reinsert the new vessel into the burner, then heat to a boil. To thin it out, sprinkle more cinnamon and a little water. Transfer the solution into a tumbler and enjoy.

Nutritional Facts

Calories 130| Carbohydrates 32 g| Protein 0 g| Fat 0 g| Sodium 0 mg |

Sodium 23 mg |

76. Detoxifying Beet Juice

Preparation time: 10 minutes

Cook time: 10 minutes

Servings: 4

Ingredients

- 1-pound beets washed
- 2 pounds carrots
- 1 bunch celery
- 2 lemons, peeled
- 1 lime peeled quartered
- 1 bunch parsley
- 1 Fuji red apple, chopped

Instructions

Wash and cut vegetables so that it fits into your juicer's feeding tube. To help in the juicing process, pump the vegetable segments into the juicer, switching rougher and milder granular chunks. Serve right away, or keep refrigerated in a tightly covered container. It's better to drink the juice within 48 hours after creating it.

Nutritional Facts

Calories 58| Carbohydrates 13 g| Protein 2 g| Fat 0 g| Sodium 4 mg |

77. Pineapple Protein Smoothie

Preparation time: 5 minutes

Cook time: 0 minutes

Servings: 4

Ingredients

- 1/2 cup of cottage cheese
- 1/2 cup of frozen pineapple
- 1/2 teaspoon of brown sugar
- 1/4 teaspoon of vanilla extract
- 1 tablespoon of ground flaxseed
- 1 cup of milk of choice

Instructions

In a blender, combine every mixture and stir until smooth. Serve right away.

Nutritional Facts

Calories 220| Carbohydrates 29 g| Protein 22 g| Fat 0.2 g| Sodium 23 mg |

78. Pina Colada Smoothie

Preparation time: 5 minutes

Cook time: 2 minutes

Serving: 1

Ingredients

- 1/2 cup of vanilla almond milk
- 1/2 cup of coconut milk
- 3/4 cup of pineapple chunks
- 1 scoop of vanilla powder
- 1 teaspoon of raw honey
- 1 teaspoon of vanilla

Instructions

In a smoothie, incorporate almond milk, coconut milk, pineapple, vanilla powder, and hona. Mash till they are entirely creamy. Serve right away.

Nutritional Facts

Calories 241| Carbohydrates 20 g| Protein 26 g| Fat 7 g| Sodium 2 mg |

79. Sunny Pineapple Smoothie

Preparation time: 5 minutes

Cook time: 5 minutes

Servings: 2

Ingredients

- 1/2 cup of fresh or frozen pineapple chunks
- 2/3 cup of almond milk
- 1/2 teaspoon of ginger powder
- 1 tablespoon agave syrup

Instructions

Assemble a smoothie and spin everything for roughly thirty seconds until and unless it's creamy and silky. Fill a glassful or Mason container midway with the mixture. Serve and have fun.

Nutritional Facts

Calories 114| Carbohydrates 37 g| Protein 1.6 g| Fat 0.36 g| Sodium 3 mg |

80. Power Boosting Smoothie

Preparation time: 5 minutes

Cook time: 0 minutes

Servings: 2

Ingredients

- ½ cup of water

- ½ cup of non-dairy topping
- 2 scoops of protein powder
- 1½ cups of blueberries

Instructions

Assemble a smoothie and spin everything for roughly thirty seconds until and unless it's creamy and silky. Fill a glassful or Mason container midway with the mixture. Serve and have fun.

Nutritional Facts

Calories 242| Carbohydrates 34.2 g| Protein 32.3 g| Fat 7.3 g| Sodium 8 mg |

81. Strengthening Smoothie Bowl

Preparation time: 5 minutes

Cook time: 0 minutes

Servings: 2

Ingredients

- ¼ cup of blueberries
- ¼ cup of plain yogurt
- 1/3 cup of almond milk
- 2 tablespoons of whey protein (powdered form)
- 2 cups of blueberries

Instructions

Insert blueberries into a stand mixer and whizz for roughly 1 minute. Process almond milk, yogurt, and protein powder until the desired consistency is achieved. Divide the mixture evenly between the two bowls. End up serving with fresh blueberries as a garnish.

Nutritional Facts

Calories 176| Carbohydrates 27 g| Protein 15 g| Fat 1.6 g| Sodium 9 mg |

82. Grapefruit Sorbet

Preparation time: 10 minutes

Cook time: 0 minutes

Servings: 2

Ingredients

- ½ cup of granulated sugar
- ¼ cup of water
- 1 fresh thyme sprig

For the sorbet

- Juice of 6 grapefruit
- ¼ cup of thyme syrup

Instructions

To make the simple thyme syrup

Combine the sugar, water, and thyme in a small frying pan or skillet. Bring to a boil, turn off the heat, and refrigerate the thyme sprig until cold. Strain the thyme sprig from the syrup.

To make the sorbet

Merge the grapefruit juice and 1/4 cup of simple syrup in a juicer and whisk until creamy. Freeze for 3 to 4 hours, just until firm, in an airtight container. Serve.

Nutritional Facts

Calories 117| Carbohydrates 18.2 g| Protein 22.7 g| Fat 2.6 g| Sodium 12 mg |

83. Strawberry Cheesecake Smoothie

Preparation time: 5 minutes

Cook time: 0 minutes

Servings: 2

Ingredients

- 1 cup of rice milk
- 1 cup of strawberries
- 2 tablespoons of cream cheese
- ½ teaspoon of honey
- 1 teaspoon of vanilla extract
- 5 ice cubes

Instructions

Add all the ingredients to the blending machine, including rice milk, strawberries, cream cheese, honey, vanilla, and ice cubes, and process until the texture gets smooth. End up serving after processing until soft.

Nutritional Facts

Calories 114| Carbohydrates 13 g| Protein 1 g| Fat 3 g| Sodium 19 mg |

84. Pineapple Juice

Preparation time: 5 minutes

Cook time: 0 minutes

Servings: 2

Ingredients

- ½ cup of sliced pineapple
- 1 cup of fresh
- 3 cubes of ice

Instructions

Whisk all ingredients in an electric mixer and end up

serving over ice.

Nutritional Facts

Calories 135| Carbohydrates 0 g| Protein 0 g| Fat 0 g| Sodium 23 mg |

85. Watermelon Bliss

Preparation time: 5 minutes

Cook time: 0 minutes

Serving: 4

Ingredients

- 2 cups of watermelon without seed
- 1 medium-sized cucumber
- 2 mint sprigs
- 1 celery stalk
- A squeeze of lime juice

Instructions

To commence, incorporate all of the things in a blending jug. Shake it for 30 seconds, until and unless it's evenly miscible. End up serving cold

Nutritional Facts

Calories 156| Carbohydrates 12 g| Protein 14 g| Fat 0 g| Sodium 45

Conclusion

Inflammation is the body's natural defense against infection, illness, and damage. Because of the inflammatory reaction, your body creates more white blood cells, immune system cells, and cytokines that help fight infection. Redness, discomfort, heat, and swelling are signs of acute (short-term) inflammation.

On the other hand, the body may acquire chronic (long-term) inflammation without symptoms. All of these conditions may be brought on or worsened by chronic inflammation. Obesity and stress may also lead to inflammation. Blood markers of inflammation include C-reactive protein, homocysteine, TNF alpha, and IL-6.

Your finger becomes red and swollen when you cut it. Swollen and inflamed knees are the result of knee injuries. Some inflammation is beneficial in the healing process, but too much of it may cause disease. Many diseases, including cancer, heart disease, Alzheimer's disease, and depression, have been linked to chronic inflammation.

Inflammation may be triggered by certain daily habits, particularly those repeated. Sugar and high-fructose corn syrup in large quantities are exceedingly harmful. Insulin resistance may lead to various health problems, including insulin resistance, diabetes, and obesity.

According to researchers, refined carbohydrate diets, such as white bread, have been linked to inflammation, insulin resistance, and obesity. The endothelial cells lining your arteries may be damaged by Trans fats found in processed and packaged meals.

There is a good chance that many processed meals include vegetable oils. Omega-6 and omega-3 fatty acid imbalances have been linked to an increase in inflammation, according to some specialists.

Inflammation may also be induced in the body by consuming large quantities of alcohol and processed meat. Sedentary behavior is another important non-dietary risk factor for inflammation.

Consume less inflammatory foods and more anti-inflammatory substances to minimize inflammation. Processed foods should be avoided in favor of whole, nutrient-dense meals high in antioxidants. You'll be able to accomplish your objectives using the recipes in this book.

Made in United States
Troutdale, OR
09/12/2023